# Social Software Engineering

## Development and Collaboration with Social Networking

# Social Software Engineering

Development and Collaboration with Social Networking

**Jessica Keyes**

CRC Press is an imprint of the
Taylor & Francis Group, an **informa** business
AN AUERBACH BOOK

CRC Press
Taylor & Francis Group
6000 Broken Sound Parkway NW, Suite 300
Boca Raton, FL 33487-2742

First issued in paperback 2019



ISBN-13: 978-1-4398-5375-7 (hbk)
ISBN-13: 978-1-138-38207-7 (pbk)



**Visit the Taylor & Francis Web site at**
**http://www.taylorandfrancis.com**

**and the CRC Press Web site at**
**http://www.crcpress.com**

# Dedication

This book is dedicated to my family and friends.

I would especially like to thank those who assisted me in putting this book together. As always, my editor, John Wyzalek, was instrumental in getting my project approved and providing great encouragement.

# Contents

# Preface

The world is a changed place. The collaborative web has caught our collective imagination and there is no turning back, particularly in the business world. Some have taken to calling this use of collaborative technologies in business Enterprise 2 (E 2.0). Wikipedia may have been the first company to popularize the phenomenon of user-generated knowledge, but this encyclopedia is just the tip of the iceberg. Companies far and wide are wiki-izing. Nokia hosts a number of wikis, some of which are used internally to coordinate technology research. Dresdner Kleinwort, an investment bank, operates the largest corporate wiki. About 50% of Dresdner staff use this wiki to make sure that all team members are on the same project management page.

E 2.0 is more than just wikis, of course. It constitutes the entirety of social networking applications including blogs, discussion boards, workspaces, and anything else that is sharable, and even combinable (i.e., mashups). IBM uses E 2.0 for everything from collaborative document production to internal project collaboration. Nokia uses it for all-purpose teamware. A whole host of companies use it for knowledge management. Honeywell was one of the first to use E 2.0 to perform knowledge discovery, research, and sharing across miles—regardless of whether users even know each other. It would appear, then, that E 2.0 using social networking technologies has wide applicability to all things business—including software engineering.

Software development projects are usually complex and often mission critical. Successful software development projects usually have something in common. Each of these projects, in some way, shape, or form, follows one or more principles of applied software engineering methodology. However, the precepts of software engineering have been around for decades. While advances in computer hardware and software have accelerated with breathtaking speed over these past decades, advances in software engineering have not quite kept pace. Modern systems that now integrate multiple platforms, multiple architectures, and usually seek a global reach via the Internet require modern software engineering methods.

Software engineering is an inherently collaborative set of socio-technical activities that permit distributed developers to discuss and share knowledge and artifacts using appropriate supportive processes and tools. This can be referred to as social software engineering.

The goal of this book is to examine the new field of software engineering through the spectrum of the social activities that compose it. Computer science must be fused with psychology, sociology, and mathematics, and wrapped around the principles of knowledge engineering, to develop an appropriate infrastructure (i.e., tools, applications, and environments) to support a software engineering discipline capable of developing twenty-first century applications.

# Author

**Jessica Keyes** is president of New Art Technologies, Inc., a high-technology and management consultancy and development firm started in New York in 1989.

Keyes has given seminars for such prestigious universities as Carnegie Mellon, Boston University, University of Illinois, James Madison University, and San Francisco State University. She is a frequent keynote speaker on the topics of competitive strategy and productivity and quality. She is former advisor for DataPro, McGraw-Hill's computer research arm, as well as a member of the Sprint Business Council. Keyes is also a founding board of director member of the New York Software Industry Association. She completed a two-year term on the Mayor of New York City's Small Business Advisory Council. She currently facilitates doctoral and other courses for the University of Phoenix and is a member of the Faculty Council for the College of Information Systems & Technology. She has been the editor for Warren, Gorham & Lamont's *Handbook of eBusiness* and CRC Press' *Systems Development Management* and *Information Management*.

Prior to founding New Art, Keyes was the managing director of R&D for the New York Stock Exchange and has been an officer with Swiss Bank Co. and Banker's Trust, both in New York City. She earned a master's in business administration from New York University and a doctorate in management. A noted columnist and correspondent with more than 200 articles published, Keyes is the author of the following books:

*The New Intelligence: AI in Financial Services*, HarperBusiness, 1990
*The Handbook of Expert Systems in Manufacturing*, McGraw-Hill, 1991
*Infotrends: The Competitive Use of Information*, McGraw-Hill, 1992
*The Software Engineering Productivity Handbook*, McGraw-Hill, 1993
*The Handbook of Multimedia*, McGraw-Hill, 1994
*The Productivity Paradox*, McGraw-Hill, 1994
*Technology Trendlines*, Van Nostrand Reinhold, 1995
*How to be a Successful Internet Consultant*, McGraw-Hill, 1997
*Webcasting*, McGraw-Hill, 1997
*Datacasting*, McGraw-Hill, 1997

*The Handbook of Technology in Financial Services*, Auerbach, 1998
*The Handbook of Internet Management*, Auerbach, 1999
*The Handbook of eBusiness*, Warren, Gorham & Lamont, 2000
*The Ultimate Internet Sourcebook*, Amacom, 2001
*How to Be a Successful Internet Consultant, 2nd ed.*, Amacom, 2002
*Software Engineering Handbook*, Auerbach, 2002
*Real World Configuration Management*, Auerbach, 2003
*Balanced Scorecard*, Auerbach, 2005
*Knowledge Management, Business Intelligence, and Content Management: The IT Practitioner's Guide*, Auerbach, 2006
*X Internet: The Executable and Extendable Internet*, Auerbach, 2007
*Leading IT Projects: The IT Manager's Guide*, Auerbach, 2008
*Marketing IT Products and Services*, Auerbach, 2009
*Implementing the Project Management Balanced Scorecard*, Auerbach, 2010

# Chapter 1

# Why Social Networking?

The *2009 Standish Group Chaos Report* painted a dismal picture of the state of software development. The Boston, Massachusetts, research firm surveyed 400 organizations and found a decrease in IT project success rates and an increase in IT project failure rates in a short two-year period. Only 32% of surveyed projects were considered successful (i.e., on time, on budget, and with required functionality and feature sets). Nearly one quarter of IT projects were considered failures. The rest were considered to be challenged—a euphemism for late, over budget, or implemented without the full set of promised functions and features. It should be noted, however, that many dispute the *Chaos Report* findings. What's undisputed is that a large number of projects do fail.

Many things can and do go wrong with software development efforts. McConnell (1996) neatly categorized the issues as shown in Table 1.1. Hyvari (2006) provides an updated view, as shown in Table 1.2. The names may have changed but the problems remain more or less the same. As you can see, a host of reasons can negatively impact project success and high on the list is the human element. Ewusi-Mensah (2003) states simply that, "the software development enterprise is a purely abstract and conceptual endeavor, and as such places an undue burden on all the stakeholders to collaborate with a clear vision of what is to be achieved, how it is to be achieved, and at what cost and in what time frame."

Having the right people on a project team is certainly key to the success of a project. In a large pharmaceutical company, the lead designer walked off a very important project. Obviously, that set the team back to a large extent because no one else had enough experience to do what he did. Even if the IT staff stays put, it is always possible that a "people" issue will negatively affect a project. For example, a change in senior management may mean that the project you are working on gets canned or moved to a lower priority. A project manager working for America

**Table 1.1 Classic Software Development Project Problems**

| *People-Related Mistakes* | *Process-Related Mistakes* | *Product-Related Mistakes* | *Technology-Related Mistakes* |
|---|---|---|---|
| Undermined motivation | Overly optimistic schedules | Requirement gold-plating, i.e., too many product features | Silver-bullet syndrome, i.e., latching onto new technology or method that is unproven for project |
| Weak personnel | Insufficient risk management | Feature creep | Overestimated savings from tools or methods |
| Uncontrolled problem employees | Contractor failure | Developer gold-plating, i.e., use of technology for the sake of using that technology | Switching tools in middle of project |
| Heroics | Insufficient planning | Push me–pull me negotiation, i.e., constantly changing schedule | Lack of automated source code control |
| Adding people to late project | Abandonment of planning under pressure | Research-oriented development, i.e., stretching limits of technology | |
| Noisy crowded offices | Wasted time before project starts, i.e., approval and budgeting processes | | |
| Friction between developers and customers | Shortchanged upstream activities, e.g., requirements analysis, etc. | | |

**Table 1.1 (continued) Classic Software Development Project Problems**

| | | | |
|---|---|---|---|
| Unrealistic expectations | Inadequate design | | |
| Lack of effective project sponsorship | Short-changed quality assurance | | |
| Lack of stakeholder buy-in | Insufficient management controls | | |
| Lack of user input | Premature or too frequent convergence, i.e., product released too early | | |
| Politics over substance | Omitting necessary tasks from estimates | | |
| Wishful thinking | Planning to catch up later | | |
| | Code-like-hell programming | | |

Online-Time Warner had just started an important new project when a new president was installed. The new president did what all new presidents do. He engaged in a little housecleaning. Projects—and some people—were swept away. When the dust settled, the project manager faced a whole new set of priorities and a bunch of new team members. As you can see, today's dynamically changing, and very volatile, business landscape can play havoc with software engineering efforts and going global adds an entirely new dimension to the mix. What we need, then, is a whole new paradigm of software development that places the human aspect at the center of software engineering.

## The Social Network

Social networking is a hot topic. More than 30 billion pieces of content are shared on Facebook each month and Nielsen researchers say that consumers spend more than 5½ hours on social networking sites per day. So I am sure it doesn't come as a surprise that social networking has made its way into the workplace.

**Table 1.2 Success and Failure Factors**

| **Factors related to project** |
|---|
| Size and value |
| Having clear boundary |
| Urgency |
| Uniqueness of project activities |
| Density of project network (in dependencies between activities) |
| Project life cycle |
| End-user commitment |
| Adequate funds and resources |
| Realistic schedule |
| Clear goals and objectives |
| **Factors related to project manager and leadership** |
| Ability to delegate authority |
| Ability to trade off |
| Ability to coordinate |
| Perception of role and responsibilities |
| Effective leadership |
| Effective conflict resolution |
| Relevant past experience |
| Management of changes |
| Contract management |
| Situational management |
| Competence |
| Commitment |
| Trust |
| Other communication |
| **Factors related to project team members** |
| Technical background |
| Communication |
| Troubleshooting |
| Effective monitoring and feedback |
| Commitment |

**Table 1.2 (continued) Success and Failure Factors**

| Factors related to organization |
|---|
| Steering committee |
| Clear organization and job descriptions |
| Top management support |
| Project organization structure |
| Functional manager's support |
| Project champion |
| **Factors related to environment** |
| Competitors |
| Political environment |
| Economic environment |
| Social environment |
| Technological environment |
| Nature |
| Client |
| Subcontractors |

As early as 2008, AT&T released the results of a research study it commissioned in Europe. The study conducted by Dynamic Markets found that the use of social networking tools led to an increase in efficiency. Of the 2,500 people surveyed in five countries, 65% said that use of these tools made them or their colleagues more efficient and 46% insisted that networking tools sparked ideas and creativity (AT&T, 2008).

Deep Nishar is vice president of products and user experience at LinkedIn and manages a group of data researchers who look at everything from data center behavior to trends in search and mobile communications. His eclectic staff have experience in such fields as brain surgery, computer science, meteorology, and poetry. According to Nishar, machine-based systems like Google can't keep up with organizing the data they capture. Interesting and important problems will be solved by looking at social networks (Hardy, 2010).

In 1976, science fiction author Richard Dawkins coined the term *meme* to describe an idea that moves from person to person and onward. With social networking tools, staff can check to see what ideas people discuss within an organization. Some refer to the activity as a "meme broadcast tool." Where marketers have Twitter to communicate with people outside the company, business people can use services such as Yammer (yammer.com) to share information within a company, discuss relevant issues, and more. Table 1.3 lists some of the more popular social networking tools in use today.

Leading-edge organizations have already figured out how to make social networking profitable. SolarWinds, a network management company, built a 25,000-member user community of network administrators who help each other with various problems. This allows the company to support a customer base of over 88,000 companies with only two customer support people. Cisco created employee councils and shifted decision making down to these levels through the support of collaborative technologies. Indeed, Cisco's CEO, John Chambers, insists that most of the progress made during the past 2 years has resulted from the use of collaborative and social technologies.

When IBM transformed an Intranet into a social network, it provided each of IBM's 365,000 employees a voice and identity that not only helped increase

**Table 1.3 Social Networking Tools**

| | |
|---|---|
| Social networking | Facebook, Friendster, LinkedIn, Ning, Orkut, Bebo, KickApps, OpenACircle, Vyew, MOLI, Fast Pitch!, Plaxo, Yammer, Eurekastreams.org, researchgate.net/ |
| Publishing | TypePad, Blogger, Wikipedia, Joomla |
| Photo sharing | Radar.net, SmugMug, Zooomr, Flickr, Picasa, Photobucket, Twitxr |
| Audio | iTunes, Rhapsody, Podbean, Podcast.com |
| Video | Youtube, Metacafe, Hulu, Viddler, Google Video, Brightcove |
| Microblogging | Twitxr, Twitter, Plurk |
| Livecasting | SHOUTcast, BlogTalkRadio, TalkShoe, Justin.tv, Live365 |
| Virtual worlds | There, SecondLife, ViOS, ActiveWorlds |
| Productivity | ReadNotify, Zoho, Zoomerang, Google Docs |
| Aggregators | Digg, Yelp, iGoogle, Reddit, FriendFeed, TiddlyWiki |
| Rich site summary (RSS) | RSS 2.0, Atom, PingShot |
| Search | Technorati, Redlasso, EveryZing, MetaTube, IceRocket, Google Search |
| Mobile | Jumbuck, CallWave, airG, Jott, Brightkite |
| Interpersonal | WebEx, iChat, Meebo, Acrobat Connect, Goto Meeeting, Skype |

effectiveness and productivity but also helped workers transcend national cultures (How social networking, etc., 2009). IBM uses a variety of social networking tools. Long before Facebook graduated from college, IBM created its own internal social networking site called BluePages. It lists basic information about individual employees, their views, who reports to them, to whom they report, what organization they are in and what communities they are parts of. Employees can self-edit their listings and even add pictures. Clicking on an entry allows someone to send an instant message.

Perhaps the most powerful feature is social tagging, also called social bookmarking. Clicking on an employee not only brings up identifying data, it also brings up his or her tags, i.e., blog feeds, RSS feeds, communities joined, social networks joined, recent forum entries, and wiki participation. Ethan McCarty, former editor in chief of IBM's intranet, describes it, "If you think of the phases of the intranet and even Internet communication, first it's about access to information, then it's about transacting with it—like e-business—and now it's more about people."

The people we refer to as the millennials come into the workplace with cell phones glued to their ears and fingers firmly glued to keyboards as they tweet and Facebook to friends and strangers alike. They think that talking on the phone is passé. Some don't even have landlines. They communicate via social networks, instant messages, Twitter, and smartphones. However, their older brothers and sisters of Gen-Y are working to convince technology management of the values of these new technologies, according to a Forrester Research survey of 2,000 IT professionals. This isn't all that surprising as a 2010 Pew report found that Internet users from all age groups increased their usage between 2008 and 2010. While 83% of those between 18 and 33 use social networking, those 45 and older more than doubled their Internet participation (Major trends, 2010).

## The Software Engineering Social Network

The development of software systems has long been considered a social activity. Software is developed using a team model and the work is divided among the various team members. Several studies suggest that developers of large projects spend 70 to 85% of their time working with others. Thus, it is important that a team collaborate effectively to achieve a common goal.

One of the earliest to research the psychology and sociology behind software engineering was Gerald M. Weinberg in 1971. His seminal book on the psychology of programming was radical for its time. Aside from coining the "egoless programming" phrase, Weinberg's book on micro organizational behavior delves deeply into the concept of programming as a social construct and offers advice on dealing with team dysfunction.

Much of the literature on the psychology of software development concludes that most of the social problems inherent in development teams can be solved by a critical analysis of the dynamics among the people involved. This sort of introspective analysis can be helpful to explain (1) why certain people are excluded from group decision making, (2) why someone always resists the decisions of project leadership, (3) why certain kinds of people should never be grouped together to avoid group fragmentation, (4) why groups often divide themselves into subgroups, and (5) the difference between the "real" chain of command and the formal one (Ahmadi, Jazayeri, Lelli, and Nesic, 2008).

Fischer (2005) discusses the individual and social perspectives that affect design. Individuals often worry about whether they are interested enough to be effective during the span of a project. They also worry about whether they have something relevant to add to a group and can express it clearly so that others might understand them. On the other hand, the group is interested in hearing from a wide variety of stakeholders. Thus, the group is concerned with encouraging individuals to contribute, preventing voices from being lost because too much information is available, avoiding illegitimate voices, preventing getting stuck in group think, and eliminating sources of exclusion.

A multitude of studies have discussed the vast amounts of time spent on communication and collaboration with others. Because software development is an inherently collaborative and distributed process involving teams of developers working intra- and inter-organizationally and globally, it is logical that these teams require toolsets designed specifically for the collaborative, distributed nature of their work.

## Collaborative Applications

The computer-supported cooperative work (CSCW) community has been studying computer-assisted collaboration for some time. CSCW researchers have developed a number of frameworks that seek to categorize the requirements of the collaborative toolset. Whitehead (2007) categorizes collaborative software engineering tools into four groups: (1) model-based collaboration tools, (2) process support tools, (3) collaboration awareness tools, and (4) collaboration infrastructure tools. Sarma's (2005) framework classifies tools based on the required effort to collaborate effectively. The framework consists of five layers and three strands, as shown in Figure 1.1. The layers are tools and the strands are critical needs that permeate all aspects of collaboration.

As is often the case, many of the toolsets discussed in the literature are experimental and not offered for use by those in the field. In 2003, Booch and Brown surveyed both experimental and commercial collaborative development environments (CDEs). Their definition of a CDE is a virtual space wherein all the stakeholders of a project, even if distributed by time or distance, may negotiate, brainstorm, discuss, share knowledge, and generally labor together to carry out some task, most often to create an executable deliverable and its supporting artifacts. As encompassing as this definition is, it does not necessarily distinguish private and public (open

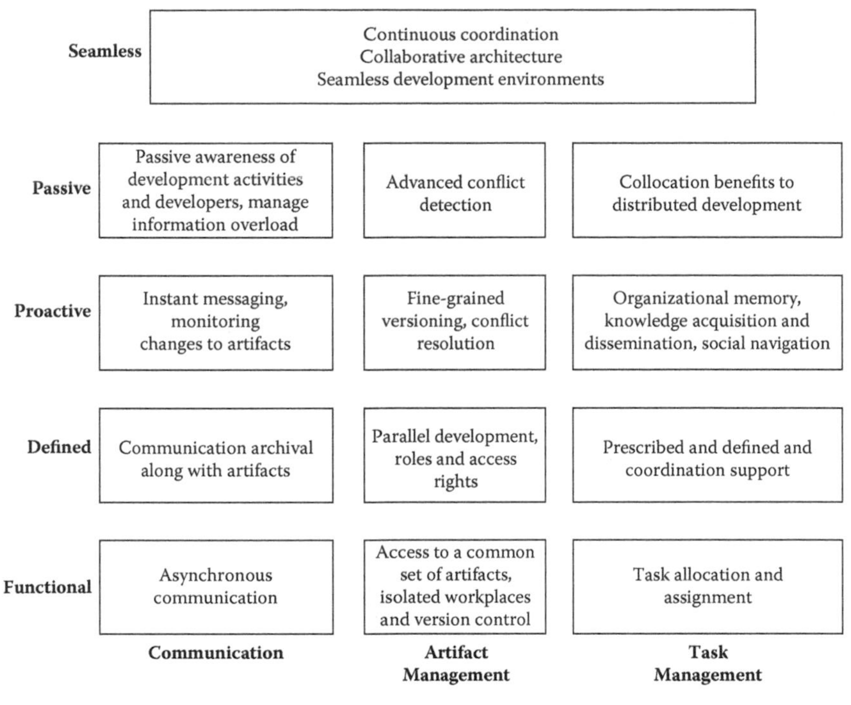


**Figure 1.1 Collaboration framework.**

source) projects and does not necessarily stress software development. Still, their analysis of the requirements of a CDE is worthwhile to discuss. They base their requirements list on Fournier (2001). Table 1.4 lists the combined Fournier and Booch and Brown requirements for this sort of environment.

Web 2 technologies have finally given a voice to the collaborative needs of software developers and can lend a hand toward building the type of CDE envisioned in Table 1.4. Web 2 engages users to build collective intelligence. One of the most common examples of this is the wiki (*wiki* is a variant of the Hawaiian *wicki* meaning *fast*). Wikis are so ubiquitous that the learning curve is minimal. Many organizations use this tool, specifically IT departments within organizations, and several articles were written about the use of wikis to promote software reuse within IT departments. However, wikis have their own attendant problems. Insufficient usage and decaying structures must be addressed if wikis are to be successful.

The advent of social networking services such as LinkedIn, Facebook, and MySpace demonstrate the power of social networks and provide insights into what could be created specifically for software engineering. Of course, the current state-of-the-art social networks present some limitations, as Ahmadi et al. (2008) thoroughly describe. Chief among the described problems is the lack of interoperability

**Table 1.4 Recommended Feature Set of Collaborative Development Environment**

| Coordination |
|---|
| Centralized information management |
| Configuration control of shared artifacts |
| Online event notification |
| Calendaring and scheduling |
| Project resource profiling |
| Project dashboards and metrics (Booch and Brown) |
| Searching and indexing of resources and artifacts |
| Electronic document routing and workflow |
| Virtual agents and scripting of tasks (Booch and Brown) |
| **Collaboration** |
| Threaded discussion forums (Booch and Brown) |
| Virtual meeting rooms |
| Instant messaging |
| Online voting and polling |
| Shared whiteboards |
| Co-browsing of documents |
| Multiple levels of information visibility (Booch and Brown) |
| **Community Building** |
| Personalization capabilities (Booch and Brown) |
| Established protocols and rituals |
| Well-defined scope and leadership |
| Self-publication of content (Booch and Brown) |
| Self-administration of projects (Booch and Brown) |

among social networks. The authors suggest leveraging semantic web technologies, one of which is the ontology, as a solution to this problem. An ontology is a formal representation of specific domain concepts and the relationships of those concepts. Several ontologies (e.g., www.foaf-project.org, www.sioc-project.org, http://www.semanticdesktop.org/ontologies/pimo/) have become universally recognized and it is expected that at some point interoperabilities of social networks using ontologies will become standard practice.

Indeed, some researchers have advocated for the use of ontologies to improve the discipline of software development. Mavetera and Kroeze (2010) discuss the different ontology types that can be used. A domain ontology describes the knowledge to be captured during the requirements analysis phase of software development. Method ontologies capture the knowledge and reasoning needed to perform a task. Status ontologies, either dynamic or static, capture the status characteristics of a system. Intentional ontologies model the softer aspects of living things such as beliefs, desires, and intentions. Process ontologies capture (1) enterprise knowledge (processes, organizational structure, IT structure, products, customers); (2) domain knowledge (terms, concepts, relationships); and (3) information knowledge (document types and structures). Finally, social ontologies describes the organizational structures and interdependencies among the social actors (analyst, tester, developer, etc.).

## We've Reached the End of Chapter 1

Sure, we can all use Microsoft Sharepoint, Oracle Beehive, or glue together any number of social networking tools such as wikis and blogs to effect a viable software solution. We're going to discuss many of these in this book, and even show you how to use them. You'll find that several good social networking tools exist. When I first approached writing this book, I thought that the subject was a problem in search of a software solution. However, the more research I did, and the more people I spoke with, the more I became convinced that the issue is really a problem in search of a process.

The goal of the rest of this book, therefore, is to fuse software engineering methodology and toolsets to the underpinnings of social networking—knowledge sharing and transfer. Along the way, we will delve into psychosocial constructs such as action learning, action research, and action science. This trifecta, popularized in the annals of psychology and used to improve productivity and spur creativity among management types, fits well within the rubric of "social engineering."

## References

Ahmadi, N., Jazayeri, M., Lelli, F., and Nesic, S. (2008). A survey of social software engineering. *23rd IEEE/ACM International Conference on Automated Software Engineering Workshops*. pp. 1–12.

AT&T. (2008). *Social networking in the workplace increases efficiency*. http://www.att.com/gen/pressoom?pid=4800&cdvn=news&newsarticleid=26293

Booch, G. and Brown, A.W. (2003). Collaborative development environments. *Advances in Computers*, 59: 2–29.

Ewusi-Mensah, K. (2003). *Software Development Failures*. Cambridge, MA: MIT Press.

Fischer, G. (2005). Social creativity: making all voices heard. *Proceedings of HCI International Conference*, Las Vegas, July, CD. http://l3d.cs.colorado.edu/~gerhard/papers/social-creativity-hcii-2005.pdf

Fournier, R. (2001). Teamwork is the key to remote development. *Infoworld.* http://www.itworld.com/IW010305tcdistdev

Hardy, Q. (2010). LinkedIn plots career success paths. http://www.forbes.com/forbes/2010/0830/e-gang-linkedin-social-networking-deep-nishar-be-the-boss.html

How social networking increases collaboration at IBM. (2009). *Strategic Communication Management,* 14: 32–35. Retrieved from ABI/Inform Complete.

Hyvari, I. (2006). Success of projects in different organizational conditions. *Project Management Journal,* 37(4): 31–42.

Major trends in online activities (2010). Pew Research. http://pewinternet.org/Reports/2010/Generations-2010/Trends/Social-network-sites.aspx

Mavetera, N. and Kroeze, J.H. (2010). An ontology-driven software development framework. *Proceedings of 14th International Business Information Management Association Conference*, Istanbul, June, pp. 1713–1724.

McConnell, S. (1996). *Rapid Development: Taming Wild Software Schedules.* Redmond, WA: Microsoft Press.

Sarma, A. (2005). A survey of collaborative tools in software development. Institute for Software Research, University of California, Irvine. http://citeseerx.ist.psu.edu/viewdoc/download?doi=10.1.1.126.671&rep=rep1&type=pdf /

Whitehead, J. (2007). Collaboration in software engineering: a roadmap. In *Future of Software Engineering,* New York: IEEE Computer Society, pp. 214–225.

# Chapter 2

# Social Networking Tools at Work

Most professionals, when they think of social networking at all, think in terms of Facebook and Twitter. CIOs see great potential in these sorts of tools. IBM conducted a worldwide study of 2,500 CIOs in late 2010. The collective take on collaboration tools is that they must be institutionalized to meet the demands of business. Surprisingly, as we will shortly show, and with some effort, all of these tools can be institutionalized to enhance the productivity of the software engineering discipline. Based on the popularity of these types of tools among consumers, it is no wonder that a variety of such tools are geared to specific business disciplines.

## Tools that Provide Networking Capabilities

Salesforce.com, the enterprise CRM giant, has begun to provide social networking capabilities. Its new Chatter service is available on Salesforce's real-time collaboration cloud. Users establish profiles and generate status updates that may be questions, bits of information and/or knowledge, or relevant hyperlinks. All of this information is then aggregated and broadcast to co-workers in their personal networks. Essentially, a running feed of comments and updates flow to those in a particular network. Employees can also follow colleagues throughout a company, not just in their own personal networks, enabling cross-organizational knowledge sharing. Toward that end, Chatter also provides a profile database that users can tap into to find needed skills for a particular project. Chatter is accessible via desktop or mobile.

Like Salesforce.com, more than a handful of well-known software companies have developed collaboration tools, all for a fee. Oracle's Beehive provides a spate of tools such as instant messaging, email, calendaring, and team workspaces. Microsoft's SharePoint is heavily used within IT departments. Microsoft's Lync Server product that permits users to communicate from anywhere via voice, video, or document share is also becoming a contender. One of the first companies to dabble in the collaborative market—indeed they created it—was Lotus. Now owned by IBM, Lotus Notes brings together a wide array of tools: instant messaging, team rooms, discussion forums, and even application widgets.

A wide variety of free tools are available and may adapted for various purposes. LinkedIn has been widely used to provide networking capabilities for business people. A relevant feature is the LinkedIn group that may be created for any purpose, with permission required to join. Thus, project teams can make use of the already developed facilities LinkedIn provides. For example, the Tata Research Development and Design Centre (TRDDC) was established in 1981 as a division of Tata Consultancy Services Limited, India's largest IT consulting organization. TRDDC is today one of India's largest research and development centers for software and process engineering. TRDDC has its own membership-by-request LinkedIn group. It is very easy to create a members-only LinkedIn group for a particular project and limit it to specific members, as shown in Figure 2.1.

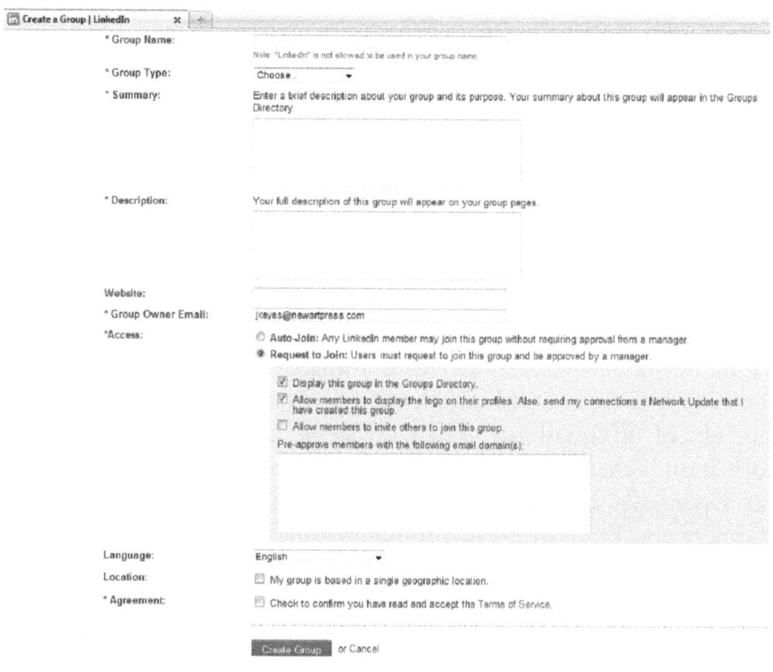


**Figure 2.1 Creating members-only LinkedIn group.**

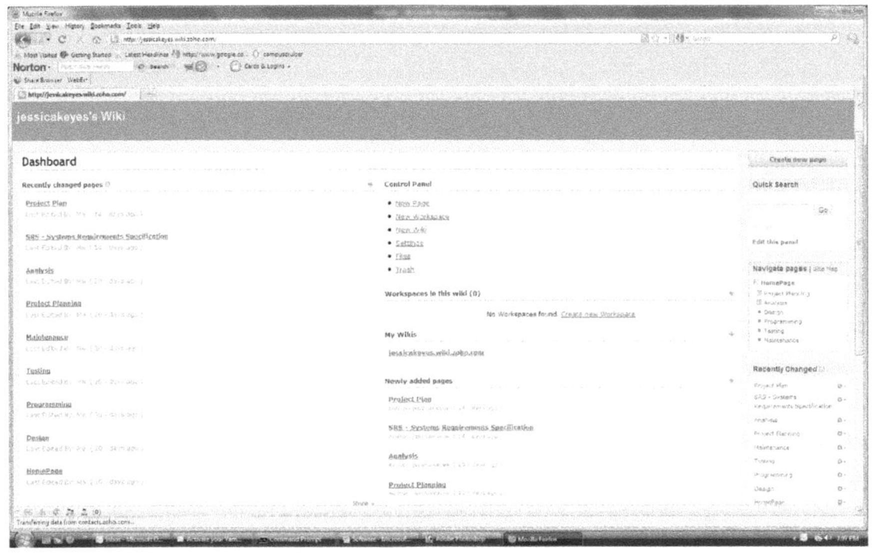


**Figure 2.2 Project artifact wiki.**

Of all of the collaborative tools available, particularly those that are free, wikis are the most commonly used. Zoho.com provides a wide range of tools, including chats, discussions, meetings, and projects, but it is their wiki tool I will focus on. Figure 2.2 is a wiki I created to store all the artifacts for a typical project, i.e., project plan, systems requirement specifications, analysis documents, etc. Figure 2.3 shows the project plan artifact in wiki form. Note the ability to post comments.

Twitter, a social networking application made famous by celebrities who tweet hourly updates on what they are doing (eating lunch, shopping, etc.), has morphed into an enterprise social networking application called Yammer. With the ability to integrate with tools such as SharePoint, Yammer provides a suite of tools including enterprise microblogging, communities, company directories, direct messaging, groups and knowledge bases. SunGard employees actually started using Yammer on their own to share information about projects they were working on. Now Yammer has been rolled out to all 20,000+ employees. Much of what Yammer offers is free with its basic service. A gold subscription provides such corporate niceties as security controls, administrative controls, broadcast messages, enhanced support, SharePoint integration, keyword monitoring, and virtual firewall solutions. Yammer can be used by the software development team to interactively discuss any aspect of a project, as shown in Figure 2.4.

Project groups have used wikis in some creative ways: writing personal research and making comments on others' research, asking questions, posting links to resources that may be of interest to others in the group, adding details for upcoming events and meetings, letting each other know about activities, adding comments to

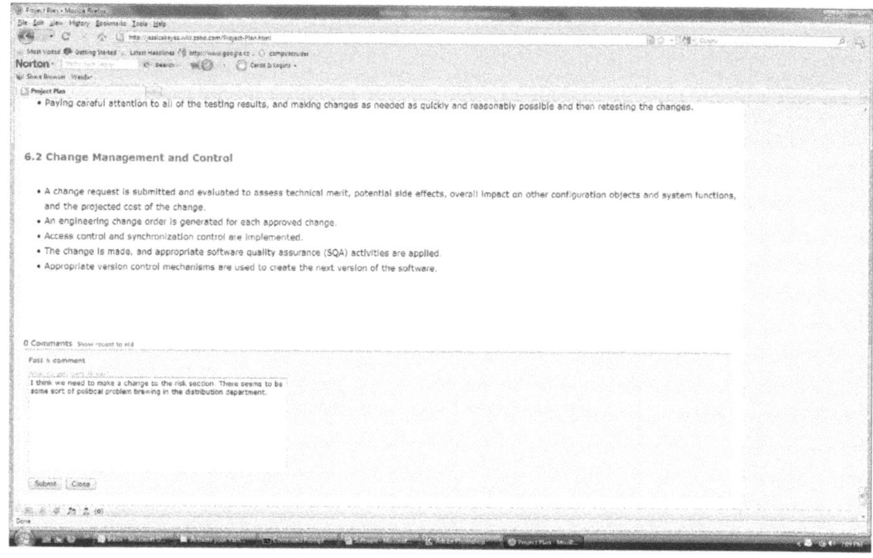


**Figure 2.3 Project plan wiki demonstrating ability to include comments.**

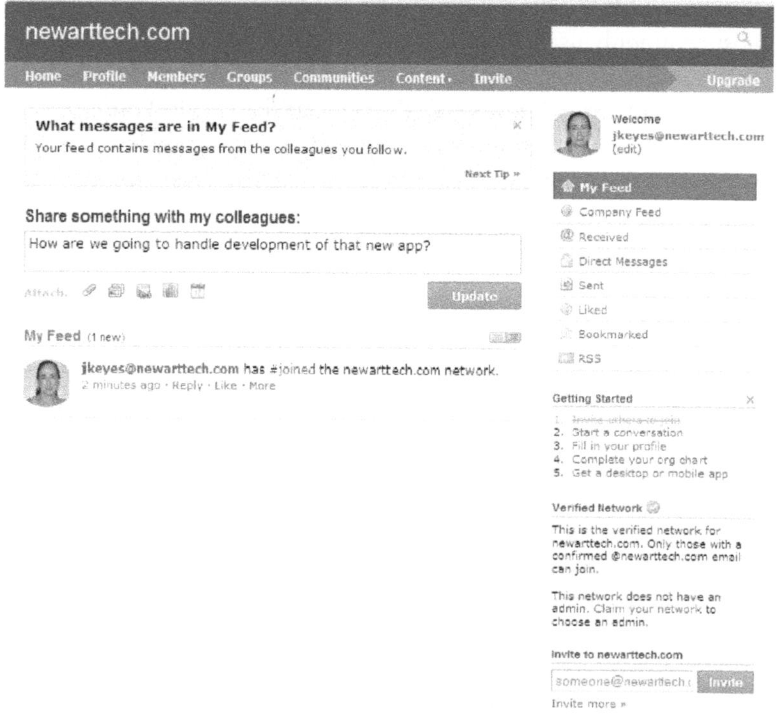


**Figure 2.4 Dynamic discussion using Yammer.**

other team members' information and pages, and recording minutes of meetings in real-time. One may expect that use of these sorts of ad hoc discussion tools would degenerate into chaos. In truth, this rarely happens—even in social networks of anonymous users. Anderson (2006) talks about the fact that the largest wiki of all, Wikipedia, is fairly resistant to vandalism and ideological battles. He stresses that the reason is "the emergent behavior of a Pro-Am [professional and amateur] swarm of self-appointed curators." This group of curators has self-organized what Anderson terms the most comprehensive encyclopedia in history—creating order from chaos. Welcome to the world of "peer production."

## Wikis in Action

Intellipedia (https://www.intelink.gov/wiki) is an online system for collaborative data sharing used by the United States intelligence community (IC). It consists of three different wikis with different levels of classification: Top Secret, Secret, and Sensitive But Unclassified. The levels used by individuals with appropriate clearances from the 16 agencies of the IC and other national-security-related organizations, including Combatant Commands and other federal departments. The wikis are not open to the public.

Intellipedia includes information on the regions, people, and issues of interest to the communities using its host networks. Intellipedia uses MediaWiki, the same software used by the Wikipedia free-content encyclopedia project. Officials say that the project will change the culture of the U.S. intelligence community, widely blamed for failing to "connect the dots" before the September 11, 2001 attacks.

The Secret version predominantly serves Department of Defense and Department of State personnel, many of whom do not use the Top Secret network on a day-to-day basis. Users on unclassified networks can access Intellipedia from remote terminals outside their workspaces via a VPN in addition to their normal workstations. Open Source Intelligence (OSINT) users share information on the unclassified network.

Intellipedia was created to share information about some of the most difficult subjects facing U.S. intelligence and bring cutting-edge technology into its ever-more-youthful workforce. It also allows information to be assembled and reviewed by a wide variety of sources and agencies, to address concerns that pre-war intelligence did not include robust dissenting opinions about Iraq's alleged weapons programs. Some view Intellipedia as risky because it allows more information to be viewed and shared, but most agree that the result is worth the risk.

The project was greeted initially with a lot of resistance because it runs counter to past practice that limited the pooling of information. Some encouragement has been necessary to spur contributions from the traditional intelligence community. However, the system appeals to the new generation of intelligence analysts because this is how they like to work and it represents a new way of thinking.

The wiki provides so much flexibility that several offices throughout the community use it to maintain and transfer knowledge about daily operations and events. Anyone with access to read it has permission to create and edit articles. Because Intellipedia is intended as a platform for harmonizing the various views of the agencies and analysts of the IC, Intellipedia does not enforce a neutral point of view policy. Instead, viewpoints are attributed to the agencies, offices, and individuals participating, with the hope that a consensus view will emerge.

During 2006 and 2007, Intellipedia editors awarded shovels to users to reward exemplary wiki "gardening" and encourage others in the community to contribute. A template with a picture of the limited-edition shovel (actually a trowel) was created to place on user pages for Intellipedians to show their "gardening" status. The handle is imprinted: "I dig Intellipedia! It's wiki wiki, baby." The shovels have now been replaced with mugs bearing the tag line "Intellipedia: it's what we know." Different agencies have experimented with other ways of encouraging participation. For example, CIA managers have held contests for best pages and awarded prizes such as free dinners.

Chris Rasmussen, a knowledge management officer at the Defense Department's National Geospatial Intelligence Agency (NGA), argues that "gimmicks" like the Intellipedia shovel, posters, and handbills encourage people to use Web 2.0 tools like Intellipedia and are effective low-tech solutions to promote their use. Also, Rasmussen suggests that social software-based contributions should be written in an employee's performance plan.

## Meaning-Based Computing

Even before the advent of social networking, the shear amount of data needed to be processed by a worker was overwhelming. Researchers and writers talked about information overload decades ago. Now data arrives from many more directions, much of it unstructured and unordered (email, IM, video, audio, etc.). Wall Street technologies have a solution for such data overload. They user powerful computers to speed-read news reports, editorials, company websites, blogs, posts, and even Twitter messages. Intelligent software then parses all the input and figures out what it means for the markets. If only we could have smart software like this for our IT-oriented blog, wiki, discussion group, and other types of messages!

Autonomy.com is a leader in the movement toward finding a way to add a sort of autonomy to this disorganized chaos of data. Termed meaning-based computing, the goal is to give computers the ability to understand the concepts and context of unstructured data, enabling users to extract value from the data where none could be found earlier. Meaning-based computing systems understand the relationships between seemingly disparate pieces of data and perform complex analyses of such data, usually in real-time. Key capabilities of meaning-based computing systems are automatic hyperlinking and clustering that enable users to connect to documents, services, and products that are linked contextually to the original text. The ability to collect, analyze, and organize data automatically to achieve this end requires these computer systems to extract meanings. Autonomy's meaning-based computing platform known as IDOL is capable of processing any type of information from any source. IDOL can aggregate hundreds of file formats including voice, video, document management systems, email servers, web servers, relational database systems, and file systems.

Google's most recent plans for "augmented humanity" will most certainly give Autonomy.com something to think about. According to Google CEO Eric Schmidt, Google knows pretty much everything about us: "We know roughly who you are, roughly what you care about, roughly who your friends are." Schmidt sees a future in which people simply don't forget anything because the computer (read that Google) remembers everything. Some of this ability is already available if you use Google tasks, contacts, calendar, and documents. Your searches are stored and accessible by Google. If you use Google e-mail and chat, this data lives on Google servers as well. Google's plan is to be able to suggest what you should do based on what your interests or knowledge requirements are. It intends to use this knowledge to suggest ideas and solutions that you may have found if you performed your own analysis. Some writers are comparing this eventuality as a clone or "your own virtual you" (Elgan, 2010). Coupled with Google's new voice synthesizer that can replicate an individual voice, it's not much of a stretch to find that one day you will go on vacation and your clone will give your team a call to set up a project meeting.

## Semantic Web

Google cloning is actually an extension of technology that exists today. Tim Berners-Lee, who invented the World Wide Web and HTML, also came up with the idea of a semantic web as shown in Figure 2.5. The semantic web represents

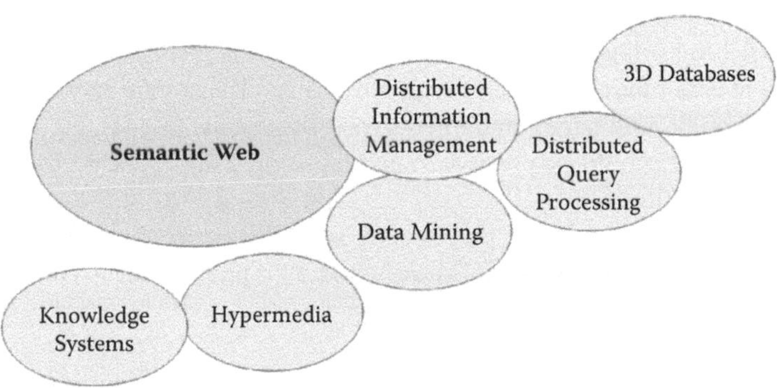


**Figure 2.5 Semantic web.**

a synthesis of all corporate and external data including results from data mining activities, hypermedia, knowledge systems, etc. It uses a common interface that makes data easily accessible by all (e.g., suppliers, customers, employees).

The semantic web is sometimes called the defined web and serves as an ultimate repository of all content and knowledge on the web. It uses XML (Extensible Markup Language, a formalized version of HTML) to tag information on intranets, extranets, and the Internet. Tim Berners-Lee explains the semantic web as follows:

> At the doctor's office, Lucy instructed her semantic web agent through her hand-held web browser. The agent promptly retrieved information about mom's *prescribed treatment* from the doctor's agent, looked up several lists of *providers*, and checked for the ones *in-plan* for mom's insurance within a *20-mile radius* of her *home* and with a *rating* of *excellent* or *very good* on trusted rating services. It then began trying to find a match between available *appointment times* (supplied by the agents of individual providers through their web sites) and Pete's and Lucy's busy schedules.

Hewlett-Packard's Semantic Web Research Group frequently circulates items of interest such as news articles, software tools, and links to websites; they are called snippets or information nuggets (Cayzer, 2004). Because email is not the ideal medium for this type of content, the group had to find a technique for decentralized, informal knowledge management. They began a research project to create a system capable of aggregating, annotating, indexing, and searching a community's snippets. The required characteristics of this for this system include:

- Ease of use and capture.
- Decentralized aggregation. Snippets will be in a variety of locations and formats. It will be necessary to integrate them and perform a global search of the results.
- Distributed knowledge. Information consumers should be able to add value by enriching snippets at the point of use by adding ratings, annotations, etc.
- Flexible data model. Snippets are polymorphic. The system should be able to handle email, web pages, documents, text fragments, images, etc.
- Extensible. It should be possible to extend snippet data schema to model the changing world.
- Inferencing. It should be possible to infer new metadata from old. For example. A machine should "know" that a snippet about a particular HP Photosmart model is about a digital camera.

Some have suggested that blogs make ideal tools for this type of content and knowledge management. However, today's blogging tools offer only some of the capabilities mentioned. Traditional blogging has many limitations but the most important one is that metadata is used only for headline syndication in a blog. Metadata is not extensible, not linked to a risk-flexible data model, and incapable of supporting vocabulary mixing and inferencing.

The researchers, therefore, looked to the semantic web for a solution. As discussed, the premise of the semantic web is that data can be shared and reused across application, enterprise, and community boundaries. RSS1.0 (web.resource.org/rss/1.0) is a semantic web vocabulary that provides a way to express and integrate with rich information models. The semantic web standard Resource Description Framework (RDF) specifies a web-scale information modeling format (www.w3.org/RDF). Using these tools, researchers devised a prototype (http://www.semanticblogging.org/blojsom-hp/blog/default/) for creating what they called a semantic blog. The prototype has some interesting searching capabilities. For example, snippets can be searched for via their own attributes ("I'm interested in snippets about HP") or via the attributes of an attached blog entry ("I'm interested in snippets captured by Bob").

## Virtual Worlds

Perhaps the most interesting of all social-based community software is Linden Labs' Second Life (http://www.secondlife.com). While Second Life is used primarily for such fun activities as fantasy role-playing (pirates, Goths, science fiction, etc.), the software has a serious side.

In 2008, IBM's Academy of Technology held a virtual world conference and annual meeting in Second Life, as shown in Figure 2.6. The virtual meeting conference space had room for breakout sessions, a library, and areas for community

**Figure 2.6 Using Second Life to host conference.**

gathering. IBM estimates that the return on investment for the virtual world conference was about $320,000 and that the annual meeting cost one-fifth that of a real-world event (http://work.secondlife.com/en-US/successstories/case/ibm/). Just think of the possibilities. Project team members near and far can use Second Life to hold virtual but tactile team meetings and even work with end users.

## Knowledge Management Tools

Knowledge management (KM) has been defined as the identification and analysis of available and required knowledge and the subsequent planning and control of actions to develop these into "knowledge assets" that will enable a business to generate profits and/or increase its competitive position. The major focus of knowledge management is to identify and gather content from documents, reports, and other sources and be able to search such content for meaningful relationships. A variety of business intelligence, artificial intelligence, and content management methodologies and tools constitutes the framework under which knowledge management operates. While we will discuss the relationship of knowledge management (KM), social networking, and software engineering in more depth later, it is worthwhile to briefly address the best-known KM construct now.

Groups of individuals who share knowledge about a common work practice over time, while not parts of a formally constituted work team, are considered "communities of practice" (CoPs) that generally cut across traditional organizational boundaries. They enable individuals to acquire new knowledge faster. They may also be called communities of interest if the people share an interest in a common task but do not necessarily perform the work on a daily basis. For example, in one government agency, a group of employees who were actively involved in multi-party, multi-issue settlement negotiations began a monthly discussion group during which they explored process issues, discussed lessons learned, and shared tools and techniques. CoPs can be more or less structured, depending on the needs of the membership (see Appendix B).

CoPs provide mechanisms for sharing knowledge throughout one organization or across several organizations. They lead to improved networks of organizational contacts, supply opportunities for peer-group recognition, and support continuous learning, all of which reinforce knowledge transfer and contribute to better results. They are valuable for sharing tacit (implicit) knowledge. To be successful, CoPs require support from organization(s). However, if management closely controls their agendas and methods of operation, they are seldom successful. This issue is more applicable to CoPs within organizations.

CoPs can be used virtually anywhere within an organization: within one organizational unit or across organizational boundaries, with small or large groups of people, in a single or multiple geographic locations. They can also be used to bring together people from multiple companies, organized around a profession, shared roles, or common issues. They create value when tacit information, if shared, produces better results for individuals and the organization. CoPs are also valuable in situations where knowledge is constantly gained and sharing it is beneficial to the accomplishment of an organization's goals.

CoPs serve a number of purposes. Some develop best practices, some create guidelines, and others meet to share common concerns, problems, and solutions. They can connect in different ways: personally, in small or large meetings, or electronically. These virtual communities of practice are called VCoPs.

VCoPs (as well as face-to-face CoPs) need a way to capture their collective experiences for online examination. Daimler AG does this via its EBOK (Engineering Book of Knowledge) system that provides best practice information on almost every issue related to the manufacture of cars. Tech CoPs share knowledge related across car processes and then consolidate it into the EBOK system.

CoPs provide a great amount of what academics call social capital that provides the motivation and commitment required to populate knowledge stores such as EBOK. CoP has historically been used for small team interaction. More recently, some organizations are attempting to use it for large group interventions, although some dispute whether this can be effectively done at all. In experiments, up to 300 people were brought together within a CoP to work through organizational issues. While it would be unusual for a software engineering effort to involve such large populations, it would not be out of the question to have to develop a system in which team members and stakeholders together approached this number. A variety of CoP-based designs apply to groups of this size. The World Café is perhaps the best known and most popular; others are Open Space Technology, Participative Design, and Wisdom Circles.

The World Café (http://www.theworldcafe.com/) describes its process as an innovative yet simple methodology for hosting conversations. These conversations link and build on each other as people move among groups, cross-pollinate ideas, and discover new insights into the questions and issues raised. As a process, the World Café can evoke and make visible the collective intelligence of any group, thus increasing capacity for effective action in pursuit of a common aim.

In a face-to-face environment, the way to do this is simple. Tables allow seating for a series of conversational rounds lasting from 20 to 45 minutes, each of which intends to tackle a specific question. Participants are encouraged to write, doodle, or draw key ideas and themes on the tablecloths, as shown in Figure 2.7. At the end of each round, one person remains at the table as the host and the others travel to new tables. The hosts welcome the newcomers and share the table's conversation so far. The newcomers share what they discussed from the tables they've already visited and so on. After the last round, participants return to their individual tables to integrate all the information. At the end of the session, everyone shares and explores emerging themes, insights, and learning. The process serves to capture the collective intelligence of the group (Raelin, 2008).

Visiting the World Café's website demonstrates how the construction was modified to suit the online environment. One output of this type of brainstorming

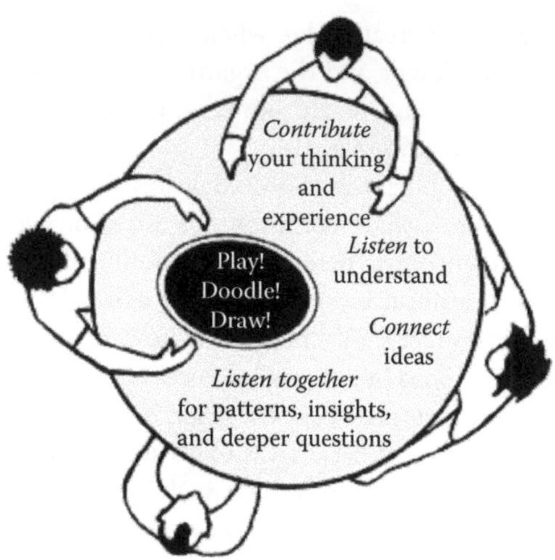


**Figure 2.7 World Café methodology.**

**Figure 2.8 Tag cloud.**

session might be a "tag cloud" or visual depiction of user-generated tags based on discussions. Tags are usually single words, usually listed alphabetically. The importance of a tag is shown by font sizes or colors as shown in Figure 2.8.

Tag clouds were popularized by websites such as Flickr and Technorati. They actually serve a very useful purpose for software engineers by providing methods to classify, organize, and prioritize the results of meetings. Because individual tags may be hyperlinks, it is possible to tag clouds to store increasingly granular levels of information. Perhaps the best-known cloud tag generator is Wordle (http://www.wordle.net/create ).

## Mashups

Web developers have long been engaged in what is known as service composition—the practice of creating value-added services by reusing existing service components. Mashups represent an emerging paradigm of Web 2.0 that enables developers and very talented end users to create new web-based applications and services that address specific needs and interests. *Mashup* implies fast integration. This is achieved by using open APIs and data sources to produce enriched results that were not necessarily the original reasons for producing the raw source data. Mashup tools generally support visual wiring of GUI widgets, services, and components together.

Some tech leaders have discontinued their mashup tool offerings (Microsoft's Popfly in 2009 and Google's Mashup Editor in 2009). However, Yahoo Pipes (http://pipes.yahoo.com/pipes/) is still supported. As Yahoo describes it:

> Pipes is a free online service that lets you remix popular feed types and create data mashups using a visual editor. You can use Pipes to run your own web projects, or publish and share your own web services without ever having to write a line of code. You make a Pipe by dragging preconfigured modules onto a canvas and wiring them together in the Pipes Editor. Each Pipe consists of two or more modules, each of which performs a single, specific task. For example, the Fetch module will retrieve a feed URL, while the Sort module will re-order a feed based on criteria you provide (you can find a complete list of available modules in the documentation). You can wire modules together by clicking on one module's output terminal and dragging the wire to another module's input terminal. Once the terminals are wired together, the output from the first module will serve as input to the second module. In addition to data feeds, Pipes also lets you add user input fields into your Pipe. These show up at runtime as form fields that users of your Pipe can fill in.

JackBe Corporation is a privately held software provider of enterprise mashup software. JackBe's flagship product is an enterprise mashup platform called Presto (http://www.jackbe.com/products/), with support for Microsoft SharePoint. JackBe launched its Enterprise App Store product in July 2010 as a platform for creating internal enterprise application stores. Enterprise App Store is aimed at non-developers, allowing them to create new business applications and share them with other users. JackBe is a founding member of the Open Mashup Alliance

(OMA) that promotes enterprise mashup interoperability and portability. JackBe was the original contributor and continues to be a key supporter of OMA's Enterprise Mashup Markup Language (EMML), an XML markup language for creating enterprise mashups (see Appendix H). These software applications consume and "mash" data from variety of sources, often performing logical or mathematical operations as well as presenting data. Mashed data produced by enterprise mashups is presented in graphical user interfaces as mashlets, widgets, or gadgets. EMML is an open language specification promoted by OMA. EMML is fairly easy to understand and use because it is a derivative of the now-familiar XML. For example, the EMML code below joins Yahoo! News, Financial News, and Reuters feeds.

```
<merge inputvariables="$YahooRSS, $FinancialNewsRss,
    $ReutersRSS"
  outputvariable="$NewsAggregate"/>
```

EMML provides a common command to invoke any publically accessible web service or website using the <directinvoke> operation. The following code shows how this operation can be used to access the Google Finance web page and retrieve the financial information for the ticker through the web clipping feature provided by EMML. Web Clipping converts the HTML result of any URI into XHTML and gives you a clip of the required content from the web page (Viswanathan, 2010):

```
<foreach variable="value" items="$itemNames/records/record">
  <template expr="http://finance.google.com/
    finance?q={$ticker}" outputvariable="wholeURL"/>
  <!-- invoke the Google Finance web page that has stock
    information -->
  <directinvoke outputvariable="clipresult"
    endpoint="$wholeURL"/>
  <assign fromexpr="$clipresult//xhtml:div[@class='g-section
    sfe-break-bottom-8']" outputvariable="clipresult2"/>
  <assign fromexpr="$clipresult2//xhtml:h3/string()"
    outputvariable="$company"/>
  <assign fromexpr="$clipresult//xhtml:span[@class='pr']"
    outputvariable="clipresult3"/>
  <assign fromexpr="$clipresult3//xhtml:span/string()"
    outputvariable="$price"/>
  <assign fromexpr="$clipresult//xhtml:div[@id='price-
    change']" outputvariable="clipresult4"/>
  <assign fromexpr="$clipresult4//xhtml:span[@class='chg']/
    string()" outputvariable="change"/>
</foreach>
```

Detailed documentation for EMML can be found on the OMA website (http://www.openmashup.org/omadocs/v1.0/index.html).

## We've Reached the End of Chapter 2

As you can see, a wide variety of tools are available to support social software engineering and you can choose from three methodologies when making a platform decision: (1) off-the-shelf, (2) mashup, and (3) build your own. This chapter has provided information to start you moving in a direction that is the most suitable for your organization. If you do decide on a do-it-yourself (DIY) solution, you will find the user interface design guide in Appendix K very useful.

## References

Anderson, C. (2006). *The Long Tail.* New York: Hyperion.

Cayzer, S. (2004). Semantic blogging and decentralized knowledge management. *Communications of ACM*, 47(12): 47–52.

Elgan, M. (2010). How Google plans to clone you. *Computerworld.* http://www.computerworld.com/s/article/9199638/

Raelin, J.A. (2008). *Work-Based Learning: Bridging Knowledge and Action in the Workplace.* San Francisco: Jossey-Bass.

Viswanathan, A. (2010, April 12). Mashups and the Enterprise Mashup Markup Language (EMML). *Dr. Dobb's: The World of Software Development.* http://deepakalur.wordpress.com/2009/09/24/omg-we-launched-oma-and-emml/

# Chapter 3

# Preparing Team to Collaborate

Jaron Lanier, the inventor of virtual reality, often criticizes the claimed omniscience of collective wisdom. In fact, he refers to the collective wisdom of the Internet as the "hive mind"—certainly not a compliment and very reminiscent of Star Trek's Borg. Lanier's argument is with the anonymity and perhaps combined level of expertise of the collective experience. Social software engineering, if done properly, should avoid the pitfalls cited by Lanier. The goal of software engineering is to produce quality software efficiently. Further, the goal of social software engineering is to enhance the quality and productivity aspects of the software engineering experience and achieving it requires us to pay special attention to software engineering productivity factors, particularly as they relate to teaming.

## Nontechnological Issues in Software Engineering

Although much of the emphasis in the literature is on the technical issues of software engineering, a number of substantive nontechnological problems pose dangers to effective practice. A lack of software engineering productivity can be caused by managerial, organizational, economic, political, legal, behavioral, psychological, and social factors. To achieve an acceptable level of software engineering productivity, as much emphasis must be placed on people issues as on technological issues. The human aspect of software engineering provides by far the largest source of opportunity for improving software productivity.

It is important to recognize that the process of software engineering is sufficiently confused and incoherent in that nontechnological factors impede the effective application of technology. The software engineering profession for the most part has not developed a sufficient block of competent managers. In spite of a concerted effort to make software development an engineering discipline, it is still very much of an individual creative activity whose practitioners sometimes thwart all efforts toward effective collaboration. Little has been done to reduce performance differences among individuals or across teams.

Poor management leads to a wide variety of problems. An inexperienced or unskilled project manager may well produce project plans that are unrealistic due to improper scheduling or estimation. Staff may become unmotivated because their creativity is unappreciated or underutilized. Effective teamwork may be lacking because of the inability of the project manager to build and manage effective teams. The project manager may engage in micromanagement, leading to inadequate delegation and ineffective organization of the project team. This problem may extend to inadequately trained staff due to a short-sighted rather than long-term perspective. Finally, the project manager may not have sufficient technical background to support a team engaged in a highly sophisticated software development effort.

A number of easy-to-implement solutions can address some of these problems. While dual career paths for technical and managerial staff are great solutions for many IT jobs, they do not represent a perfect solution for a project manager. This job needs someone who is equally savvy in both technical and managerial areas. If you have to choose one ability over the other for an open project management position, it's probably best to select someone who is technical and then provide training in managerial skills and techniques. The best approach is to institute an active mentoring and supervision program within IT, so that new project managers can tap into the expertise of seasoned professionals. In all cases, the project manager should be encouraged to delegate responsibility and matching authority wherever appropriate.

We will discuss knowledge-sharing problems in more detail in the next chapter. However, we will touch on some of the reasons for lack of effective teamwork here because this issue fits neatly into our nontechnological discussion. Many IT folks have a real desire for autonomy, and many have an unusual need for privacy. Organizational culture rewards individual efforts more than team efforts, so this behavior is reinforced. The problem is the concentration of key application knowledge by too few individuals. Aside from the fact that this can prove disastrous should one of these chosen few decide to leave or become ill, any teaming effort is destined to be lopsided as knowledge and expertise are bunched up in one or two team members. Experts have more organizational clout and power than nonexperts, so decision making becomes problematic. For example, it is not unusual for a key team member to vote down any approach that he or she did not initiate or does not personally endorse. Thus, a team's solution may reflect the ideas and decisions of the experts instead of the best approach.

Solving these teaming problems is not simple. Aside from egoless programming touted in Gerald Weinberg's now-classic tome on the psychology of programming, the best technique is to modify the organizational culture to condone and reward group efforts. Because IT departments are probably consigned to change, we can at least attempt to devise some objective assessments of team contributions and tie these assessments to appropriate rewards. Most importantly, we must make an active effort to disperse crucial application knowledge across the project staff and improve communication and coordination across organizational layers. Happily, the social form of software engineering does a good job on both fronts.

The large performance differences among individuals obviously negate productivity increases. Experts estimate that productivity ranges of 3:1 to 5:1 are typical, and some studies documented differences as high as 26:1 among experienced programmers. This variability arises for a number of interesting reasons. The most obvious is misguided staffing. Some managers simply do not know how to hire a good technical person. Even if all individuals have stellar credentials, it is quite possible that productivity may plummet due to ineffective management as discussed above. Poor team development and inattention to the critical role of motivation are also factors.

Several tactics may prove effective in trying to increase programmer productivity. Improved management and performance recognition, as mentioned, are obvious techniques. Often overlooked is the importance of making sure that the right person is selected for every job. Skills testing is paramount to ensure that the applicant's resume reflects actual skill rather than a skill in progress. You'll also want to be sure that the person is matched to the correct job and that some form of career progression is offered along with the job. Because the value of a developer equates to the number of acronyms he or she has mastered, training and professional development opportunities should be continuous. From a technology standpoint, adherence to standard practices and investment in productivity-enhancing tools and methods such as social software engineering can certainly help.

Of all of the techniques that can be used to improve productivity, the most important may be special care to achieve effective team composition. Heterogeneous teams based on experiences and skill sets have been proven to be the most effective. However, for a heterogeneous team to be truly effective, the management and knowledge sharing problems already discussed must be resolved.

## Creativity Development

Have you ever attended a trade show and walked onto the floor before the doors were open to the public? If you have, you've witnessed some energy-boosting exercises (involving lots of arm waving and yelling) that many sales managers think leads to increased sales. Software engineering as a discipline requires those practicing it to be creative, so creativity-boosting techniques have real value.

The most obvious technique is to survey staff to obtain perceptions of the environment for creativity and innovation. Based on the results, a training workshop can be used to discuss ways to generate creativity within the organization, department, and team. Facilitated by someone outside the organization, staff should be asked to keep "creativity logs" to track their creativity improvements based on workshop activities. A single workshop may be effective, but continuing workshops on a single subject matter may prove more beneficial. Aside from discussing ways to improve creativity, some creativity-inducing exercises discussed below may be helpful.

An analogy is a statement about how objects, people, situations, or actions are similar in process or relationship. Metaphors, on the other hand, are merely figures of speech. Both techniques can be used to create fictional situations for gaining new perspectives on problem definition and resolution. In the "blue slip" technique, ideas are individually generated and recorded on 3-inch by 5-inch sheets of blue paper. The recording is usually done anonymously to make people feel more at ease so that they readily share ideas. Because each idea is on a separate paper, the sorting and grouping of like ideas is facilitated. Thus, a technique or approach already used by the organization is stretched via extrapolation to apply to a new problem.

By moving through progressively higher levels of abstraction, it is possible to generate alternative definitions from an original problem. When a problem is enlarged in a systematic way, it is possible to generate many new definitions that can then be evaluated for utility and feasibility. After an appropriate level of abstraction is reached, possible solutions are more easily identified.

The 4Ws and H is the traditional and journalistic who–what–where–when–how approach that serves to expand a person's view of a problem and helps make sure all related aspects of the problem have been addressed and considered. The strength of force field analysis comes from its ability to identify forces contributing to or hindering a solution to a problem. This technique stimulates creative thinking by (1) defining direction, (2) identifying strengths that can be maximized, and (3) determining weaknesses that can be minimized. Peaceful setting is not so much of a technique as an environment. Taking people away from their hectic surroundings enables "a less cluttered open mental process."

Reversing a problem statement often provides a different framework for analysis. For example, in attempting to find ways to improve productivity, try considering the opposite aspect: how to decrease productivity. Most of us have played the game in which a person names a person, place, or thing and asks for the first thing that pops into the second person's mind. The linking of combining processes is another way of expanding the solution space. Wishful thinking enables people to loosen analytical parameters to consider a larger set of alternatives. By permitting a degree of fantasy into the process, the result may be a new and unique approach. In all cases, follow-up sessions should be scheduled for reinforcement. These sessions are primarily staff meetings and employees should be invited to identify results of creative activities. In addition to facilitated creativity-inducing workshops, several managerial techniques can be used to spur innovation, as shown in Table 3.1.

**Table 3.1 Promoting Innovation**

| *Technique* | *Definition or Example* |
|---|---|
| Commitment to problem solving | Ability to ask "right" questions; allow time for research and analysis |
| Commitment to openness | Analytical and cultural flexibility |
| Acceptance of out-of-box thinking | Seek and encourage different views, even radical ones! |
| Willingness to reinvent products and processes already in place | Create "blank slate" opportunity map, even for processes that appear battle tested and comfortable |
| Willingness to listen to everyone (employees, customers, vendors) | "Open-door" policy to show respect for data and perspectives without regard to seniority or insider status |
| Keeping informed of industry trends | Constantly scanning business publications and trade journals; clipping articles of interest; "FYI" activities among managers |
| Promotion of diversity, cross-pollination | Forward-thinking team formation that also attempts to foster diversity; sensitivity to needs of gender, race, work style |
| Changes of management policies | Instill energy and "fresh-start" thinking by revising established rules |
| Provision of incentives for all employees (not only researchers and engineers) | Compensation schemes to align individual performance with realization of goals |
| Use of project management | Clear goals and milestones; use of tracking tools; expanded communication |
| Transfer of knowledge within organization | Commitment to aggregating and reformatting key data for "intelligence" purposes |
| Provision for off-site teaming | Structured meetings and socialization outside office to reinforce bonds of key team members |
| Provision for off-site training | Development of individuals through education and experiential learning to master new competencies |
| Use of simple visual models | Simple but compelling frameworks and schematics to clarify core beliefs |
| Use of the Internet for research | Fluency and access to websites (e.g., competitor home pages) |
| Development of processes for implementing new products and ideas | Structured ideation and productization; clear release criteria; senior management buy-in |
| Championing products | Identify and prioritize products that represent best possible chances for commercial success; personally engage and encourage contributors to strategic initiatives |

## Communications and Group Productivity

Communications can dominate productivity. Most project problems arise from poor communications between workers. If a team is composed of $n$ workers, it has $n(n - 1)$ possible interfaces that may lead to communications problems. A highly motivated individual working alone is not interrupted by fellow group members and therefore can achieve very high productivity. It is estimated that one programmer working 60 hours a week can complete a project in the same calendar time as two others working normal hours, but at three-quarters of the cost.

Small groups of experienced and productive software developers can create large systems. Some years ago, I wrote about a very forward-thinking technology company that scoured the country for the best analytical thinkers. Its senior programmers typically earned well over six digits a year and were paid bonuses of two to three times that amount. They worked in small teams, never more than five people, to produce large, complex systems. In comparison, most IT departments produce large systems using normal development teams with developers of average ability. In general, the difference between the cost to produce an individual program to be run by the program author and the cost to produce a system developed by a software group, is about 1:9.

At a certain point, coordination overhead outweighs any benefit that can be obtained by adding staff. Statistics that support this were pioneered in military organizations during the nineteenth century. Research indicated that as the number of workers who had to communicate increased arithmetically from 2 to 3 to 4 to 5 and so on, the number of communication channels among them increased geometrically, from 1 to 3 to 6 to 10. The study concluded that the upper limit of effective staff size for cooperative projects was about 8; when the number of staff increased to 12 or more, the efficiency of the group decreased to less than 30%. The optimum group size for a software development team is 5 to 8 members. The overall design of any system should be partitioned into successively smaller chunks until the development group has a chunk of software to develop that minimizes intra- and inter-group communications.

## Productivity through Shared Information Technology

Organizations have made large investments in shared information technology (SIT) over the years under the guise of electronic mail systems, distributed databases, group decision support systems, and now social software engineering. Thus, it is important that a corporate culture must support sharing of information across boundaries. Two organizational prerequisites for successful investment in SIT are (1) the "right" organization culture, appropriate for and supportive of the sharing of information, and (2) timely access to shared information.

"Excellent" companies foster a great deal of communication among people in different functional areas. Communication may involve cross-functional management of cost, quality, and scheduling. This implies that communication occurs across traditional organizational boundaries and that information is shared. In traditional American businesses, the organization follows a hierarchical structure in which corporate norms dictate that communications paths follow the hierarchy. This allows certain managers to monopolize information. SIT, in contrast, allows workers to function cooperatively across traditional organizational boundaries.

If a culture does not encourage information sharing, the answer may be to plan and implement an improvement program that focuses on a single, measurable objective of strategic importance (such as quality improvement) and requires involvement by everyone in the organization. The objective is to develop a culture in which everyone is concerned with continuous improvement, measurable results, and shared information. It is essential to ensure that management behavior is consistent with the objectives of the program and that the organization's reward system encourages information sharing.

If the improvement program is successful, the next step is to develop a plan for implementing SIT. This requires development of an information infrastructure with standardized definitions of key data elements, an information technology infrastructure that provides access to both corporate and external databases, a uniform set of user-friendly tools that includes tools establishing communication protocols among individuals, and reinforcement of the new collaborative norms.

## Promoting Collaboration

A number of techniques can help promote collaboration. Pausing actually slows down the "to and fro" of a discussion. Participants have fewer "frames per second": to deal with. The technique provides precious wait time that has been shown to dramatically improve critical thinking. Pausing and the acceptance of moments of silence creates a relaxed but purposeful atmosphere. Silence, however initially uncomfortable, can be an excellent indicator of productive collaboration. Pausing also signals to others that their ideas and comments are worth thinking about. It dignifies their contributions and implicitly encourages future participation. Pausing enhances discussion and greatly increases the quality of decision making.

To paraphrase is to re-cast or translate into one's own words, to summarize, or to provide an example of what has just been said. The paraphrase maintains the intention and the accurate meaning of what has been said expressed by different words and phrases. The paraphrase helps members of a team hear and understand each other as they evaluate data and formulate decisions. Paraphrasing is also extremely effective for reducing group tension and individual anger. The paraphrase is possibly the most powerful of all nonjudgmental verbal responses because it indicates that "I am attempting to understand you" and that "I value you."

Probing seeks to clarify something that is not yet fully understood. More information may be required or a term may need to be more fully defined. Clarifying questions can be either specific or open-ended, depending on the circumstances. Gentle probes increase the clarity and precision of a group's thinking and contribute to trust building because they communicate to group members that their ideas are worthy of exploration and consideration. It takes a degree of self-confidence and courage to put forward an idea, and it is vital that collaborative groups nurture such self-confidence and courage. Ideas are the heart of a meaningful discussion. Groups must be comfortable to process information by analyzing, comparing, predicting, applying, or drawing causal relationships.

Collaborative work is facilitated when each team member is explicitly conscious of self and others. This includes awareness of what he or she is saying, how it is said, and how others are responding. Understanding how we create different perceptions allows us to accept others' views as simply different, not necessarily wrong. The more we understand about how others process information, the better we can communicate with them.

Presuming positive presuppositions is the assumption that other members of the team are acting from positive and constructive intentions despite possible disagreement with their ideas. This type of presumption is not a passive state; it must become a regular manifestation of one's verbal responses. The assumption of positive intentions permits the creation of such sophisticated concepts as "loyal opposition" and allows one group member to play the "devil's advocate." The technique builds trust, promotes healthy cognitive disagreement, reduces the likelihood of misunderstanding, and decreases affective and emotional conflicts.

Inquiry and advocacy are both necessary components of collaborative work. Highly effective teams are aware of this and consciously attempt to balance them. Inquiry provides for greater understanding. Advocacy leads to decision making. One common mistake that collaborative teams may make is to bring premature closure to problem identification (inquiry for understanding) and rush into problem resolution (advocacy for a specific remedy or solution). Maintaining a balance between advocating for a position and inquiring about the positions held by others further inculcates the ethos of a genuine learning community.

Any group that is too busy to practice the skills of collaboration is also a group that is too busy to improve. Ironically, the groups most in need of the skills of collaboration are often those most resistant to them. Groups functioning most effectively recognize the need for regular collaboration training; those in trouble are very often too busy to examine how they work together—or fail to work together.

One excellent way of developing the skills of collaboration is round-robin reflection. The activity works best when groups are relatively small (fewer than 8 people) and a time limit (20 to 30 minutes) is set. Round robin is also more effective the second or third time it is used, as participants become more comfortable with the process of reflection. At first, the paraphrasing may seem forced, artificial, and even tedious. However, the more it is used, the greater the likelihood that it will become part of an individual's unconscious repertoire of collaborative strategies. Round robin enables groups to think about how they function as a collaborative team.

Following a meeting or problem-solving discussion, a team should take 20 or 30 minutes to follow the steps outlined below:

1. Each member of the group is assigned a letter: A, B, C, etc.
2. Person A begins by briefly describing how his participation has affected the group's work. No interruptions or questions are permitted. Maximum time is 2 to 3 minutes.
3. Person B asks Person A a probing question or briefly paraphrases what A said. Again, no interruptions or questions are permitted.
4. Person B briefly describes how his or her participation has affected the group's work. Again, no interruptions or questions are permitted.

This activity continues in a round-robin fashion until all members have had opportunities to describe how their participation affected the group. Following the round robin, the group should briefly discuss what was said.

## Collaboration and Knowledge Management

Software engineering is an inherently collaborative process. Teaming problems are only exacerbated by collaborating virtually, so it is important for managers to find ways to promote inter- and intra-team knowledge transfer. That this is based on knowledge management should come as no surprise. Knowledge management can be defined in three dimensions: (1) knowledge (experience), (2) information (context), and (3) data (facts). Note that data represents an explicit form of knowledge and knowledge is a tacit form. Knowledge is converted between the tacit and explicit forms, as shown in Table 3.2. If knowledge includes the experience and understanding of the people in the organization along with the information artifacts available within the organization and outside the organization, knowledge management must have a way to identify, collect, store, and transfer that knowledge within the organization, as shown in Figure 3.1.

Siemens (n.d.) developed a Knowledge Management Maturity Model (KMMM) loosely based on the Software Engineering Institute's widely used Capability Maturity Model (CMM). As shown in Table 3.3, the CMM framework closely

**Table 3.2 Converting between Tacit and Explicit Knowledge Forms**

| *Conversion* | *Process* | *Examples* |
|---|---|---|
| Tacit to tacit | Socialization | Team meetings and discussions |
| Tacit to explicit | Externalization | Team dialogs; answering questions |
| Explicit to tacit | Internalization | Learning from reports |
| Explicit to explicit | Combination | Emailing reports |

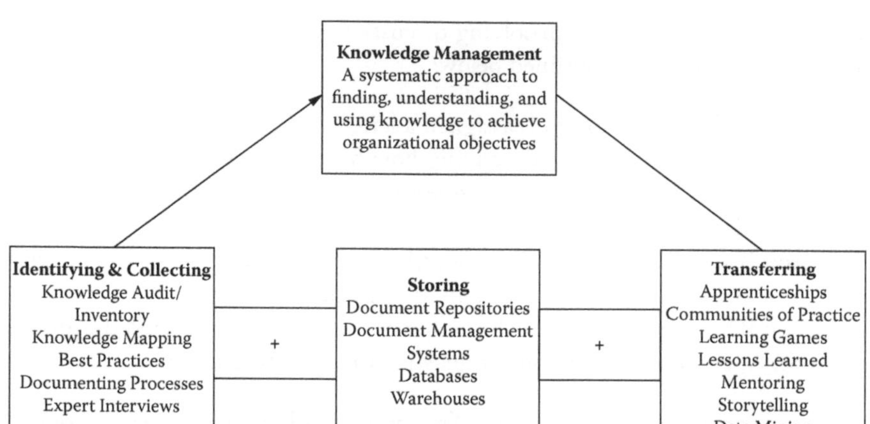


**Figure 3.1 Knowledge management process.**

**Table 3.3 Software Engineering Institute's Capability Maturity Model**

| *Level* | *Focus* | *Key Process Areas* |
|---|---|---|
| 5 – Optimizing | Continuous process improvement | • Defect prevention<br>• Technology innovation<br>• Process change control |
| 4 – Managed | Product and process quality | • Process measurement and analysis<br>• Quality management |
| 3 – Defined | Engineering process | • Organization process focus<br>• Organization process definition<br>• Peer reviews<br>• Training program<br>• Inter-group communication<br>• Software product engineering<br>• Integrated software management |
| 2 – Repeatable | Project management | • Software project planning<br>• Software project tracking<br>• Software subcontract management<br>• Software configuration management<br>• Requirement management |
| 1– Initial | Putting out fires | • Ad hoc |

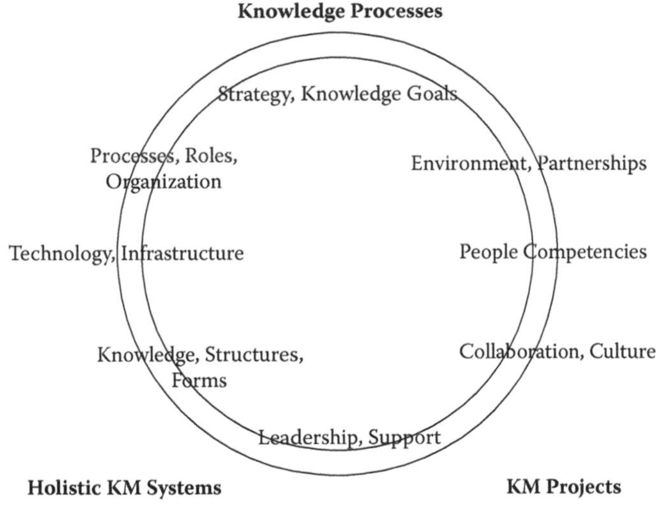


**Figure 3.2 KMMM analysis model.**

followed by those who practice rigorous software engineering methodology, consists of five levels. Siemens' KMMM utilizes the same five levels: initial, repeated, defined, managed, and optimizing in its development model. The KMMM also has an analysis model as shown in Figure 3.2 that creates transparency in all the key areas of knowledge management and thus provides a vehicle for improvement. The development model provides the methodology for reaching the next level.

Project teams must be able to effectively share and transfer knowledge and collaborate toward a solution. However, this is more easily said than done. Many individual developers closely guard their information. Some knowledge management exercises and practices will be useful to prepare the project team to effectively work together and share information.

## Best Practices

Best practices require an organization to identify and use processes or practices that result in excellent products or services. Best practices, sometimes called preferred practices, often generate ideas for improvements in other work units. Best practices represent ways of doing business and developing processes, methods, and strategies that yield superior results. They have been implemented and honed over time to a point where they are viewed as exemplary and should or could be adopted more widely. A formal "benchmarking" process is often used to identify best practices. A full description of this technique is beyond the scope of this chapter, but many books and other resources cover the subject.

Identifying and sharing best practices allow an organization to incorporate the knowledge of some into the work of many. Organizational structures tend to promote "silo" thinking by which locations, divisions, or functions focus on maximizing their own accomplishments and rewards, guarding their information, and thus sub-optimizing the whole organization. Silo thinking lacks the mechanisms for sharing of information and learning. Identifying and sharing best practices help build relationships and common perspectives among people who do not work side by side. Best practices can also spark innovative ideas and generate suggestions for improving processes, even if a practice cannot be adopted completely. The process of identifying ideas can also benefit employee morale. By highlighting or showcasing their work, employees enjoy organization-wide recognition.

## Expert Interviews

An expert interview engages one or more people considered experts in a particular subject, program, policy, or process to meet with others to share knowledge. Expert interviews can capture the knowledge of those scheduled to leave an organization, conduct debriefings to discover lessons learned, identify job competencies, and even videotape the reflections of recent retirees about the reasons for successes and failures.

Expert interviews make tacit knowledge more explicit. A person can describe what was done and why, and also provide context and explain the judgment behind the action. Interviews are often easier for experts than documenting all the details and nuances of their subjects. Learners can ask questions and probe more deeply to ensure understanding. Making time for these sessions is probably the biggest challenge for both the experts and learners. In formal sessions involving large groups of learners, some participants may be intimidated and need coaching.

Expert interviews apply in many situations. The best place to begin is with people who have unique knowledge developed over a long period and may leave the organization soon. The next step may be identifying mission-critical processes or programs in which only one or two staff members have high levels of technical knowledge. Expert interviews are probably most effective when someone facilitates the experience, setting the stage with participants, facilitating the exchange of any information prior to the interview, and handling scheduling and other logistics.

Identify the experts and learners who should participate and the knowledge you want to transmit. Discuss with the experts the reasons for the interviews, who will be involved, and the focus of the interview. If learners must prepare for the session, the expert can identify how to do this and what resource materials would be helpful. It is also essential to ask the learners what they want to learn from the expert. If they have specific questions, provide these to the expert in advance so he or she can be prepared. If a session is formal and involves large numbers of experts and learners, a facilitator can help keep the session focused and on time. If the interview is a one-on-one meeting, a facilitator is probably not needed. Audio or video taping should be arranged in advance and equipment should be tested to ensure that all participants can be heard.

## Job Aids

Job aids are tools that help people perform tasks accurately. They include checklists, flow diagrams, reference tables, decision tree diagrams, and other materials that provide specific, concrete information and serve as quick reference guides to performing tasks. Job aids are not the tools such as computers, measuring devices, and telephones that perform work. A job aid can take many forms but basically it is a document containing information or instructions about performing a task. It guides a user to work correctly and is used during performance of a task when an individual needs information about a procedure. Types of job aids include

- Step-by-step narratives or worksheets sequencing a process
- Checklists that may detail items to be considered when planning or evaluating
- Flowcharts that lead a user through a process and assist the user in making decisions and completing a task based on a set of conditions
- Reference resources such as parts catalogs and telephone listings

Job aids are usually inexpensive to create and easy to revise. Using job aids can eliminate the need for employees to memorize tedious or complex procedures. When a job aid is easy to access, it can help increase productivity and reduce error rates. Job aids must be written clearly and concisely and leave nothing open to interpretation. They also must be updated regularly. Finding the time to create job aids can be a challenge, but good job aids produce benefits over the long term.

Consult with knowledgeable users to identify job aids to develop. Create job aids that include only the steps or information required by users. Keep the information and language simple; use short words and sentences. Do not include background or other information extraneous to performance of the task; keep that in another location. Use graphics or drawings when appropriate to demonstrate detail. Use bold or italicized text to highlight important points. Use colors to code different procedures or parts of a process. Make sure the job aid is sturdy and readily available. A laminated wall chart hung near a worksite can be consulted more quickly than a paper stored in a file.

Job aids are most appropriate for complex tasks or steps that are not performed frequently. Tasks involving many steps that are difficult to remember or may cause errors that can lead to high costs can benefit from accessible job aids. Also, job aids save time and reduce chances of errors for tasks that change frequently. They can serve as good supplements to classroom training because they provide users with information to rely on as they do a job.

## Knowledge Audits and Knowledge Fairs

Knowledge audits help an organization identify its knowledge assets including what is available and what is needed. Audits provide information on how knowledge assets are produced and shared, and reveal needs for internal transfers of knowledge. Knowledge fairs showcase information about an organization, department, topic, or project. They can be used internally to provide a forum for sharing information or externally to educate customers and other stakeholders about important information.

A knowledge fair is a showcase for information about an organization or a topic. It can be organized to include speakers, demonstrations, or more commonly, booths displaying information of interest to the attendees. One example is Xerox Corporation's annual Team Day showcasing the work of various quality improvement teams. A large amount of information can be made available and attendees can focus specifically on what they are interested in learning. They may interact directly with presenters to get immediate answers to their specific questions. They also can establish contacts for further exploration of topics if needed.

Attendees often network with one another, and booth developers often strengthen their teamwork skills. Knowledge fairs also provide opportunities to draw attention to best practices and recognize employee and team achievements. Depending on scope and size, an event may require large amounts of staff time for creating booths, compiling information for displays, and handling organization and logistics. The costs for space, materials, and resources can be high. The potential exists for participants to become overwhelmed with information.

Consider a knowledge fair when you have a lot of information to share with a lot of people and participants need broader perspectives and opportunities to interact on a one-on-one basis on specific topics. A knowledge fair is an alternative to traditional presentations if more interactive experiences are desirable.

## Knowledge Maps and Inventories

Knowledge maps and inventories catalog information available in an organization and where it is located. They point to information but do not contain it. An example is an expert or resource Directory that lists people with expert knowledge who can be contacted by others in need of their knowledge. Knowledge mapping is particularly useful for the analysis phase of a software development lifecycle.

Knowledge mapping involves surveying, assessing, and linking the information, knowledge, competencies, and proficiencies of individuals and groups within an organization. Organizations use knowledge maps for various purposes, for example, compiling company locators to find internal and external resources and identifying knowledge sharing opportunities or knowledge barriers within cross-functional work groups. Many organizations use knowledge mapping before developing formal communities of practice. The knowledge mapping process does not have the goal of mapping how knowledge flows throughout an organization. The process consists of the following steps:

- Discover locations, ownerships, values, and uses of knowledge artifacts.
- Learn the roles and expertise available.
- Identify constraints to the flow of knowledge.
- Highlight opportunities to leverage existing knowledge.

A knowledge map describes what knowledge is used in a process and how it flows around the process. It serves as a basis for determining knowledge commonalities and areas where knowledge is used across multiple processes. A map describes who has the knowledge (tacit), where the knowledge resides (infrastructure), and how the knowledge is transferred or disseminated (social). Knowledge mapping is used to focus on the strategic and tactical knowledge assets of an organization. On an enterprise level, it should focus on strategic, technical, and market knowledge along with the cross-functional linkages of divisions or business groups. On a tactical level, the focus should be on working groups and the processes within the groups. At all levels, a knowledge map assesses existing or required knowledge and information as follows:

- What knowledge is needed?
- Who has this knowledge?
- Where does this knowledge reside?
- Is the knowledge tacit or explicit?
- Is the knowledge routine or nonroutine?
- What issues does it address?

The American Productivity and Quality Center (APQC) developed a Road Map to Knowledge Management (www.apqc.org) consisting of five stages for implementing knowledge management (KM): (1) getting started; (2) develop strategy; (3) design and launch KM initiatives; (4) expand and support; and (5) institutionalize KM. Within this context, knowledge mapping is recommended at stage 2 or stage 3.

Process knowledge mapping analyzes a business process or method to identify

- Design milestones (when knowledge is needed)
- Knowledge requirements (what knowledge is needed)
- Routes for access and retrieval of knowledge (through people and technology)
- Gaps between current and required skills

Questions to be asked during this process include

- What do you need to know?
- Where does the knowledge come from?

- Who owns it?
- What knowledge, tools, templates exist today?
- What knowledge, tools, templates should be created?
- What barriers or issues exist?

The method for mapping the process or focus area consists of

- Reviewing critical processes
- Identifying individual steps within each process
- Determining routine and nonroutine tasks
- Identifying key decision points, hand-offs
- Locating owners of and stakeholders in high-value processes
- Following knowledge pathways through the organization via interviews or brainstorming
- Inventorying types of knowledge utilized and needed; categorizing knowledge content (explicit, tacit, embedded), social capital (trust, interpersonal relationships, cultural norms), and infrastructure (processes, tools, roles and responsibilities, incentives)
- Identifying gaps, lacks of connectivity, and information overloads
- Developing plans to collect, review, validate, store, and share knowledge
- Creating measurement criteria for each critical process step

A sample knowledge process map might look like Table 3.4. Completed maps should be analyzed. For each process step, the knowledge resources should be reviewed to determine

- Do we leverage this today?
- Is the knowledge available and accessible to everyone who needs it?
- Are decisions based on all the right knowledge?
- Where should we focus our improvement efforts?

Finally, summarize the analysis for creating a list of key strengths and key opportunities.

## Learning Games

Learning games are structured learning activities used to make learning fun and more effective, review material presented earlier to strengthen learning, and evaluate how much learning occurred. Games can also be used to

- Help people prepare for learning by testing current levels of knowledge.
- Apply a newly learned skill.

**Table 3.4 Sample Knowledge Map**

| *Process Step* | *1 – Conduct design session* | *2 – Document product gap* | *3 – …* |
|---|---|---|---|
| Objective of step | Gather requirements for software | Clarify requirements not met by package | Etc. |
| Infrastructure | Methods and tools database; deliverables database; project management guidelines | Vendor-supplied methods; methods and tools database; deliverables database | |
| Social capital | Consultant discussions; connecting with subject matter experts | Vendor and technical consultant discussions | |
| Tacit knowledge | Knowledge of previous design sessions; estimating experience | Knowledge of developers' skills and package capabilities | |

- Learn as they play the game.
- Practice what has been presented to reinforce the learning.

Games improve knowledge transfer by

- Increasing participation among all involved
- Improving the learning process by creating an environment where people's creativity and intelligence are engaged
- De-stressing learning by making it fun
- Addressing the different ways in which different people best learn, through movement, hearing, and seeing
- Adding variety to a training program to keep people actively involved

When games are used as an end in themselves and not a means to an end, they waste time and can hamper learning. In addition, too many games can destroy learning effectiveness. Games are usually used in conjunction with other learning methodologies such as presentations and discussions. When you use them and if you use them will depend on the learning you want to convey and whether games will help meet your learning objectives.

Games used at the beginning of a program can measure existing knowledge and build immediate interest in the training material. Games used during a program can help people discover the learning (which strengthens recall and commitment), practice using new knowledge or skills, and reinforce initial learning. Games used near the end of a program can test knowledge gained and the ability of participants to apply the learning in their work settings. To be effective, games must

- Relate to the workplace by providing knowledge, reinforcing attitudes, and initiating actions important to job success.
- Teach people how to think, access information, react, understand, and create value for themselves and their organizations.
- Be enjoyable and engaging without being overly simplistic or silly.
- Allow collaboration among learners.
- Be challenging but not unattainable.
- Permit time for reflection, feedback, dialog, and integration (debriefing).

Examples of games include

- Quizzes
- Scavenger hunts
- Quiz show games including those modeled on television game shows such as *Jeopardy* or *Family Feud*
- Board games such as GOER's Supervision Central
- "Name that" games
- Sports-related games
- Twenty questions

## Lessons-Learned Debriefings

Debriefings allow participants to identify, analyze, and capture experiences and discuss what worked well and what needs improvement to enable others to learn from their experiences. For maximum impact, lessons-learned debriefings should be held immediately after an event or on a regular basis, with results shared quickly among those who can benefit from the knowledge gained. Hewlett Packard refers to lessons-learned sessions held to share knowledge during and after projects as "project snapshots."

Session(s) conducted at the completion of a project or activity, or at strategic points during a project or work team's ongoing work, where members of the team or group evaluate the process used and the results. They identify what was done right and what could be done better the next time. These sessions identify and capture the things that went well and the things that could be improved so that team or workgroup members are aware of and can use the broader team/group's learning in their future projects or work activities. Results can also be shared with future teams or other workgroups so they can learn from the experiences of others.

Making the time to conduct lessons-learned debriefing sessions and documenting the results are the biggest challenges. The sessions should convene as soon as possible (within 30 days) after the completion of the project or activities or be conducted at any strategic point during a project. A lessons-learned session work bests as a formal review held in a functional meeting room, using facilitator(s) and an assigned note taker. It is essential to develop ground rules for the session, e.g., listen for understanding, respect others' contributions, prohibit blaming, and ensure full participation and include appropriate people:

- Project sponsor
- Project or work unit manager
- Project team or work unit staff
- Customers
- Stakeholder representatives including manager responsible for project oversight
- Other appropriate executive management
- Others (based on nature of the project or work, e.g., maintenance, information systems, technical services, and operations staff)

Additional considerations include

- Ensuring lists of lessons learned are process oriented and aimed at improving work processes, not individual performances
- Requiring feedback to be constructive
- Describing specific behaviors and their effects
- Acting nonjudgmentally
- Identifying actions and behaviors that may be more effective
- Recognizing positive contributions
- Reviewing lessons-learned forms

As an alternative, have groups of six to ten people answer the following questions and consolidate responses for all the groups. You may want to consider the commonality or strength of agreement on the responses. Select questions from the following or develop your own. Open-ended questions usually elicit the best responses.

- What worked best on the project or activity?
- What could have been better on the project or activity?
- How can we improve the methodology to better assist in the successful completion of future projects or work activities?

- What parts of the project or work resulted in meeting the specified requirements and goals? What helped assure these results?
- What parts did not meet specifications and goals? What could have been done to ensure that these were met?
- How satisfied were the customer(s) with results? What was particularly good? What could have been done to improve customer satisfaction?
- Were cost budgets met? Why or why not? What helped or hindered staying within budget?
- What contributed to meeting the schedule? What hindered it?
- What appropriate risks were identified and mitigated? What additional risks should have been identified or what additional actions should have been taken to mitigate risks?
- What communications were appropriate and helpful? What additional communications would have been helpful?
- How did the project or activity management methodology work? What worked particularly well? What could have been done to improve it?
- What procedures were particularly helpful in producing deliverables? What could have been improved? How can we improve or streamline processes?

Another method is to develop, post, and use a list of eight to ten items or objectives considered most important for success. The team leader, work unit leader, and facilitator may develop this list in advance or develop it with participants at the start of the session. Possible items to help keep the discussions focused include

- Meeting customer expectations
- Achieving all specifications
- On-time completion
- Within-budget completion
- Achieving return on investment
- Meeting organizational goals
- Positive experiences for group members

Management should determine how well these items were accomplished (fell short, met, exceeded expectations) and identify actions that contributed to or hindered the accomplishment of each objective. See below for a possible meeting notes template. Another strategy is to identify eight to ten major strategies, activities, or processes that helped the project or work unit and eight to ten major problems encountered during the project or activity, then determine what may be done to address or prevent the problems in the future.

The project or work unit manager is responsible for (1) making all arrangements, (2) ensuring that the appropriate people attend, (3) ensuring that the necessary materials and documentation are available, and (4) communicating results to appropriate right people throughout the organization. The facilitator handles typical facilitation responsibilities.

Surveys can replace or supplement meetings. Consider professional assistance for developing and administering a survey to a large group or to people outside the organization. The survey could be in the form of a written questionnaire mailed to respondents or administered during a meeting. Consider the method of administration and recipients (sponsors, team or workgroup members, customer representatives, consumers, or other stakeholders). Survey goals include

- Reviewing product delivered against baseline requirements and specifications
- Determining how well customer needs were met
- Learning whether the product or service was delivered effectively and efficiently
- Finding areas needing improvement

## Storytelling

Storytelling involves the construction of fictional examples or the telling of real organizational stories to illustrate a point and effectively transfer knowledge. An organizational story is a detailed narrative of management actions, employee interactions, or other intra-organizational events communicated informally within an organization. When used well, storytelling is a powerful transformational tool for an organization. The technique uses two types of anecdotal examples to illustrate a point and effectively transfer knowledge. Organizational stories (business anecdotes) are narratives of management or employee actions, employee interactions, or other intra-organizational events communicated formally or informally. Future scenarios create a vision for the enterprise that describes how life will be different after a particular initiative or change fully implemented and provide a qualitative way to describe the value of an initiative even before it starts. Storytelling has many benefits; for example, stories

- Capture context that gives them meaning and makes them powerful
- Are natural, easy, entertaining, energizing, and comfortable
- Help us make sense, understand complexities, and assist us to see our organizations and ourselves in a different light
- Are easier to remember than recitations of facts
- Are nonadversarial and nonhierarchical
- Engage our feelings and our minds and are thus more powerful than logic alone
- Complement abstract analysis
- Reveal similarities of listeners' backgrounds, contexts, fields of experience, and thus help them to see the relevance of their own situations
- Act as powerful transformational tools
- Are only as good as the underlying idea

- Require good presentation skills because they are usually presented orally
- Are seldom used alone and are normally combined with other approaches such as quantitative analysis, best practices, and knowledge audits
- Impart meaning and context to ideas, facts, and other kinds of knowledge derived from other knowledge management tools
- Can support decision making, aid communications, engage buy-in, or market an idea or approach
- Are best used early to engage listeners or achieve buy-in if they are used to illustrate the value of a way of thinking or explain an idea

In using storytelling, the message, plot, and characters must be considered. Determine what underlying message is to be conveyed (e.g., importance of organizational goals, impacts of changes, end benefits associated with change effort, mechanics of new process). How does the story illustrate the underlying message (plot)? Who was involved in the story (characters)? Think about the audience. At whom is the story aimed? What will each audience do with the story's message? What message will be told to each audience? How do we tell each desired story? According to Denning (2001), four different structures for using stories have been developed:

- Open with a springboard story, and then draw out its implications.
- Tell a succession of stories. Multiple stories can enhance the chances that the audience will co-create a follow-up. For example, if you want to describe the benefits of a proposed change effort, tell a story that only partly serves your purpose and then extrapolate with an anecdote (e.g., future scenario) that describes how the story will play out when the change is fully in place. Alternatively, tell a series of related stories that, taken together, illustrate various ways in which a change effort will pay off.
- Accentuate the problem. Start by describing the nature of a problem, tell a story, and draw out the implications.
- Simply tell the story. This is useful when time is very limited and you want to plant a seed.

A story should

- Be relatively brief and reveal only enough detail for the audience to understand it. Listeners will get caught up in too much detail and miss the message.
- Be intelligible to a specific audience and be relevant.
- Be inherently interesting, maybe because the problem is difficult and old ways of resolving it no longer work; tension exists between characters in the story, or unexpected events or elements of strangeness are present.
- Embody the idea you want to convey and provide an easy mental leap from the facts of the story to its underlying message.
- Have a positive ending, to avoid creating negative or skeptical reactions.

- Convey an implicit change message, especially if the audience is skeptical or resistant; the audience can then discover the change message and consider it their own idea
- Feature a protagonist with whom the audience can identify—a protagonist typical of the organization and its main business.
- Deal with a specific individual or organization.

True stories are generally more powerful than invented stories and can serve as jumping-off points for future scenario stories. Stories should be tested on individuals or small groups before they are used on large groups or in high-risk settings. A story must be simple, brief, and concise. It should represent the perspectives of one or two people in a situation typical of the business so that it is familiar to the audience. Similarly, a story should be plausible and "ring true" to listeners. It must be alive and exciting, not vague and abstract. Including a strange or incongruous aspect allows a listener to visualize a new way of thinking or behaving. A story should help listeners extrapolate from the narrative to their own situations. Finally, a storyteller must believe (own) the story and tell it with conviction or the audience will not accept it.

## We've Reached the End of Chapter 3

It always amazes me that IT management seems to throw ITers on a team without adequately preparing the team and its members for the difficult task of working collaboratively. This chapter covered the problems of teaming and hopefully offered effective solutions to team problems.

## References

Denning, Stephen. (2001). The *Springboard: How Storytelling Ignites Action in Knowledge-Era Organizations*. Woburn, MA: Butterworth-Heinemann.

Siemens Corporation. (n.d.). Knowledge management maturity model: KMMM. http://www.kmmm.org/objects/KMMM_Flyer.pdf

New York State Department of Civil Service. (2002). *Report of Knowledge Management Transfer Work Group*. http://www.cs.state.ny.us/successionplanning/workgroups/knowledgemanagement/knowledgemanagetransfer.html

# Chapter 4

# Knowledge Sharing and Software Engineering Teams: A Study

Nonaka (1994) defined knowledge as a justified belief that increases an entity's capacity for effective action. In this chapter, we will demonstrate how knowledge management, in particular its knowledge sharing component, directly affects the success of any social software engineering framework deployed by IT.

## Knowledge Management

Davenport and Prusak (2003) define knowledge management as the processes that support knowledge collection, sharing, and dissemination. Knowledge management is expected to improve growth and innovation, productivity and efficiency reflected in cost savings, customer relationships, decision making, innovation, corporate agility, rapid development of new product lines, employee learning, satisfaction and retention, and management decision making (Pollard, 2005; Alavi, Kayworth, and Leidner, 2005 and 2006).

The sources of competitive advantage migrated from their bases on economies of scale to being based on economies of expertise derived by leveraging knowledge distributed in an organization network through intra- and inter-organizational relationships. Subramani and Venkatraman's (2003) study found that while physical asset specificity was a determinant of governance in the industrial age, domain knowledge specificity has the potential to be a key determinant in a knowledge-driven economy.

Many senior managers emphasize knowledge management as an important means of innovation (Parikh, 2001; Paraponaris, 2003; Suh, Sohn, and Kwak, 2004). In organizations, it is essential to address effective knowledge flow among employees and knowledge collaboration across organizational boundaries while limiting knowledge-sharing barriers (Lee and Ahn, 2005; King, Marks, and McCoy, 2002; Parikh, 2001; Paraponaris, 2003). Weiss, Capozzi and Prusak (2004) cited an International Data Group (IDG) report estimating that an organization with 1,000 workers might easily incur a cost of more than $6 million per year in lost productivity when employees failed to find existing knowledge and recreated knowledge that was available but could not be located. On average, 6% of revenue as a percentage of budget is lost from failure to exploit available knowledge (So and Bolloju, 2005).

Leaders of businesses can use these findings to develop new processes and procedures for overcoming resistance to knowledge sharing that may eventually translate to increased innovation, productivity, and competitive advantage.

The recognition that knowledge is a key strategic asset for organizations of all sizes is discussed throughout the literature (Oltra, 2005). It follows then that knowledge management is also widely discussed (i.e., advantages and disadvantages, successes and failures). Carneiro (2000) asserts that, with a few exceptions, few viable strategic knowledge systems exist within organizations.

A variety of reasons explain knowledge management implementation problems. Oltra (2005) found that the emphasis is on cultural, organizational, and human aspects as potential levers or inhibitors of knowledge management. However, Oltra also notes the relatively minor consideration of cultural and people issues in the knowledge management literature. A key reason for lack of knowledge management viability is the unwillingness of employees to share their knowledge effectively with their peers (Lee and Ahn, 2005). Modern project teams are often agile. Problems may arise because software engineering teams have different members at different times. Bushe (2010), who writes on leadership and organization development, points out four possible problems:

1. *Loss of knowledge.* The longer someone stays on a team, the more knowledge he or she acquires about the project, problem domain, and stakeholders. Loss of a team member means loss of experience and knowledge. The best approach is to ensure that the team has some stable team members.
2. *Thinking differently.* When a group of people work together for any length of time, they develop a way of synchronized thinking. New team members may need some time to adapt to this shared thinking. Use of knowledge management systems or social networking technologies (knowledge bases, wikis, blogs) can greatly accelerate a new team member's trip along the learning curve.

3. *Low commitment.* If you know that your term on a team will be short, it may be difficult to feel totally committed to the team's efforts. Motivation is the key to solving this problem. A reward system is one method to overcome low commitment. Both positive and negative rewards can be used. While positive reward systems (days off, bonus pay, etc.) are common, negative reinforcement approaches should be considered as well.
4. *Lack of cohesion.* Team members may experience problems in building a sense of identification with a team whose membership changes constantly. Bushe's solution is to find a way for workers to identify with other people who do the same job at the same company. He calls these groups practice centers, and the technique is a derivative of the knowledge management community of practice (CoP) concept that joins workers across organizational lines to discuss common goals.

One way around this problem, as suggested by the authors of *The 2020 Workplace*, is hiring an entire team. Meister and Willyerd, the authors of *2020*, predict that a highly cooperative and engaging social atmosphere will dominate the workplace of the future. Along with replacing outsourcing with crowd sourcing, the authors suggest that companies recruit teams of employees to work on projects and assert that some companies already do this. As this trends grows, the authors visualize the formation of guilds that move as groups from one company to another.

## Knowledge Management Issues

Knowledge and knowledge workers are considered intellectual capital of a company and a key factor in its sustainable development. Carneiro (2000) asserts that managers must be able to embed more knowledge value in their decisions to produce a new, improved, or even better alternative than their competitors. Knowledge management has become a strategic tool in most organizations.

Siemens Corporation has fully adopted knowledge management as a strategic tool. At Siemens, knowledge is regarded as the means for effective action. At companies like Siemens, knowledge management systems are considered socio-technical systems (Halawi, McCarthy, and Aronson, 2006). These systems encompass competence building, emphasis on collaboration, ability to support diverse technology infrastructures, use of partnerships, and knowledge codification for all documents, processes, and systems.

Siemens is widely known as a company built on technology and an early adopter of knowledge management. The company's goal is to share existing knowledge in a better way and create new knowledge more quickly. Siemens' holistic approach clearly demonstrates the importance of people, collaboration, culture, leadership, and support. Absence of these critical success factors reduces the likelihood of knowledge-sharing success. Siemens is considered a knowledge management success story. However, Green (2006) asks whether most businesses in the knowledge era have truly institutionalized the leveraging of knowledge adequately to manage and control the intangible assets that contribute 70% of the value to a typical business.

## Knowledge Management and Knowledge Sharing

Knowledge can be defined as a fluid mix of framed experiences, values, contextual information, and expert insight that provides a framework for evaluation and incorporating new experiences and information (Davenport and Prusak, 2000). The knowledge in an organization is embedded in the minds of its employees and in organizational routines, processes, practices and norms, sometimes referred to as socially constructed templates (Guzman and Wilson, 2005).

The realization of organizational knowledge depends on people who interpret, organize, plan, develop, and execute the socially constructed templates. Most importantly, organizational knowledge depends on specific situations and does not always rely on absolute truths or quantitative facts. Thus, one can conclude that organizational knowledge has some soft features that are related to the subtle, implicit, embedded, sometimes invisible knowledge, presumptions, values, and ways of thinking that permeate employee behaviors, decisions, and actions. Ultimately, organizational knowledge is complex and ambiguous.

Effective management of these ambiguous layers of knowledge in organizations is a primary factor for success in a knowledge economy in which harvesting knowledge is a key to remaining competitive and innovative (Abdullah, Kimble, Benest, and Paige, 2006). Studies reveal that many large organizations engage in knowledge management to improve profits, remain competitively innovative, respond to a perceived *brain drain*, or simply survive (Lau, Wong, Hui, and Pun, 2003; Davenport and Prusak, 2000). Keskin (2005) stated that "firms have become much more interested in stimulating knowledge, which is considered as the greatest asset for their decision making and strategy formulation" (p. 169). Knowledge then is considered by most firms as the key to competitive advantage.

Knowledge is a well-organized combination of information, assimilated within a set of rules, procedures, and operations learned through experience and practice (Keskin, 2005). The literature classifies knowledge as tacit and explicit. Explicit knowledge may be seen, shared, and easily communicated to others. Most explicit knowledge is in the form of raw data such as documents containing the work experiences of staff, descriptions of events, interpretations of data, beliefs, guesses, hunches, ideas, opinions, judgments, and proposed actions (Choo, 2000).

Tacit knowledge is more difficult to share because it is embedded in individual memories. DeLong and Fahey (2000) described tacit knowledge as what we know but cannot explain. They explain that tacit knowledge is (1) embodied in mental processes, (2) originates from practices and experiences, (3) expressed through ability applications, and (4) transferred in the form of learning by doing and watching.

Knowing how to solve a problem using tacit knowledge thus involves personal interpretation, ability, and skill (Abdullah et al., 2006). Ardichvili et al. (2006) argues that sharing and internalizing tacit knowledge require active interaction among individuals, using knowledge management techniques such as storytelling. Tacit knowledge sharing is affected by distributive justice, procedural justice, and cooperativeness, indirectly via organizational commitment, and also by instrumental and expressive ties via trust in co-workers (Lin, 2006).

Knowledge management is a broad discipline that may be divided into several themes: knowledge management procedures, knowledge management techniques, knowledge management technologies, and knowledge sharing issues, the last of which has ramifications for successful social software engineering. Knowledge sharing can be compared to organizational citizenship behavior or pro-social organizational behavior—positive social acts carried out to produce and maintain the well-being and integrity of others (Connelly and Kelloway, 2003). Pro-social behaviors include acts such as helping, sharing, donating, cooperating, and volunteering. Knowledge sharing is not necessarily synonymous with pro-social behavior. Indeed, knowledge sharing may involve significant effort or sacrifice. Yet, one of the critical success factors for knowledge creation, transfer, and sharing is that employees willingly contribute their knowledge or expertise to a company (DeTienne, Dyer, Hoopes, and Harris, 2004).

In general terms, research about knowledge sharing barriers covers several basic concepts: (1) cultural background (age, ethnicity, educational level) affects knowledge sharing (Ardichvili, Maurer, Li, Wentling, and Stuedemann, 2006; Ojha, 2005; Riege, 2005); (2) organizational culture affects knowledge sharing (Lin and Lee, 2006; Connelly and Kelloway, 2003; Bock and Kim, 2002); and (3) IT support affects willingness to share knowledge (Flanagin, 2002; Lin and Lee, 2006; Connelly and Kelloway, 2003). Riege (2005) considered 36 knowledge sharing barriers based on an extensive literature review and categorized the barriers as (1) individual, (2) organizational, and (3) technological.

Reige's (2005) findings were reinforced by an extensive survey by Sveiby and Simons (2002) of 1,180 staff members of the Australian Transport Union (ATU). They determined that the ATU culture was not conducive to knowledge sharing for a variety of reasons including (1) absence of support systems, (2) lack of training, (3) job security, (4) employee competition, (5) organizational culture, and (5) lack of recognition. Many of the barriers Reige described were revealed in the results of the survey; organizational culture yielded the lowest score.

Group compatibility and knowledge sharing are related. The more compatible a person is with the group in terms of age, gender, and other factors, the more likely he or she is to practice knowledge sharing (Ojha, 2005). Conversely, individuals who perceive themselves in a minority based on gender, marital status, education, etc., are less likely to participate in knowledge sharing. Of particular note is the finding that female participants required a more positive social interaction culture before they perceived a knowledge sharing culture as positive (Connelly and

Kelloway, 2003). Sun and Scott (2005) confirmed Ojha's findings. The list of compatibility variables included more than the obvious traits of age, gender, ethnicity, and educational level. Personality differences, communication skills and individual values also factored into the equation (Ojha, 2005).

Interestingly, Ojha (2005) also found a relationship between organizational tenure and knowledge sharing. A long organizational tenure had a negative effect on knowledge sharing. One employee commented in a study by MacKinlay (2002) that he felt he was asked to give himself away when asked to share his knowledge. There are many reasons for this type of fear. For example, long-term employees may feel threatened by those they consider their potential replacements, or they may feel of discomfort in dealing with newer and often younger arrivals.

Several studies employed age as one of many variables (Ojha, 2005; Riege, 2005). For the most part, researchers noted that the more age-compatible a team is, the more likely the team will engage in effective knowledge sharing. However, age diversity is often present. Older workers are sometimes technology resistant or may feel threatened by younger employees they consider rivals. Slagter (2007) recommends a more proactive management style toward older employees to facilitate successful use of knowledge management.

Ardichvili et al. (2006) discusses cross-cultural differences in knowledge-sharing patterns based on three criteria: individualism versus collectivism, in-group versus out-group orientation, and fear of losing face. Individualism is the tendency of people to place their personal goals ahead of the goals of the organization, while individuals from collectivist cultures tend to give priority to the goals of the larger collective, group, or company to which they belong. Essentially, members of individualist cultures like those in the United States view themselves as independent of others. Members of collectivist cultures such as in China, Brazil, and Russia see themselves as interdependent with other members of their groups.

Collectivists tend to distinguish sharply between in-group and out-group members. Chow, Deng, and Ho (2000) compared factors influencing knowledge sharing behaviors of American and Chinese managers and found that Chinese nationals were much more reluctant to share with out-group members than employees in the United States were. Hwang, Francesco, and Kessler (2003) found that individualists were more concerned with gaining face (impressing colleagues) than collectivists. They found that individuals who wanted to gain face were more likely to use formal communications channels to show their knowledge and ability; those who feared losing face preferred informal communication channels. This has ramifications for the use of formal knowledge sharing systems like intranets and blackboards because collectivists may resist using them. The possible cultural barriers to successful knowledge sharing include age, gender, organizational tenure, culture, and ethnicity as key factors.

## Organizational Culture's Effect on Knowledge Sharing

Organizational culture consists of the shared values, beliefs, and practices of people in an organization. Beyond the mission statement and stated values lies a deeper level of culture that is embedded in the way people act, what they expect of each other, and how they interpret each other's actions (McDermott and O'Dell, 2001). Culture is rooted in core values and assumptions; it is taken for granted and is thus often hard to articulate. Essentially, some aspects of organizational culture are confusing or even invisible to organization members.

Some organizations exhibit little awareness or realization of the value and benefit of possessed knowledge to others. Hierarchical, position-based status and formal power issues may also act as inhibitors. In other organizations, a general lack of time and resources may affect the sharing of knowledge (Riege, 2005). Sun and Scott (2005) categorized organizational culture-related barriers as organizational relationships, organizational climate, organizational structuring, and organizational imperative.

Organizational culture influences knowledge-related behaviors in four ways. First, cultures and particularly sub-cultures heavily influence what is perceived as useful, important, or valid knowledge in an organization. Second, culture mediates the relationships among levels of knowledge, i.e., it dictates what belongs to the organization and what knowledge remains in control of individual employees; it determines who is expected to control specific knowledge, who must share it, and who can hoard it. Third, culture creates a sub-text for social interaction in that it represents the rules and practices that determine the environment within which people communicate, i.e., the cultural ground rules. Finally, culture shapes the creation and adoption of new knowledge (DeLong and Fahey, 2004). Thus, organizational culture (and its related sub-cultures) affects the level of collaboration within an organization, and collaboration is the key to successful knowledge sharing.

As noted by Sveiby and Simmons (2002), the collaborative climate is a major factor that influences the effectiveness of knowledge programs as it improves knowledge sharing and organizational effectiveness. It was suggested that a culture audit be conducted to determine the extent to which organizational culture exhibited the values of collaboration, empowerment, action taking, and informality (Albert and Picq, 2004).

Collaboration in software development organizations usually takes the form of teaming. Team performance increases with the amount of knowledge that employees share (Kayworth and Leidner, 2005, 2006; Wang, 2004). A positive relationship between individual self-interest concerns (e.g., competition, job security) and reduction in knowledge sharing intentions was also identified (Wang, 2004). Riege (2005) reinforced this finding by claiming a relationship between apprehension or fear that sharing may reduce or jeopardize job security and a lack of knowledge sharing intentions. Knowledge sharing imposes costs on knowledge contributors. Under intensive competition for rewards, status, and promotions, employees often regard their unique knowledge as power. If others gain power, they fear they will lose theirs (Lee and Ahn, 2005). It takes a great deal of trust to make an employee share this level of power.

Interestingly, Foos, Schum, and Rothenberg (2006) found a positive correlation between knowledge sharing and trust among team members. Ultimately, successful teams overcome these fears. This may be attributed to workplace ethics—knowledge sharing is considered the right thing to do (Wang, 2004).

Some companies may be tempted to reward knowledge sharing behavior as a spur to successful collaboration and teaming. However, Albert and Picq (2004) assert that most companies do not provide individual rewards based solely on the ability to learn or to share knowledge. Bock and Kim (2002) found no relationship between the use of rewards and knowledge sharing. Instead, they conclude that promoting a positive attitude toward knowledge sharing triggers a positive intention to share knowledge. However, Hutchings and Michailova (2004) recommend rewarding the group rather than the individual. Kwok and Gao (2005/2006) theorized that extrinsic motivation is not an influential variable; thus, it should not be necessary to establish reward systems. They suggest that more effort should be given to reinforcing employee absorptive capacity (the ability to acquire, assimilate, and use knowledge) and knowledge transmission mechanisms. They suggest that employees with closely aligned knowledge bases work together more frequently for knowledge sharing purposes. They assert that greater learning performance resulting from their large absorptive capacities will lead to favorable attitudes toward knowledge sharing and outstanding sharing achievement.

Organizational factors, such as hierarchy, power, available resources, support, reward systems, and ultimately attitude about knowledge sharing, may either impede or promote knowledge sharing behaviors. Willem and Scarbrough (2006) discuss the potentially negative effects of power and organizational politics on the role that social capital plays in knowledge sharing. They argue that the role of power is under-explored in the literature. They also assert that the effects of power are diverse, making it a highly complex factor in knowledge sharing.

## IT Support's Effect on Knowledge Sharing

Knowledge management systems are often driven by technology. McDermott and O'Dell (2001) analyzed the relationship between information technology (IT) support and knowledge sharing within an organization. They found a relationship between IT support and the *perceived* relative advantage (degree to which knowledge sharing was perceived to benefit the conduct of business) of knowledge sharing and the perceived compatibility (fit to business processes). They also concluded that IT support negatively affected the perceived complexity of knowledge sharing. Like McDermott and O'Dell (2001), Bock and Kim (2002) identified a positive relationship between the level of information technology use by individuals and their knowledge sharing behaviors. Indeed, most research evidenced a positive relationship between the use of technology and knowledge sharing intentions.

Devedzic (2001) listed the technologies thought to be knowledge sharing and knowledge management enablers. These included ontologies, document retrieval software, groupware, intranets, knowledge-based systems, pointers to people, decision support systems, data mining, and intelligent agents. However, Alavi, Kayworth, and Leidner (2005, 2006) found that the values of organizational members influenced the ways in which technologies were used, implying that organizations cannot expect uniform use of knowledge management tools by different groups.

King, Marks, and McCoy (2002) studied knowledge management practitioners and found that the success of knowledge management rested on an IT infrastructure. Such applications included (1) knowledge repositories—databases that allow the storage and retrieval of knowledge; (2) best-practices and lessons-learned systems—knowledge repositories used specifically to explicate, store, and retrieve best practices and make lessons learned available to others; (3) expert networks—electronically accessible experts who can be contacted by others who have questions related to the experts' fields of expertise; and (4) communities of practice defined as electronically enabled networks of self-organizing groups whose members share professional interests.

It is important to stress that a poor understanding of the relationships of sources of knowledge and users of knowledge that may overlap can lead to one of two extremes: a focus on IT as the only tool or absence of a dedicated IT resource (Al-Ghassabi, Kamara, Anumba, and Carillio, 2004). Those researchers also suggested that cultural implications may produce IT systems that are not compatible with the environment of an organization and its structure. For example, they found that gender significantly affected knowledge management usage, with males more likely to use such systems than females (Taylor, 2003).

Lam and Chua (2005) studied the mismanagement of knowledge management and found the key factors to be technological ignorance, technical over-complexity, lack of technical infrastructure scalability (i.e., inability to support the required volume of users), and techno bias (i.e., believing that technology solves all problems). Abdullah et al. (2006) extensively evaluated the role of knowledge-based systems in knowledge management and asserted that such systems had fallen out of favor due to organizational and managerial issues. However, they recommended reevaluation of the contributions of these systems to knowledge management.

Few new technologies are used by employees who have not received training or support from management (Connelly and Kelloway, 2003). The researchers cited a study in which employees had no incentives to use a new system; in fact, they were afraid of giving their expertise to colleagues who might use this knowledge to get promoted. A wide variety of information technologies fit within the knowledge management rubric, particularly for software engineering professionals. However, several factors can lead to the success or failure of implementation, for example, training, management support, and even age, gender, and culture of employees.

## Techniques for Promoting Knowledge Sharing

Two hotel companies found four main ways to increase knowledge sharing: motivation, feedback, communication, and socializing (A problem shared, 2005). By inspiring employees to increase their feelings of belonging to an organization, motivation for knowledge sharing increased. The authors projected a multiplier effect among employees as the benefits of sharing permeated through an organization. Most organizations send employees through various training programs. The authors found that these training sessions could have a greater effect if employees shared the knowledge gained through debriefing sessions with their peers. These debriefing sessions were also good examples of enhanced, informal, channels of communications by which ideas and knowledge could be communicated. Finally, the authors proposed that organizations should enable frequent socialization through events, outings, and mentoring programs. These methods engendered experience sharing and built trust.

Cross, Parker, Prusak, and Borgatti (2001) proposed mapping knowledge flows across organizational boundaries to yield critical insights about areas where management should target efforts to promote collaboration. Four relational qualities were found to promote effective knowledge sharing. Knowing what someone else knows (knowledge) is a precursor to seeking a specific person when faced with a problem for which a solution is needed. However, knowing to whom to turn is useful only if timely access to that person is possible. Access is influenced by the closeness of the relationship, physical proximity, organizational design, and use of collaborative technology. When access is available, knowledge can be shared only if the expert understands the problem experienced by the person seeking assistance (engagement). At this point, the expert can shape his or her knowledge to help solve the problem. Finally, the safety of the person seeking knowledge is of utmost concern. The ability to admit a lack of knowledge and seek assistance results in creativity and learning.

Cross et al. (2001) found it particularly important to identify points of knowledge creation and sharing that hold strategic relevance. Potential domains that might yield this benefit include senior management networks, collaborative initiatives, joint ventures and alliances, and communities of practice (CoPs).

CoPs constitute a common knowledge sharing or transfer method. In a CoP, groups of individuals share knowledge about a common work practice over time even though they are not members of a formally constituted work team. CoPs often cut across traditional organizational boundaries. The purpose of this organizational structure is to enable individuals to acquire new knowledge more quickly. Jakobson (2008) documented the use of CoPs at the Des Moines-based Weitz Company that implemented the communities to enable its workforce, which exhibited a wide diversity in ages, to collaborate more effectively. Weitz invested in its employees through a variety of methods, including job rotation, shadowing programs, executive internships, and mentoring. Older Weitz employees were suspicious that the mentoring program was designed to drain their experience before terminating them. To counter this negative feeling, Weitz created CoPs in which junior and senior employees came together to share best practices to prevent senior employees from feeling that they were simply offloading knowledge.

Widen-Wulff and Suomi (2007) developed a framework for creating an organization-wide knowledge sharing information culture that included sources, organizational learning, and business process re-engineering. They stressed that the organization needed to provide basic resources like technology. When resources were made available, the organization must ensure that the basic resources were turned into competencies, i.e., employees knew how to exploit them. The authors also asserted that the concept of organizational learning must be embedded in an organization, and it was imperative to recognize that an organization's workforce was more than a mere collection of expert individuals. The experts had to hone their skills to adapt and distribute their expertise through official and unofficial networks. Thus, the authors suggested that effective knowledge sharing be rewarded.

Major benefits of knowledge flow freely throughout an organization, but a number of cultural, social, and technological barriers often limit effective flows of knowledge among workers. The age variable affects knowledge sharing (Ojha, 2005). Team members of similar ages are likely to band together and interact more freely within their subgroup. It should also be noted that individuals who perceive themselves in a minority were less likely to participate in team-level knowledge sharing. Sun and Scott (2005) concluded that barriers to knowledge sharing arose from at least fourteen sources; the major ones were organizational relationships, organizational climate, organizational structuring, and organizational imperative. Finally, Lin and Lee (2006) identified a positive relationship between the use of technology and knowledge sharing. The key is that management cannot expect knowledge sharing to occur spontaneously. Management must initiate knowledge sharing within an organization.

## IT Worker Study

I decided to put these theories to the test and interviewed twenty-one IT practitioners over a 1-month period. Our discussions focused on three major research questions:

1. What are the cultural reasons that cause employees to resist the sharing of knowledge?
2. What are the organizational reasons that cause employees to resist the sharing of knowledge?
3. What are the key reasons employees list for not wanting to share their expertise?

All participants were engaged in some aspect of high-tech industries and could be considered knowledge workers. The spread of the sample by age (Question 4), gender (Question 5), and position (Question 1) demographics is detailed in Tables 4.1

**Table 4.1 Distribution of Subjects by Age (Question 4)**

| *Age of Subject* | *Number* |
|---|---|
| 21 to 30 | 0 (0.0%) |
| 31 to 40 | 2 (9.5%) |
| 41 to 50 | 10 (47.6%) |
| 51 or more | 9 (42.8%) |

**Table 4.2 Distribution of Subjects by Gender (Question 5)**

| *Gender of Subject* | *Number* |
|---|---|
| Female | 7 (33%) |
| Male | 14 (66%) |

**Table 4.3 Distribution of Subjects by Position (Question 1)**

| *Position of Subject* | *Number* |
|---|---|
| Non-management | 4 (19%) |
| Middle manager | 12 (57%) |
| Senior manager | 5 (24%) |

**Table 4.4 Tenure in Company versus Tenure in Industry**

| *Years* | *Tenure in Company* | *Tenure in Industry* |
|---|---|---|
| 0 to 10 | 15 (71.0%) | 4 (19.0%) |
| 11 to 20 | 1 (4.7%) | 5 (23.8%) |
| 21 to 30 | 4 (19.0%) | 6 (28.5%) |
| 31 or more | 1 (4.7%) | 6 (28.5%) |

through 4.3, respectively. Table 4.4 compares participants' tenures to tenures in the industry (Questions 2 and 3, respectively). Most participants were senior staff members with lengthy tenures in their companies and many years in their industries. Their senior status was reflected in their educational attainments as shown in Table 4.5.

Thus, the sample for this study consisted of highly educated knowledge workers with lengthy tenures in their industries and organizations. Their expertise was readily evidenced during the interviews. The participants were uniformly cooperative and reflective. They were knowledgeable about knowledge management and fully

**Table 4.5 Distribution of Degrees**

| *Degree* | *Number* |
|---|---|
| Doctorate | 7 (33%) |
| Master's | 5 (24%) |
| Bachelor's | 6 (29%) |
| Some college | 3 (14%) |
| No college | 0 |

understood the ramifications of sharing or failing to share knowledge. Question 7 specifically addressed the importance of knowledge sharing. Each participant provided a thoughtful response to this question. All articulated the importance of knowledge sharing to the organization and to them.

## Question 1: What are the cultural reasons that cause employees to resist the sharing of knowledge?

Age, education, ethnicity, gender, and tenure with the company and industry were examined to determine whether these factors affected the sharing of knowledge. Table 4.6 summarizes the cultural reasons the participants suggested for knowledge sharing problems in their respective companies. None of the study participants felt that tenure (organizational or within the industry) impacted knowledge sharing. Of the remaining cultural factors, education had a moderate impact while ethnicity and age had the most pronounced effects on knowledge sharing.

While most study participants noted no significant knowledge sharing problems related to age, some interesting perspectives were uncovered. Mature, less-educated participants felt that younger colleagues did not adequately share

**Table 4.6 Cultural Factor Summary**

| *Cultural Factor* | *Number of Sources* | *Number of References* |
|---|---|---|
| Ethnicity | 8 (38%) | 13 (29%) |
| Education | 3 (14%) | 4 (8%) |
| Age | 7 (33%) | 8 (18%) |
| Gender | 2 (10%) | 3 (7%) |
| Tenure, organization | 0 | 0 |
| Tenure, industry | 0 | 0 |

knowledge. Participant 7, who was over 50 and did not complete college, clearly articulated this: "Some younger people are not personable. There is no respect. They don't even say hello to me in the hall."

Two of the twenty-one participants emphasized the concept of respect. While this was only casually mentioned by 19% of the other participants, respect—or the lack thereof—appeared an important factor in knowledge sharing.

Participant 14, a senior manager with an advanced degree in computer science, confirmed the fact that age may be a variable to be considered in knowledge sharing: "Age-wise we're fairly homogeneous so we really don't have knowledge sharing problems." Nineteen percent of the participants observed that older employees had more problems sharing and obtaining knowledge for their own use. Participant 19, a computer engineer, shared this insight: "Knowledge is power and people are trying to hold onto some of their advantage over other employees. I think older people have this problem more."

Participant 5, a senior manager in his 50s, noted that some older employees may lack a command over modern technologies and thus run the risk of exclusion from the knowledge sharing loop. "I have my phone. I use it as a phone. I don't text. People in their 20s and 30s are texting like crazy. The younger crowd is more technically involved. There is definitely a risk for people over 50 for being kept out of the loop. I see them struggling."

Advanced degrees were held by 57% of the participants in the study. Most participants (about 86%) indicated that education had little to do with knowledge sharing. Participant 8, the CEO of the case study firm, said, "I had several people working for me with advanced degrees. There were no problems with knowledge sharing. What's important is you're only as good as your last project. When the guy stops hitting home runs, he's fired. What matters here is how good you are, not the degrees you have."

There were dissenters, however. Participant 19 noted that those with higher educations shared more: "If you work with someone who has less than a bachelor's degree, they might want to share less because that's just their upbringing, and they might feel more threatened."

Ethnicity was a difficult subject for many of the participants. Some feared labeling as racists if they articulated their true feelings. Many participants worked in culturally diverse metropolitan areas and felt that few real knowledge sharing problems related to the levels of diversity aside from the language barriers. However, 24% of the participants cited problems in this area.

Participant 7, who worked in a company located in the New York area and labeled by the press as the most diverse in the United States, said: "We have a diverse workforce. However, knowledge sharing is impeded by inability to speak proper English. They are just hard to understand. You can't get a point across." The same participant added: "With different ethnicities, there is no common ground, so it is hard to share information with them."

Common ground was a recurring theme in the discussion. Participant 9, a nonmanagerial employee who did not complete college, had this to say about her diverse workplace: "In terms of the comfort factor, if you have different cultures trying to get along, it could put up a barrier because you don't feel comfortable relating. In terms of knowledge sharing, there has to be some sort of comfort factor that you will be understood what you are trying to share."

Some participants pointed to the reticence of some cultural groups to communicate. Asians were singled out on two occasions. Participant 10, a senior project manager who is pursuing a doctorate, said: "Some cultures may be more reticent to communicate. Just a natural quietness. Sometimes I run into some folks of Asian background that tend to be less communicative. But that's just my experience."

The cultural factors studied included ethnicity, education, age, gender, and tenure. Tenure within the organization or industry had no effect on knowledge sharing. On the other hand, the research demonstrated that education somewhat impacted knowledge sharing. While 86% of participants felt that education did not impact knowledge sharing, some participants felt that the higher the educational level, the more likely a person was to share knowledge. Consequently, the lower the educational level, the less likely a person was to share knowledge, possibly due to fear that he or she lose the only thing that constituted value to the company.

The research uncovered a more definite relationship between age and knowledge sharing, and between ethnicity and knowledge sharing. Thirty-three percent of the participants noted a divide between older and younger workers, with the younger workers less willing to share with older workers. Nineteen percent of the participants indicated that long-tenure workers who also tended to be older felt threatened by younger workers and as a result did not share knowledge with them. As Participant 17 said: "They don't want to be taken over."

Participant 5 brought up an interesting issue concerning the fact that younger people might be more technologically adept. For example, younger people tend to use text messaging to stay in constant communication. Like many of the older participants, Participant 5 preferred face-to-face and email communication and feared that his lack of "technological savvy" about communication media may keep him out of the loop.

The research found that ethnicity was a factor in knowledge sharing. The ability to understand what was communicated, cultural mores that define the ways different groups communicate, and work ethics were cited as barriers to knowledge sharing by the participants. Trust, comfort, and respect figured prominently in the interviews. The participants uniformly asserted that these factors had to be present in the cultural mix if knowledge sharing were to succeed in their organizations.

## *Question 2: What are the organizational reasons that cause employees to resist the sharing of knowledge?*

Table 4.7 maps the participants against the various organizational factors examined in the study. "Number of Sources" indicates the number of participants who

**Table 4.7 Organizational Factor Summary**

| *Organizational Factor* | *Number of Sources* | *Number of References* |
|---|---|---|
| Job security | 4 (19%) | 7 (7%) |
| Metrics, use of | 1 (4%) | 1 (1%) |
| Organizing | 2 (9%) | 3 (3%) |
| Politics | 8 (38%) | 10 (10%) |
| Time | 7 (33%) | 7 (7%) |
| Organizational, general | 19 (90%) | 44 (44%) |
| IT support | 15 (71%) | 23 (23%) |

mentioned this factor. "Number of References" indicates the number of times the factor was cited during the interview. Ten percent of the participants indicated that they withheld knowledge due to job security issues and 19% mentioned that they knew of others who had this problem. Participant 16, a chief technology officer with a master's degree, had this to say: "Technology people are not often the best in terms of sharing knowledge or communicating. My team members do have that problem. I think it's job security. They haven't been trained or led to believe that it's important to do that. It's a lot of desire to keep things to themselves because then they have this particular power over others." It was understandable that office politics would figure prominently in the discussions. More than 38% of the participants mentioned politics in their interviews. Participant 1 summed this up by stating simply that "knowledge is power."

Two aspects of politics are fear and control. Participant 18 stressed that sharing "knowledge opens people up and makes them vulnerable... it might open me up to criticism." Participant 13, a senior manager pursuing his doctorate, continued: "In some cases, people may hesitate because of the political arena... so to speak. They may be fearful to speak up about something that others may not agree with... They might be afraid that what they say will not be well received by others—whether it's someone above them or just their colleagues."

Thus, fear was a factor: fear of disagreements or fear of looking foolish. Control was the most common aspect of corporate politics. Participant 12, a computer engineer with a master's, summed up the thoughts of most participants. "There are egos involved. There are control freaks—someone wants absolute control so they keep information from others."

Perhaps the most corrosive political problem preventing knowledge sharing was a work environment that, as Participant 90 said, "has a survivor mentality." She remarked: "People do not want to share between departments. There is a definite 'survivor'-type feeling. They do things to make themselves look good. I think it's much healthier for us to work together and share information, but we can't. We are wary about giving other departments information, because they'll utilize it to make us look bad."

Participant 9 stated that management influenced corporate politics. Participant 15 said: "In a small company, it comes from the CEO. The CEO creates that kind of culture. In a larger company, it's more departmental because people don't have that sort of visibility. Who is the top guy or woman that this person's career is influenced by and that's the person whose culture that they create drives those sorts of behaviors." Participant 15 clearly stated that management set the tone for effective knowledge sharing within the organization. However, as Participant 4, a project manager with a master's, stated: "I'm not real sure if management really recognizes their responsibility or that there may be a problem."

Thirty-three percent of the participants indicated that their managements did not actively support knowledge management practices. As Participant 10 explained: "Corporate sees a different world. It's just perspective. You can't appreciate or understand something you can't perceive." Some participants viewed management as the principal problem. Participant 9 said: "The head of the company was hired to bring back the money. He has pets, shows favoritism. He is very political. He is playing one group against the other. He comes across as wanting all of this. He seems very interested in a good culture and sharing. But he's really interested in playing the game. He is just interested in looking good with the Board of Directors so that his contract will be extended. We are very fragmented. I find out much of my information third hand. The head of the company comes across as very involved. He wants all of this Kumbaya. He wants all this knowledge sharing—openness. That's his philosophy. But he doesn't implement it."

Participant 14 talked about management's inertia and the ad hoc nature of any attempts at knowledge sharing: "The company could benefit from officially supporting knowledge sharing. I don't know why there is a problem. Some of it may be political. Some of it may be because it's never been done. Senior management is aware of it; they just don't do it. There was some talk, but nothing happens. There's a level of inertia. It's mentioned and then there's not really a follow-through. If it were going to be organizational wide, it should be top down, bottom up. There is no pilot program. No one leading it. It's just kind of ad hoc."

Even when management supported knowledge sharing, other factors had to be overcome if employees were to share knowledge effectively. Twenty-nine percent of the participants mentioned time constraints. Participant 13 described this problem. "Time limitations are a definite factor. People are busy. They've got other priorities. It's difficult to have a structure that's ongoing that brings people out of their daily routine that gets them talking and sharing."

Participant 20 noted that knowledge sharing was impeded by "sleep deprivation" caused by too much work. Participant 3, a CEO and holder of a doctorate, linked the problems of time to the problems of effective organizing: "No problem in doing this but staff has problems organizing stuff, making it available, always time issues, what's the priority."

Most organizations maintain a variety of databases. Those practicing knowledge management may also have multiple knowledge bases. Organizing the knowledge bases for effective knowledge sharing may be a challenge, although fewer than 10% of the participants indicated this as a major hurdle. Participant 12 asserted that knowledge silos created problems and led to redundant information and work efforts: "Two weeks ago I went to a meeting. This room had a bunch of poster boards in there. I said, "Hey, this is just what we're working on." I talked to one of my colleagues. I said, "You know about that project up there. Isn't it the same thing that we're doing?" I said, but why weren't we collaborating? I am not sure what the barrier is. They were a totally different group. But why weren't we collaborating? We are working in silos.

Only one of the participants worked at a company that emphasized knowledge sharing. Participant 16 said: "We have a department called Center for Leadership and Organizational Excellence. Knowledge sharing is their charter. It's ingrained in the culture. All managers are required to take certain training that explains the importance of knowledge sharing and how do they have to promote it to their direct reports."

Participant 15, whose company did not actively promote knowledge sharing, had advice for management on how to promote effective knowledge sharing within the organization: "One way they do this is by tying people's business goals together. In my organization, people get compensated, and they get bonuses and their bonuses are based on certain metrics. And I think that the best way to promote the sharing of information is to tie people's metrics together down to the line item. If I get compensated for something and a peer that I collaborate with doesn't, he might not share information with me or seek information from me. By tying people's goals together, you get the best cooperation."

All of the participants indicated that one of the major ways organizations could promote effective knowledge sharing was by providing technologies to assist in this area. Most participants indicated that their organizations provided some of these technologies. Participant 4 talked about his company's use of intranet-based technologies to support this effort: "Managers have web pages where they can post solutions to problems. This way we can all be on the same page and knowing what each other are doing."

A variety of collaborative technologies including Microsoft Sharepoint, Centra for white boarding and video, and WebEx were used for video-enhanced distributed meetings and document sharing. Despite the wealth of technology available, other participants indicated that their organizations were not particularly forward thinking in this area. Participant 18 said: "We're so behind the curve that we needed to have a meeting on how to share your calendar in Outlook. I would like a more intuitive and user-friendly knowledge-sharing product."

Other participants described how post 9/11 security concerns forced IT departments to take stringent measures at the request of management. As Participant 12, a computer engineer at a firm with government contracts, emphasized: "There's a whole lot of ill feelings between the people that run the computer networks and the computer users because they put the network security in place as if computers are used for one purpose—word processing and email. It doesn't really facilitate engineering and science. The security restrictions have gotten bad since 9/11. However, if this system ever did get used, it would be very valuable as much of the information cannot be found in any book. Computer networks are great, but this is where the barrier has been put up. When 9/11 happened they put this big barrier up. They took away all of the file sharing. We went from Ethernet to sneakernet. No chat. Period. That's just a no-no. We don't have collaborative technologies. We have to pass files around via email."

Several organizational factors either support or impede effective knowledge sharing in an organization. These include job security, use of metrics, organizing, office politics, lack of time, organizational, management issues, and IT support. Nineteen percent of the participants indicated that the issue of job security was twofold: (1) fear of losing face if they provided incorrect information or others disagreed with them and (2) the desire to control situations or people by sharing or withholding information.

Office politics was another factor discussed by 38% of the participants. Politics may produce corrosive effects, particularly if management spearheaded a political problem or overlooked it. As Participant 15 stated: "Who is the top guy or woman that this person's career is influenced by, and that's the person whose culture drives those sorts of behaviors."

Lack of time and the inability to organize properly the vast information stores these organizations possess were also cited as factors that inhibited the effective sharing of knowledge by 29% of the participants. Participant 15 advised that the only way knowledge sharing could be effective was to add it to the goals of the organization and measure its use. Organizational issues related to management generated the most discussion. Thirty-three percent of the participants stressed that many of those in charge of companies did not effectively promote knowledge sharing. Some did not endorse it at all (by inaction), and some paid it "lip service" but did not provide the support required. One notable exception, Participant 16, stated that knowledge sharing was engrained in his company's corporate culture and pointed to a department created solely for this purpose.

All the participants discussed the technology tools in use at their organizations; they ran the gamut from email to collaborative whiteboards. Some participants mentioned problems in using these technologies, including high-level security infrastructures that precluded easy sharing of files and "being behind the curve" in the use of technologies.

## *Question 3: What are the key reasons employees list for not wanting to share their expertise?*

Questions 1 and 2 enumerated the general cultural and organizational factors that impeded or enhanced effective knowledge sharing in an organization. Question 8

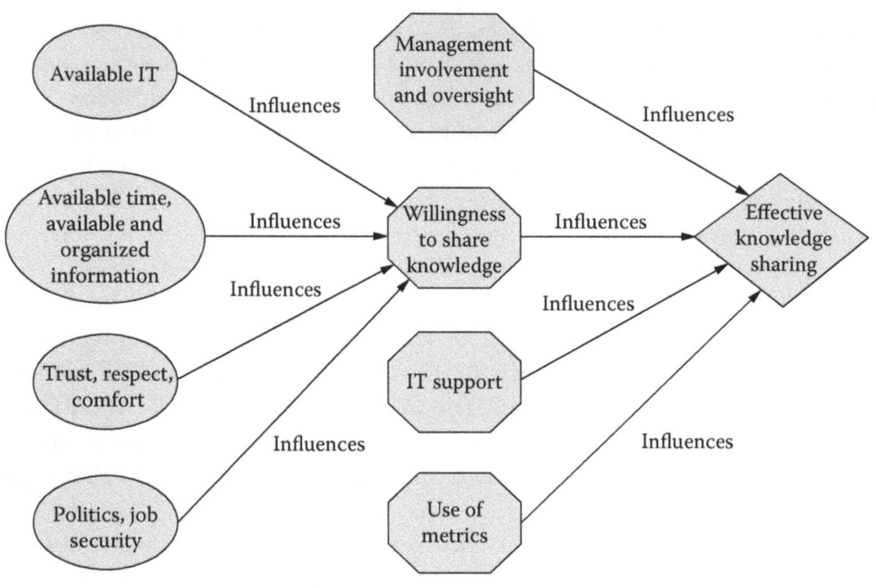


**Figure 4.1 Key factors affecting knowledge sharing.**

in the interview attempted to elicit the key reasons for knowledge sharing problems. Many were addressed in the discussions in the preceding sections and are diagrammed in Figure 4.1.

A variety of factors affected the willingness to share knowledge in the sample population. Workers first needed to feel secure in their jobs. They needed to know that the act of sharing knowledge with their co-workers would not diminish their jobs in any way. Perhaps, more importantly, office politics served as a potential barrier to effective collaboration and knowledge sharing, diminishing any eagerness for knowledge sharing. One participant even mentioned the survivor-type mentality in her office, an allusion to the popular television program that pits teams against each other.

Trust, respect, and comfort were mentioned as variables that also affected the willingness to share knowledge. The participants stated that workers needed to trust and respect their co-workers. Based on the diversity of the modern organization, one of the most important factors that seemed to affect willingness to share knowledge was the level of comfort in dealing with others. In the presence of a language or cultural barrier, that level of comfort did not effectively exist, thereby diminishing effective knowledge sharing.

More than a few of the participants indicated that they simply did not have sufficient time to share knowledge; they were too busy getting their base-level work completed. Several participants also complained about the lack of knowledge organization within their companies. Essentially, they felt that it was difficult to find the information they needed so that they could effectively collaborate and share knowledge.

Lack of available information technology assets was another factor in affecting willingness to share knowledge. Modern collaborative software, such as lessons-learned databases, wikis, and other technologies, were simply not available. One participant complained about post 9/11 enforced security restrictions that effectively rendered his network useless.

Willingness to share knowledge is only one of four factors that affect effective knowledge sharing. The other three are (1) management involvement and oversight, (2) IT support, and (3) use of metrics. Many participants indicated that their senior management was not actively involved in promoting knowledge management in their companies; in fact, knowledge management was not mentioned at all. Other participants indicated that their senior managers talked about supporting knowledge management but did little else to promote it or integrate it into performance management and measurement programs. One participant suggested that a company could promote a more effective knowledge sharing atmosphere by utilizing metrics to measure how and when knowledge was shared and how effective sharing was.

Finally, IT support was seen as critical to effective knowledge sharing. In some cases, IT departments were seen as barriers, effectively limiting what information could be shared across teams and among members of teams. In other cases, IT was castigated for not providing modern technologies that supported knowledge sharing (wikis, whiteboards, etc.). Some participants, however, indicated that IT fully supported the move into these technologies. Figure 4.2 lists the technologies used by the participants and the technologies that they desired to use.

Face-to-face (F2F) contact is still the predominant method of knowledge sharing, with email a close second. Participant 19 talked about F2F communication: "I might be old-fashioned in that I just like face-to-face. There are just more nuances that can be given face-to-face. You can see if the person is receiving it and understanding it properly that way."

Although everyone in the sample used email, some complained about it. Participant 3 said: "Emails have problems. Communicating orally and through email can be very time consuming, depending on the people who are on the team. They get files lost and they have to send again. Timeliness is a barrier." Participant 8 agreed: "I don't like email because so many misunderstandings take place on email. How one-dimensional it is. Because people walk away from the opposite impression of what was meant. Many people don't read emails and then they miss the point. They don't get the inflection. They don't get the sarcasm. You got to have the back and forth."

Chat was less popular than expected, although many project leaders used it with their younger project teams, but not without complaints. Participant 3 had this to say: "What I find a little difficult with chat is that sometimes you are overlapping your thoughts. You are asking a question while the other person is answering the last question. Or you're making a comment while the other person is making another comment. Might be transferring the wrong knowledge."

In all cases, technology was a fundamental component of the way information was transferred in these organizations. In many cases, the participants recommended

| Participant Number | Technology Desired | Technology Used |
|---|---|---|
| 1 | 0 | F2F, online forums, email, intranet |
| 10 | Blogs | Email, wiki |
| 11 | Wiki | F2F, bulletin board |
| 12 | 0 | Email |
| 13 | 0 | F2F, email, chat, whiteboard |
| 14 | Wiki, repository | F2F |
| 15 | Whiteboard | Sharepoint, intranet, email, cell phone |
| 16 | 0 | F2F, email |
| 17 | 0 | F2F, whiteboard |
| 18 | 0 | Email, chat, WebEx |
| 19 | 0 | F2F, email, chat, intranet |
| 2 | 0 | Email, web-based conferences, F2F |
| 20 | 0 | Email |
| 21 | 0 | Email |
| 3 | Wiki | Chat |
| 4 | 0 | F2F, email, web pages |
| 5 | 0 | F2F, email, conference calls |
| 6 | 0 | Chat |
| 7 | 0 | Cell phone, email |
| 8 | 0 | F2F |
| 9 | 0 | Email, F2F, shared drive |

**Figure 4.2 Technology desired by and used in sample organizations.**

more cutting-edge technologies such as blogs and wikis, although none seemed to be aware of the many knowledge sharing technologies and techniques available. IT support, therefore, is a critical factor in effective knowledge sharing.

The research uncovered a moderate relationship between education and knowledge sharing. While most participants felt that education did not impact knowledge sharing, some stated that higher educational levels made people more likely to share knowledge. The lower the educational level, the less likely a person was to share knowledge, possibly due to fear of losing the only skill that made them valuable to the company.

The research uncovered a more definite relationship between age and knowledge sharing, and between ethnicity and knowledge sharing. Some participants noted a divide between older and younger workers, with the younger workers less willing to share with older workers. Other participants indicated that long-tenure workers who tended to be older felt threatened by younger workers and, as a result, did not share knowledge with them. One participant said: "They don't want to be taken over."

Another participant brought up the interesting issue that younger people may be more technologically adept. For example, younger people used text messaging to stay in constant communication. Like many older participants, this participant preferred face-to-face and email communications and feared that his lack of knowledge about communications media might keep him out of the loop.

The research found that ethnicity was somewhat a factor in knowledge sharing. The ability to understand material communicated, cultural mores related to communication, and work ethics were cited as barriers to knowledge sharing by the participants. Trust, comfort, and respect figured prominently. The participants uniformly asserted that these three factors were required in the cultural mix if knowledge sharing were to be successful in their organizations.

It was expected that corporate culture would impact the willingness to share knowledge. The variables affecting willingness included trust, management commitment, involvement, perception, rewards, leadership, resources provided, job title, tenure, and others. Lin and Lee (2006) discussed organizational climate in the context of how knowledge sharing fit into business processes, the degree to which knowledge sharing was perceived to benefit the conduct of business, and management's intention to encourage knowledge sharing.

Connelly and Kelloway (2003) discussed management commitment to knowledge sharing and the individual perception that a positive social interaction culture would be more likely to perceive a positive knowledge-sharing culture. Bock and Kim (2002) posited that if employees believed they could contribute to an organization's performance, they would develop a more positive attitude toward knowledge sharing.

The study addressed a variety of organizational factors that supported or impeded effective knowledge sharing within an organization: job security, use of metrics, organizing, office politics, lack of time, organizational and management issues, and IT support. Several participants indicated that job security involved fear of providing incorrect information, fear of losing face if others disagreed, and the desire to control situations or people by sharing or withholding information.

Office politics was another factor discussed by many participants. Politics may produce corrosive effects, particularly if management initiates or overlooks a political problem. According to Participant 15: "Who is the top guy or woman that this person's career is influenced by, and that's the person whose culture drives those sorts of behaviors."

Lack of time and inability to organize the vast information stores these organizations possess were also cited as factors that inhibited the effective sharing of knowledge. Participant 15 advised that the only way knowledge sharing could be effective was to add it to the goals of the organization and to measure its use. Organizational issues related to management generated the most discussion. The research found that many of those in charge of companies did not effectively promote knowledge sharing. Some did not endorse it and some talked about it but did not support the effort. One notable exception, Participant 16, stated that knowledge sharing was vital to his company's corporate culture and the company created a department to manage it.

All participants pointed to the technology tools use by their organization, from email to collaborative whiteboards. Some of the participants pointed out problems in using these technologies, including high-level security infrastructures that precluded easy sharing of files and "being behind the curve" in the use of technologies.

It was also expected that IT support would have an impact on willingness to share knowledge. Flanagin (2002) discussed the tendency to reduce knowledge complexity artificially with the use of technologies for knowledge management. Lin and Lee (2006) found a positive causal relationship between use of technology and knowledge sharing. Connelly and Kelloway (2003) mentioned the perception of a positive knowledge sharing culture due to the presence of technology.

The study found that IT support affected willingness to share knowledge and noted a distinction between willingness to share knowledge and effective knowledge sharing, as shown in Figure 4.3. Several factors affected willingness to share knowledge in the sample population. Workers first needed to feel secure and know that sharing knowledge with their co-workers would not diminish their work. Furthermore, office politics had the potential to become a barrier to effective collaboration and knowledge sharing, diminishing any eagerness toward knowledge sharing. One participant even mentioned the survivor-type mentality in her office, an allusion to the popular television where teams were pitted against teams.

Trust, respect, and comfort were mentioned as variables that also affected willingness to share knowledge. It was stated that workers needed to trust and respect their co-workers. One important factor that seemed to affect willingness to share knowledge was the level of comfort in dealing with others. If there were a language

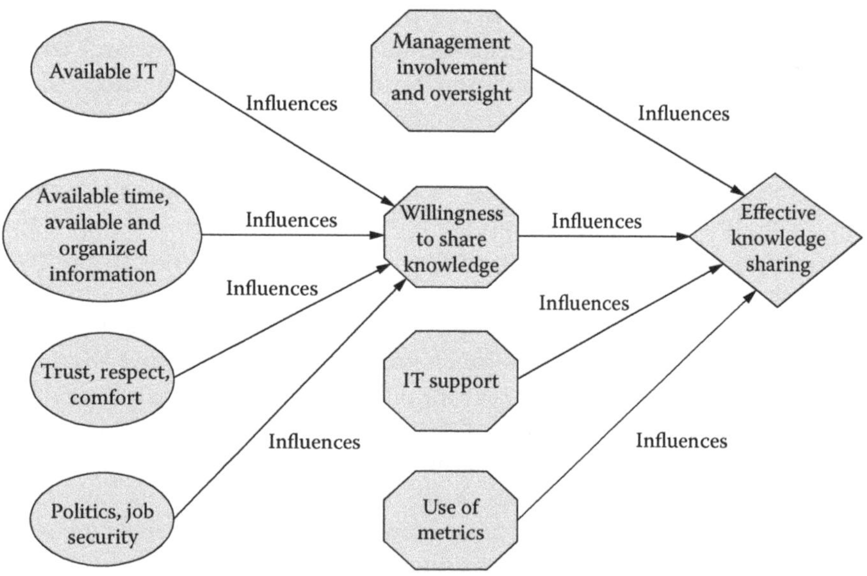


**Figure 4.3 Key factors affecting knowledge sharing.**

or cultural barrier, that level of comfort was absent, thus diminishing the level of effective knowledge sharing.

More than a few of the participants in the sample indicated that they simply did not have sufficient time to share knowledge; they were too busy with their base-level work. Several participants also complained about the lack of knowledge organization; they felt that it was difficult to find the information they needed so that they could effectively collaborate and share knowledge.

Lack of available information technology assets was another factor affecting willingness to share knowledge. Modern collaborative software such as lessons-learned databases, wikis, and other technologies were not available. One of the participants complained about the post 9/11 enforced security restrictions that effectively rendered his network useless.

Willingness to share knowledge was just one of four factors that affected effective knowledge sharing. The other three factors were management involvement and oversight, IT support, and use of metrics. Several participants indicated that senior staff was not actively involved in promoting knowledge management. Other participants indicated that their senior managers stated that they supported knowledge management but did little else to promote it or integrate it into the organization's performance management and measurement programs. One participant suggested promoting a more effective knowledge sharing atmosphere by using metrics to measure how it was used, when it was used, and how effective it was.

IT support was seen as critical to effective knowledge sharing, although IT was sometimes seen as a barrier by limiting information that could be shared across teams and among team members. Some participants castigated IT for failure to provide modern technologies to support knowledge sharing. However, some participants indicated that IT fully supported advanced technologies. IT support clearly is critical for effective knowledge sharing.

According to Pollard (2005), the expectations for knowledge management and, by definition, knowledge sharing were improvements in growth and innovation; productivity and efficiency reflected in cost savings; customer relationships; employee learning, satisfaction, and retention; and management decision making. Knowledge sharing could meet the goals if embedded in an organization using a bottom-up approach rather than a top-down approach. Top-down approaches forced on employees are usually resisted or even ignored. The bottom-up approach is similar to viral marketing: one person becomes enthusiastic about a product or service and tells someone who tells someone else. By providing the tools, methodologies, training, and support on a unit or department level, employees are encouraged to capture, share, and archive their knowledge for the good of the organization.

However, knowledge management requires a focus. Pollard (2005) found that knowledge management's safe haven seemed to be the IT department. This is a natural fit based on the definition of knowledge management to include organizational learning, technology transfer, competitive intelligence, data warehousing, business intelligence, document management (Davenport and Prusak, 2003), and a dependence on information technology resources. Pollard suggested a number of techniques to disseminate knowledge sharing practices:

1. Don't force people to adapt. They must be self-motivated.
2. Change the jobs of knowledge professionals. Enable everyone to carry on the task of knowledge management.
3. Consider localized knowledge bases. There is no reason to prevent employees from storing their domains of knowledge in their own private databases. Pollard made a good point about respecting the privacy and confidentiality of personal information. People do not like to share what provides a personal competitive edge.
4. Help people connect to experts inside and outside the organization.

The current emphasis on a balanced scorecard (Kaplan and Norton, 1996) and performance management and measurement may be used as a lever to further embed knowledge sharing in an organization. A balanced scorecard uses four perspectives to define a set of objectives, measures, targets, and initiatives to achieve goals. We will delve into adapting this to social software engineering in Chapter 7. While the learning and growth perspective was a natural fit for knowledge sharing, the remaining perspectives should also be considered. Adding goals, metrics, and other measures for knowledge sharing activities is a sure way to motivate departments to consider the use of knowledge sharing.

Sunassee and Sewry (2003) proposed a framework for organizational knowledge management that consists of three main interlinked components: knowledge management of the organization, knowledge management of the people, and knowledge management of the infrastructure and processes. They indicated that an organization must achieve a balance among these three subsystems to successfully manage knowledge and that it is critical to align the knowledge management of the organization to its overall business strategy. A close second in importance was an effort to make people feel involved in the change process when knowledge management is implemented by emphasizing individual learning and innovative thinking. The model also proposed a set of critical success factors that aid successful implementation:

1. Align knowledge management strategy with business strategy.
2. Ensure top management support.
3. Create and manage knowledge culture.
4. Use a pilot project.
5. Create and manage organizational learning.
6. Manage people.
7. Choose the right technology.
8. Include double-loop learning.

Argyris (1976) proposed double-loop learning theory related to changing underlying values and assumptions. The theory focuses on solving problems that were complex, poorly structured and changed as problem solving advanced. Double-loop learning figures prominently in action learning—the focus of the next chapter.

## Recommendations for Making It Work

The study produced some intriguing results, consistent with most of the prevailing research on this topic (Ardichvili et al., 2006; Bock and Kim, 2003; Connelly and Kelloway, 2003; Flanagin, 2002; Lin and Lee, 2006; Ojha, 2005; Riege, 2005). It focused on high-tech workers, mostly in the information technology arena. Due to the team-focused nature of work in this industry, collaboration and knowledge sharing are necessary if a worker expects to achieve success. A good example of this was the 2006 Netflix challenge. The company offered a million-dollar award to the person or team that created a movie-recommending algorithm 10% better than its own. The competitors were startlingly open about the methods they used. One even posted a complete description of his algorithm. When asked about this surprising openness in the face of a million-dollar prize, the general response was that the primary prize was learning and interacting with other teams (Ellenberg, 2008).

In 2006, IBM took this concept to the next level. Over 150,000 people from 104 countries participated in the IBM Innovation Jam intended to review and reexamine the company's core values. IBM has been "jamming" with employees since 2001 and decided to open its collaborative brainstorming session to the public. Since 2001, IBM jams have created a number of products and services:

- Smart health-care payment systems
- Simplified business engines
- Intelligent transportation business
- Digital Me

Digital Me simplifies secure, managed, and long-term access to personal content and was utilized by the designers of the popular animated movie *Despicable Me* to enable collaborative digital media content.

The pro-collaboration nature of technology workers made them attractive subjects for studies to determine how their collaborative mindset might be transferred to other types of knowledge workers. To promote knowledge sharing, senior management must be proactive and fill a visible role in supporting the development of a knowledge management framework within an organization (Corcoran and Robison, n.d.). The most important aspect of this framework is designing a process for creating and sharing knowledge. Not only should a vision and mission be similar to other strategic efforts, but incentives (compensation, promotions, give-aways) that will influence others to adopt the vision and mission must be determined.

Performance measurement is another critical success factor, as some of the study's interview participants suggested. Kaplan and Norton (1996) developed the balanced scorecard approach to compensate for the perceived shortcomings of using only financial metrics to judge corporate performance. They recognized that it was also necessary to value intangible assets and urged company managers to measure such esoteric factors as quality, customer satisfaction, learning, and knowledge sharing.

In the scorecard scenario, a company organizes its business goals into discrete, all-encompassing perspectives: financial, customer, internal process, and learning/growth. The next step is determining cause–effect relationships, e.g., satisfied customers bought more goods, thus increasing revenue. Next, the company lists measures for each goal, pinpoints targets, and identifies projects and other initiatives to help reach the targets. Departments create scorecards tied to the company's targets. Employees and projects have scorecards tied to their department targets. This cascading nature provides a line of sight between individuals, their work, the units they support, and the impacts on the strategy of the whole enterprise. Table 4.8 lists recommended metrics from a sample of knowledge management artifacts.

The interviews uncovered techniques that participants used or wished to use to promote effective knowledge sharing. Any organization uses a number of techniques to identify, store, and transfer knowledge. Some strategies work better in one organization than another. Some may not be appropriate for specific businesses. The challenge is to identify and develop complementary ways to further knowledge management and transfer in an organization. Some of these techniques were addressed in Chapter 3 (storytelling, CoPs, etc.).

Knowledge management requires computer technologies to effectively support knowledge sharing and collaboration. All participants in this study had access to email, which is now universally available. However, not everyone had access to newer collaborative technologies such as whiteboards, corporate intranets, and innovative products like Cisco's Telepresence. Electronic whiteboards permit two or more employees to work together synchronously on a project artifact (memo, plan, specification), even if they work thousands of miles apart. New commercial software is geared to the knowledge sharing paradigm. One study participant discussed the use of Basecamp (http://www.basecamphq.com/). This project management software enables collaboration on internal and client projects. More importantly, it allows the creation of threads by which each project can be discussed online via a web-based client.

While corporate intranets are becoming increasingly popular, for the most part, they are used for human resources activities (401k participation, scheduling vacation time, payroll matters). Because a corporate intranet is web-enabled and available to employees on and off site, it is the perfect venue for the databases and discussion boards mentioned earlier. Wikis, blogs, best practices, communities of practice, documenting processes, knowledge maps, and lessons learned can all be enabled on the intranet, although an IT department must support its use by implementing database and knowledge base software for this purpose.

**Table 4.8 Recommended Knowledge Sharing Metrics**

| *Knowledge Management Initiative* | *Key System Measures* |
|---|---|
| Best-practice directory | Number of downloads<br>Number of users<br>Number of contributions<br>Contribution rate |
| Lessons-learned database | Number of downloads<br>Number of users<br>Total number of contributions<br>Contribution rate |
| Communities of practice or special interest groups | Number of contributions<br>Frequency of update<br>Number of members<br>Number of members versus number of contributors |
| Expert or expertise directory | Number of site accesses<br>Frequency of use<br>Number of contributions<br>Contribution or update rate over time |
| Portal | Searching precision and recall<br>Usability survey |
| Collaborative systems | Latency during collaborative process<br>Number of users |

IT departments play a pivotal role in the transformation of information to knowledge and the resultant transformation to a knowledge-based company. IT must take a leadership role in seeking out collaborative technologies, learning how to use them, implementing them, and supporting them. A number of participants said that their preferred method of knowledge sharing was still face-to-face. They insisted that important communication nuances were lost when personal discussions were replaced with the collaborative technologies available today. Thus, the marketplace must be continually monitored to ensure that technologies that overcome these limitations may eventually become available.

Toward this end, a chief knowledge officer whose role is to promote knowledge management with emphasis on knowledge sharing should be appointed. This person would be responsible for implementing many of the recommendations discussed in this section. Chief knowledge officer is not a new job description. Many companies have such officers. However, the dot.com "bust" coupled with slow economic growth caused organizations to cut costs. One of the first cuts was the chief knowledge officer. Desouza and Raider (2006) asserted the importance of this job and offered some suggestions for linking it to the bottom line, including increasing the drive toward business value and the use of metrics. Table 4.8 lists recommended knowledge sharing metrics. Desouza and Raider (2006) suggested adding metrics for customer retention, employee retention, innovation rates, customer evaluations, and speed to market. They maintain that these metrics represent measurable results that display the value of knowledge management initiatives. Metrics and related issues will be covered in subsequent chapters.

## We've Reached the End of Chapter 4

This chapter presented an attitudinal study that demonstrates obstacles to effective knowledge sharing within an IT organization, most particularly a team of IT people working together on a project. What probably surprised you (or maybe not) is that knowledge sharing was not generally effective in our sample survey population. The factors discussed produce several negative consequences for the effectiveness of an IT project team. The goal is to impress upon readers the importance of fixing such problems before they engage in social software engineering endeavors.

## References

A problem shared: following in the footsteps of Marriott and Ritz-Carlton. (2005). *Strategic Direction,* 21(5), 15–17.

Abdullah, M.S., Kimble, C., Benest, I., and Paige, R. (2006). Knowledge-based systems: a re-evaluation. *Journal of Knowledge Management,* 10(3), 127–142.

Alavi, M, Kayworth, T.R., and Leidner, D.E. (2005–2006). An empirical examination of the influence of organizational culture on knowledge management practices. *Journal of Management Information Systems,* 22(3), 191–224.

Albert, M. and Picq, T. (2004). Knowledge-based organizations: perspectives from San Francisco Bay area companies. *European Journal of Innovation Management,* 7(3), 169–177.

Ardichvili, A., Maurer, M., Li, W., Wentling, T., and Stuedemann, R. (2006). Cultural influences on knowledge sharing through online communities of practice. *Journal of Knowledge Management,* 10(1), 94–107.

Argyris, C. (1976). *Increasing Leadership Effectiveness.* New York: Wiley.

Bock, G.W. and Kim, Y.G. (2002). Breaking the myths of rewards: an exploratory study of attitudes about knowledge sharing. *Information Resource Management Journal,* 15(2), 14–21.

Bushe, R. (2010). When people come and go. *The Wall Street Journal,* August 23.

Carneiro, A. (2000). How does knowledge management influence innovation and competiveness? *Journal of Knowledge Management,* 4(2), 87.

Choo, S.W. (2000). Working with knowledge: how information professionals help organizations manage what they know. *Library Management,* 21(8), 395.

Chow, C., Deng, F., and Ho, J. (2000). The openness of knowledge sharing within organizations: a comparative study in the United States and the People's Republic of China. *Journal of Management Accounting Research,* 12, 65–95.

Corcoran, M.E. and Robison, C.A. (n.d.). Successful management of the corporate knowledge base: checklist for top management. http://scientific.thomson.com/quantum2/media/pdfs/q-chklst.pdf.

Connelly, C.E. and Kelloway, E.K. (2003). Predictors of employees' perceptions of knowledge sharing cultures. *Leadership and Organization Development Journal,* 24(5/6), 294–301.

Cross, R., Parker, A., Prusak, L., and Borgatti, S.P. (2001). Knowing what we know: supporting knowledge creation and sharing in social networks. *Organizational Dynamics,* 30(2), 100–120.

Davenport, T.H. and Prusak, L. (2000). *Working Knowledge: How Organizations Manage What They Know.* Boston: Harvard Business School Press.

Davenport, T.H. and Prusak, L. (2003). *What's the Big Idea?* Boston: Harvard Business School Press.

DeLong, D. and Fahey, L. (2000). Diagnosing cultural barriers to knowledge management. *Academy of Management Executive,* 14(4), 113–127.

Desouza, K.C. and Raider, J.J. (2006). Cutting corners: CKOs and knowledge management. *Business Process Management Journal,* 12(2), 129–134.

DeTienne, K, Dyer, G., Hoopers, C., and Harris, S. (2000). Toward a model of effective knowledge management and directions for future research, culture, leadership and CKOs. *Journal of Leadership and Organizational Studies,* 10(4), 26–43.

Devedzic, V. (2001). Knowledge modeling: state of the art. *Integrated Computer-Aided Engineering,* 8(3), 257–281.

Ellenberg, J. (2008). The Netflix challenge. *Wired,* March, 25–26.

Flanagin, A.J. (2002). The elusive benefits of technology support of knowledge management. *Management Communication Quarterly,* 16(2), 242–248.

Foos, T., Schum, G., and Rothenberg, S. (2006). Tacit knowledge transfer and the knowledge disconnect. *Journal of Knowledge Management,* 10(1), 6–18.

Green, A. (2006). The transformation of business knowledge into intangible assets. *Vine,* 36(1), 27–34.

Guzman, G.A.C. and Wilson, J. (2005). The "soft" dimension of organizational knowledge transfer. *Journal of Knowledge Management,* 9(2), 59–74.

Halawi, L.A., McCarthy, E., and Aronson, J.E. (2006). Knowledge management and the competitive strategy of the firm. *The Learning Organization,* 13(4), 384–397.

Hutchings, K. and Michailova, S. (2004). Facilitating knowledge sharing in Russian and Chinese subsidiaries: role of personal networks and group membership. *Journal of Knowledge Management,* 8(2), 84–94.

Hwang, A., Francesco, A., and Kessler, E. (2003). The relationship between individualism–collectivism, face, and feedback and learning processes in Hong Kong, Singapore, and the United States. *Journal of Cross-Cultural Psychology,* 34(1), 72–91.

Jakobson, L. (2008). Save the knowledge. *Incentive,* 182(2), 42–43.

Kaplan, R.S. and Norton, D.P. (1996). *The Balanced Scorecard: Translating Strategy into Action*. Boston: Harvard Business School Press.
Keskin, H. (2005). The relationships between explicit and tacit oriented knowledge management strategy, and firm performance. *Journal of American Academy of Business,* 7(1), 169–175.
King, W.R., Marks, P.V., and McCoy, S. (2002). The most important issues in knowledge management. *Communications of ACM,* 45(9), 92–97.
Kok, A.H. and Gao, S. (2005-2006). Attitude toward knowledge sharing behavior. *Journal of Computer Information Systems,* 46(2), 45–51.
Lam, W. and Chua, A. (2005). The mismanagement of knowledge management. *Aslib Proceedings,* 57(5), 424–433.
Lau, H.C.W., Wong, C.W.Y., Hui, I.K., and Pun, K.F. (2003). Design and implementation of an integrated knowledge system. *Knowledge-Based Systems,* 16(2), 69–76.
Lee, D.D. and Ahn, J.H. (2005). Rewarding knowledge sharing under measurement inaccuracy. *Knowledge Management Research and Practice,* 3, 229–243.
Lin, C. (2007). To share or not to share: modeling tacit knowledge sharing, its mediators and antecedents. *Journal of Business Ethics,* 70, 411–428.
Lin, H.S. and Lee, G.G. (2006). Effects of socio-technical factors on organizational intention to encourage knowledge sharing. *Management Decision,* 44(1), 74–88.
MacKinlay, A. (2002). The limits of knowledge management. *New Technology, Work and Employment,* 17(2), 76–88.
McDermott, R. and O'Dell, C. (2001). Overcoming culture barriers to knowledge sharing. *Journal of Knowledge Management,* 5(1), 76–85.
Meister, J.C. and Willyerd, K. (2010). *The 2020 workplace: How innovative companies attract, develop and keep tomorrow's employees today.* New York: HarperBusiness.
Nonaka, I. (1994). A dynamic theory of organizational knowledge creation. *Organization Science,* 5(1), 14–37.
Ojha, A.K. (2005). Impact of team demography on knowledge sharing in software project teams. *South Asian Journal of Management,* 12(3), 67–78.
Oltra, V. (2005). Knowledge management effectiveness factors: role of HRM. *Journal of Knowledge Management,* 9(4), 70–86.
Parikh, M. (2001). Knowledge management framework for high-tech research and development. *Engineering Management Journa*l, 13(3), 27–33.
Paraponaris, C. (2003). Third generation R&D strategies for knowledge management. *Journal of Knowledge Management,* 7(5), 96–106.
Pollard, D. (2005, January). The future of knowledge management. *Executive Action,* 130. http://www.conference-board.org/publications/describe_ea.cfm?id=920
Riege, A. (2005). Three-dozen knowledge sharing barriers managers must consider. *Journal of Knowledge Management,* 9(3), 18–35.
Slagter, F. (2007). Knowledge management among the older workforce. *Journal of Knowledge Management,* 11(4), 82–96.
So, J.C.F. and Bolloju, N. (2005). Explaining the intentions to share and reuse knowledge in the content of IT service operations. *Journal of Knowledge Management,* 9(6), 30–41.
Subramani, M. and Venkatraman, N. (2003). Safeguarding investments in asymmetric interorganizational relationships: theory and evidence. *Academy of Management Journal,* 46(1), 46–62.
Suh, W., Sohn, J.H.D., and Kwak, J.Y. (2004). Knowledge management as enabling R&D innovation in high tech industry: the case of SAIT. *Journal of Knowledge,* 8(6), 5–15.

Sun, P.Y. and Scott, J.L. (2005). Investigation of barriers of knowledge transfer. *Journal of Knowledge Management,* 9(2), 75–90.

Sveiby, K.E. and Simons, R. (2002). Collaborative climate and effectiveness of knowledge work. *Journal of Knowledge Management,* 6(5), 420–433.

Wang, C. (2004). The influence of ethical and self-interest concerns on knowledge sharing intentions among managers: an empirical study. *International Journal of Management,* 21(3), 370–381.

Weiss, L.M., Capozzi, M.M., and Prusak, L. (2004). Learning from the Internet giants. *MIT Sloan Management Review,* 45(4), 79–84.

Widen-Wulff, G. and Suomi, R. (2007). Utilization of information resources for business success: knowledge sharing model. *Information Resources Management Journal,* 20(1), 46–67.

Willem, A. and Scarbrough, H. (2006). Social capital and political bias: exploratory study. *Human Relations,* 59(10), 1343–1370.

# Chapter 5

# Action Learning Teams

Both action research and action learning are based on the principles espoused in action science. As described by Raelin (2008), the goal of action science is to "improve the level of discourse in groups and organizations." Advocates of action science point to the rather parochial, standardized policies of most organizations that inhibit learning and stifle productive discourse. Action science seeks to create an environment that enables people to engage in participatory communications that permit them to delve deeply into their own behaviors and modes of thought using self-reflective techniques, described by Argyris and Schon (1978 cited in Raelin, 2008, p. 111) as Model II behavior. While Model I behavior (typified by defensiveness, need to win, and suppression of emotions) is the norm in most organizational settings, Model II behavior enables people to learn at the emancipatory level of knowledge (Habermans, 1971 cited in Raelin, 2008, p. 113). This is exactly the type of knowledge and learning needed to create a group cohesive enough to thrive in a knowledge sharing intensive, social software engineering environment.

## Action Learning

Emancipatory knowledge is an example of third-order learning. According to Raelin (2008), learning can be defined on three levels: first order or single loop, where the focus is on data; second order or double loop, where the focus is on context; and third order, where the focus is on the context of contexts. At this highest level of learning we can finally understand and ultimately question the meaning of our standard responses to situations. Thus, action science can be said to be the study of how people craft their responses to particular situations. Raelin (2008) explains that action science "decontextualizes practice" so that people can examine in-depth their belief systems. The goal is participatory discourse.

Action research is essentially a reflexive process of progressive problem solving led by individuals working in teams or within a community of practice (CoP). Kurt Lewin coined the term in the 1940s. Then a researcher at MIT, he described a spiral of steps, each of which is composed of a circle of planning, action, and fact-finding related to the result of an action.

Action learning is based on this level of in-depth self-examination. Raelin (2008) describes action learning as a group-based educational strategy that promotes learning by engaging in the solution of real-time, work-related problems. Action learning can be seen in practice in many organizations in the form of CoPs, often included within the rubric of an organization's knowledge management practice. A CoP consists of a team of individuals who work together to resolve each other's work-related problems. Garratt (1991 cited in Raelin, 2008, p. 85) noted that adults learn best from working on real projects involving support and constructive criticism from their colleagues. Raelin (2008) stressed that the team must offer a safe environment to share and resolve problems.

Action learning is based on the team approach as a pathway to learning. Team members support and also challenge each other to find solutions to difficult problems. However, as Raelin (2008) pointed out, solving the problem is not as important as what is learned from the experience.

Action research is closely related to action learning. Reason and Bradbury (2001 cited in Brydon-Miller , Greenwood, and Maguire, 2009, p. 10) defined action research as a "participatory, democratic process concerned with developing practical knowing.... It seeks to bring together action and reflection, theory and practice, in participation with others, in the pursuit of practical solutions to issues of pressing concern." Where action learning seems to focus on individual learning and self-reflection, action research appears to focus on collaborative learning. Raelin and Coghlan (2006) summarized the differences: action learning "aims at helping managers learn through primarily second person experience. Action research aims at contributing to dialectical knowledge.... The learning in action of managers can lead to research in action and to producing actionable knowledge."

Many describe action research as "a work in progress." Working collaboratively with others leads to organizational and personal changes. Techniques that can be used to promote these behaviors are closely aligned to techniques used for knowledge management: visualization, Socratic dialog, concept mapping, data mapping—all active techniques that lead to knowledge from the act of "doing."

The key to action learning, science, and research is the art of reflection—self-reflection and collaborative reflection. Both are vital to the success of a software development team. Raelin (2008) talked about five principal skills: being, speaking, disclosing, testing, and probing. Reflection means stepping back and pondering. Thus, the first step in the process of reflection is, according to Raelin, "to experience" or simply "to be." Being requires us to experience and describe situations,

**Table 5.1 Comparison of Defensive and Reflective Postures**

| *Defensive Posture* | *Reflective Posture* |
|---|---|
| Maintaining unrealistic standards | Realistic expectations |
| Expressing doubt | Displaying tolerance |
| Concentrating on self-expression | Using listening techniques |
| Being self-absorbed | Conveying humility |
| Feeling out of depth | Feeling open to learn |
| Feeling out of context | Feeling open to experience |

including our own involvement in them. The reflection process of being can be beneficial in the software engineering process. Developers often see what they want to see and hear what they want to hear. Learning to develop a more reflective style lets them see a problem as it was meant to be seen, and not colored by personal perceptions and biases. Thus, it can be said that the reflective response is in direct contrast to the usual defensive posture, as shown in Table 5.1. The being skill is both inquisitive and nonjudgmental, for example, a project team ready to start programming a new system. The project manager who pushed for a particular design wonders out loud whether something has been overlooked or whether the team might take one more look at the design.

The second reflective skill is speaking, defined as using language to help people slow down and understand each other. It is collective in nature, as is the third reflective skill of testing. That skill is based on open-ended queries and directed to the group as a whole. Its goal is to uncover new ways by using the collective dynamic. All these skills represent facilitated modes of reflection. A designated facilitator can use several methodologies to promote the testing skill, such as asking for a process check, playing devil's advocate, or acting out a scenario. For example, if a team reaches an impasse, a facilitator might ask the members to stop defending their own positions for a moment and search for ways to solve the impasse.

The two remaining reflective skills are individual in nature. Disclosing promotes the sharing of doubts or voices passion. The goal is to help the group learn more about its own membership. The last reflective skill is individual testing by using open-ended queries to uncover new ways of thinking and behaving. The real goal is to draw out facts, assumptions, reasons, and consequences.

## Leaderful Practice

Raelin was very specific in defining the shared model of leadership he calls "leaderful" practice. In his treatise on using action learning to "unlock the capacity of everyone in the organization," he implies that collaborative leadership is a form of just-in-time leadership under which any employee who has the capacity and willingness to lead, will. According to Raelin, collaborative leadership is based on a simple humanistic precept: people who have a stake in a venture and participate in that venture will be fully committed to it. Collaborative leadership requires this type of full commitment that extends itself to leadership and decision making across all levels and processes.

For the most part, and in spite of the popularity of the "flat" organizational structure, leadership remains hierarchical. Raelin poetically describes "a coterie of subordinates" who "await their marching orders from detached bosses." In an organization made rich by leaderfulness, the subordinates may be leaders and the bosses are no longer detached. Instead, bosses and subordinates collaborate toward a specific end.

Raelin's shared model of leaderful practice is based on four operational perspectives: concurrent, collective, collaborative (called "mutual" in his 2006 article) and compassionate (the four *c*'s). Concurrent leadership may be the *c* that causes the most trouble in a typical organization. Concurrent leadership allows several people to lead at the same time. This is not traditional practice, so an organizational bent on employing the action learning paradigm would have to retrench and relearn. Collective leadership means that anyone and everyone on a team can be a leader. Collaborative leadership puts everyone in control and able to speak for the team. The last two perspectives are not all that uncommon in practice. Leaderless teams are common and have been discussed in the literature.

The last perspective is perhaps the most important. In compassionate leadership, team members strive to maintain the dignity of all members by carefully considering each individual whenever any decision is made. Raelin's belief is that action learning in this way creates an organization in which everyone participates in leadership. If they choose to become leaders, employees need not stand by and be dependent. Raelin further asserted that the link between work-based learning and leaderful practice creates a "spirit of free inquiry" such that employees go beyond the problem itself in often divergent, creative, and often profitable ways.

Action learning has great potential. It can produce more "aha" moments than traditional methods. However, engaging in such methods would probably entail a major paradigm shift by current organizational leaders and staff. Such "culture shock" issues are far more pronounced when dealing with global cultures. Raelin describes many cultural challenges. For example, in many cultures, learners are viewed as passive and dependent, and teachers as active and authoritarian. Cross-cultural studies also point out the problems with originating, distributing, and sharing feedback. My own studies on the effects of ethnicity on knowledge sharing run parallel to the studies cited by Raelin. The ability to understand what was communicated, and cultural mores that affect the ways different groups communicate, and work ethics were cited as barriers to knowledge sharing by the participants in my studies. Trust, comfort, and respect figure prominently in all studies on this issue.

Certainly some solutions can solve culture clash problems. Yiu and Saner, as cited in Raelin (2008), found they had to make cultural modifications to a training program to adapt it to the Chinese culture. Modifications included personal coaching, identifying the right individuals to work on teams, modifying reflective activities to focus on more tasks and methodologies than individual challenges and relationships, and training senior supervisors to support action learning projects. It is evident that a careful examination of each "host"culture is required to germinate the seeds of action learning and collaborative leadership.

The four leaderful perspectives require those assuming leadership positions (anyone who wants to be a leader) to be concurrent, collective, mutual, and compassionate. While we may not see this model deployed in the real world of big business at the highest levels, it is certainly viable and may be very effective for a CoP, volunteer organization (e.g., open source group), or work-related teams.

Most organizations, even software organizations, use traditional models of leadership, at least at top levels. Apple's Steve Jobs is a case in point. His leadership style has been described as charismatic and transformational. He is a true visionary, a magnet for creative people. However, he is legendary for being difficult to work with. Bill Gates, on the other hand, is an authoritarian leader. I must say that most of the CEOs I have worked with are also authoritarian and would not deign to share leadership in any way, shape, or form. To do so would mean a real loss of power and power is everything to them.

However, some leaders appear to be moving in this direction. Herb Kelleher is the former CEO of Software Airlines. He asserts that lodging control within a single executive is a strategic blunder. Raelin cites research that states the return on investment from action learning at anywhere from 5 to 25 times its cost. While I don't expect Gates, Jobs, and the "smartest guys in the room" on Wall Street to share power any time soon, I would expect them to at least endorse action learning and leaderful practice at the lower rungs of their organizations.

Johnson & Johnson now utilizes an action learning culture. The CEO introduced a strategic, collaborative process called FrameworkS. The *S* signifies the multiple frames through which a team may view its project mission. The system involves choosing ten to twelve employees based on technical, geographic, or organizational perspectives to serve on a team and sending them off site. The employees were not necessarily high ranking, and no leader was appointed. Meetings were run democratically. After the initial gathering, subcommittees and task forces were formed to research the issues and take action. FrameworkS led the company to move into new markets, new technologies, new businesses, and even new values. It expanded into strategic areas not explored earlier. Team members expanded their individual knowledge and the company as a whole expanded its organizational knowledge.

## Action Projects

From an action project perspective, a typical software engineering project is ideally suited to the principles of action learning. Projects in this environment are best designed when team members understand that their actions will produce a real impact. Based on this result, many arguments support the idea that team members should select their project and also determine its direction. This is a sea change from the way most project teams work now: team members are assigned based on availability.

It is presumed that IT staffers are members of at least one learning set; this is also the premise of a CoP. The learning set might also include individuals not in IT (end users, external vendors, etc.). The learning set may be cross-departmental and even cross-functional or mixed (including participants of different skill levels). Research has shown that mixed sets are beneficial. Inexperienced members benefit from the experiences of veterans, and the veterans report high degrees of satisfaction from mentoring newer team members. The learning set will be presented with a list of available projects for evaluation. Raelin (2008) proposes asking three questions:

1. Who knows? Learning set members pose this question to determine which members know anything about the problem and the opportunities and obstacles it might present.
2. Who cares? Which learning team member(s) feel strongly enough about the problem to want to do something about it?
3. Who can? Which team members have the requisite skills to tackle the problem? Which team members have the power and motivation to successfully solve the problem?

The learning set as a whole may decide to tackle a project. It is also feasible that one or more members may decide to venture outside the set to join a newly configured learning set to tackle a problem. However the ultimate project team is configured, the team members must have the skills and vested interest to succeed.

Some studies support housing a project team at an alternative site. Hayes and Allison (1998) talk about the problem of "strategic myopia." Without benefit of different organizational cultures (obtained by working outside a familiar IT environment), team members will exhibit limited ways to think about solutions to a problem. Working at an alternative site can encourage new ways of thinking (moving from single- to double-loop learning), reveal unexpected insights, and essentially provide opportunities to reframe a problem as knowledge and experience increase.

Social networking methodologies provide alternative environments in a virtual format—a sort of e-communication. Studies have shown that e-communication can be far more effective than face-to-face communication. Valacich and Schwenk (1995) note that e-communication promotes the sharing of information and is superior for handling divergent-thinking tasks. Other studies point to the benefits of e-communications for reducing barriers such as domination by high-status group members and inequalities of participation.

Studies also reveal problems in all virtual communications. Crede and Sniezek (2003) studied the use of face-to-face and video conferencing of 282 participants across 94 groups. The researchers found significant differences in the groups' confidence levels in their decisions. Those using video conferencing showed lower levels of confidence in their decisions. However, the researchers also found no significant differences between the two groups in terms of outcomes, i.e., accuracy, overconfidence, commitment to group decision, sizes of credible intervals, improvement over average initial individual estimates, and number of beliefs discussed or learned.

While social networking is encouraged for software engineering group work, managers must remember that it succeeds only if there is some face-to-face component. The personal contact allows team members to warm up to each other and develop the relational social and emotional links based on trust, cohesion, and group identity addressed in Chapter 4.

## We've Reached the End of Chapter 5

This short chapter covered important ground. Unfortunately, the nuggets of knowledge that encompass action learning are usually not included in IT curricula at work or at school. I felt it important to cover the concepts of the action learning set and leaderful practice as useful devices for encouraging effective collaboration within IT departments, particularly those that plan to engage in social software engineering.

## References

Brydon-Miller, M., Greenwood, D., and Maguire, P. (2009). Why action research? *Action Research*, 1(1), 9–28.

Crede, M. and Sniezek, J.A. (2003). Group judgment processes and outcomes in video conferencing versus face-to-face groups. *International Journal of Human-Computer Studies*, 59(6), 875–897.

Hayes, J. and Allinson, C.W. (1998). Cognitive style and the theory and practice of individual and collective learning in organizations. *Human Relations*, 51(7), 847–871.

Raelin, J.A. and Coghlan, D. (2006). Developing managers as learners and researchers: using action learning and action research. *Journal of Management Education*, 30(5), 670–689.

Raelin, J.A. (2008). *Work-Based Learning: Bridging Knowledge and Action in the Workplace*. San Francisco: Jossey-Bass.

Valachich, J.S. and Schwenk, C. (1995). Devil's advocacy and dialectical inquiry effects on face-to-face and computer-mediated group decision making. *Organizational Behavior and Human Decision Process*, 62(2), 158–173.

# Chapter 6

# Knowledge across Social Networks

Software engineering produces a multitude of artifacts such as specifications, use cases, and project plans along with emails, memos, interview notes, and meeting minutes. Migrating to an online social network generates even more data. Wikis, blogs, discussion boards, and other social networking toolsets can easily double the amount of data floating around. The main problem confronting intelligent integration of information is accessing diverse data residing in multiple, autonomous, heterogeneous repositories and integrating or fusing it into coherent information that can be used by developers. To make the problem even more interesting,

1. Data may be in multimedia (video, images, text, sound).
2. Sources may store data in diverse formats (flat files, network, relational or object-oriented databases, expert systems, blogs, wikis, etc.).
3. Data semantics may conflict across multiple sources.
4. Data may reside outside the enterprise, perhaps in a cloud-based environment served by Google, Amazon, or Salesforce.com.
5. Data may be of uncertain quality; source reliability may be questionable.

The goal of this chapter is to address the issues of integrating the types of cross-platform information social software engineers require in the course of doing business.

## Heterogeneity of Information

Clearly, one cannot expect to solve information integration and other large-scale system problems with monolithic and nonintegrated solutions. Rather, the system should be composed of smaller components, with each component having the requisite knowledge to perform its tasks within the larger problem-solving framework. Thus, the use of cooperative intelligent agents holds promise in helping to address, discuss, and understand the issues in building next-generation intelligent information systems.

Bird (1993) proposed an agent taxonomy based on two client–server classes (1) mobile agents (clients) for content, communications, and messaging services and (2) static agents (servers). Bird notes that distributed intelligent systems share many of the same characteristics of multi-database systems, in particular distribution, heterogeneity, and autonomy. Knowledge and data are distributed among various expert systems, knowledge bases, and databases, making problem solving a cooperative endeavor. The heterogeneity of information in systems encompasses syntactic, control, and semantic facets.

1. Syntactic heterogeneity encompasses the myriad knowledge representation formats and data definition formats to represent both knowledge and data.
2. Control heterogeneity arises from the many reasoning mechanisms for intelligent systems including induction, deduction, analogy, case-based reasoning, etc.
3. Semantic heterogeneity arises from disagreement about the meaning, interpretation, and intended use of related knowledge and data.

## Intelligent Systems

Intelligent systems originally emerged from the artificial intelligence community. The result was a great deal of interest in knowledge-based (rule-based intelligent) systems—also known as expert systems. These systems were considered flexible because rule bases could be modified easily. However, in practice the early systems were often monolithic and rule-based systems. As the intertwined rule bases grew, often with more than 1,000 interdependent rules, they often became difficult to understand and maintain. Then a more flexible, distributed, and adaptable paradigm for intelligent systems emerged: intelligent agent-based systems. While no commercial systems readily come to mind, spending a few moments discussing this technology is worthwhile because it gives us a preview of what may become the standard for handling distributed data across social networks. Intrepid readers may want to get a head start by building their own systems using a programming environment such as JACK (http://www.agent-software.com.au/products/jack/)—

an extension of Java—or a language such as GOAL (http://mmi.tudelft.nl/~koen/goal.php) or the tools mentioned below.

Agents are computer programs that act autonomously on behalf of a person or organization and their capabilities vary considerably. While much of the early research was in artificial intelligence, the growth of the Internet emphasized distributed computing. Java offers many features for distributed computing and has become a popular language for programming agent-based systems. Distributed Java technologies, in particular Remote Method Invocation (RMI) and Java Intelligent Network Infrastructure (Jini), provide distributed application infrastructures for distributed agent-based systems implemented in Java.

An intelligent agent-based system is highly distributed; agents are active concurrent objects that act on behalf of users. Agents are intermediaries between clients that are typically user interface objects and servers that are entity objects that store persistent information. Usually, several agents participate in a problem solving activity and communicate with each other. This leads to a more distributed and scalable environment. Agents may be categorized based on their mobility, intelligence, or the roles they plan in an agent-based system. One categorization is based on whether an agent is stationary or mobile. Another is based on a number of capabilities:

1. Cooperative agents communicate with other agents and their actions depend on the results of the communications.
2. Proactive agents initiate actions without user prompting.
3. Adaptive agents learn from past experience.

Agents may combine the above three capabilities (Case, Azarmi, Thint, and Ohtani, 2001) as shown in Figure 6.1. Personal agents are proactive and serve individual users. They may also be adaptive. Adaptive personal agents can search for user information in background mode and are often coupled with Internet access. Collaborative agents are both proactive and cooperative.

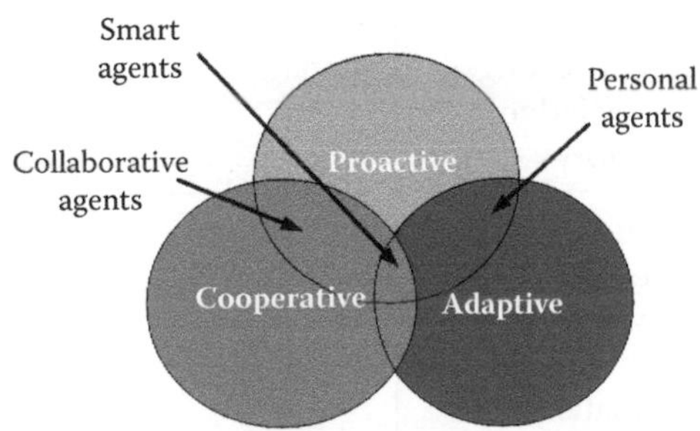


**Figure 6.1 Categorization of agents.**

In the late 1990s, Baek et al. (1997) performed significant research on developing an agent-based conceptual framework for intelligent agents that supported processes of managing project-relevant knowledge of a virtual team. The study replicates exactly what we need to do to support social software engineering data, as shown in Table 6.1. It is interesting that Baek et al. did not use sophisticated knowledge management (KM) technology to building their application. They used a combination of Adobe Cold Fusion and Microsoft Access, both of which run on a typical Windows server. Oracle Beehive, mentioned in Chapter 2, has moved in this direction. Beehive uses a single Oracle database to house collaborative documents. In 2009, Oracle submitted an object model to the Organization for the Advancement of Structured Information Standards (OASIS). An Oasis working

**Table 6.1 Roles of Intelligent Agents in Supporting Knowledge Management-Based Social Software Engineering**

| *Knowledge Management Activity* | *User Needs* | *Intelligent Agent* | *Intelligent Agent Functionality* |
|---|---|---|---|
| Create knowledge | Easily and fully represent their knowledge | User agent | Help users to create knowledge and formulate queries; remember all users' KM activities; dynamically organize content, user agendas, etc. |
| Combine knowledge | Assemble, customize, and extend material stored in knowledge repository | Knowledge agent | Index knowledge; find inconsistencies; save, retrieve, and update knowledge from one or more repositories |
| Distribute knowledge | Be aware of dynamic changes to knowledge repository | Knowledge manager | Monitor all changes in knowledge repository; forward them to user agent |
| Retrieve knowledge | Intelligently retrieve knowledge (combinations of information) based on context and/or content | Knowledge manager | Reformulate queries based on ontology; determine best alternative based on preference weighting and ranking |

group is tasked with defining a standard Integrated Collaboration Object Model (ICOM) for interoperable collaboration services (http://www.oasis-open.org/committees/tc_home.php?wg_abbrev=icom) in the hope that its object model will become the basis for this standard.

## Semantic Standards

We described the semantic web in Chapter 2. It is really an add-on to the current web. It gives information a more refined meaning and thus better enables computers and people to work together. The goal of the semantic web is to build a global information space consisting of linked data, such as you see at http://richard.cyganiak.de/2007/10/lod/imagemap.html. Major web data sources like Google, Yahoo, Amazon, and eBay have started to make their data accessible through proprietary APIs. This inspired the development of many interesting mashups that combine data from a fixed number of sources.

The key to the success of the semantic web is the development of "semantic standards." Some say the software industry is building an alphabet but hasn't yet invented a common language. A common language has appeared in the form of the ontology, discussed in earlier chapters. An ontology is an explicit specification. The term is actually borrowed from philosophy where it is defined as a systematic account of existence. From a semantic web perspective, an ontology is an explicit, formal specification of a shared conceptualization of interest. *Formal* means machine readable; *shared* indicates that the ontology captures knowledge that is not private. Essentially, ontologies represent knowledge within specific domains in a machine-readable way.

Those who develop object-oriented systems are probably familiar with ontologies because they are similar in form and structure to classes and objects. For example, in an automotive ontology, a Car class is partitioned into Two-Wheel Drive and Four-Wheel Drive classes. Objects in an ontology can be described by their assigned attributes. Each attribute has at least a name and a value, and is used to store information specific to the object to which it is attached. For example, the Ford Explorer object has attributes such as

| *Attribute* | |
|---|---|
| Name | Ford Explorer |
| Number of doors | Four |
| Engine | 4.0 L, 4.6 L |
| Transmission | Six speeds |

Examples of informal ontologies on the Internet are Yahoo categories and the Amazon.com product catalog, both of which are generalized taxonomies of "things." Essentially, ontologies are built to share a common understanding of the structure of information among people and among software components. Ultimately, ontologies enable inferencing and reasoning from data. This permits an understanding of the inter-relationships among data and allows software to reason against the data to infer new information.

A number of formal languages are available for encoding ontologies. The World Wide Web Consortium (W3C) has standardized an Ontology Web Language, also known as OWL (http://www.w3.org/TR/owl-features/) and developed as a follow-on to W3C's Resource Description Framework (RDF) specification used as a general method for modeling knowledge, through a variety of syntax formats such as XML.

The RDF metadata model (http://www.w3.org/RDF/) is based on the idea of describing resources by a subject–predicate–object expression (a triple in RDF terminology). One way to represent that "the sky has the color blue" in RDF would be as a triple. The subject is "the sky," the predicate is "has the color," and the object is "blue." A predicate is a trait or aspect of a resource that expresses a relationship between the subject and the object.

Ontology editors are used to create and maintain ontologies. Most tools permit the creation of a hierarchy of concepts (a car is a subconcept of a motor vehicle) and the ability to model relationships between the concepts (a car is driven by a person). Some editors also permit modeling or rules. Annotation tools allow the addition of semantic markups to resources. The inference engine—a staple of artificial intelligence—enables the processing of knowledge available on the semantic web. Sample ontologies can be found at SchemaWeb, a volunteer project at http://www.schemaweb.info/.

Semantic web technologies are used to develop social ontologies, important in social networks [e.g., a friend of a friend (FOAF) on networks such as Facebook]. Data may be scraped or mined from various sources such as the web, email, and bibliographic data, then stored and enhanced, usually through a reasoning or intelligent system. Finally, the data can be browsed and visualized often for the purpose of social network analysis.

Social network analysis views social relationships in terms of network theory consisting of *nodes* and *ties* (also called *edges*, *links*, or *connections*). Nodes are the individual actors within networks and ties are the relationships between actors. The resulting graph-based structures are often very complex because many kinds of ties may connect the nodes. Research in several academic fields has shown that social networks operate on many levels, from families to nations, and play a critical role in determining the way problems are solved, organizations are run, and the degree to which individuals succeed in achieving their goals. Social networks may also be used to analyze group or individual performance and observe the dynamics of community development.

## Enterprise Information Management

The semantic web is an excellent vehicle for enabling data collection and retrieval of data related to social software engineering. Some information and processes may be web based, solely client based with both information and processes encapsulated in an executable, or combine both types.

Content can be delivered to the software developer in a variety of ways—bots (robots), search, push, browsing, and portal. The process is called knowledge flow. Bots are automated agents that seek out information of interest and send it back to an end user on request by the end user. Push technology (or server push) is delivery of information that is initiated by the information server rather than by the end user. The information is "pushed" from server to end user in response to a programmed request initiated by the end user. A portal is a website that serves as a single gateway to information and knowledge. All these methodologies require some type of content management. In the world of business, it is called enterprise information management (EIM).

The four major elements of EIM are correspondence management, workflow management, document management, and records management. In a modern organization, these information assets may take the form of documents, multimedia objects, emails, discussion posts, wikis, blogs, technical documents, images, sounds, videos, databases, knowledge bases, or combinations thereof. All this data is usually spread around different types of EIM systems as shown in Figure 6.2.

- Content management system (CMS): Usually focused on intranet- or Internet-based corporate content including data and knowledge bases; may be expanded to extranet or public web-based social networking sites.
- Document management system (DMS): Focuses on the storage and retrieval of work documents (e.g., forms) in their original formats.
- Records management system (RMS): The management of both physical and electronic documents.
- Digital asset management (DAM): Similar to RMS but focused on multimedia resources such as images, audio, and video.
- Library management system (LMS): The administration of a (corporate) library's technical functions and services.
- Digital imaging system (DIS): Automates the creation of electronic versions of paper documents (e.g., PDF files) that are input to records management systems.
- Learning management system (LMS): The administration of training and other learning resources. Learning content management systems (LCMSs) combine content management systems with learning management systems.
- Geographic information system (GIS): Computer-based systems for the capture, storage, retrieval, and analysis and display of spatial (i.e., location-referenced) data).

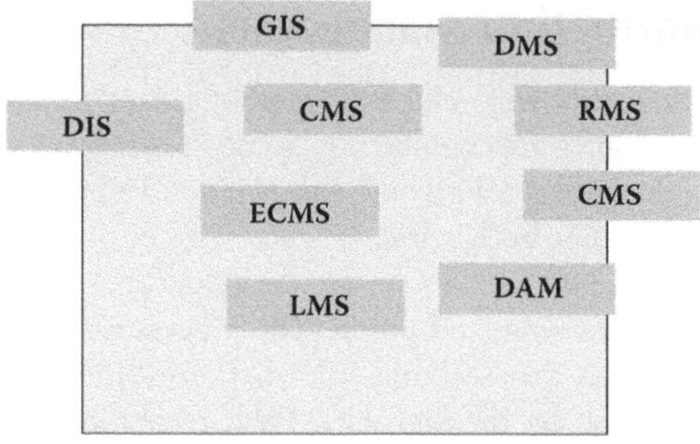


**Figure 6.2 Enterprise information system components.**

Enterprise content management systems (ECMSs) combine all of the above systems in a variety of configurations within an organizational setting. The ECMS should provide the foundation for maintaining an organization's valuable social software engineering artifacts.

## Content Management System (CMS)

This digital content life cycle consists of six primary activities: create, update, publish, translate, archive, and retire, each of which can take place on a variety of platforms. For example, digital content is created by one or more authors and may be edited over time. One or more individuals may provide some editorial oversight, thereby approving the content for publication. After publication, the content may be superseded by another form of content and thus retired or removed from use. Content management is a collaborative process by design and necessity. The process usually consists of the following basic roles and responsibilities:

- Content author: creates and edits content.
- Editor: tunes content message and style of delivery.
- Publisher: releases content for consumption.
- Administrator: manages release of content ultimately placing it into a repository so that it can be found and utilized.

A critical aspect of content management is the ability to manage versions of content as they evolve (version control). This is particularly important if a CMS is designed to be distributed across platforms or certain aspects of content are pushed to clients. Essentially, a content management system is a set of automated processes that may support the following features:

- Identification of all key users and their roles

- Ability to assign roles and responsibilities to different content categories or types
- Definition of workflow tasks often coupled with messaging so that content managers are alerted to changes in content
- Ability to track and manage multiple versions of a single instance of content
- Ability to publish the content to a repository to support the consumption of the content

A CMS allows end users to add new content in the form of articles easily. The articles are typically entered as plain text, perhaps with markups to indicate where other resources (such as pictures, video, or audio) should be placed. Hence, CMS systems are multimedia enabled. A CMS then uses rules to style an article, separating the display from the content; this has a number of advantages when articles should conform to a consistent "look and feel." The system then adds the articles to a larger collection for publishing.

The wiki is a popular example of this—a reasonable first foray into social software networking. A wiki is a web application that allows users to add content, as on an Internet forum, but also allows anyone to edit the content. The Wikipedia encyclopedia was created this way. Figure 6.3 shows a typical formatted page on Wikipedia. We discussed this in Chapter 2, but it is worthwhile to note the variety of wiki "engines" including UseMod, TWiki, MoinMoin, PmWiki, and MediaWiki. A more extensive list can be found at http://c2.com/cgi/wiki?WikiEngines. What's important is that the "intelligence" wrapped in social software engineering networks, likely composed of wikis, blogs, discussion messages, etc., should be managed in the same way as other corporate information assets.

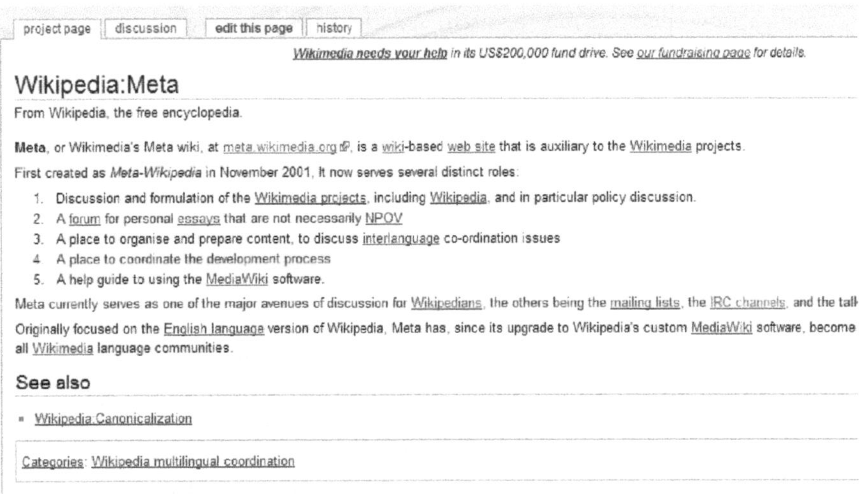


**Figure 6.3 Wikipedia page structure.**

## Document Management and Electronic Document Management Systems

The document management system (DMS), a generic form of an IT repository, focuses on the storage and retrieval of work documents (forms, specifications, programs, etc.) in their original formats. The key processes of DMS are

**Feeding** — Paper scanning or document importing.
**Storage** — Every organization has its own particular storage needs based on data volume, accessibility requirements, archival duration, and other factors. Choices include magnetic (typical desktop hard-drives, RAID), optical (CD, DVD, WORM), magneto-optical storage technologies, or a combination of these devices.
**Indexing** — Tagging each document with some code for accessibility.
**Control and security** — One of the main advantages of an EDMS is that all documents of all types reside in the same computing environment. However, during a company's daily operations, it is probable that certain groups of employees require access privileges to certain types of documents, while others may not have such needs.
**Workflow** — The EDMS is capable of mapping a company's organizational rules in the form of access controls to document databases. EDMS tool suites often provide the means to model operational procedures in the forms of workflow management utilities.
**Search** —An efficient EDMS allows users to search documents via pre-set indices, keywords, full-text search, even via thesaurus and synonym support. Usually, filters can be applied and search criteria may be nested; Boolean and comparison operators may be used. We discuss this in more depth below.
**Access** — After documents are identified for review, the EDMS must be capable of retrieving them quickly and transparently regardless of their locations. Documents may be distributed in multiple databases at multiple locations. An efficient access strategy will give end users the impression that the documents are all stored in one location on a single computer.
**Sharing** —Collaborative capabilities prevent end users from making duplicates of retrieved documents.

The document management solution allows users to deposit documents through multiple interfaces. Most users will access a document management system through a typical desktop configuration via a Web interface or proprietary application. Access can also be obtained through imaging devices or the organization's email system that archives emails as historical artifacts.

Search capabilities are typically built into the functionality of a document management system. Searches can be driven by a keyword search or other designated parameters. The web content management interface is the method of integrating documents within the document management system into the social software engineering system. Access through this Web content management interface would be independent of access directly to a document management system and defined accessibility and authentication must be established.

Originally, a document management system was a computer program (or set of programs) used to track and store images of paper documents. More recently, the term is used to distinguish imaging and records management systems that specialize in paper capture and records, respectively. Document management systems commonly provide check-in, check-out, storage, and retrieval of electronic documents often as word processor and similar files. In a typical system, the user scans the original paper document and stores its image in the document management system, although documents are increasingly starting life in digital form. An image is often given a name containing the date; a user may have to add "tags" to make retrieval of the image easier.

## Digital Asset Management

Digital asset management (DAM) is similar to RMS but focused on multimedia resources such as images, audio, and video. Digital asset management is still a new and rapidly evolving market. As a result, many different types of systems are labeled as DAMs although they are designed to address slightly different problems or created for a specific industry. Several commercial systems for DAM are available and numerous groups are trying to establish standards for DAM.

DAM systems generally support functions for ingesting, managing, searching, retrieving, and archiving assets. The systems may also include version control and asset format conversion capabilities (i.e., dynamically downsizing a large, high-resolution image for display on a website). DAM systems are related to and can be considered a superset of content management systems. A DAM is a combination of workflow, software, and hardware that organizes and retrieves a company's digital assets. It is useful for storing any audio or video components of the software engineering process such as audio or video transcripts of meetings and user interviews.

## Data Mining

Data mining toolsets are the primary devices used by a typical organization to perform business intelligence. Most typically used in strategic planning and other business analysis departments, data mining can certainly be utilized in IT for the purposes cited in this chapter. At this point, it is probably the best tool available. Data mining aids in knowledge discovery, that is, the identification of new phenomena, and is also useful in enhancing our understanding of known phenomena. One key step in data mining is pattern recognition—the discovery and characterization of patterns in image and other high-dimensional data. A pattern is an ordering or arrangement in which some organization of underlying structure can be said to exist. Patterns in data are identified using measurable features or attributes extracted from the data.

Data mining is an interactive and iterative process involving data preprocessing, searches for patterns, knowledge evaluation, and possible refinement of the process based on input from domain experts or feedback from one of the steps, as shown in Figure 6.4. The preprocessing of the data is a time-consuming but critical first step and is often domain and application dependent. However, several techniques developed in the context of one application or domain can be applied to other applications and domains. The pattern recognition step is usually independent of the domain or application. Data mining starts with raw data, usually in the form of simulation data, observed signals, or images. These data are preprocessed using techniques such as sampling, multiresolution analysis, denoising, feature extraction, and normalization.

Sampling is a widely accepted technique to reduce the size of a data set and make it easier to handle. However, in some cases, such as searching for an object that appears infrequently in the set, sampling may not be viable. Another technique is reducing the size of the data set. With multiresolution analysis, data at a fine resolution can be "coarsened" (shrunk) by removing some of the detail and extracting relevant features from the raw data set. The key to effective data mining is reducing the number of features used to mine data, so only the features best at discriminating among the data items are retained.

One great example of the value added by using data mining is in lessons-learned analysis. Post-implementation, a software development team should spend time to

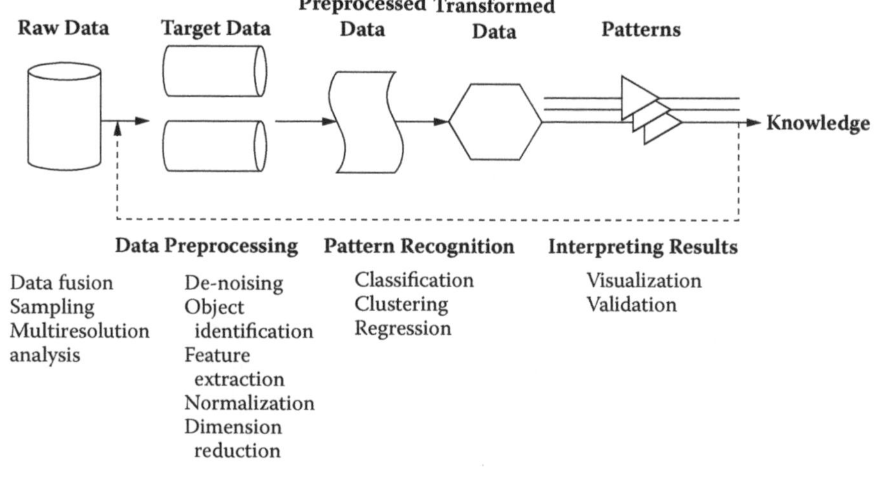


**Figure 6.4 Data mining.**

create a lessons-learned document detailing issues and problems, and their resolutions encountered during system development. Over time, hundreds of lessons learned may be recorded in this knowledge repository. When embarking on a new system, lessons learned should be reviewed so that earlier problems may be avoided. Obviously, reviewing hundreds of lessons-learned documents is a tedious process. Instead, data mining can be used to select lessons learned specific to characteristics of a new problem. After data are preprocessed or "transformed," pattern recognition software is used to find patterns (a pattern is an ordering that contains some underlying structure). The results are processed back into a format familiar to the experts who then examine and interpret the results.

## We've Reached the End of Chapter 6

IT projects are data heavy. Social networking is often data light. This chapter discussed some methodologies for integrating the full spectrum of documentation required by a typical IT project into a social software engineering framework.

## References

Baek, S.L, Liebowitz, J., Prasad, S.Y., Granger, M.J., and Lewis, M. (1997). An intelligent agent-based framework for knowledge management on the web: case study of a virtual team designing a multimedia system. *AAAI Technical Report WS-97-09.*

Bird, S.D. (1993). Toward a taxonomy of multi-agent systems, *International Journal of Man–Machine Studies*, 39, 689–704.

Case, S. Azarmi, N. Thint, M., and Ohtani, T (2001). Enhancing e-communities with agent-based systems, *IEEE Computer*, 34, 64–69.

# Chapter 7

# Measuring Social Software Engineering

IBM's 2010 study of 2,500 CIOs found that ongoing measurement is essential. IT processes have always been measured, although not always very effectively. This chapter will examine the fundamentals of balanced scorecard as it relates to the precepts of project management (PM). Readers will examine the balanced scorecard in relationship to an organization and the people, processes, technologies, and products that are components of the organization's discrete projects, programs, and collaborative efforts such as social software engineering.

## Effective Project Management

While most organizations understand the importance of effective project management, they simply do not do a good job of managing projects. This translates to less-than-stellar project outcomes. Many stakeholder groups are involved in a typical project (e.g., business process users, owners, users, business managers, clients, etc.), and each stakeholder group has different goals and objectives for assessing project outcomes. At the most basic level, the triple constraint methodology (time, cost, quality) is most often used to assess project success. However, many now believe that triple constraint does not account for the varied dimensions of projects that need to be considered in their assessments. Current research in this area finds a lack of agreement about what constitutes project success and methods for more comprehensive assessment of project outcomes (Barclay, 2008).

Based on the varied dimensionality of a typical project, some argue for the need to distinguish PM success in terms of the traditional time, cost, and quality constraints and project success aligned with the product outcome and discerned through the stakeholders. Thus, it is possible to experience product success without PM success. Obviously, the traditional project measures of time, cost, and quality must be enhanced by additional project measurement dimensions such as stakeholder benefits (customer satisfaction), product benefits (competitive advantage, financial rewards), and preparing for the future (value, personal growth) (Barclay, 2008).

## Balanced Scorecard for Project Management

A number of studies (Barclay, 2008; Lynn, 2006) suggest that adaptation of the balanced scorecard business approach to performance management measurement provides this type of enhanced vehicle. Robert S. Kaplan and David P. Norton developed the balanced scorecard approach in the early 1990s to compensate for the perceived shortcomings of using only financial metrics to judge corporate performance. They recognized that the new economy also required valuation of intangible assets, and they urged companies to measure such esoteric factors as quality and customer satisfaction. By the middle 1990s, balanced scorecard became the hallmark of a well-run company. Kaplan and Norton often compare their approach for managing a company to that of pilots viewing assorted instrument panels in an airplane cockpit—both activities require monitoring of multiple aspects of their working environments.

In the scorecard scenario in Figure 7.1, a company organizes its business goals into discrete, all-encompassing perspectives: financial, customer, internal processes, and finally learning and growth. The company then determines cause-and-effect relationships (satisfied customers buy more goods, increasing revenue). Next, the company lists measures for each goal, pinpoints targets, and identifies projects and other initiatives to help it reach those targets.

Departments create scorecards tied to the company's targets, and employees and projects have scorecards tied to their departmental targets. This cascading nature provides a line of sight between each individual, his or her current project, the work unit supported, and how these factors impact the strategy of the enterprise as a whole. For project managers, the balanced scorecard is an invaluable tool that permits them to link a project to the business side of the organization using a cause-and-effect approach. Some have likened balanced scorecard to a new language that enables project managers and business line managers to think together about steps to support or improve business performance.

A beneficial side effect of the balanced scorecard is that after all measures are reported, it is possible to calculate the strengths of relations among the various value drivers. For example, if the relation between high implementation costs and high profit levels is weak for a long time, it can be inferred that the project as implemented does not sufficiently contribute to results as expressed by other (e.g., financial) performance measures.

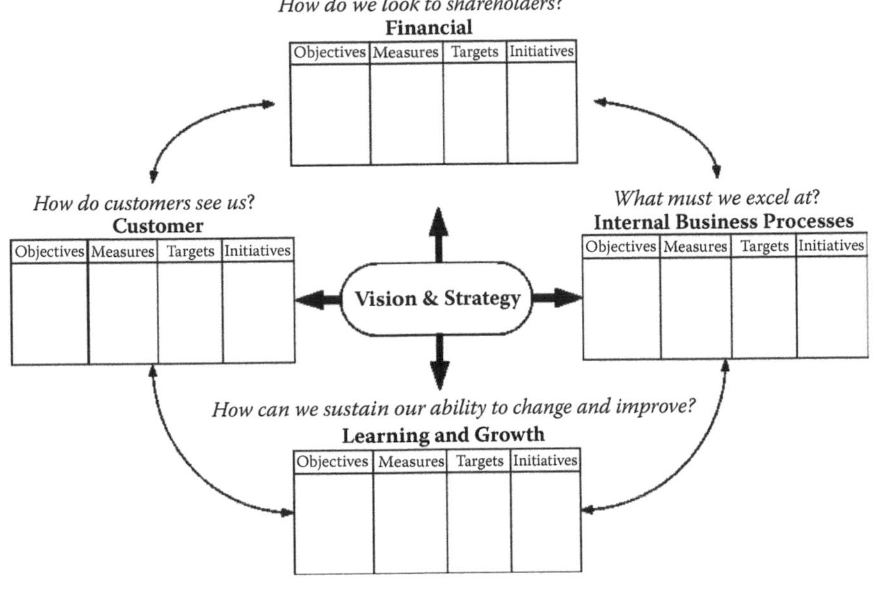


**Figure 7.1 Balanced scorecard.**

## Adopting a Balanced Scorecard

Kaplan and Norton (2001) provide a good overview of how a typical company adapts to the balanced scorecard approach:

> Each organization we studied did it a different way, but you could see that, first, they all had strong leadership from the top. Second, they translated their strategy into a balanced scorecard. Third, they cascaded the high-level strategy down to the operating business units and the support departments. Fourth, they were able to make strategy everybody's everyday job, and to reinforce that by setting up personal goals and objectives and then linking variable compensation to the achievement of those target objectives. Finally, they integrated the balanced scorecard into the organization's processes, built it into the planning and budgeting process, and developed new reporting frameworks as well as a new structure for the management meeting.

The key, then, is to develop a scorecard that naturally builds in cause-and-effect relationships, includes sufficient performance drivers, and, finally, provides a linkage to appropriate measures, as shown in Table 7.1. At the very lowest level, a discrete project may also be evaluated via a balanced scorecard. The key is the

**Table 7.1 Typical Departmental Sample Scorecard**

| *Objective* | *Measure/Metric* | *End of FY 2010 (Projected)* |
|---|---|---|
| **Financial** | | |
| Long-term corporate profitability | % Change in stock price due to earnings growth | +25% per year for next 10 years<br>+20% per year for next 10 years |
| Short-term corporate profitability:<br>1. Introduce new products<br>2. Enhance existing products<br>3. Expand client base<br>4. Improve efficiency and cost effectiveness | Revenue growth | +20% related revenue growth |
| | % Cost reduction | Cut departmental costs by 35% |
| **Customer** | | |
| Customer satisfaction:<br>1. Customer-focused products<br>2. Improve response time<br>3. Improve security | Quarterly and annual customer satisfaction surveys | +35%; raise satisfaction level from current 60 to 95% |
| | Satisfaction ratio based on customer surveys | +20% |
| Customer retention | % Customer attrition | –7%; reduce from current 12 to 5% |
| Customer acquisition | % Increase in number of customers | +10% |

| Internal | | |
|---|---|---|
| Complete M&A transitional processes<br>Establish connectivity<br>Improve quality<br>Eliminate errors and system failures | % Work completed | 100% |
| | % Workforce with full access to corporate resources | 100% |
| | % Saved on reduced work | +35% |
| | % Reduction of customer complaints | +25% |
| | % Saved on better quality | +25% |
| Increase ROI | % Increase in ROI | +20 to 40% |
| Reduce TCO | % Reduction of TCO | –10 to –20% |
| Increase productivity | % Increase in customer orders | +25 |
| | % Increase in production per employee | +15% |
| Enhance products and services | Number of new products and services introduced | 5 new products |
| Improve response time | Average hours required to respond to customer | –20 minutes; reduce from current 30 to 60 minutes to 10 minutes or less |

*(continued)*

**Table 7.1 (continued) Typical Departmental Sample Scorecard**

| *Objective* | *Measure/Metric* | *End of FY 2010 (Projected)* |
|---|---|---|
| **Learning and innovation** | | |
| Develop skills | % Spent on training | +10% |
| Initiate leadership development and training | % Staff with professional certificates | +20 |
| | Number of staff attending colleges | 18 |
| Innovative products | % Increase in revenue | +20% |
| Improved processes | Number of new products | +5 |
| R&D | % Decrease in failures and complaints | –10% |
| Performance measurement | % Increase in customer satisfaction based on survey results | +20 |
| | % Projects passing ROI test | +25% |
| | % Staff receiving bonuses on performance enhancement | +25% |
| | % Increase in documentation | +20% |

**Table 7.2 Simple Project Scorecard Approach***

| *Perspective* | *Goals* |
|---|---|
| Customer | Fulfill project requirements<br>Control cost of project<br>Satisfying project end users<br>**Collaborating with end users** |
| Financial | Provides business value (e.g., ROI, ROA, etc.)<br>Project contributing to organization as a whole<br>**Reduction in costs due to enhanced communications** |
| Internal processes | Adheres to triple constraints: time, cost, quality—including a **reduction in time required to build systems** |
| Learning and growth | Maintain currency<br>Anticipate changes<br>Acquire skillsets<br>**Promote collaboration and knowledge sharing** |

* *Bolding indicates goals that may be applicable to social software engineering.*

connectivity between the project and the objectives of the organization as a whole as shown in Table 7.2. The internal processes perspective maps neatly to the traditional triple constraints of project management using many of the same measures. For example, we can articulate the quality constraint using the ISO 10006:2003 standard that provides guidance on applying quality management to projects of varying complexity, small or large, of short or long duration, in different environments, and regardless of product or process involved. The standard bases quality management of projects on eight principles:

- The customer focus
- Leadership
- Involvement of people
- Process approach
- System approach to management
- Continual improvement
- Factual approach to decision making
- Mutually beneficial supplier relationships

Table 7.3 illustrates sample characteristics. The characteristics of a variable (quality, time, etc.) are used to create key performance indicators (KPIs) or metrics used to measure the success of a project. Based on Tables 7.1 through 7.3, we have a

**Table 7.3 ISO 10006 Definition of Quality Management for Projects**

| *Quality Characteristic* | *Sub-Characteristic* |
|---|---|
| Customer focus | 1. Understand future customer needs<br>2. Meet or exceed customer requirements<br>Social software engineering promotes close collaboration with various stakeholder groups. |
| Leadership | 1. Set quality policy and identify objectives (including quality objectives) for project<br>2. Empower and motivate all project personnel to improve project processes and product<br>Social software engineering may promote leaderful teams, as discussed Chapter 5. |
| Involvement of people | 1. Personnel in project organization have well-defined responsibility and authority<br>2. Competent personnel are assigned to project organization<br>The use of collaborative social technologies evolves naturally and will hopefully lead to improving products and processes. |
| Process approach | 1. Identify appropriate processes for project<br>2. Clearly identify interrelations and interactions among processes<br>Social software engineering environments enable team to more effectively articulate system processes and provide excellent means to document processes of systems development. |
| System approach to management | 1. Clearly divide responsibility and authority between project organization and other relevant parties<br>2. Define appropriate communication processes<br>Social software engineering provides a systematized method for more effective management of development effort and enhanced communications among various stakeholder groups. |
| Continual improvement | 1. Treat projects as processes rather than as isolated tasks<br>2. Provide for self-assessments<br>Social software engineering provides means for constant assessment via group workspaces. |
| Factual approach to decision making | 1. Base effective decisions on analysis of data and information<br>2. Record information about project progress and performance<br>Social software engineering allows easy tracking of project progress and performance. |
| Mutually beneficial supplier relationships | 1. Investigate possibility of a common supplier for a number of projects |

**Table 7.4 Representative Social Software Engineering Metrics**

| *Learning and Growth* | *Number of Wikis* |
|---|---|
| | Number of blogs |
| | Number of group workspaces |
| | Number of collaborative project plans |
| | Number of collaborative spreadsheets |
| | Number of teams using social software engineering |
| | Number of team members using social software engineering |
| | Maturity of collaboration |
| | Degree of communication efficiency |
| | Collaborative lessons learned |

number of choices for measuring the quality dimension of any particular project and directly tying in the social software aspects. More specifically, the perspectives that best fit the social software engineering paradigm are learning and growth. Possible metrics are shown in Table 7.4.

## Example: FedEx

FedEx applies three key measurement indicators. The goal of the *customer-value creation* indicator is to define a customer a customer value that is currently unmet and use technology to meet that need. Ultimately, the information produced by the system should be stored for analysis. A hallmark of the "FedEx way" is that employees really listen to their customers and create services to fulfill core needs. When FedEx initiated its overnight services in the 1970s, customers told them that they required access to more extensive delivery information. The original tracking service was a tedious, manual process requiring numerous telephone calls to a centralized customer service center. In turn, customer service had to call one or more of 1,400 operations centers to track a single package. This process was expensive and slow. Today's rapid online tracking capability was conceived to meet this need.

FedEx's tracking system also fulfills another important company requirement. The system automatically calculates whether a customer commitment was met by comparing ship date and service type to delivery date and time. This information forms the basis of FedEx's money-back guarantee and appears on customer invoices. More importantly, this statistic is aggregated for the internal index on service quality that serves as a focal point for corporate improvement activities.

Another key FedEx indicator is *performance support*. The goal is to create appropriate tools that enable front-line employees to improve their personal performance using information in FedEx's vast databases. Individual performance is then aggregated to location, geographic unit, and ultimately makes its way into corporate-wide statistics that are available on every company desktop. Performance support indicators for couriers include

1. Does the count of packages delivered equal the Enhanced Tracker's count of deliverables?
2 Does the count of revenue forms equal the Enhanced Tracker's count of shipments picked up?

As a courier closes out daily activities, he or she uses a hand-held device (Enhanced Tracker) to review a series of performance measurements. During the day, the tracker records activity information and time per activity of the courier. Information from the tracker is ported to the corporate database. The aggregated historical information is used later for manpower tracking or comparison of achievements to performance standards. Perhaps the most important indicator is *business goal alignment* designed to align employee and management incentives with corporate and customer objectives.

FedEx's entire business strategy is based on its technology. FedEx was the first company to provide automated package tracking. For a long time this gave the company "first mover" advantage. Now that other delivery companies are catching up, FedEx must work twice as hard to maintain its competitive edge. From an IT perspective, it does this by using the CollabNet Platform to respond to globalization, software proliferation, and time-to-market pressures. With the CollabNet Platform, FedEx decreased software development cycles by 50%, reduced third-party integration time by 50%, and decreased training time for project members by 90%. CollabNet is an integrated suite of Web-based tools for application lifecycle management (ALM) of distributed software development projects. It combines software configuration management (SCM), issue tracking, project management, and, most importantly from a social software engineering perspective, collaboration tools. These indicators form the basis for FedEx's balanced scorecard. The "People, Service, Profit" corporate philosophy of FedEx guides all company decisions.

## Attributes of Successful Project Management Measurement Systems

Certain attributes set apart successful performance measurement and management systems, including

1. A conceptual framework is needed for a performance measurement and management system. A clear and cohesive performance measurement framework that is understood by all project managers and staff and supports objectives and the collection of results is needed.
2. Effective internal and external communications are the keys to successful performance measurement. Effective communication with employees, process owners, end users, and stakeholders is vital to the successful development and deployment of project management-oriented performance measurement and management systems.
3. Accountability for results must be clearly assigned and well understood. Project managers must clearly identify what factors determine success and ensure that staff understand their responsibilities for achieving these goals.
4. Performance measurement systems must do more than compile data. They must provide intelligence for decision makers. Performance measures should relate to strategic goals and objectives and provide timely, relevant, and concise information for use by decision makers at all levels to assess progress toward predetermined goals. These measures should produce information on the efficiency with which resources (people, hardware, software, etc.) are transformed into goods and services, how well results compare to a program's intended purpose, and the effectiveness of activities and operations in terms of their specific contributions to program objectives.
5. Compensation, rewards, and recognition should be linked to performance measurements. Performance evaluations and rewards must be tied to specific measures of success by linking financial and nonfinancial incentives directly to performance. Such linkage sends a clear and unambiguous message about what activities and results are important.
6. Performance measurement systems should be positive, not punitive. The most successful performance measurements are not "gotcha" systems; they are learning systems that help identify what works—and what does not—so as to continue with and improve what works and repair or replace what does not.
7. Results and progress toward program commitments should be openly shared with employees, customers, and stakeholders. Performance measurement system information should be openly and widely shared with employees, end users, stakeholders, vendors, and suppliers.

Note that a number of attributes listed above seem to be made for social networking environments. Performance measurement systems should be communicated openly throughout an organization. What better place for communication than the enterprise social networking environments promoted in this book. In all cases, however, balanced scorecard must be carefully planned and executed to work effectively.

## Project Management Office

Project management consists of a set of discrete steps that takes a project from inception to closure as shown in Figure 7.2. A particular project is only one of many that will be implemented at any given time by a typical organization. A project might be one of many included in a specific program. A program is related to a corporate strategy, for example, becoming an e-book publisher. The entry into e-publishing may involve multiple projects. One project might be development of a website where e-books could be sold. Another might be developing software to convert print books into e-books. Most organizations have several ongoing programs in play at one time and all relate to one or more business strategies. It is conceivable that hundreds of projects in various stages of execution may be ongoing at any one time.

Portfolio management is needed to provide the business and technical stewardship of all of these programs and their projects, as shown in Figure 7.3. The requirement to manage multiple projects at one time creates several thorny issues (Dooley, Lupton, and O'Sullivan, 2005); the most salient ones are shown in Table 7.5. Many may be resolved using the social engineering techniques discussed in this book. Inter- and intra-project communications and maintaining motivation across project teams are critical. Maintaining all project documentation online makes it possible to record lessons learned. Thus, the knowledge gleaned from past projects would never be lost. Finally, information could move through the system quickly and reach team members without delay or loss.

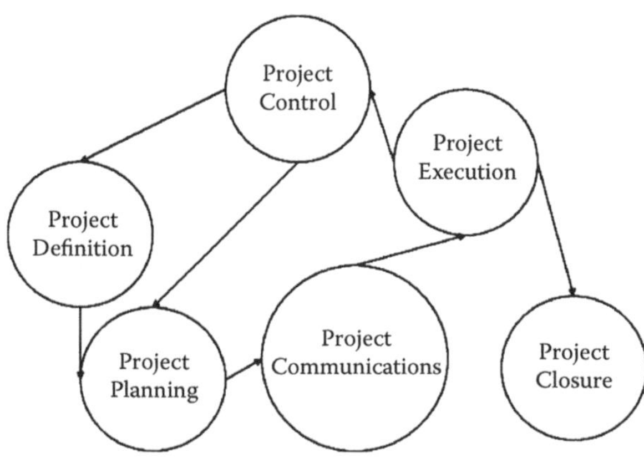


**Figure 7.2 Project management perspectives.**

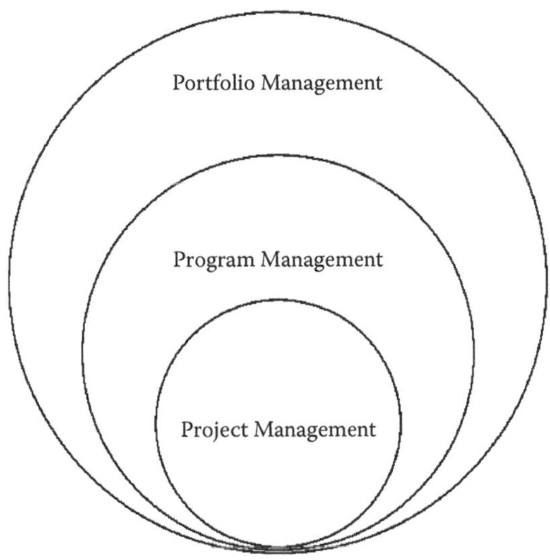


**Figure 7.3 Portfolio management.**

**Table 7.5 Multiple Project Management Issues**

| *Responsibility* | *Issue* |
|---|---|
| Alignment management | • Balancing individual project objectives with organization's objectives |
| Control and communication | • Maintaining effective communications within project and across multiple projects<br>• Maintaining motivation across project teams<br>• Resource allocation |
| Learning and knowledge management | • Inability to learn from past projects<br>• Failure to record lessons learned for each project<br>• Lack of timely information |

Portfolio management is usually performed by a project management office (PMO)—a department or group that defines and maintains the standards of process within the organization. The PMO strives to standardize and introduce economies of repetition in the execution of projects. It acts as the source of documentation, guidance, and metrics to aid project management and execution. While most PMOs are independent of the various project teams, it may be worthwhile to assign oversight of the social software engineering effort to the PMO to ensure a degree of standardization of use throughout an operation. A good PMO will base project management principles on accepted, industry-standard methodologies. Increasingly, influential industry certification programs such as ISO9000 and the Malcolm Baldrige National Quality Award, government regulatory requirements such as Sarbanes-Oxley, and business process management techniques such as balanced scorecard have propelled organizations to standardize processes.

If companies manage projects from an investment perspective with a continuing focus on value, risk, cost, and benefit, reduced cost should engender attendant increases in value. This is the driving principle of portfolio management. By now it should be obvious that the emphasis of PMO is standardization. To this end, the PMO employs robust measurement systems. The following metrics might be reported to indicate process responsiveness:

1. Total number of project requests submitted, approved, deferred, and rejected
2. Total number of project requests approved by a portfolio management group through the first project request approval cycle to provide an indicator of quality of project requests
3. Total number of project requests and profiles approved by the portfolio management group through secondary and tertiary prioritization approval cycles to determine baseline of effort versus return on investment for detailed project planning time
4. Time and cost through the process
5. Changes to project allocations after portfolio rebalancing (total projects, projects canceled, projects postponed, projects approved)
6. Utilization of resources: percentage utilization per staff resource (over 100%, 80% to100%, under 80%, projects understaffed, staff-related risks)
7. Projects canceled after initiation (project performance, reduced portfolio funding, reduced priority, and increased risk)

We will want to compare some of these statistics for projects using social software engineering and those that are not to determine productivity and quality gains based on this process. Interestingly, PMOs are not all that pervasive in industry. However, they are recommended if an organization is serious about enhancing performance and standardizing project management performance measurement. Implementation of a PMO is a discrete project involving three steps:

**Inventory** — A complete inventory of all initiatives should be developed. The inventory should list the project's sponsors and champion, stakeholders, strategic alignment with corporate objectives, estimated costs, and potential project benefits.

**Analyze** — After the inventory is completed and validated, all projects on the list should be analyzed. A steering committee should be formed, and members should have enough insight into the organization's strategic goals and priorities to place projects within the overall strategic landscape. The output of the analysis step is a prioritized project list, and priority is based on criteria set by the steering committee. This step is different for different organizations. Some companies may

**Table 7.6 Sample Process-Related Metrics**

| *Process* | *Sub-Process* | *Associated Sample Metric* |
|---|---|---|
| Initiating project (IP) | IP1 Planning Quality | Requirement error rate |
| | IP2 Planning Project | % Resources devoted to planning and review of activities |
| | IP3 Refining Business Case and Risks | % Definitional uncertainty risk |

consider strategic alignment to be the most important criterion; others may decide that a cost–benefit ratio is a better criterion for prioritization.

**Manage** —Portfolio management is not a one-time event. It is a constant process that must be managed. Projects must be continually evaluated based on changing priorities and market conditions.

The *analyze* step is where the balanced scorecard should be created, then fine-tuned in the *prioritize* step, and actually used in the *manage* step. In all likelihood, the PMO will standardize the project management methodologies based on two major sets of standards. The Project Management Body of Knowledge (PMBOK), which is most popular in the United States, recognizes five basic process groups typical of almost all projects: initiating, planning, executing, controlling and monitoring, and closing. Projects in Controlled Environments (PRINCE2) is the *de facto* standard for project management in the United Kingdom and popular in more than 50 other countries. It defines a variety of sub-processes and organizes them into eight major processes: starting a project, planning, initiating a project, directing a project, controlling a stage, managing product delivery, managing stage boundaries, and closing a project.

Both PRINCE2 and PMBOK consist of a set of processes and associated sub-processes that may be used to craft relevant metrics as shown in Table 7.6. Because the PMO is the single focal point for all aspects of project management, it is natural that the balanced scorecard should be within the purview of the PMO.

## Project Management Process Maturity Model ($PM^2$) and Collaboration

The $PM^2$ model determines and positions an organization's relative project management level with those of other organizations (Kwak and Ibbs, 2002). The various project management process maturity models are all based on work done by the Software Engineering Institute at Carnegie Mellon University intended to improve

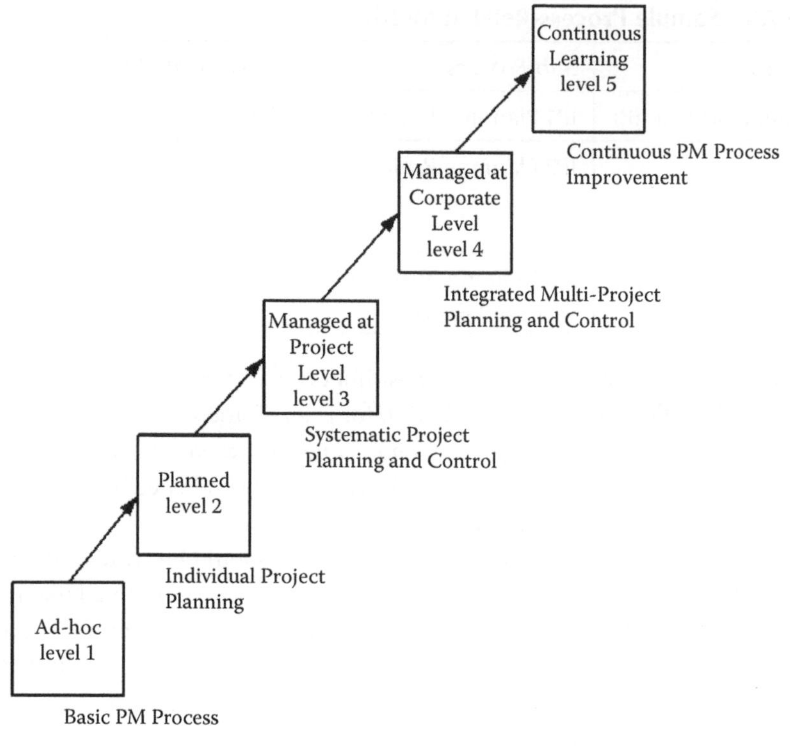


**Figure 7.4 PM² model.**

the quality of the software development process. The PM2 model defines five steps as shown in Figure 7.4.

Unfortunately, a number of organizations are still hovering somewhere between the ad hoc and planned levels. They continue to use some very basic project management techniques, usually limited to project management tools such as Microsoft's Project. Even then, tasks and methods are usually subject to the whims of a project manager and are not standardized across the company as a whole. Introduction of a PMO goes a long way toward moving up the ladder to the planned level, particularly if performance measurement and management are thrown into the mix (level 4).

Companies that are serious about improving performance strive to achieve level 5 (continuous learning). This requires a company to compare itself to others in its peer grouping—the goal of PM² and similar systems. In the PM² model, key processes, organizational characteristics, and key focus areas are defined as shown in Table 7.7. Each maturity level is associated with a set of key project management processes, characteristics of the processes, and key areas on which to focus. When mapped to the four balanced scorecard perspectives, PM² becomes a reference point or yardstick for PM best practices and processes.

**Table 7.7 Key Components of PM² Model**

| *Maturity Level* | *Key PM Processes* | *Major Organizational Characteristics* | *Key Focus Areas* |
|---|---|---|---|
| Level 5 (Continuous Learning) | PM processes continuously improved | Project-driven organization | Innovative ideas to improve PM processes and practices |
| | PM processes fully understood | Dynamic, energetic, fluid organization | |
| | PM data optimized and sustained | Continuous improvement of PM processes and practices | |
| Level 4 (Managed at Corporate Level) | Multiple PM (program management) | Strong teamwork | Planning and controlling multiple projects in professional manner |
| | PM data and processes integrated | Formal PM training for project team | |
| | PM data quantitatively analyzed, measured, and stored | | |
| Level 3 (Managed at Project Level) | Formal project planning and control systems managed | Team oriented (medium) | Systematic and structured project planning and control for individual project |
| | Formal PM data managed | Informal training of PM skills and practices | |

*(continued)*

**Table 7.7 (continued) Key Components of PM$^2$ Model**

| *Maturity Level* | *Key PM Processes* | *Major Organizational Characteristics* | *Key Focus Areas* |
|---|---|---|---|
| Level 2 (Planned) | Informal PM processes defined | Team oriented (weak) | Individual project planning |
| | Informal PM problems identified | Organizations possess strengths in doing similar work | |
| | Informal PM data collected | | |
| Level 1 (Ad Hoc) | No PM processes or practices consistently available | Functionally isolated | Understand and establish basic PM processes |
| | No PM data consistently collected or analyzed | Lack of senior management support | |
| | | Project success depends on individual efforts | |

While the PM$^2$ model determines and positions an organization's relative project management level with those of other organizations, it is worthwhile to note the recent shift toward more decentralized and distributed project teams—some completely virtual and others working in partnerships with teams from other companies. Thus, measurement across collaborative, distributed partners must be considered in any measurement program.

Several interest groups and partnerships in the automotive industry were formed to develop new project management methods and processes that worked effectively in a collaborative environment (Niebecker, Eager, and Kubitza, 2008). The German Organization for Project Management (GPM e.V.), the PMI automotive special interest group, the automotive industry action group (AIAG), and others have embarked on projects to develop methods, models, and frameworks for collaborative product development, data exchange, quality standards, and project management. One recent output from this effort was the ProSTEP-iViP reference model to manage time, tasks, communications in cross-company automotive product development projects (http://www.prostep.org/en/).

A set of drivers and KPIs for a typical stand-alone project can be seen in Table 7.8. Using guidelines from the ProSTEP reference model, Niebecker, Eager,

**Table 7.8 Representative Drivers and KPIs for Standard Project**

| *Balanced Scorecard Perspective* | *Drivers* | *KPIs* |
|---|---|---|
| Finances | Project budget<br>Increase of business value<br>Multiproject categorization<br>Project management | Human resources<br>Share of sales<br>Profit margin<br>Savings<br>Return on investment<br>Expenditure |
| Customer | Customer satisfaction | Cost overrun<br>Number of customer audits<br>Change management<br>Process stability |
| Process | Adherence to schedules<br>Innovation enhancement<br>Minimizing risks<br>Optimization of project structure<br>Quality | Adherence to delivery dates<br>Lessons learned<br>Number of patent applications<br>External labor<br>Quality indices<br>Duration of change management<br>Product maturity<br>Percentage of overhead<br>Number of internal audits<br>Project risk analysis |
| Development | Employee satisfaction<br>Employee qualification enhancement | Rate of employee fluctuation<br>Travel costs<br>Overtime<br>Index of professional experience<br>Continuing education costs |

and Kubitza (2008) reoriented the drivers and KPIs in Table 7.8 to account for the extra levels of complexity found in a project involving two or more companies in a networked collaborative environment. This suits the social software engineering construct very well, as shown in Table 7.9.

**Table 7.9 Drivers and KPIs for Collaborative Project (CP)**

| *Balanced Scorecard Perspective* | *Drivers* | *KPIs* |
|---|---|---|
| Finances/ Project | Project cost<br>Increase of business value<br>Categorization into CP management<br>Project maturity | Product costs<br>Production costs<br>Cost overruns<br>Savings<br>Productivity index<br>Turnover<br>Risk distribution<br>Profit margin<br>Feature stability<br>Product maturity index |
| Process | Adherence to schedules<br>Innovation enhancement<br>Minimizing risks<br>Adherence to collaboration process<br>Quality | Variance to schedule<br>Changes before and after design freeze<br>Duration until defects removed<br>Number and duration of product changes<br>Number of postprocessing changes<br>Continuous improvement process<br>Project risk analysis<br>Maturity of collaboration process<br>Frequency of product tests<br>Defect frequency<br>Quality indices |
| Collaboration | Communication<br>Collaboration | Number of team workshops<br>Checklists<br>Degree of communication efficiency<br>Collaborative lessons learned<br>Maturity of collaboration<br>Degree of lessons learned realization |

**Table 7.9 (continued) Drivers and KPIs for Collaborative Project (CP)**

| *Balanced Scorecard Perspective* | *Drivers* | *KPIs* |
|---|---|---|
| Development | Team satisfaction | Employee fluctuation |
| | Team qualification enhancement | Project-focused continuing education |
| | Trust among team members | Employee qualification |

Niebecker, Eager, and Kubitza's recommendations expand upon the traditional balanced scorecard methodology, providing an approach for monitoring and controlling cross-company projects by aligning collaborative project objectives with the business strategies and project portfolios of each company. Appendix F provides an extensive set of scorecard metrics that incorporate the collaborative aspects of social software engineering.

## We've Reached the End of Chapter 7

"You can't know where you're going unless you know where you've been." That old adage clearly shows why it is important to measure. In this chapter, we advocated use of the balanced scorecard, tied to knowledge management and social software engineering performance metrics.

## References

Barclay, C. (2008). Toward an integrated measurement of IS project performance: the project performance scorecard. *Information Systems Frontiers*, 10, 331–345.

Dooley, L., Lupton, G., and O'Sullivan, D. (2005). Multiple project management: a modern competitive necessity. *Journal of Manufacturing Technology Management*, 16(5), 466–482.

Kaplan, R.S. and Norton, D.P. (2001). On balance (interview). *CFO, Magazine for Senior Financial Executives*. February.

Kwak, Y.H. and Ibbs, C.W. (2002). Project management process maturity ($PM^2$) model. *Journal of Management in Engineering*, 18(3).

Lynn, S.C. (2006). Project management methodologies and strategic execution. www.asapm.org/asapmag/articles/Lynn12-06.pdf

Niebecker, K., Eager, D., and Kubitza, K. (2008). Improving cross-company management performance with a collaborative project scorecard. *International Journal of Managing Projects in Business*, 1(3), 368–386.

# Chapter 8

# Social Engineering Paradigm Remixed

More than a decade ago, Lipnack and Stamps (2000) wrote a book about virtual teams, stressing that they would represent the future of corporate networking and ultimately lead to what they called the "intelligent organization." The key to this intelligence is shared knowledge. Working in groups can make the most of shared knowledge as shown in Figure 8.1, which is patterned after Hutchins et al.'s (1996) model of collaboration stages and cognitive processes.

Software engineering teams are composed of individuals, each with a "take" on information required for any particular team-based project. The way a team member visualizes or interprets the meaning of this information (i.e., knowledge construction) may be at odds with the ideas of other team members or the team as the whole. In the collaborative team problem-solving phase of this model, the team works to integrate individual knowledge toward a common understanding. Essentially, the goal is a convergence of individual mental models into a team mental model. In the team consensus phase, the team negotiates solution alternatives. This is a critical phase as it may require individual team members to share hidden knowledge—perhaps reluctantly. In the final outcome evaluation and revision phase, the team picks a solution and adjusts it to fit the goals of the problem.

Virtual communications permit team members to gain wider access to experience, promote the sharing of best practices, encourage collaborative solutions to problems, and make learning a natural by-product of working. Any tools and processes we can muster to promote this level of collaboration can only increase the knowledge capital of the team, IT, and the organization as a whole. How can

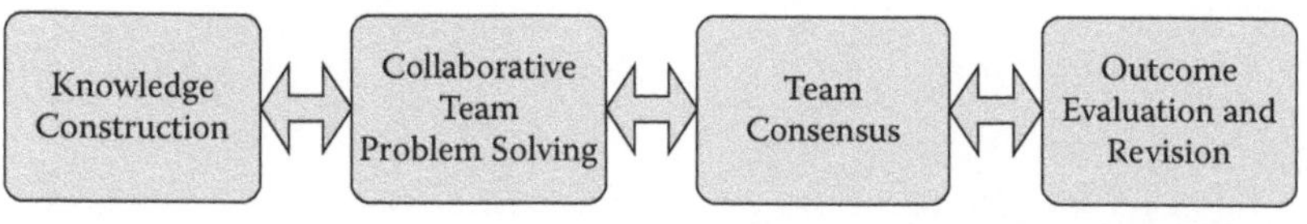


**Figure 8.1 Team sharing model.**

software engineering be reconfigured to take advantage of the social software engineering paradigm? Among a number of software engineering methodologies, the agile ones are well suited for adaptation to the social networking techniques we espouse. Let's take a closer look.

## Scrum

We will combine the agility of the Scrum methodology to the flexibility of Socialtext software to provide an example of how reconfiguration may be done. Socialtext 4.5 (http://socialtext.com) is representative of Enterprise (E 2.0) social software that is making its way into the marketplace.

Socialtext, which is SaaS based but can be hosted on site via a hosted appliance, provides what is sure to become the standard fare in enterprise-level social networking environments. Social networking people profiles enable staff to pinpoint exactly who has specific expertise within an organization and enables staff members to get to know each other.

Microblogging enables groups to stay in touch so that they are all on the same page, while internal blogs can be used to share knowledge across the organization or across teams. A team can carve out its own private real estate in the social network through the use of groups. Wiki Workspaces are group-editable workspaces that enable a team to brainstorm and then store the results of their ideas. Social spreadsheets can serve many purposes, one of which is to enable the team to dynamically and collaboratively track their deliverables and schedules. The dashboard is essentially a social intranet homepage within a group, across groups, or covering an entire organization.

Scrum is an agile framework used by software developers who often have to tackle large, complex projects. According to the Scrum Alliance (scrumalliance.org), Scrum consists of three roles, four ceremonies, and three artifacts, each of which will be described here. The product owner is the person (or persons) responsible for the business value of a project. The person who ensures that the team is functional and productive is the Scrum master. Finally, the team—the focus of the Scrum methodology—self-organizes to get the work done.

If a project starts with a Scrum master, he or she may want to use social networking people profiles to populate the team with individuals who have the most suitable skillsets for the project. It is important to keep current the profiles showing education and skills of everyone in the company (not only IT staff). Although, in the parlance of this methodology, the product owner is responsible for the business value of the project, the team will invariably need to tap into multiple levels of business expertise to build the assigned system. Simply picking any available end user is a sure road to project failure. Having the ability to pick just the right people is paramount if a project is to be successful.

The product owner and end users must be tightly integrated into the project team. Informational updates can be done via microblogging via group channels. If the entire company must be kept in the loop, an internal blog can be used. Because this form of blogging permits two-way, open dialogs, input from all levels of employees and even individuals outside the company is possible.

Completing the work involves four processes—ceremonies in Scrum speak. During sprint planning, the team meets with the product owner to choose a work set to deliver during a sprint. A virtual, asynchronous meeting can be of help via Socialtext or Wiki Workspace. With both systems, user stories can be discussed and selected at this point. The stories selected are the ones the team believes it can complete during the sprint. They are decomposed into tasks and estimates are provided for each of these tasks. The resulting task schedule can be loaded to the social spreadsheet, where it can be dynamically updated.

After the team starts work (coding, texting, reviewing, etc.), it meets every day via a Wiki Workspace to discuss progress and problems. Typically, three questions are asked and answered. What did you do yesterday? What will you do today? Did you meet any roadblocks? This process is called the daily scrum. Anyone may attend a daily scrum but only team members may speak. With Socialtext Workspace, people do their work on group-editable web pages that are visible to authorized users. Team members who are away may contribute via email, the contents of which can be posted to a Workspace by including the e-mail address of the Workspace in the address bar of the email.

Periodically the team will show the product owner what it accomplished during the current sprint. This is the sprint review. The product owner and end users can be notified of a sprint review via blog or a Dashboard announcement. If the product under development is standards based, it is possible that Socialtext Connect can be used to integrate the system under development or prototype into the Socialtext environment. Finally, the team will get together during a sprint retrospective to discuss ways to improve both process and product. The retrospective may also occur virtually via Wiki Workspace or Group. A sprint will usually last 2 to 4 weeks. Throughout a spring, the Scrum master keeps the team focused on the goal and tracks progress via the social spreadsheet. This process repeats until enough items in the product backlog have been completed, a deadline arrives, or the budget is depleted. The goal of Scrum is to make sure that the most valuable work has been completed when a project is terminated.

As is the case with all methodologies, various documentation types evolve during the sprints and the development of a product. The product backlog is a list of desired project features (requirements) that may be stored in a social spreadsheet. The backlog is dynamic, that is, items may be deleted, changed, or added at any time. Essentially, there is no scope creep, a problem common in traditional project management methodologies. The product backlog is prioritized, thus ensuring that highest-priority items are always completed first.

A sprint backlog is a set of features from the product backlog that the team has agreed to work on during a particular sprint. This backlog is further broken down into discrete tasks. The burndown chart is a visual aid that may be reproduced using the Socialtext tools; it shows the remaining work.

Several agile principles are actively endorsed in this methodology, according to the Agile Manifesto (agilemanifesto.org). Customer collaboration is preferred over contract negotiation. Completed functionality is more important than comprehensive documentation. It is more important to respond to change than follow a plan. Finally, and the reason for discussing Scrum in this book, is that individuals and interactions are valued over processes and tools. Toward that end, the technologies of social software engineering provide a firm foundation to enhance Scrum interactions.

## Extreme Programming (XP)

XP is a software methodology developed by Kent Beck (1999) to help software developers design and build systems more efficiently and successfully. XP is a disciplined and well-planned approach to software development. What makes it so popular is that it is one of the first lightweight methodologies. A lightweight methodology has only a few rules and practices that are easy to follow. XP does not require any additional paperwork, and the programmers do not have to test tons of methods. XP stresses customer satisfaction and can be used when a customer is not certain of his requirements or when new technology is to be introduced. XP applies four rules in developing software projects: communication, simplicity, feedback, and courage, and all may be supported by social software engineering tools.

The programmer communicates with the customer and elicits the customer's requirements, thus emphasizing customer satisfaction. The programmers also communicate with fellow workers, thus emphasizing teamwork. We already mentioned a host of social networking tools in the discussion on Scrum. The same tools may be used here, and other possibilities are equally intriguing. In Chapter 2, we talked about Second Life (Figure 8.2).

IBM utilizes virtual teams whose members have never met but are very productive. They use Second Life avatars to meet in a virtual office. Picture a meeting with an end user in a virtual environment. Organizations with global, distributed workforces really benefit from this type of social networking technology.

Simplicity in design is another XP rule. Overcomplicated designs result when developers work in a vacuum with little or no oversight. Social software engineering

**Figure 8.2 Using Second Life to collaborate with team members and end users.**

goes a long way toward solving this problem. A third tenet of XP is that software is tested and feedback obtained from the very outset and necessary changes are made. The process is cyclical. Feedback and change tracking naturally lend themselves to social tools.

Courage—a rather strange term to use in a software engineering context— is the final XP construct. It simply means that programmers are allowed to make changes at the final stages and implement new technologies as and when they are introduced. While this is certainly anathema to traditional methodologies in which scope creep is a dirty phrase, the idea is a good one and can be used in moderation to construct a system that users actually want and need.

## Collaborative Development Environment (CDE)

CDEs (Booch and Brown, 2003) were envisioned to be frictionless based on the need of developers to switch back and forth across environments and applications to communicate and work with each other. The CDE was envisioned to incorporate a project workspace with a standardized tool set to be used by global software teams. The earliest CDEs were developed within the open source community because, as expected, open source developers have always been composed of widely dispersed individuals and teams. SourceForge (http://sourceforge.net/) from CollabNet (http://www.collab.net/) is the most popular CDE, with well over a million users and tens of thousands of hosted projects. SourceForge offers a variety of free services: web interface for project administration, trackers, discussion forums, mailing lists, shell functions and compile farms, wikis, blogs, code hosting, and configuration management. The commercial version includes desirable features like measuring and reporting.

A group of scientists from the University of Manchester and the University of Southampton developed a portal that makes finding, using, and sharing scientific workflows and other research objects and building communities easy. While designed primarily for researchers, myExperiment (http://www.myexperiment.org/) is worth a mention as its approach is similar to the systems described in this chapter. The myExperiment project team followed a user-driven, agile approach of scientific software design consisting of six key principles: fit in, don't force change; jam today and more jam tomorrow; just in time and just enough; act local, think global; enable users to add value; and design for network effects. myExperiment was written using the Ruby on Rails web application development framework. The developers insist that it represents a middle ground between conventional, highly formalized software engineering and "hacking" that inscribes collective improvisation. The agile approach adopted by the myExperiment team affords a balance between structured orderliness that ensures timely delivery of whole projects, improvisation that enables responsiveness to new and changing user requirements, and exploitation of a rapidly expanding array of Web 2.0-based components and technologies.

As explained by the developers, a range of mechanisms and tools are used to help myExperiment team members to collaborate with the goal of delivering value quickly (Lin et al., 2008). Members may meet face-to-face or utilize computer-mediated meetings to cope with distributed teamwork. To coordinate activities routinely, developers working from different sites have a 1-hour Skype chat daily at 5 p.m. to test changes; discuss and review technical strategies, priorities, and schedule changes; and review new requirements and options for realizing or rejecting them. The topics are based on the developers' daily activities, and the chats enable them to inform each other of progress and work on and solve problems together. A chat usually begins with greetings and social talk, then progresses to the main topic. The conversation flow is fast paced; the participants are accustomed to typing and instant messaging. It is interesting that project teams prefer typing over talking when using Skype. One reason may be that Skype functions like a shared wall or whiteboard that allows participants to draw information from as many sources as possible (URLs, multimedia objects, copy-and-paste email texts). Skype recently introduced the SkypeKit (http://developer.skype.com/public/skypekit), a collection of software and APIs that allows Internet-connected devices or applications to offer Skype voice and video calls. Organizations intent on developing their own voice-enabled social networking environments should investigate this.

At weekly meetings, core members in managerial positions track development and reevaluate priorities. Monthly team meetings allow a wider membership to take part and meet face-to-face. Because members are in different places, collaboration tools such as instant messaging are used for these meetings and for ad hoc interactions on a daily basis. A wiki provides a persistent and shared semi-formal record for notes, task lists, and decisions, and team members have frequent virtual meetings with users.

Two mailing lists (one open for general discussion, one limited to the core team) and a wiki (with open and secure areas) are also available. The open mailing list has a dual role, serving as a mechanism for users to comment on existing features and raise new requirements and a way for developers to announce progress and openly talk with users about dealing with new requests.

Interestingly, Lin et al. (2008) assert that their studies suggest that agility and top-down management approaches (next section) are well balanced and not necessarily conflicting or contradictory. Because software engineering must deliver systems and eliminate as many problems and risks as possible, the myExperiment methodology, which is similar to the social software engineering methodology espoused in this book, is well suited to facilitate accountable management of software development.

## Traditional Software Methodologies and Social Networking

Most organizations do not use agile methodologies. Traditional methodologies still rule. In general, the traditional approaches may be categorized as follows. Note that more than one may be used at one time.

**Linear** — This is a phased, structured approach to systems development, sometimes called the waterfall method. The phases include requirements feasibility, analysis, system design, coding, testing, implementation, and testing. Note that the names of these phases may vary. The phases are usually performed sequentially although some potential for overlap is present. This approach is used commonly in industry.

**Iterative (prototyping)** — In the linear approach, the time to market can be months or even years. During development, requirements may change and the final deliverable may be outmoded. To prevent this, it is a good idea to try to compress the development cycle to shorten time to market and provide interim results to the end user. The iterative model consists of three steps: listen to customer, build and revise a mock-up, have customer "test drive" the mock-up, return to step 1.

**Rapid Application Development (RAD)** — This is a form of the iterative model. The key word is *rapid*. Development teams try to get a first version of a system to an end user within 60 to 90 days. To accomplish this, the normal seven-step SDLC is compressed into business modeling, data modeling, process modeling, application generation and testing, and turnover. RAD uses *application generators* to describe what were formerly called CASE (computer-assisted software engineering) tools.

**Incremental model** — The four main phases of software development are analysis, design, coding, and testing. If we break a business problem into increments, we can use an overlapping, phased approach to software development. For example, we can start the analysis of increment 1 in January, increment 2 in June, and increment 3 in September. As increment 3 starts, increment 1 is at the testing stage and increment 2 is at the coding stage.

**Joint Application Development (JAD)** — JAD is more of a technique than a complete methodology. It can be utilized in conjunction with any of the other methodologies discussed here. The technique consists of one or more end users who are "folded" into the software development team. Instead of an adversarial software developer–end user dynamic, the team gains the continued, uninterrupted attention of the person(s) who will ultimately use the system.

**Reverse Engineering** — This technique is used to first understand a system from its code, generate documentation based on the code, and finally make desired changes to the system. Competitive software companies often try to reverse engineer their competitors' software.

**Re-engineering** — Business goals change over time. Software must change to meet the goals. Re-engineering utilizes many of the techniques already discussed in this section. Instead of building a system from scratch, re-engineering retrofits an existing system to new business functionality.

**Object Oriented** — An object is a fundamental building block on which an object-oriented paradigm rests. The four pivotal concepts behind object orientation are encapsulation, message passing, dynamic binding, and inheritance. A tool or language that incorporates these concepts becomes qualified as an object-oriented toolkit.

All these traditional methodologies can be retrofitted to incorporate social software engineering methods for enhanced productivity and improved quality. This section will retrofit the base methodology of the software development life cycle (SDLC) using the traditional linear approach. Instead of discussing specific product as in the section on agile technologies, we will use the *group workspace* term to encompass any combination of group discussion boards, wikis, blogs, etc. Any of the tools already mentioned above or listed in Appendix A can be used, even "social network makers" such as Socialgo as shown in Figure 8.3. The group workspace will have the abilities to store documents, store multimedia such as audio and video transcripts and podcasts, make comments, whiteboard, launch surveys, and link to external resources such as databases and other file systems.

The idea phase of the SDLC is the point at which the end user, systems analyst, and various managers meet for the first time and the scope and objectives of the system are fleshed out in a high-level document. Meetings with end users usually utilize a brainstorming format. Using the IBM approach, a virtual environment such as Second Life can be used for this purpose. If that is not feasible, face-to-face meetings can be enhanced by using the group workspace where notes and documents can be stored.

Next, a team composed of one or more system analysts and end users tries to determine whether the system is feasible. A system may not be feasible because it is too expensive, it utilizes technology not yet available, or the developers lack

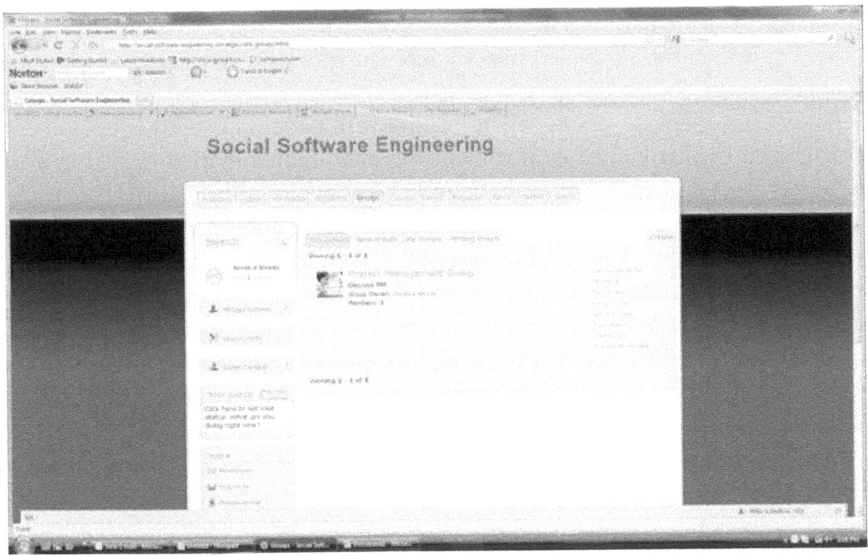


**Figure 8.3 Using a "social network making" tool to create a social software engineering network.**

sufficient experience to create the system—these are only a few reasons for not implementing a system. Reasons for and against a system can be documented in the workspace or wiki, with interested stakeholders responding to questions raised or commenting on negative or positive findings. All this activity becomes input into a formal feasibility study that can then be published online or make its way through corporate channels for approval.

Systems analysis is initiated after a system is determined to be feasible. At this point, the analysts try to ferret out all the rules and regulations of the system. What are the inputs? What are the outputs? What kind of interface is required? What kind of reports would be generated? Will paper forms be required? Will any hook-ups to external files or companies be required? How shall this information be processed?

Normally, this information is obtained using one or more information-gathering techniques. The most common technique is the interview. Questionnaires can also be used. Other techniques include observation and a review of available documentation (policy documents, memos, emails, etc.). Most of these tasks can be performed virtually. The only two that are not straightforward are observation and review of available documentation. However, because most work now is done online, it is possible to use technology to "observe" end-user activities online using a keystroke logger, a screen capture software that records screen and audio activity as videos (http://camstudio.org/, http://www.zdsoft.com/) and quality assurance tools that automatically generate test scripts (HP Quality Center software ). Accessing all available documentation is usually easy because most of it is available online. In all cases, this data should be fed directly into the group workspace for review and discussion.

Traditional software development occurred in a vacuum, with little end-user involvement. The artifact or deliverable of the requirement-gathering phase is the requirements specification. Because the end users have seen little until this point, a big difference may separate what the end users expected and what the requirements specification describes. The collaborative SDLC should eliminate this problem.

After all the unknowns are known and fully documented in the requirements specification, the systems analyst can put flesh on the skeleton by creating both high-level and detailed designs. Throughout the process, the accuracy of all of these documents should be verified by having the end users and analysts review and discuss them when they are posted to the group workspace.

Implementation can begin after a complete working design is delivered to the programmers and a new group of stakeholders becomes active in the group workspace. To this point, the programmers monitored the group workspace but had no active involvement in the discussions. Their goal was to become familiar with the system to reduce their learning curves as close to zero as possible.

The detailed design document posted to the group workspace contains the details (along with associated diagrams, database descriptions, screen designs, etc.) for the system and an itemized listing of human resources assigned to each task, including start and stop dates of all tasks. Many organizations use Microsoft Project for project planning. The server version of Microsoft Project is built on SharePoint, which is integrated to at least one of the social networking platforms we discussed (i.e., socialtext.com).

Programmers will use the group workspace for a variety of purposes: (1) codes that can then be reviewed and discussed by the programming team (the "walk-through"), (2) status reports to update end users and managers on progress of the development effort, and (3) question-and-answer sessions and links to interim deliverables for end user review. Of course, end users are expected to monitor the group workspace frequently, if not daily, so that they can respond quickly to any questions and comment on deliverables they have reviewed.

The step after coding is testing. Programmers will first perform unit testing to ensure that the coding follows the directions they were given. Systems testing, parallel testing, and integration testing are all forms of testing that involve end users, managers, and programmers. Again, the group workspace is used for this purpose. Test scripts should be developed on a joint basis and the results of the testing of these scripts reviewed collaboratively as well. Many companies have QA (quality assurance) departments that use automated tools to test the veracity of new systems. Thus, the QA department also needs access to the group workspace.

After a system is fully tested, it is turned over to production (changeover). Usually before this occurs, the end-user departments (not only team members working on the project) are trained and manuals are distributed. Modern manuals are not usually paper-bound. Online manuals and help facilities are now the norms. They should be stored in the group workspace and reviewed before publication.

By now, it is probably obvious that I recommend that some if not all training be accomplished online. One only has to browse Youtube.com to see how ubiquitous training videos have become. Short (minutes only) videos tied to specific functionalities of a system are recommended. For example, http://www.youtube.com/watch?v=bkJmB56GBfg&feature=related is a short video on making Microsoft documents look interesting. Obviously, these videos also should be stored in the group workspace.

We can now summarize the development from a knowledge perspective. At the end of the effort, the group workspace contains all the information nuggets that constitute the effort—specifications, brainstorming session results, questions and answers, and training videos. Ultimately, a lessons-learned log will be added to the mix. The log details what went right and what went wrong with the project. At the outset of a new project by an organization, the lessons-learned logs of earlier projects should be reviewed. All this information represents a "gold mine" of knowledge if it is made accessible for future iterations (maintenance) of the current project and for new endeavors. Some social networking toolsets accomplish this task, at least in a modified fashion. While no one yet has the ability to do what Wall Street traders do with their intelligent news-sniffing software, Socialtext's integration to Sharepoint, its API that enables an organization to build its own news-sniffing tool, and Yammer's ability to turn "conversations" into fully searchable knowledge bases come close to enterprise-level social software engineering nirvana.

## We've Reached the End of Chapter 8

In this chapter we realigned several tried and tested software development methodologies to the social software engineering construct. We saw how to incorporate different types of social networking tools into the different phases of three different methodologies.

## References

Beck, K. (1999). *Extreme Programming Explained.* Boston: Addison-Wesley.

Booch, G. and Brown, A.W. (2003). Collaborative development environments. *Advances in Computers,* 59, 2–29.

Hutchins, S. G., Bordetsky, A., Kendall, T., and Bourakov, E. (1996). Empirical assessment of a model of team collaboration. *12th International Command and Control Research and Technology Symposium,* Newport, RI.

Lin, Y., Poschen, M., Procter, R., Voss, A., Goble, C., Bhagat, J., De Roure D., Criickshank, D., and Rouncefield, M. (2008). Agile management: strategies for developing a social networking site for scientists. *4th International Conference on e-Social Science*. http://www.mygrid.org.uk/outreach/publications/lin2008/

Lipnack, J. and Stamps, J. (2000). *Virtual Teams: People Working across Boundaries with Technology*. New York: Wiley.

# Chapter 9

# Mobile Social Software Engineering

The list of best products of 2010 published by *The Wall Street Journal* ranked Apple's iPad in the top spot; the iPhone 4 and Samsung's Galaxy S smartphone tied for third place. The list also included 4G wireless networks. iPads, and iPhones — and all things mobile — were best sellers over the 2010 holiday season. It's now hard to find anyone without a smartphone or two or four. Some have even predicted the imminent death of the PC, to be replaced by the ubiquitous smartphone. Gartner, the king of all IT research firms, estimates that 1.2 billion people used smartphones as of the end of 2010.

One would think that a smartphone is simply too small to handle enterprise-level computing, let alone enterprise-level social networking. MIT recently published its year-in-computing review (Simonite, 2010). Innovations on the market, or soon to arrive there, include touchscreens that touch back, virtual controls for forearms, eye tracking for mobile control, mobile phone mind control, computers that run on light instead of electricity, and cloud services that let small devices act like much more powerful ones. It's no wonder that these advances represent the fifth wave of computing.

Modern smartphones have morphed into tiny, full-fledged computers and compete by including sophisticated features and thousands of application options. For that reason, we will discuss mobile social software engineering n this chapter.

## Pervasive (Ubiquitous) Computing

Some time ago I wrote a book about the "extended Internet" and described some exciting innovations. We're not exactly there yet, but I thought I would introduce some of these technologies so that you can see the new directions that will provide expanded capabilities for workers using smartphones.

Sony and Philips are co-inventors of near-field communication (NFC). It works by magnetic field induction and operates within the globally available and unregulated radiofrequency band of 13.56 MHz. With one tap of a mobile device equipped with an NFC chip, a user can make purchases, access information and services, set up conference calls with colleagues, and do much more—without menus, wires, or complex set-ups. According to Philips, touching is the clearest way to tell a device where to connect. For example, touching a stadium turnstile means "let me in." Touching a band's "smart poster" means "let me hear a sample" and touching a book asks it to read a sample.

People in Germany use NFC-enabled cellphones to buy, store, and use tickets for mass transit systems. Football fans in the Netherlands have turned in their club cards for NFC phones they use to enter stadiums, buy food and drinks, and purchase souvenirs. In France, residents use their phones to pay for shopping and parking, pick up tourist information, and download ringtones and bus schedules from smart posters. At the Philips Arena stadium in Atlanta, Georgia, a major NFC-based trial allows fans to enter the grounds by waving their NFC phones. Another wave allows them to buy goods at concession stands and apparel stores just as easily.

Many forces are pushing us to adopt the extended Internet—another way of saying interconnectivity everywhere! VoIP (voice over Internet Protocol) is catching on in many companies. Computer telephony integration that passes information seamlessly from a telephone to a customer service representative's computer is becoming standard practice. The eXtensible Business Reporting Language (XBRL) allows exchanges of business data between systems on the Internet without rekeying. Broadband over power lines (BPL) may bring high-speed Internet access to any location that has access to a power grid so that any device plugged into the grid has the potential for Internet connectivity. The goal is to have almost every device have the ability to link to the Internet.

Japan is on the leading edge of mobile Internet capabilities. More non-PC devices are now connected to the Internet than are PCs. The reason is Japan's early adoption and successful implementation 3G (third-generation technology). 3G provides the ability to transfer both voice (phone calls) and non-voice (email, instant messaging) data. Japan's push into 4G technology that is just now becoming available in the United States enables user to connect all kinds of objects and devices to their "truly ubiquitous network."

Japanese telecoms introduced a variety of services, some requiring refinements of the handsets used by subscribers. NTT (Nippon Telegraph and Telephone) DoCoMo launched the i-mode service in 1999, which required a handset specifically geared for downloading email and accessing services such as Internet banking and ticket reservation. In 2001, DoCoMo launched the first Java-enabled handsets offering the i-appli service that enables subscribers to download and run small Java applets. Some stand-alone applications such as games may be saved in the handset. Others such as stock quotes require connection to a server.

Location-based services in Japan were introduced by NTT in the late 1990s. Ima-doko (which translates to "now where") uses technology that estimates a caller's distance from a wireless transmission tower. DoCoMo's i-area service provides weather, dining, traffic, and other information for 500 areas in Japan, based on location-service technology. Japanese companies and researchers are investigating or using a wide variety of other pervasive technologies beyond cell phones (Srivastava, 2004):

Electronic tags are currently used as alternatives to bar codes for plant distribution management. A study group was formed in 2003 to develop measures to promote the advanced use of electronic tags in fields such as health care and education. RFID (radio frequency identification tags) are tiny chips that act as transponders (transmitters and responders). A chip continuously waits for a radio signal sent by a transceiver. When a transponder receives a signal, it responds by transmitting a unique ID code. RFID tags are widely used to track the locations of tagged items. In Japan, this technology has been used to great acclaim in a library. Staff can locate a book even if it has been removed from its shelf.

In 2003, DoCoMo tested its R-Click service that delivers information specific to a subscriber's location using RFID tags. The prototype of R-Click has three modes: Koko Dake Click enables the user to stand in one of ten to twenty areas (cells) in the test area. He or she can click a button on the device to receive information about that area. Mite Toru Click enables a user to receive information about a product or service advertised on an electronic board that shows commercials. Buratto Catch automatically emails area information as it detects movements of a user around the test area. The system actually anticipates the movements and emails the information about an area before the user enters it.

Some DoCoMo mobile phones contain integrated circuit (IC) cards that enable the phones to be used as tickets or cash for services such as transportation and concert tickets. The 2D code developed by Japan's DENSO Corporation allows fast reading of large amounts of text. DoCoMo released several phones that use digital camera technology in the phone to scan text. Japan's T-Engine Forum (http://www.t-engine.org/english/whatis.html), a nonprofit organization open to companies from all countries, developed the Ubiquitous Communicator (UC) for business use. It communicates via TCP/IP, VoIP, Bluetooth, infrared, and other technologies.

The Rutgers University Wireless Internet Network Laboratory (WINLAB) (http://www.winlab.rutgers.edu/pub/Index.html) is working on a multimode wireless sensor known as MUSE, a multi-chip module that includes a sensor, RF communications circuitry, a modem, a CPU, and supporting circuits. WINLAB also developed a wireless sensor network. Its SOHAN (self-organizing hierarchical ad hoc network) offers significant capacity improvements over conventional ad hoc wireless networks.

The European MIMOSA consortium (www.mimosa-fp6.com) developed an overall architecture specification for a mobile device-centric, open technology platform for ambient intelligence. In the MIMOSA vision, the personal mobile phone serves as the intelligent user interface to ambient intelligence and a gateway between the sensors, network of sensors, public network, and the Internet. According to Allan (2006), wireless sensor techniques will eventually mature to permit the seamless interconnection of the physical and virtual worlds. Wireless network technologies like WiMedia Ultra-Wideband (UWB) (http://www.wimedia.org/en/index.asp) will enable end users to download an entire television show in 1 minute. High data rate UWB can enable wireless monitors, transfer data efficiently from digital camcorders, enable wireless printing of digital pictures from a camera without the need for an intervening personal computer, and transfer files among cell phone handsets and other hand-held devices like personal digital audio and video players.

Gartner (www.gartner.com) researchers predict a surge in mobile collaboration by 2011. They see a world dominated by communication and social interactions within communities that will require careful coordination. Communication will not be limited to voice. Video, shared documents, messaging, email, and mobile virtual (tele)presence will become commonplace. To achieve these advances, Gartner predicts nothing less than a complete re-architecting of our communication and collaboration platforms by 2020. New device types and user interfaces will be needed to support object recognition, biometrics, gestures, body area networks, multi-screens, photo-conferencing, mobile virtual worlds, and proactive contextual notification based on location and context

We're not there yet, but recent applications may be loaded to corporate smartphones that do some of the collaborative processing. Gartner notes that some smartphone makers are now building in the "smarts" for collaboration. The Samsung Strive enables users to create groups of fellow texters to exchange messages simultaneously. Texts appear as "chat-style" threaded messages for easy conversational reading. However, if an organization plans to proceed down this path, it must carefully coordinate and structure a secure mobile portal.

Based on the projected numbers of instant messaging streams, those engaged in social software engineering, a service such as BeeJive (http://www.beejive.com/) might be useful. BeeJive is a multi-protocol instant messaging client that connects a mobile user to the major instant messaging networks. The BeeJive application available for a wide range of mobile devices weaves together the different messaging services. If you start a discussion on Facebook, you will be able to continue it on Yahoo messaging. Currently, BeeJive supports AIM/MobileMe, MSN/Windows Live, Yahoo!, GoogleTalk, Facebook, MySpace, and Jabber. Of course, the system is useful only if these services are used. The ability to integrate private networks via an API will probably be available in the future from BeeJive or from a more enterprise-level competitor. Virgin Mobile is in the game too. Virgin's Connect enables users to link to Facebook, MySpace, YouTube, and Flickr all at the same time.

Perhaps the most interesting application is Viewdle (http://www.viewdle.com/), which was demonstrated at the Consumer Electronics Show in early 2011. Viewdle uses a phone camera to pick out faces using a novel compressed faceprint technology, and tags the faces with names on-the-fly. It then links these names with social networks and other online sources so that their latest bits of information can be displayed beneath their images. Imagine taking a photo of Sam, a project stakeholder, and then having all Sam's published wisdom quickly appear beneath his picture. As you can see, real progress continues toward connectivity and integratability via a single device.

Collaboration vendors provide mobile access in a number of ways. We already covered Socialtext. Rather than building native, downloadable applications for the iPhone, BlackBerry, and other devices, the Palo Alto, California, company created a mobile website that works on all smartphones. The mobile version of Socialtext includes most features found in its downloadable application. It is possible to read colleagues' Twitter-style comments, post reply comments in Socialtext Signals, follow co-workers' activity streams, view their profiles, and also read and edit content in Socialtext's wiki workspaces. Similarly, solutions such as Microsoft Sharepoint, IBM's LotusLive suite, and more recently Chatter from Salesforce.com, are delivered as cloud-based services and accessed via desktop browsers or mobile applications.

Aepona (http://www.aepona.com), a United Kingdom-based company, focuses on mobile network enablement and stresses the importance of distinguishing "mobile enablement" from "mobile network enablement." Mobile enablement is simply the rendering of an existing web or desktop application on a mobile device. Mobile network enablement provides embedding on-demand network capabilities in an application to increase its utility, whether the application is web-, desktop-, or mobile-device based.

Enterprise collaboration services augmented with mobile cloud-based network enablers create additional value well beyond the simple act of making an existing application portable. Think of a cloud collaboration service such as Chatter augmented with network-derived location and presence information, allowing members of a group to see each other's real-time whereabouts and current status and make decisions on the best way to interact based on this information. By using the messaging and call control capabilities of the mobile network, a user can set up an instant or scheduled group call without the need to book a conference bridge and distribute dial-in details and passcodes. Aepona's solution is to extend the base enterprise collaboration service using APIs provided by mobile operators or cross-network mobile cloud providers. The advantage of enablement via mobile cloud providers lies in the ability to reach all employees regardless of the mobile operator to which they subscribe.

As smartphones become increasingly common and the workforce becomes more mobile, spending more time away from the office, it is important that employees have access to vital information regardless of their locations. AHG's (http://www.ahg.com) Absolutely! mobile knowledge management software enables employees to access and contribute information from anywhere. Absolutely! combines the benefits of a traditional KMS (organization and distribution of knowledge) with collaboration and integration of wikis and social networks. Integration with Google Apps provides immediate access to the power of cloud computing and allows collaborative synchronous work on documents along with sophisticated sharing options and a powerful editing interface. Absolutely! allows employees to collaborate to create and edit knowledge base articles including documents, spreadsheets, flashes, videos, audios, interactive flow charts, and diagrams.

## Mobile Social Software Engineering

Most of the collaborative tools discussed have been or soon will be ported to many mobile environments or at least their cloud equivalents, and users should be able to socialtext, yammer, or chatter on any smartphone available, and many improvements are expected. We can expect all key technology players to develop new products if they haven't already done do. If you look beyond the traditional technology companies, you may find solutions that will surprise you.

FirstClass (http://ww.firstclass.com) by OpenText is primarily a tool for academic institutions looking to provide distance education to students. Distance education has been around for at least a decade, and a few strong tools developed for that purpose provide many of the capabilities business users seek. FirstClass Mobile offers intriguing features. At the core of its collaboration capabilities are FirstClass Conferences (for large groups or departments) and WorkSpaces (for smaller project teams). Both are permission-based, shared spaces that facilitate topic-based discussions, emails, group calendars, knowledge bases, communities of interest, document repositories, peer-to-peer networking, and more.

## Software Platforms

Organizations intent on building proprietary social software engineering applications that take advantage of mobile platforms can choose from a few feature-rich, extensible operating systems that support third-party applications. All these software platforms provide a set of APIs, programming tools, and software emulators that permit testing without the need for a physical device.

Symbian OS is supported by several large cell phone companies including Nokia (http://symbian.nokia.com/), Ericsson, and Samsung. The Symbian OS defines several UI reference models for different types of devices. Its OS is a real-time, multithreaded preemptive kernel that performs memory management, process and thread scheduling, hardware abstraction, interprocess communications, and process-relative and thread-relative resource management. Symbian OS uses EPOC

C++ as the supporting programming language for both system services implementations and APIs. It also allows Java applications for mobile devices to run on top of a small Java runtime environment. The Windows Phone 7 mobile OS is built upon existing Microsoft tools and technologies such as Visual Studio, Expression Blend®, Silverlight, and the XNA Framework (http://create.msdn.com/en-US/education/catalog/article/wp7_jump_start). Developers already familiar with those technologies and their related tools will be able to create new applications for the Windows Phone without a steep learning curve, as shown in Figure 9.1. You can see how easy it is to populate the UI of the application with the familiar TextBlock, TextBox, and Button controls by dragging the controls from the toolbox onto the design surface of Visual Studio 2010.

Android is a software stack for mobile devices that includes an operating system, middleware, and key applications, as shown in Figure 9.2. The Android SDK (http://developer.android.com/sdk/index.html) provides the tools and APIs necessary to begin developing applications on the Android platform using the Java language. The Google API's add-on extends your Android SDK to give your applications access to Google libraries such as Maps. Using the Maps library, you can quickly add powerful mapping capabilities to your Android applications. Android Cloud-to-Device Messaging is a service that allows you to send lightweight messages from your application server to an Android application on a device. You can use the service to tell the application to contact the server for updates, for example.

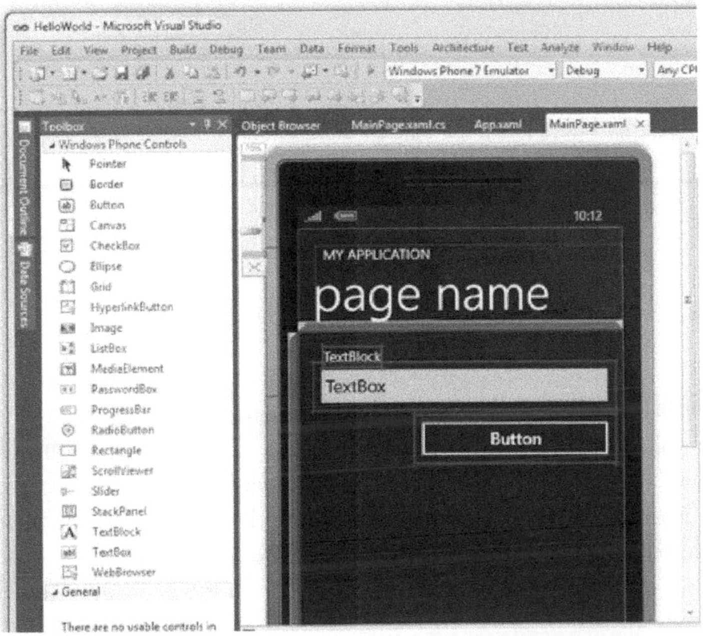


**Figure 9.1 Populating UI of a Microsoft phone using Visual Studio.**

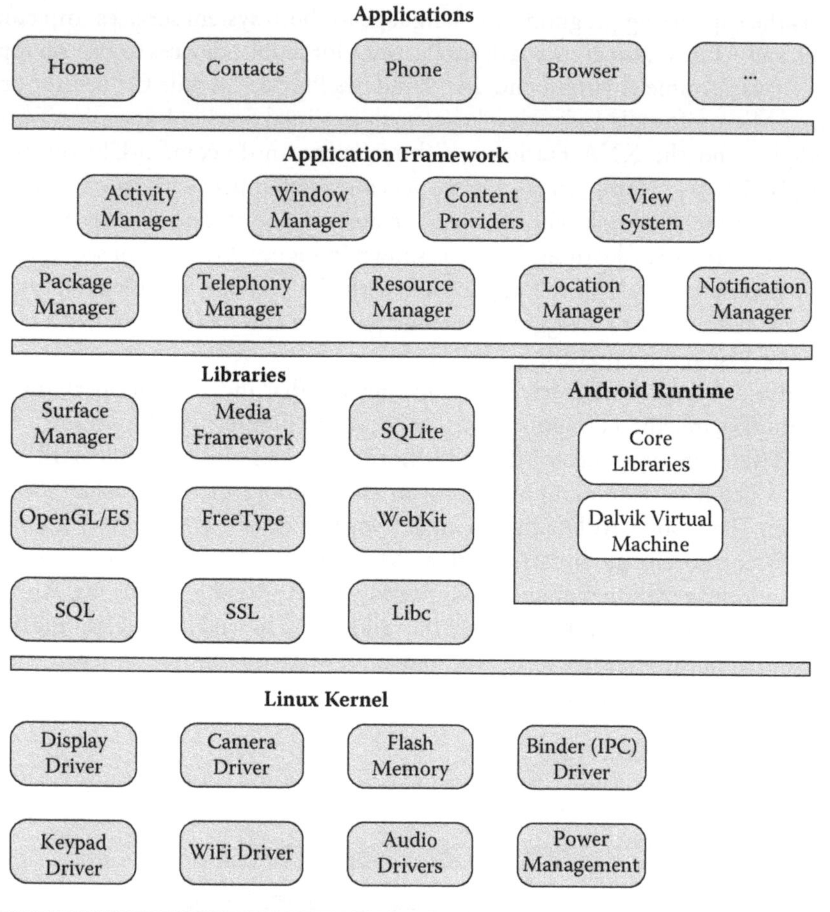


**Figure 9.2 Android architecture.**

## Security

We all use our smartphones as if we had absolutely no concern about security issues. Security will be addressed in Chapter 10, but some mention here is worthwhile. Your smartphone is not secure, whether you use it for personal business or for mobile social software engineering. In 2010, Nicolas Seriot, a Swiss software engineer, published a paper on the topic of iPhone privacy (http://seriot.ch/resources/talks_papers/iPhonePrivacy.pdf). He described the software he wrote to access private data on the iPhone, including the twenty most recent searches on the Safari web browser, the user iPhone ID, email address, and history of connections to a wireless server that reveals data about a user's location. Based on these possible security breaches, it is a good idea to limit access via mobile devices.

## We've Reached the End of Chapter 9

The world is going mobile. Software engineering needs to morph to support what the mobile platform developers will expect. In this chapter, we addressed the technologies and issues raised by supporting social software engineering via smartphone.

## References

Allan, R. (2006). Wireless sensing spawns the connected world. *Electronic Design*, 54(7), 30.

Simonite, T. (2010). The year in computing. *Technology Review*, December 29. http://www.technologyreview.com/computing/26988/

Srivastava, L. (2004). Japan's ubiquitous mobile information society. *Journal of Policy, Regulation, and Strategy for Telecommunications, Information and Media*, 6(4), 234.

## Chapter 10

# Legal, Privacy, and Security Issues

Do these facts concern you?

- When you buy a Microsoft Kinect, you bring into your home or office a telescreen that can recognize who's in the room and interpret body language.
- A joint effort by a British university and a Canadian security company will bring to a theater near you the ability to monitor facial expressions.
- Cisco commissioned a survey of 2,600 workers and IT professionals in thirteen countries. Twenty percent of the IT leaders said that their relationships with their employees were dysfunctional—demonstrating a disconnect among IT, employees, and policies.
- A recent survey of 1,100 mobile workers found that 22% had breached their employers' strict smartphone policies when using nonmanaged personal smartphones to access corporate information.
- One in eight malware attacks is accomplished via a USB device, according to Avast Software, a security firm.
- The U.S. Department of Defense estimates that more than a hundred foreign intelligence organizations have attempted to break into U.S.-based networks (governments, universities, and businesses). Every year, hackers steal enough data to fill the Library of Congress many times over.
- A virus may be transmitted by any connected device, for example, MP3 players, cameras, fax machines, and even digital picture frames. In 2008, the Best Buy chain found a virus in the Insignia picture frames it sold.

- Companies outsourcing data storage (to a cloud) are responsible for any data breached. Make sure your cloud or data service provider is investigated carefully.
- Cybercriminals are getting smarter. They invented poisoned search results, rogue anti-viruses, social networking malware, malicious advertisements, and even built-in instant messaging clients that notify criminals when their "marks" have logged onto their online bank accounts.

Social networking raises some issues concerning content use, infringement, defamation, attribution, tort liability, privacy, and security. While most of these issues relate to public social networking sites such as Facebook and LinkedIn, most are also relevant to internal social software engineering, particularly if public platforms are integrated into the toolsets.

## Website Legal Issues

**Defamation and other torts** — Wikis, blogs, workspaces, and other IT facilities provide ample opportunities for defamation (harming the reputation of another by making a false statement to a third person). These resources should be monitored for possible defamation and other tort liabilities. Examples of damages arising from torts include intentional infliction of emotional distress, interference with advantageous economic relations, fraud, and misrepresentation.

**Trademarks** — Trademark or service mark notices should be notably displayed wherever required. If a mark has been registered with the U.S. Patent and Trademark Office (http://www.uspto.gov/), the "registered" (®) symbol should be displayed; otherwise, the trademark (™) or service mark (SM) symbol should be displayed. Organizations should be vigilant in protecting their trademarks and service marks and equally vigilant in preventing infringements on the marks of others. Content that resides on an organization's servers should be audited to ensure no trademark infringement is taking place.

**Copyrights** — Copyright is a form of protection provided to the authors of "original works of authorship" including literary, dramatic, musical, artistic, and other types of intellectual works such as software, both published and unpublished. The 1976 Copyright Act generally gives the owner of a copyright the exclusive right to reproduce the copyrighted work, prepare derivative works, distribute copies or audio recordings of the copyrighted work, perform the copyrighted work publicly, and display the copyrighted work publicly. A copyright protects the form of expression rather than the subject of the writing. For example, a description of a machine could be copyrighted, but doing so would only prevent others from copying the description; it would not prevent others from writing their own descriptions or from making and using the machine.

It is important for organizations to audit data residing in their social networks to make sure that any content, data, and information is not violating copyrights of other individuals or organizations. One example is dynamically accessing Google and downloading research results to a social network. Because Google's content is copyrighted to Google, you would need to take care not to violate any copyrights. Using third-party content without permission can result in both criminal and civil liability, including treble damages and attorney fees under the U.S. Copyright Act. Essentially, the best tactic is to periodically review network content to screen for possible copyright violations.

**Computer Fraud and Abuse Act** — Most organizations provide their employees with PCs capable of wireless Internet access. Many companies and home users have installed wireless Internet connectivity. It is not usual for people to seek out unsecured "hot spots," as these wireless connections are known. Several computer equipment manufacturers have developed inexpensive, small hot-spot locaters for this purpose. The Computer Fraud and Abuse Act (CFAA) makes punishable whoever intentionally accesses a computer without authorization. Organizations must develop very clear policies warning employees against using corporate-supplied PCs in this manner.

**Corporate content** — Not long ago, a Congressman made a secret trip to Iraq. Upon arrival, he tweeted a message that he had just landed. His trip was no longer a secret. While we have not focused on the use of Twitter as a social software engineering tool, we expect Twitter or its Yammer corporate equivalent to be used. Because these systems enable almost instantaneous communication with an entire network of people within and outside an organization, users must be very careful about exactly what they communicate.

## Developing Your ePolicy

It is important that the organization develop an ePolicy that addresses how employees use email, Internet access, and all social networking activities. The policy should be comprehensive, appear in the employee handbook, and be reviewed with all new employees. It is also a good idea to refresh the memories of all employees annually by sending an email instructing them to review the ePolicy. The policy should be stored on the corporate intranet as well and one staff member should be assigned as the main point of contact for the ePolicy if questions or problems arise. Some points to address in an ePolicy include

- Whether employees may use the Internet for personal use.
- Whether external social networking services such as Facebook, LinkedIn, and Yammer may be used.
- Notice that email is monitored (if it is not, it should be). Let employees know that the email and social networking systems they use are owned by the organization and they can expect that management or designated staff may access email, workspaces, blogs, wikis, etc.

- Descriptions of the types of content that can be maintained within internal or external social networking site, e.g., copyrighted materials.
- Netiquette policies for using email and social networking websites.
- Details of corporate discrimination and sexual harassment policies, particularly as they relate to online environments.
- The expectation that individual employees will respect the privacy of the individuals whose information they may access and use all available security methods to preserve the integrity and privacy of information within their control.
- A directive that specifies that employees are not to engage in any activity that alters or damages data, software, or other technological-related resources belonging to the organization or to someone else; compromise another individual's ability to use technological-related resources; or intentionally disrupt or damage corporate technology resources.
- A stipulation that individuals who observe potential abuse are expected to report it for appropriate resolution.

## Security Issues

In 2008, Cisco commissioned a study on security in the workplace. The study findings will probably not surprise you:

- One of five employees altered security settings on work devices to bypass IT policy to access unauthorized web sites. More than half said they simply wanted to access the sites; a third indicated that the sites they accessed "were no one's business." Seven out of ten IT professionals said employee access of unauthorized applications and Web sites ultimately resulted in as many as half of their companies' data loss incidents. This belief was most common in the United States (74%) and India (79%).
- Two of five IT pros dealt with employees accessing unauthorized parts of a network or facility. Of those who reported this issue, two-thirds encountered multiple incidents in the past year and 14% encountered it monthly.
- One in four employees admitted verbally sharing sensitive information with nonemployees such as friends, family, and even strangers. When asked why, the most common answers included, "I needed to bounce an idea off someone," "I needed to vent," and "I didn't see anything wrong with it."
- Almost half of the employees surveyed share work devices with others, including nonemployees without supervision.
- Almost two of three employees admitted using work computers daily for personal use. Activities included music downloads, shopping, banking, blogging, and participating in chat groups. Half of the employees used personal email to reach customers and colleagues; only 40% said such use was authorized by IT.

- At least one in three employees left computers logged on and unlocked when they left their desks. They also tended to leave laptops on their desks overnight, sometimes without logging off, creating potential for theft and allowing unauthorized access to corporate and personal data.
- One in five employees stored system log-ins and passwords in their computers or wrote the information and left it on their desks, in unlocked cabinets, or pasted on the fronts of their computers.
- Almost one in four employees carried corporate data on portable storage devices outside the office.
- More than one in five employees allowed nonemployees to roam around offices unsupervised. The study average was 13%; 18% allowed unknown individuals to "tailgate" behind employees into corporate facilities.

As you can see, information systems are vulnerable to many threats that can inflict various types of damage, resulting in significant losses. This damage can range from errors harming database integrity to fires destroying entire systems centers. Problems can arise inside the company (employees) to the more common scenario—outsiders intent on harm. All manner of hardware and software is at risk, including mobile devices. In 2010, we all awoke to the news that iPad users' email addresses and device IDs were exposed. In 2009, security experts identified thirty security flaws in the software and operating systems of smartphones. Also in 2010, two European university researchers extracted an entire database of text messages (including deleted messages) from an iPhone using a corrupt website they controlled.

Losses from these exploits can stem, for example, from the fraudulent actions of supposedly trusted employees, from outside hackers, or from careless data entry. An organization should develop an information systems security program to implement and maintain the most cost-effective safeguards to protect against deliberate or inadvertent acts, including

1. Unauthorized disclosure of sensitive information or manipulation of data
2. Denial of service or decrease in reliability of critical information system (IS) assets
3. Unauthorized use of systems resources
4. Theft or destruction of system assets

Appendix J contains an extremely detailed checklist of best practices for security compiled by the U.S. Department of Defense. It covers access control, confidentiality, integrity, availability, non-repudiation, protection, detection, reaction to incidents, configuration management, vulnerability management, personnel security, physical security, and security awareness and training. All of these topics should be reviewed before initiating any social software engineering program to set the parameters for its use. The checklist should also be used on a periodic basis to ensure the security of the social software engineering platform on an ongoing basis. The organization should develop an IS security plan to meet the following goals:

1. Achieve data integrity levels consistent with the sensitivity of the information processed.
2. Achieve systems reliability levels consistent with the sensitivity of the information processed.
3. Comply with applicable state and federal regulations.
4. Implement and maintain continuity of operations plans consistent with the criticality of user information processing requirements.
5. Implement and follow procedures to report and act on IS security incidents.

Organizations should conduct periodic security reviews to ensure that

1. Sufficient controls and security measures are in place to compensate for any identified risks associated with the program/system or its environment.
2. The program/system operates cost effectively and complies with applicable laws and regulations.
3. The information in the program/system is properly managed.
4. The program/system complies with management, financial, information technology (IT), accounting, budget, and other appropriate standards.

Two types of security assessments of computer facilities must be conducted periodically: risk assessments and security reviews. A risk assessment is a formal, systematic approach to assessing the vulnerability of computer assets, identifying threats, quantifying potential losses from threat realization, and developing countermeasures to eliminate or reduce threats and potential losses. Risk assessments should be conducted whenever significant modifications are made to the system.

The three major IT security components are management controls, operational controls, and technical controls. The *management controls* address matters deemed managerial. The *technical controls* are security measures that should be implemented on systems that transmit, process, and store information. The *operational controls* address security measures implemented by employees that directly support the technical controls and processing environment.

**Management controls** are necessary to manage a security program and its associated risks. They are nontechnical techniques, driven by policy and process, and are intended to meet IT protection requirements. Program security policies and system-specific policies are developed to protect sensitive information transmitted, stored, and processed within system components. Program security policies are broad and are developed to establish a security program and enforce security at the program management level. System-specific security policies are detailed and developed to enforce security at the system level. The information, applications, systems, networks, and resources must be protected from loss, misuse, and unauthorized modification, access, and compromise. All organizations that process, store, or transmit information must develop, implement, and maintain IT security programs to ensure protection of their information. The program security policy establishes the program, assigns the appropriate personnel, and outlines the duties and responsibilities of all individuals in the program.

**Operational controls** focus on controls implemented and executed to improve the security of a particular system. Media controls address the storage, retrieval, and disposal of sensitive materials that should be protected from unauthorized disclosure, modification, and destruction. Media protection is composed of two security requirements: computer output controls and electronic media controls. Computer output controls apply to all printout copies of sensitive information and specify that all printout copies of sensitive information should be clearly marked. Electronic media controls should encompass all the controls of printout materials; however, procedures must be established to ensure that data cannot be accessed without authorization and authentication from electronic media that contain sensitive information.

All personnel with responsibilities for the management, maintenance, operations, or use of system resources and access to sensitive information should have the appropriate management approvals. Organizations should institute personnel security procedures to specify responsibilities of the security personnel and users involved in the management, use, and operation of systems. The IT staff must be alert and trained in offensive and defensive methods to protect the organization's information assets. Adequate staffing and key position back-up are essential in maintaining a secure environment. Personnel security also includes establishing and maintaining procedures for enforcing personnel controls, including

- Determining appropriate access levels (logically and physically)
- Ensuring separation of duties (logically and physically) to prevent compromise of system data and attempts to thwart technical controls
- Conducting security training and providing awareness tools for all staff
- Issuing and revoking user identifications (IDs) and passwords

**Technical controls** focus on security controls that the computer system executes and they rely on the proper configuration and functionality of the system. The implementation of technical controls always requires significant operational considerations. Technical controls should be consistent with the management of security within the organization. When updating a security plan, the organization should refer to the security issues and questions in Table 10.1 to ensure its plan remains current.

**Table 10.1 Internet Security: Checklist of Issues to Address**

| |
|---|
| 1. Describe the functions (data transfer, forms-based data entry, browser-based interactive applications, etc.) the Internet will perform. |
| 2. Describe your application categories and how they are integrated with your production systems (information access = hypertext, multimedia, soft content and data; collaboration = newsgroups, shared documents, videoconferencing; transaction processing = Internet commerce and links to IT applications). |
| 3. What communication protocols are in use? FTP, HTTP, telnet, or a combination? |
| 4. How do you control access, identification and authorization (I&A), sensitive or private information, no repudiation, and data integrity? |
| 5. Are firewalls or proxy servers present? If so, describe the software used. |
| 6. Is data encryption used? Is it hardware or software based? |
| 7. What application languages (HTML, XML, JavaScript, etc.) are used? Are they static, semidynamic, or dynamic? |
| 8. What database connectivity or application program interfaces (APIs) are in place? |
| 9. Do you have separate Web servers? Describe hardware and software. |
| 10. Describe the controls in effect for shared resources, including password protection, user groups, smartcards, biometrics, data encryption, callback systems, virus scanners, vulnerability scanners, and intelligent agents. |
| 11. Are user logons and passwords challenged frequently via a multilevel protection scheme? Do you allow synchronization of passwords for a single sign-on? |
| 12. Are passwords changed regularly? How often? Is change system-controlled or manual? |
| 13. How many people have administrative rights to the application, telecommunications, and web servers? Are these rights separated by function, or can a single person access all servers? |
| 14. Are Internet application files and data files backed up? How often? |
| 15. Is a contingency plan in place? Has it been tested? How often is it updated? |

## Web Server Security

Securing the operating system that runs the Web server is the initial step in providing security for the server. The Web server software differs only in functionality from other applications that reside on computers. However, because the Web server may provide public access to the system along with organization-wide access, it should be configured securely to prevent it and the host computer from compromise by intruders.

One precaution to take when configuring a web server is to never run the Web service as a root or administrative user (super user). Web services or applications should never be located at the root of a directory structure. They should be in a component-specific sub-directory to provide optimum access management. The Web service should be run with the permissions of a normal user to prevent the escalation of privilege if the web server were compromised. Also, the file system of the Web server (directories and files) should be configured to prevent write access for any users other than employees who require such access. Other precautions and secure configuration issues to consider when configuring a public Web server are

- The Web server should be on a separate local area network separated from other production systems by a firewall configuration or demilitarized zone (DMZ).
- The Web server should never have a trust relationship with any other server that is not also an Internet-facing server or server on the same local network.
- The Web server should be treated as an untrusted host.
- The Web server should be dedicated to providing Web services only.
- Compilers should not be installed on the Web server.
- All services not required by the Web server should be disabled.
- The Web server should utilize the latest vendor software, including hot fixes and patches.

A Web browser is usually a commercial client application used to display information requested from a Web server. It should be a standard browser approved for use within the system environment. Because of the security holes in scripting languages such as JavaScript and ActiveX (Microsoft), it is recommended that all scripting languages not required for official systems operation be disabled within the browser.

Network security addresses requirements for protecting sensitive data from unauthorized disclosure, modification, and deletion. Requirements include protecting critical network services and resources from unauthorized use and security-relevant denial-of-service conditions.

Firewalls provide greater security by enforcing access control rules before connections are made. These systems can be configured to control access to or from the protected networks and are most often used to shield access from the Internet. A firewall can be a router, a personal computer, or a host appliance that provides additional access control to the site. The following firewall requirements should be implemented:

- Firewalls that are accessible from the Internet are configured to detect intrusion attempts and issue an alert when an attack or attempt to bypass system security occurs.
- Firewalls are configured to maintain audit records of all security-relevant events. The audit logs are archived and maintained in accordance with applicable records retention requirements and security directives.
- Firewall software is kept current with the installation of all security-related updates, fixes, and modifications as soon as they are tested and approved.
- Firewalls should be configured under the "default deny" concept. This means that activation of a service or port must be approved for specific use. By default, the use of any service or communications port without specific approval is denied.
- Only the minimum set of firewall services necessary for business operations is enabled and only with the approval of IT management.
- All unused firewall ports and services are disabled.
- All publicly accessible servers are located in the firewall, DMZ, or an area specifically configured to isolate these servers from the rest of the infrastructure.
- Firewalls filter incoming packets on the basis of Internet addresses to ensure that any packets with internal source addresses received from external connections are rejected.
- Firewalls are located in controlled access areas.

Routers and switches provide communication services that are essential to the correct and secure transmission of data on local and wide area networks. The compromise of a router or switch may result in denial of service to the network and exposure of sensitive data that can lead to attacks against other networks from a single location. The following best-practice solutions should be applied to all routers and switches throughout an application environment:

- Access to routers and switches is password-protected in accordance with policy guidance.
- Only the minimum set of router and switch services necessary for business operations is enabled and only with the approval of IT management.
- All unused switch and router ports are disabled.
- Routers and switches are configured to maintain audit records of all security-relevant events.
- Router and switch software is kept current by installing all security-related updates, fixes, and modifications as soon as they are tested and approved for installation.
- Any dial-up connections via routers must be performed by a method approved by IT management.

All systems should use anti-virus (AV) utilities or programs to detect and remove viruses and other malicious codes. The AV software must be kept current with the latest available virus signature files installed. AV programs should be installed on workstations to detect and remove viruses in incoming and outgoing email messages and attachments, and also actively scan downloaded files from the Internet. Workstation and server disk drives should be routinely scanned for viruses. The specific restrictions outlined below should be implemented to reduce the threat of viruses on systems:

1. Traffic destined to inappropriate websites should not be allowed.
2. Only authorized software should be introduced on systems.
3. All media should be scanned for viruses before introduction to the system. This includes software and data from other activities and programs downloaded from the Internet.
4. Original software should not be issued to users but should be copied for use in copyright agreements. At least one copy of the original software should be stored according to configuration management controls.

Table 10.2 outlines the topics of a systems security plan. During development of a security plan, the following questions should be asked and answered:

1. Does the plan address the logical and physical security of the system?
2. Does the logical security include password protection, data encryption (if applicable), and access profiles, to preclude access to data by unauthorized personnel?
3. Does the logical security allow supervisory intervention if needed (determined case by case)?
4. Are negotiable documents or authorizations stored securely?
5. Does the physical security address both equipment security and building security?
6. Does the physical security address safety and environment issues?
7. Does the security plan address data and application back-up procedures?
8. Does the security plan include disaster preparedness and recovery procedures? (They may appear in a separate plan.)
9. If a department or organization-wide security plan exists, is the point where the system security plan stops and the organization plan takes over (and vice versa) delineated clearly?
10. Does the logical security include separation of duties among functions to prevent potential fraud situations?

## Protecting Mobile Devices

A careful reading of Chapters 9 and 10 demonstrates that many people ignore security policies pertaining to their smartphones. They seem not to realize how they

**Table 10.2 Systems Security Plan**

| **Topic Outline** |
|---|
| 1. Scope — Describe site, giving location, configuration, operations, processing supported, and identify IT units and applications covered by plan |
| 2. Definitions — Explain terms that may not be familiar to all readers |
| 3. Overall security assessment — Discuss policies and practices, addressing assignment of security responsibilities, personnel security clearance policies, audit reports, and training; also assess current activities and plans for next year |
| 4. Site plan and equipment schematic diagrams |
| 5. Obtain the following information for each sensitive application system: date of last system evaluation, date of last system certification or recertification, date of next evaluation or recertification |
| 6. Summary of risk analysis reports |
| 7. Continuity plan(s) |
| 8. Summary of security reviews for all processing platforms in use |
| 9. Training needs with action schedules |
| 10. Other supporting documents (terminal security rules, local security procedures, user handbooks, etc.) |
| **Policies and Procedures** |
| 1. Physical security of resources |
| 2. Equipment security to protect equipment from theft and unauthorized use |
| 3. Software and data security |
| 4. Telecommunications security |
| 5. Personnel security |
| 6. Continuity plans to meet critical processing needs during short- or long-term interruption of service |
| 7. Emergency preparedness |
| 8. Designation of IT security officer or manager |

may be exposing themselves, their companies, and their companies' stakeholders to harm. While mobile devices cannot be totally secured, certain measures afford some measure of security:

1. Do not use hotel wireless networks to access sensitive information.
2. Hotel wired networks are often open to eavesdropping. All packets for a set of rooms, a floor or several floors, or even an entire hotel can be seen by all other systems on the network. Unprotected packets are prime targets for capture, analysis, and data extraction. A company should invest in wireless broadband equipment for employees who must travel and bring their work with them.
3. Encrypt all data on a device in case it is stolen or lost—a common occurrence. Better yet, store information on the server or in the cloud, not on the device.
4. Configure devices to block external snooping. Firewalls are required and are available for many hand-held devices.
5. Back up critical information. This sounds obvious, but employees on the road may neglect to do this. If the organization does not have a mobile-accessible back-up server, use a cloud service such as Microsoft Skydrive (skydrive.login.com).
6. Do not start a laptop with a USB device attached. This can result in direct loading of malware ahead of antivirus software.
7. Secure all wireless access points. Strong, mixed passwords should be used and changed frequently.

## We've Reached the End . . . of This Book

We spent some time together discussing details of social software engineering. I hope that you now have a good sense of what's possible and why social software engineering is a valuable approach. We're not done yet, however. Eleven interesting appendices follow this chapter. Happy social software engineering!

# Appendix A

# Social Software Engineering Tools

## Blogs

Blogs permit team members to create stream-of-consciousness notes on any subject.

### *Qumana Inc.*

URL: http://www.qumana.com/about.php
Email address: info@qumana.com

Qumana Software, Inc., is a leading developer of tools and services for bloggers. Its industry-recognized tools include Qumana, a blog editor for online publishing; Q Reader (Lektora), an RSS Reader; and Q Ads, an advertising network for bloggers integrated into the Qumana tool.

Qumana Software develops tools for every blogger: PC and Mac users, expert and novice, and multilingual. Qumana Software is headquartered in Vancouver, British Columbia, Canada.

### *Zoundry LLC*

URL: http://www.zoundry.com/
Email address: contact@zoundry.com

Whether you're a beginner or active blogger, Zoundry helps you do more with your weblog: recommend products; drop in pictures; tag your posts; earn cash rewards for yourself or charities when readers buy from your recommendations.

## Brainstorming

Brainstorming is a method used to create new ideas by suspending judgment.

### *Axon Research*

URL: http://web.singnet.com.sg/~axon2000
Email address: axon2000@singnet.com.sg

The Axon Idea Processor is a sketchpad for visualizing and organizing ideas. The Idea Processor exploits visual attributes such as color, shape, size, scale, position, depth, shadow, link, icon, etc. Visual cues facilitate recall, association, and discovery. Diagrams help users model and solve complex problems. Visualization reinforces your short-term memory.

### *Banxia Software Ltd.*

URL: www.banxia.com
Email address: info@banxia.com

Decision Explorer is a proven tool for managing "soft" issues (qualitative information that surrounds complex or uncertain situations). It allows you to capture in detail thoughts and ideas, explore them, and gain new understanding and insight, resulting in a fresh perspective, time saved through increased productivity, release of creativity, and better focus.

### *Bosley Group*

URL: www.mindmapper.com
Email address: info@mindmapper.com

MindMapper software lets you perform mind mapping on your personal computer. It is an effective and proven technique for note taking and more. It is also easy to learn and use and was designed for use by anyone from beginners to experts utilizing mind mapping. Thick manuals were replaced by an intuitive menu system.

### *CoCo Systems Ltd.*

URL: www.visimap.com
Email address: enquiries@visimap.com

VisiMap supports the way you work. It allows you to quickly and efficiently enter, visualize, restructure, print, transfer, present, and communicate information using a simple, powerful graphical metaphor called a visual map—essentially a hierarchical, two-dimensional graphic representation similar to idea maps or brain maps. VisiMap is easy to use, enhances creativity, and boosts production for visual organization, brainstorming, problem solving, document outlining and management, meeting facilitation, planning, HTML and website generation, personal organization, and many other day-to-day tasks.

## Innovation House

URL: www.brainstorming.co.uk
Email address: info@brainstorming.co.uk

Brainstorming Toolbox is software dedicated to brainstorming sessions. It was designed to complement and enhance the free training offered at the site. It gives instant access to the techniques described and brings them to life interactively. To brainstorm more effectively, try Brainstorming Toolbox free for 30 days and discover what an excellent tool it is for generating new ideas.

## Mindjet LLC

URL: http://www.mindjet.com
Email address: info@mindjet.com

MindManager is award-winning software that boosts team dynamics and increases productivity visually. It has powerful features to boost team dynamics for increased productivity by allowing users to communicate visually and make decisions faster, collaborate on projects via Internet conferencing, and brainstorm online in real-time, quickly, efficiently, and visually.

## ParaMind Software

URL: http://www.paramind.net
Email address: paramind@paramind.net

ParaMind works differently from other writers' aids on the market. It was built on the concept of brainstorming (compiling every idea that can be expressed in language) by "meaningfully exhausting the interactions of words" in any specific subject area. Unlike other brainstorming programs, you can configure ParaMind to suit your individual needs.

Concept Mapping is a structured process focused on a topic or construct of interest. It involves input from one or more participants and produces an interpretable pictorial view (concept map) of their ideas and concepts and how they interrelate.

## Classification

Classification employs a set of preclassified examples to develop a model that can classify the population of stored information.

### *Attrasoft*

URL: http://attrasoft.com/decision
Email address: webmaster@attrasoft.com

DecisionMaker is Attrasoft's application of neural network technology. It can analyze tremendous amounts of information available through a database or a spreadsheet, learning relationships and patterns; it can detect subtle changes and predict results.

DecisionMaker learns by observation. It must observe enough example behavior to identify the underlying patterns. Through this ongoing, self-learning process, DecisionMaker can acquire far more knowledge than any expert in a field. For example, it can become a medical expert in any specialty in minutes.

### *Entrieva*

URL: http://www.entrieva.com/entrieva/index.htm
Email address: info@entrieva.com

Semio Taxonomy combines the automation benefits of keyword searching with the superior functionality of browsing document collections by automatically building customized browseable taxonomies, i.e., hierarchical structures of categories. It goes beyond simply placing documents within categories. Its unique lexical extraction technology allows the entire content of a document to participate in the browseable categories. Instead of receiving an overpopulated document list posing as a category, you receive a full breakdown of concepts found within the source text collection. The level of granularity this provides a browsing user allows valuable insight that remains unavailable to those using other technologies.

The proliferation of web portals and intranets means that the numbers and varieties of unfamiliar text collections has never been greater. Like a good city map, SemioMap provides a high-level visual perspective of the information available. You can navigate through key concepts and drill down to the specific content that matters most. At the same time, SemioMap provides a sense of context that allows a user to quickly observe trends, connections, and weak signals within the text. Analyses of patents, competitive intelligence data, and web portal and intranet content are all facilitated by SemioMap. The graphical web-based interface displays the interrelationships of concepts in the underlying documents. Even users who are completely unfamiliar with a subject can explore intelligently using the SemioMap interface.

### *Wincite Systems*

URL: http://www.wincite.com
Email address: ljanocia@wincitesystems.com

WINCITE is a flexible, Windows-based, multidimensional database application designed to capture, organize, manage, and distribute actionable intelligence. Its powerful user interface, reporting, and searching tools make it easy for business development, competitive intelligence, marketing, and strategic planning professionals to utilize mission-critical information. The information may then be leveraged by distribution throughout an organization via the Internet, corporate intranets, Lotus Notes, or e-mail.

### *WisdomBuilder, LLC*

URL: http://www.wisdombuilder.com
Email address: info@wisdombuilder.com

Wisdom Builder™ is the first in a family of software products that improves the effectiveness of an organization by reducing time spent to collect and manage information by freeing more time for critical analysis activities. Building on 25 years of experience in designing and developing intelligence processing solutions for the government and private sectors, Wisdom Builder allows an organization to effectively analyze, collect, and manage the glut of raw data available.

## Collaboration and Social Media

Collaborative software, also known as groupware, is application software that integrates work on a single project by several concurrent users at separated workstations (see section on computer-supported cooperative work). The pioneering system was the popular Lotus Notes. Social media tools expand upon the concept to provide collaborations of employees, partners, and customers.

### *37 Signals*

URL: http://basecamphq.com
Email address: email@37signals.com

Millions of people use Basecamp to collaborate and manage projects online.

### *Caucus Systems, Inc.*

URL: http://www.caucus.com
Email address: sales@caucus.com

Caucus is an open source, web-based eLearning and discussion platform used by universities, nonprofit and for-profit companies that require learning, conversation, and coordination to occur together.

## Collaboration Fabricators

URL: http://collabfab.com
Email address: info@collabfab.com

CollabFab is a free web-based collaboration tool designed for small workgroups. It is easily customizable and designed to run on inexpensive, low-power servers using free server software. CollabFab allows you to manage and share information about multiple projects with your clients, co-workers, customers, and suppliers, with anyone!

## Communispace Communications

URL: http://www.communispace.com/
Email address: sales@comunispace.com

Communispace provides a unique combination of software and services that connect customers, employees, and other key stakeholders. It captures their knowledge, experiences, creative ideas, best practices, and feedback. Problems are addressed quickly, new ideas surface in record time, new products ideas are implemented with greater certainty, and learning focuses on real business issues.

## Correlate Technologies

URL: http://www.correlate.com/products/
Email address: info@correlate.com

Correlate K-Map for Lotus Domino.Doc integrates completely into your Domino. Doc environment, thus leveraging your investment in Domino.Doc. This means that a Correlate K-Map containing multiple documents supports all key document management features, including check-in and check-out, versioning, audit trails, profiling, change notifications, and much more.

Correlate K-Map for Microsoft SharePoint Portal Server organizes SharePoint content into meaningful knowledge maps. You can K-map your projects, policies, and procedures; sales kits; product plans; compliance reporting; and more. The Correlate K-Map web system allows notebook users to "grab" SharePoint content and make it available offline for viewing or editing.

## Forum One Communications

URL: http://www.projectspaces.com/
Email address: sales@ProjectSpaces.com

ProjectSpaces is a simple, secure, and powerful online workspace and extranet tool to help project teams, work groups, committees, partners, and others easily connect, share, and collaborate. It provides a flexible set of online project management and community features to help busy groups manage documents, coordinate projects and activities, and share knowledge and information.

## GroupTweet

URL: http://www.longest.com/group
Email address: support@grouptweet.com

GroupTweet turns a standard Twitter account into a group communication hub where members can post updates to everyone in the group using direct messages. When the group account receives a direct message from a member, GroupTweet converts it into a tweet that all followers can see.

## IBM

URL: http://www-01.ibm.com/software/lotus/products/connections/features.html
Email: https://www14.software.ibm.com/webapp/iwm/web/signup.do?source =swgmail&S_TACT=109HD06W&lang=en_US

IBM Lotus Connections is social software for business. It empowers business professionals to develop, nurture, and remain in contact with a network of colleagues, respond quickly to business opportunities by calling upon the expertise in the network, and discuss and refine new ideas with communities of co-workers, partners, and customers.

## KickApps

URL: http://www.kickapps.com
Contact: http://www.kickapps.com/contact-us/index.php

A complete social networking application, including profiles, groups, direct messaging, videos, photos, activity feeds, widgets, etc.

## Moxie Software

URL: http://www.moxiesoft.com/
Email: http://www.moxiesoft.com/tal_about/contact_form.aspx

Enterprise social software connecting people, groups, and teams globally and across enterprises to work better and faster than ever.

## Mzinga

URL: http://www.mzinga.com/home.asp
Email address: LearnMore@Mzinga.com

OmniSocial contains hundreds of features to make community, collaboration, and knowledge sharing pervasive across a business from a single platform. OmniSocial's modules give you the tools to help your employees, customers, and partners network, interact, collaborate, and learn.

## Ning

URL: http://www.ning.com
Contact: http://hc.ning.com/ning_contact_us.php

Ning is the world's largest platform for creating social websites. Top organizers, marketers, influencers, and activists use Ning to create online destinations that weave social conversations in content.

## Open Text Corporation

URL: http://www.opentext.com/livelink/index.html
Email address: info@opentext.com

Livelink is a collaborative application that brings together the best minds in a company and connects them to business partners, suppliers, and customers, to streamline efficiencies, gain first mover advantage, and save money. As a highly scalable collaborative commerce application, Livelink delivers web-based intranet, extranet, and e-business solutions. It also removes boundaries and connects you to what matters most: people.

## Pluck

URL: http://www.pluck.com
Contact: http://www.pluck.com/resources/contact.html

Pluck's Social Application Server provides a host of services and components that relieve web developers of everything but the business-level features and operations of their online social experience. Pluck's server provides an extensible, template-based mechanism for adding functionality to its off-the-shelf product while allowing enterprises to use all the existing functionalities of the Pluck applications.

## Salesforce.com

URL: http://www.salesforce.com

Email address: https://www.salesforce.com/form/contact/contactme_cloudcomputing.jsp?

Chatter allows people to work together and know everything that's happening in a company. Updates on people, groups, documents, and application data arrive in real-time feeds.

## *SiteScape*

URL: http://www.sitescape.com
Email address: info@sitescape.com

SiteScape Enterprise Forum 6.0 is a robust collaboration platform that provides the administrative flexibility and performance required by Fortune Global 2000 organizations. It offers an effective and easy way to communicate, share, and build knowledge; and collaborate with employees, customers, or throughout an extended business network.

Users can host online discussions, share and revise documents and files, chat, and schedule meetings using shared calendars and messaging. The powerful, integrated workflow makes collaboration significantly faster, easier, and more efficient by automating repetitive processes.

Forum managers can quickly and easily customize the platform directly or modify certain sample applications to meet their needs (contact manager, sales lead manager, resume tracker, help desk, and filtered discussion forums).

Forum 6.0 optionally supports CAD and other engineering files, real-time Web conferencing, and a variety of portals including Oracle Corporation's 9i Application Server, Plumtree Software's Corporate Portal, and Viador Inc.'s E-Portal Suite. SiteScape Forum is inherently flexible and fits into any environment. It is totally Web-based and can be accessed from any desktop, laptop, or PDA device that uses an HTML-based browser.

## *SocialGo*

URL: http://www.socialgo.com/
Email address: support@socialgo.com

SocialGo can build a social networking website in minutes with drag-and-drop tools. Developer skills optional!

## *SocialText*

URL: http://www.socialtext.com/
Email address: http://www.socialtext.com/products/freetrial.php

Socialtext keeps everyone informed. People and teams are synchronized, engaged, and informed via a broad social software platform that provides the ease of SaaS and the security of an onsite appliance. Features include social networking, Wikis, microblogging, groupos, social spreadsheets, dashboards, internal blogs, mobile use, and other features.

### ThoughtWeb, Inc.

URL: http://www.thoughtweb.com
Email address: info@thoughtweb.com

ThoughtWeb is a unique web-based capability and a breakthrough in intelligent agent and analytical technology. Its purpose is to create and share knowledge and information through the use of free-thinking, proactive personal agents (success buddies) that provide intelligent, personalized advice and guidance on the web. Users share knowledge, diffuse innovation, and collaborate proactively.

ThoughtWeb focuses on developing intelligent personal agents capable of understanding personal goals and visions and can provide advice, coaching, and knowledge to help users achieve these goals. By enabling advanced collaboration between humans and computer-based intelligent agents, ThoughtWeb technology can produce enormous benefits in the fields of consumer marketing and corporate knowledge management.

## Content Management

Document management (also called content management) is the process of managing documents throughout their lifecycles: inception, creation, review, storage, dissemination, and finally destruction.

### Documentum

URL: http://www.documentum.com
Email address: info@documentum.com

Documentum eBusiness Platform is the industry standard for managing and distributing large volumes of content within and beyond an enterprise. Based on long-standing expertise for managing electronic content, Documentum provides an open, scalable, and completely reliable platform for building and deploying e-business solutions, enabling collaborative portals, meeting regulatory requirements, and powering global websites. From creation through delivery, Documentum manages the content on which a business depends.

## HiSoftware

URL: http://www.hisoftware.com/products/prodoverview.htm
Email address: info@ highsoftware.com

HiSoftware content quality and integrity management solutions are enterprise Web content testing and test management systems that enable companies to quickly and efficiently build, deploy, and maintain highly dynamic, accessible, usable and searchable Internet, intranet, and extranet Web sites regardless of content, type, format, or location.

## Hummingbird Ltd.

URL: http://www.hummingbird.com/solutions/cm/
Email address: getinfo@hummingbird.com

Hummingbird's document management and content management solutions control, organize, access, and share vital corporate information quickly, easily, and accurately. Because enterprises worldwide recognize that information is the currency of their businesses, they place tremendous value on ensuring that all corporate information in both structured or unstructured formats is captured, managed, and put to work meaningfully and efficiently. Document and content management solutions ensure that organizations get the most from their unstructured data such as information stored in text files, e-mails, multimedia, etc., and use the knowledge contained in the data to gain competitive advantage.

## IBM

URL: http://www-306.ibm.com/software/awdtools/suite/cstudio/support/
Email address: info@ibm.com

Rational Suite ContentStudio integrates a winning combination of market-leading software development tools from Rational with the best-in-class Web content management software from Vignette. Rational Suite ContentStudio unifies code and content for e-business and accelerates Web development. By integrating common tools and processes in one powerful solution, Rational Suite ContentStudio unifies the activities of everyone who contributes to a website, including project managers, analysts, software developers, content managers, web designers, and other business contributors. This comprehensive end-to-end solution unites your team around the Rational Suite team-unifying platform and enables fast and reliable deployment of changes at Internet speeds.

## Mediasurface plc

URL: http://www.mediasurface.com
Email address: info@mediasurface.com

Mediasurface 5 is an advanced content management solution that enables people within and outside an organization to interactively create content, while adhering to business processes through its flexible workflow capabilities. Mediasurface blends the best of knowledge and content management into Mediasurface, enabling the user community to intelligently store and retrieve content as and when required.

## Microsoft

URL: http://www.microsoft.com/servers/sharepoint
Email address: info@microsoft.com

Microsoft SharePoint Portal Server 2003 extends the capabilities of Microsoft Windows and Microsoft Office by offering knowledge workers a powerful new way to easily organize, find, and share information. It delivers dramatic new value as a single solution that combines the ability to easily create corporate Web portals with document management, content searching, and team collaboration features.

## Opentext

URL: http://www.opentext.com/
Email address: info@opentext.com

Web-based, enterprise scalable, and easy to deploy, Livelink for Document Management provides a single authoritative repository for storing and organizing electronic documents. It also delivers a set of sophisticated services for managing and controlling documents, including access control; version control; compound documents; audit trails; workflows for automating document change request, review, and approval processes; extensive indexing and search capabilities; and much more.

## Stellent, Inc.

URL: http://www.stellent.com
Email address: info@stellent.com

Stellent® Universal Content Management offers a flexible, robust, and scalable content management solution that allows employees, customers, and partners to collaborate, contribute, and access business content worldwide. Stellent helps companies fully maximize the value of their information and intellectual assets by bringing spreadsheets, contracts, marketing materials, CAD drawings, digital assets, records, and catalogs to the Web where they can be efficiently managed.

### *Talisma*

URL: http://www.talisma.com
Email address: info@talisma.com

Talisma Knowledgebase enables prospects, customers, partners, and employees to find fast, accurate, consistent answers to specific questions via the web, 24 hours a day, 7 days a week. It leverages corporate information stored in the structured Talisma Knowledgebase and unstructured knowledge sources including customer support, help desk, FAQs, product, and project documentation.

### *Vivisimo*

URL: http://www.vivisimo.com
Email address: usinfo@vivisimo.com

The Vivísimo Content Integrator brings federated search or meta-search capabilities to public and private organizations. Federated search allows users to perform multiple searches concurrently through as many diverse informational sources as needed, whether internal documents, intranets, partner extranets, web sources, subscription services and databases, syndicated news feeds, or intelligence portals such as Hoover's. A user enters a search query through a single search interface that acts as an intermediary to various informational repositories. The query is sent simultaneously to all designated search sources and results are returned to the user in a single list.

## Common Sense Reasoning Engine

### *OpenCyc*

URL: http://www.cyc.com/cyc/opencyc/overview
Email address: info@cyc.com

OpenCyc is the open-source version of the Cyc technology, the world's largest and most complete general knowledge base and common-sense reasoning engine. Cycorp set up an independent organization, OpenCyc.org, to disseminate and administer OpenCyc, and committed to a pipeline through which all current and future Cyc technology will flow into ResearchCyc (available for R&D in academia and industry) and then OpenCyc.

## Data Mining

Data mining, also known as knowledge discovery in databases (KDD), is the practice of automatically searching large stores of data for patterns. It uses computational techniques from statistics and pattern recognition to perform searches.

### *Alterian, Inc*

URL: http://www.alterian.com
Email address: info@alterian.com

Alterian's technology is designed to help companies derive maximum value from even the largest corporate databases. The Alterian suite (Alterian Engine, Alterian Developer, and Alterian Distributor) can perform in-depth analysis of huge volumes of data and generate detailed reports in a variety of formats. Because even the most complex analysis can be completed in seconds, Alterian supports train-of-thought analysis to drive improved business performance. The product can be tailored to lead users through complex processes one step at a time. Multitasking facilities allow train-of-thought analyses while long processes run in the background.

### *ANGOSS Software Corporation*

URL: http://www.angoss.com
Email address: info@angoss.com

KnowledgeSTUDIO is a data mining tool that includes the power of decision trees, cluster analysis, and several predictive models to allow users to mine and understand their data from various perspectives. It includes powerful data visualization tools to support and explain the discoveries.

### *Attar Software*

URL: http://www.attar.com
Email address: info@attar.co.uk

XpertRule Miner is Attar Software's next-generation product evolved from the established Profiler scalable client/server data mining software. Using ActiveX technology, the Miner client can be deployed in a variety of ways. Solutions can be built as stand-alone mining systems or embedded in other vertical applications under MS Windows. Deployment can also be over intranets or the Internet. The ActiveX Miner works with Attar's high-performance data mining servers to provide multitier client/server data mining against very large databases. Mining can be performed directly against the data in situ or by high-performance mining against tokenized cache data tables.

### Attrasoft

URL: http://attrasoft.com/
Email address: webmaster@attrasoft.com

Predictor is Attrasoft's application of neural network technology. Predictor analyzes tremendous amounts of information available through a company's databases or spreadsheets, learning relationships, and patterns to detect subtle changes and predict results.

### Cygron DataScope

URL: http://www.cygron.com/
Email address: info@cygron.com

Cygron DataScope is a powerful, easy-to-use data mining and decision support tool. It utilizes innovative data visualization technology that leverages the natural human ability to see patterns in pictures rather than numbers. The results are decision-provoking database graphics easily understandable by specialist and non-specialist users. By seamlessly integrating state-of-the art data mining and decision support algorithms with its data visualization, it offers an analysis environment powerful enough to meet the needs of the most demanding desktop users.

### Dynamic Information Systems Corp

URL: http://www.disc.com/home/
Email address: info@disc.com

OMNIDEX is state-of-the-art information access technology that unlocks the door to corporate data. It delivers high-performance applications for database marketing, data warehousing, decision support, client/server uses, e-commerce, and other web applications. It is an enterprisewide data access solution that enhances existing databases, flat files, and document files, including relational databases such as Oracle on open systems platforms.

### Google

URL: http://www.google.com/enterprise/gsa/index.html
Email address: info@google.com

The Google Search Appliance is a hardware and software product designed to offer large businesses the productivity-enhancing power of Google search. It's as simple and powerful as Google itself. Search Appliance makes the sea of lost data on web servers, file systems, and relational databases instantly available with one mouse click. Simply point it toward the content, add a search box to your site, and in a matter of hours, users will be able to search through more than 220 file formats in any language. The system indexes up to 15 million documents, and its security features ensure that users see only documents to which they have proper access.

## *InterLeap Inc*

URL: http://www.interleap.com
Email address: sales@interleap.com

InterLeap for Windows is a new tool for data miners that allows generation of dynamically linked tables from multidimensional data structures. Tables can be drilled down, inserted as objects in other software, linked to scatterplots, and saved for use with different data.

## *Megaputer Intelligence Inc.*

URL: http://www.megaputer.com
Email address: info@megaputer.com

PolyAnalyst is a complete data mining workspace that provides all the tools needed for an analyst to find new patterns in data to enhance business intelligence. Unlike OLAP tools that reveal only patterns that are known in advance, data mining software uses the latest machine learning techniques to find hidden relationships within data. PolyAnalyst provides more machine learning techniques than any other data mining package, making it the most flexible business intelligence solution on the market.

## *Script Software*

URL: http://www.knowledgeminer.net
Email address: info@knowledgeminer.net

KnowledgeMiner is a data mining tool that enables anyone to use its unique form of modeling to quickly visualize new possibilities. It is an artificial intelligence tool designed to extract hidden knowledge from data easily. It was built on the cybernetic principles of self-organization: learning a completely unknown relationship between output and input of any system in an evolutionary way from very simple to optimally complex results.

## *Spotfire*

URL: http://www.spotfire
Email address: info@spotfire.com

Spotfire DecisionSite is a highly configurable analytical application that allows interactive visualization and information analysis, enabling decision makers to make decisions in etime. The world's leading research companies have integrated Spotfire's highly graphical environment and interactive displays for visualizing, querying, and analyzing information from any source into their mission-critical work processes.

### SPSS Inc.

URL: http://www.spss.com/clementine
Email address: info@spss.com

It takes in-depth business understanding to find effective solutions to business problems. Clementine's interactive data mining process incorporates valuable business expertise at every step to create powerful predictive models that address specific business issues.

### Veritas

URL: http://www.veritas.com/Products/www?c=product&refId=322
Email address: info@veritas.com

VERITAS Enterprise Vault™ software provides a flexible archiving framework to enable the discovery of content within email, file systems, and collaborative environments, while reducing storage costs and simplifying management.

## Mashups

Mashups represent an emerging paradigm of Web 2.0 that enables developers and talented end users to create new web-based applications and services addressing specific needs and interests.

### JackBe

URL: http://www.jackbe.com
Contact: http://www.jackbe.com/about/contact_form.php

JackBe's flagship software product, Presto, is an enterprise platform that includes functionality for creating and syndicating enterprise mashups. JackBe launched a cloud-based version of its Presto product in March 2010. It is hosted on Amazon EC2.

### Yahoo Pipes

URL: http://pipes.yahoo.com/pipes/

Pipes is a powerful composition tool to aggregate, manipulate, and mashup content throughout the web.

## Text Mining

Text Mining is looking for patterns in natural language text and may be defined as the process of analyzing text to extract information for specific purposes. Text mining recognizes that a complete understanding of natural language text, a long-standing goal of computer science, is not immediately attainable and focuses on extracting small amounts of information from text with high reliability. The information extracted may be an author name, title, and date of publication of an article, acronyms defined in a text, or articles cited in a bibliography.

### *Leximancer*

URL: http://www.leximancer.com
Email address: enquiries@leximancer.com

Leximancer produces concept maps of text data collections and can be used for knowledge discovery, subscription services, and document organization.

### *Megaputer Intelligence Inc.*

URL: http://www.megaputer.com/products/tm.php3
Email address: info@megaputer.com

Making correct decisions often requires analyzing large volumes of textual information.

## Social Web Browsers

A few web browsers include extensions for social networking applications.

### *Flock*

URL: http://www.flock.com/
Email address: shawn@flock.com

People use the web far more differently now than they did a decade ago. However, web browsers—applications at the center of all activities online—have not kept pace with the changes in online behavior. Flock was founded on the vision that a web browser can and should enable the richest user experience possible across information gathering, sharing, communication, self-expression, and interaction functions.

## *Rock Melt*

URL: http://www.rockmelt.com/
Email address: questions@rockmelt.com

RockMelt is a browser built on Chromium, with extensions for Facebook and Twitter.

*Appendix B*

# Community of Practice Practitioner's Guide*

## Contents



* This appendix was adapted from the NAVSEA Community of Practice Practitioner's Guide. May 2001. http://knowledge.usaid.gov/documents/cop_practicioners_guide.pdf

# 1 Introduction

The *Community of Practitioners Guide* presents information in the same order that you should follow as you roll out your plans for communities of practice (CoPs).

# 2 Getting Started: How to Create a Community

## *Purpose*

Where do you start? How do you translate the concept of "community" into a functioning body that provides value to its members and the enterprise? How do you facilitate a group of individuals, possibly from different organizations, backgrounds, and locations, into a viable, living source of relevant knowledge available to all members? This transformation—from concept to working reality—is the goal of this section.

## *Expected Outcomes*

- Clear understanding of the roles and responsibilities involved in a community
- Community identity
- Foundation for community activities

## Product(s)

- Established collaborative work environment (instant messenger, chat, email, corporate document management system [CDMS] work space, facilities, community experience locator, etc.)
- Orientation workshop for community members
- Assessment of community viability

## Key Tasks

1. Conduct core planning
2. Prepare for initial community workshop
3. Host initial community workshop
4. Check community progress
5. Build community experience locator

### Key Task 1: Conduct core planning

The core group (working group of key community members) should conduct a meeting to determine what building blocks must be in place to launch a community. This section addresses the following building blocks as agenda items for a core group planning meeting:

- Community identity
- Community type
- Community roles and responsibilities
- Community membership
- Collaborative work environment

Each of these areas is discussed in detail. Additionally, a sample core planning agenda is provided as a tool at the end of this section. It is essential that individuals who participated in the community originating sessions that identified critical knowledge needs attend the planning meeting as well. The community's functional sponsor, community leader, and facilitator should also attend (if not included in the originating group). (See Community and Corporate Roles and Responsibilities section for detailed descriptions of the functional sponsor and community leader).

#### Lay groundwork
#### Agenda item: Create community identity

One building block for working together is a collective understanding or identity for the community. The identity should address the community purpose, how the community supports the company's mission and goals, how the community determines whether it adds value, what members need from the community, and what cultural norms or conventions will be honored.

To save members' time, the core group may choose to develop a strawman model to address community identity and purpose. By investing time up-front, the core group develops a community identity for use during the initial community workshop. Conversely, the community may best be served by fleshing out these ideas. The exercise of thinking collaboratively may help form a shared sense of community among members. For both approaches, the collective identity is a useful tool for generating interest and membership in the community.

*Tip: If the core group chooses a strawman model approach, it must be open to a change in direction after presentation to the community. Try to avoid "pride of ownership" issues.*

## Understanding intent of community
## Agenda item: Types of communities

A collective understanding of the intent of the community is useful in further clarifying its identity and purpose. The four types of communities and their specialties are

1. Helping communities provide a forum for community members to aid each other in solving everyday work problems.
2. Best practice communities develop and disseminate best practices, guidelines, and procedures for member use.
3. Knowledge stewarding communities organize, manage, and steward a body of knowledge from which community members can draw.
4. Innovation communities create breakthrough ideas, knowledge, and practices.

Determining the primary intent for a community will help to determine how it will be organized (key activities to be undertaken, community structure, and leadership roles). Although communities may serve more than one purpose, most communities focus on one type and develop their structures with that specific intent in mind.

## What roles are played in a community?
## Agenda item: Clarify roles and responsibilities

Communities may be supported by "corporate" roles that provide resources and infrastructure support or may fill the roles within their own groups. Useful community roles include a functional sponsor, core group, community leader, facilitator, and logistics coordinator. These roles are for getting a community up and running, creating and maintaining tools to foster collaboration, planning community events, creating or capturing knowledge, sharing knowledge, and providing continued focus and support. Typical community and corporate roles and responsibilities are described at the end of this section.

### Who should be included? Agenda item: Identify community members

Anyone who wants to participate should be welcome at community events. Notwithstanding this openness, it is recommended that prospective community members (individuals who may learn from each other and have a stake in the community's success) be identified and cultivated. Consider those who hold positions in the organization who could contribute and benefit from sharing knowledge about their roles.

### Without members, there is no community

The members represent the essence of a community. Membership is voluntary rather than prescribed. Members are self-organizing and participate because *they get value* from their participation.

### Participation should not be mandated

The core group and community leader should personally invite prospective members to the initial workshop and subsequent forums until the community takes on momentum. When encouraging participation, emphasize that the goal is not another task force or project team. Communities do not produce task plans or deliverables. Stress that membership is voluntary and individuals are encouraged to participate only if they see the community purpose as meaningful and believe they could gain from or contribute to the community.

### What makes a good member?

Good members embrace and appreciate diversity of thought and perspective, and are key thought leaders.

*Tip: A technique for identifying individuals in your organization who "connect" the informal networks already operating in your organization is social networking and knowledge flow diagramming. Looking at a network of relationships can help you identify integrators or employees who are seen by many as experts or trusted as information sources. Recruiting such individuals for your community will make your communication effort easier because such people have a wide reach in the informal communication network of the organization.*

*Tip: An alternative technique would be to use the knowledge needs supply mapping technique to identify thought and opinion leaders in your organization. A discussion of this technique is provided as a tool at the end of this section.*

*Tip: Publicize commencement of new communities and stress benefits for members. The core group could write a short article for publication in an internal magazine or bulletin, describing the outcomes of community interaction and what the community sees as the next milestone in its development. This public declaration can set up a creative tension that will help motivate the community to advance.*

## Agenda item: Define collaborative work environment

The community will need an operational environment in which to collaborate. The core group must determine what mechanisms are available and can be put in place.

### How will members work together?

Some companies use a corporate document management system (CDMS) as the standard for document management, workflow, and shared workspaces. Another possibility is the use of chat room and instant messaging capabilities. The community leader must arrange for meeting rooms. Depending on membership, video conferencing may also be required.

### *Key Task 2: Prepare for initial community workshop*

First and foremost, the goal of the initial community workshop should be to engage member interests and stimulate continued involvement—not increase workloads of members. The first workshop should also serve to begin building relationships among members. Careful planning can help ensure the success of the initial community workshop. The agenda for the initial workshop should include at least the following points. A sample agenda is provided as a tool at the end of this section.

- Solidify community identity
- Clarify community intent
- Begin building relationships (exercise)
- Clarify roles
- Provide overview of methods to create, capture, and share knowledge
- Provide overview of how selected tools such as CDMS may be used to further community goals
- Identify highest priority knowledge needs
- Identify next steps to satisfy specific knowledge needs

The functional sponsor should join the workshop to welcome members, encourage participation, and spark dialogue.

### Let the core group establish themselves as members, not directors

*Tip: Consider facilitator services for at least the initial community workshop. The facilitator should be involved in planning the community orientation and assist in developing the agenda.*

### An email invitation could easily be lost in the shuffle

*Tip: Simply sending an email invitation to prospective members is not enough. The core group and community leader must reach out personally or by telephone to begin building personal relationships. Personal invitations provide an opportunity to distinguish the community from other requests for time and stress what the individual can gain from the experience.*

### Don't burden members with "administrivia"

*Tip: The community should be free to focus on its purpose—building its knowledge base. The importance of this focus cannot be overstated. The organization does not want the community to be "turned off" by procedural or administrative duties before it even starts.*

### Give them a reason to keep coming

*Tip: To jump-start the community, invite a guest speaker to share a best practice or innovation in an area of particular interest to the community.*

### Optimum location is critical

The optimum location for a workshop is off site so that interruptions can be controlled. The most successful arrangements include a U-shaped table for participant seating with a facilitator table in the front for projection equipment and facilitator supplies. The room size should reflect the number of team members. If a room is too small, people will feel cramped and trapped. If a room is too large, intimacy will be difficult to establish.

If flipcharts will be used, solid, smooth walls are required for posting and maintaining the *group memory* (discussions and decisions made by the group and documented on flipchart paper). Electronic means such as whiteboards to capture group memory are also useful.

#### *What supplies will you need?*

- Three or four easel boards with extra pads of papers (one for each possible subgroup)
- Markers

- Masking tape
- Name tents
- Access to a copier and/or printer
- Laptop computer

### *Key Task 3: Host initial community workshop*

The initial community workshop presents a *one-time opportunity* to engage member interest. Remember that first impressions are the most lasting. This orientation should convince members that leadership is ready to invest in the community.

A sample agenda is provided as a tool at the end of this section. The following tips for a successful workshop are cross-referenced to the appropriate agenda items.

#### Agenda item: Provide a guest speaker

An interview may generate more interest than a canned briefing. Consider conducting an interview with your guest speaker rather than having him or her deliver a formal briefing. Not only will this approach to knowledge exchange more closely resemble the desired give-and-take of community interactions, but it will also demonstrate a useful community technique for gathering knowledge. Members of the core group should serve as provocateurs. Interview questions designed to stimulate interesting dialogue should be prepared.

*Tip: Have questions on hand to spark dialogue during the question-and-answer period.*

*Tip: A good learning technique is for the group to collectively list the key or salient points surfaced during the guest speaker's presentation or interview. This serves to reinforce concepts. Key points should be posted on a flipchart and recorded as a possible new knowledge nugget for posting in the shared workspace. A variation might be to perform this exercise at the end of the workshop and summarize key points learned throughout the session.*

#### Agenda item: Solidify community identity

Community identity has several components and every one must be clarified and agreed upon. The components are common purpose, relationships, success criteria, and norms for interacting. A community is a network of relationships. The first workshop is a good opportunity to begin the process of building person-to-person relationships among members. The human relationships will sustain the community over time and provide a sense of reciprocity and obligation among members. To foster this, it is suggested that a relationship-building exercise be included in the initial and subsequent workshops. A sample exercise is provided as a tool at the end of this section. Additional exercises can be found in Section 3, "Creating Knowledge."

### A common purpose unifies and creates a sense of urgency

The best way to unify a community is for its members to share a common purpose. The purpose should center around knowledge areas that carry a sense of urgency and incite passions. The purpose should be directly connected to the challenges its members face in their work.

### Success criteria guide community evolution

It is essential that the community realize that it—not the enterprise leadership—is responsible for determining its own success. Members must set their own success criteria because (1) it raises the sense of ownership in the CoP and (2) individuals who develop their own performance measures set more demanding targets. Some general success criteria include

- Sustained mutual relationships
- Quick mobilization for discussion
- Shared methodology
- Rapid flow of information and fostering of innovation
- Acknowledged participant base
- Knowledge of what others know, what they do, and how they contribute
- Mutually defined identities
- Ability to assess appropriateness of actions and products
- CoP-developed (or -sustained) tools, language, and definitions
- Open communication channels
- Satisfaction of specific knowledge goals
- Reduction of time needed to solve problems
- Decreased rework
- Number of innovative/breakthrough ideas
- Member satisfaction survey results
- Transfer of best practices from one member to another
- Adoption of best practices or innovations that were "not invented here"
- Less redundancy of effort among members
- Avoidance of costly mistakes
- Quantitative measures
- Success stories

### A word on quantitative measures

Quantitative measures are most valuable when tracked over time and compared against a baseline recorded at the start of an initiative. For this reason, it is advisable to try to leverage existing measures if possible. Metrics are particularly important to knowledge management (KM) because a KM return on investment often takes significant time to appear. Putting a KM program into effect will impact other business processes as the organization learns to use and leverage the new KM capabilities. This acculturation can take eighteen to thirty-six months in some cases. In no case should a KM program be expected to show a return in less than twelve months.

### Leverage existing metrics: use available baseline data

If one organizational goal is to improve customer satisfaction, an existing baseline metric for tracking customer satisfaction should be available. The KM initiative should leverage the process already in place to monitor customer satisfaction to observe progress toward the goal.

### Anecdotes or stories can be more powerful than numbers

A story about how knowledge was leveraged in the organization to achieve value accomplishes two tasks. First, it creates an interesting context around which to remember the measure described. Second, it educates readers or listeners about alternative methods that they may employ to achieve similar results, thus helping "spread the word" about the KM program and speeding the cultural change. Qualitative measures such as stories, anecdotes, and lessons learned often achieve a primary benefit of KM measurement: allocation of resources and support for the community's KM pilot project.

### Link to business objectives

It is critical that a community be able to link its purpose to specific business drivers or objectives of the organization. By establishing this link, the community can demonstrate direct value to the organization.

### Norms help keep a community connected

When people work together or sit close enough to interact daily, they naturally build a connection. They find commonalities in the problems they face, see the value of each other's ideas, build trust, and create a common etiquette or set of norms for interacting that simply emerges from their regular contact. When building intentional communities, it is tempting to jump right to "official community business" before the community has had time to form. During community events, allow time for "technical schmoozing" so that members can share immediate work problems and begin helping each other.

Although norms will evolve over time, some initial conventions can easily be discussed and possibly adopted by the community in the initial workshop. Here are some examples:

- Relevant information will be shared as soon as possible
- One conversation at a time during discussions
- Member preferences for regular meeting times, places, etc.
- Frequency of events (schedule or standard such as second Wednesday of every month)
- Open meeting policy; with few exceptions, anyone can attend any meeting
- Agendas for all planned workshops; each agenda should list standard points of discussion such as action item assignments and tracking
- Identifying areas of interest for evolving agenda items
- Use of facilitators
- When and how documentation will be prepared; possible rotating role among members

*Tip: Once the community agrees to its identity, the message should be posted in the workspace as a "welcome" to prospective members.*

*Tip: Attendees at workshops should be polled to identify individuals who may benefit from and contribute to the community's knowledge base.*

## Member agreement on knowledge needs is key to continued involvement

### Agenda item: Prioritize knowledge needs

The community must have a shared understanding about the knowledge it needs. Although the preceding analyses identified needed knowledge, skills, and information (KSIs), it is wise to build consensus around which KSIs are most critical to community members. The *community* should prioritize its knowledge needs.

*Tip: In a large group, an effective prioritization method is multi-voting. Allow each member to cast five votes based on what he or she believes are the five highest priorities (no more than one vote on any single item). This will quickly identify areas of the most energy and urgency.*

*Tip: Another prioritization technique is to build consensus on decision criteria, e.g., mission need, safety, cost, and risk. After consensus is reached on the criteria, the prioritization of knowledge against mutually agreed-to criteria will foster commitment and build ownership of the community process.*

## How will we transform a knowledge need into a knowledge nugget?

### Agenda item: Plan of action

After the most vital knowledge needs have been decided, the community should decide how it wishes to satisfy the needs. For example, must the community conduct a search to acquire needed knowledge? Would a problem-solving session produce the needed knowledge?" (See Section 3, "Creating Knowledge," for suggested techniques.) A plan of action should address the who, what, when, and how of satisfying the knowledge needs.

## Open members' minds to possibilities of collaborative work tools

### Agenda item: Collaborative environment

This agenda item is intended to provide members with an overview of available collaborative technology. The goal is to explore collaborative tools and how they can be used to promote interactions of members and the knowledge base, not provide training.

## Schedule the next community forum before you end for the day

### Agenda item: Wrap-up

To close the session, the community should agree to next steps, at a minimum confirming a date for the next session and suggesting agenda items.

*Tip: If action items are identified, the core group should volunteer for as many as possible. The core group should be seen as a resource for the community, not the other way around.*

*Tip: In closing, conduct a roundtable (each participant shares his or her thoughts) to solicit "gut" reactions, initial reservations, enthusiasm, etc. Be sure to listen rather than defend.*

## *Key Task 4: Check community progress*

The community leader and core group should conduct a short progress check after the community's first event to ensure the community is on the road to success. "Yes" should be the answer to all the following questions. "No" answers present potential barriers to success. A solution should be developed and implemented for each identified barrier.

1. Does the community have a common purpose?
2. Is the purpose compelling to leadership, prospective members, and their functional managers?
3. Is the common purpose aligned with the organizational strategy?
4. Is the right sponsorship in place—a respected leader who is willing to contribute to the community?
5. Does the functional sponsor agree with the community's scope, purpose, and membership?
6. Are core group members and the community leader strong content experts, enthusiastic, and able to develop the community?

7. Do members' functional managers agree that time away from the job for this purpose is valuable?
8. Does the community have the right content experts to provide perspective and meaning to the membership?
9. Is there a shared space and context for dialogue, advice, and work?
10. Does the community have enough members to stay alive?
11. Are collaborative tools in place?
12. Are members set to use them?
13. Are needed resources (meeting rooms, VTC, conference attendance fees, travel funds, etc. available?

### Lessons learned provide valuable insight

A second valuable exercise for the core group and/or community leader is holding a lessons-learned discussion to evaluate the initial workshop. This information will help improve the community's next event and also be beneficial when the next community is initiated. A sample form for collecting lessons learned is provided at the end of this section.

### *Key Task 5: Build community experience locator*

Another useful tool for rapidly getting the right information to the right person at the right time is creating a community experience locator. The locator may be resident on a community's shared computer workspace and could include key information about members' significant experience such as three significant jobs held. Key word search capability may be a feature of the tool. A sample CoP experience locator template is provided at the end of this section.

*Tip: Consider developing an experience locator and hosting it in CDMS.*

## *Tools*

- Sample Core Group Planning Meeting Agenda
- Community and Corporate Roles and Responsibilities
- Social Networks and Knowledge Flow Technique
- Knowledge Needs/Supply Map
- Sample Community Workshop Agenda (Orientation)
- Suggested Exercise: Building Relationships
- Community of Practice Early Progress Checklist
- Lessons Learned Report Template
- Community of Practice/Experience Locator Template

## Sample Core Group Planning Meeting Agenda

Objectives:
- Clarify community origination and purpose
- Identify prospective community members
- Determine best methods for community collaboration

Opening activities:
- Welcome
- Introductions (if applicable)
- Review objectives and/or agenda

Create community identity:
- Clarify purpose
- Review prioritized knowledge needs
- Consider success criteria
- Consider community norms

Clarify community intent:
- Review types of communities
- Determine intent and focus of community

Clarify roles and responsibilities:
- Review functional sponsor role
- Review community leader role
- Review core group role
- Review logistics coordinator role
- Review facilitator role

Identify community members:
- Review members identified in preceding analysis
- Brainstorm additional prospective contributors
- Devise methods to "get the word out"

Define collaborative work environment:
- Explore capability for shared workspace (electronic)
- Evaluate chat room and discussion tools
- Identify meeting rooms (VTC capabilities)

Wrap-up:
- Review next steps and action items
- Review meeting objectives

## Community and Corporate Roles and Responsibilities

Within the KM context are two types of roles: (1) those associated with a specific CoP and (2) those that support and link multiple CoPs and/or other KM initiatives, e.g., building infrastructure for knowledge transfer. Corporate roles are not specific to a particular community. As the KM strategy evolves and communities are rolled out, corporate roles (acting as "infomediaries") may gain more prominence.

Certainly some communities will form as "grass-roots" movements and will not use corporate resources; some may already be in place and successful. Roles, in this context, do not equate to job positions; they can be viewed as wearing different hats to accomplish different tasks. These role descriptions are provided as guides and should be tailored to suit your community's needs and resources.

### *Functional sponsors pave the way for community success*

Every community must have a functional sponsor—typically someone who can pave the way for community success. A sponsor believes in the value of knowledge sharing and commends participation in community activities. He or she also promotes the value of membership across an organization, thus encouraging community growth and commitment of organizational resources. Sponsorship may be shared by more than one person; this may be important if community membership spans multiple organizations. The functional sponsor

- Makes community participation a priority for its members
- Builds support for community with top management, functional managers, and opinion leaders
- Bolsters community membership; spreads the word
- Plans and coordinates allocation of resources (ensures funding for awards and other purposes)
- Acts as champion for the community
- Sets direction and provides guidance
- Resolves issues
- Works with community leader to track progress

### *Core group is instrumental in establishing effective work methods for the community*

The core group subset of the community is a working group that initially performs start-up tasks such as planning. The group consists of expert and experienced members of the community. After the community is established, the core group continues to provide ongoing organizational support. For example, core group members may use their knowledge of a discipline to judge what is important, groundbreaking, and useful and enrich information by summarizing, combining, contrasting, and integrating it into the existing knowledge base. The group:

- Participates in community
- Gains support of functional managers
- Ensures infrastructure can meet knowledge objectives of the community
- Builds community experience locator

- Creates collaborative environment
- Harvests and/or creates new knowledge
- Establishes taxonomy
- Prescribes tool usage/functionality

## *Community leader provides day-to-day support while serving as a contributing member*

The community leader, an active member of the community, has an integral role in community success. He or she energizes the process and provides continuous nourishment for the community. The leader must continuously strive to further the community's goals:

- Serves as a subject matter expert on the community focus
- Plans and schedules community activities
- Connects members
- Proposes new ideas when the community starts to lose energy
- Interfaces with functional sponsor
- Bolsters community membership; spreads the word
- Represents community
- Acts as liaison with other communities
- Recognizes contributions
- Manages day-to-day activities of community (collateral duty)
- Tracks budget expenditures (if applicable)

## *No community is possible without members*

The essence of a community is its members. Membership is voluntary rather than prescribed. Members are self-organizing and participate because *they get value* from participation. A member:

- Enjoys continuous learning as a result of participation
- Bolsters community membership; spreads the word
- Populates community experience locator (if applicable)
- Works on relevant business processes; acts as expert on data, processes, or both
- Looks outside community to identify relevant information
- Conducts interviews to capture knowledge
- Presents new information to community to determine value added
- Acts as content owner by updating, creating, replenishing, and owning data in repository
- Scans best practice materials
- Performs benchmarking

- Develops rules governing assets; assures documentation consistency
- Participates in face-to-face knowledge-sharing experiences
- May be core group member
- May document community proceedings

### *A facilitator can serve as a resource for a community*

A facilitator can ensure that community activities productive for all members by acting as an independent CoP process expert. He or she

- Helps create and foster a collaborative environment
- Provides process analysis expertise
- Provides tool expertise
- Provides expertise about group dynamics and techniques to help community solve problems and evolve over time

### *Functional support provides "backbone"*

Functional support enables the storing of knowledge in a collaborative environment. He or she

- Provides on-the-spot expertise on the CoP building process
- Provides help desk services for building the CoP and specific tool support
- May document community proceedings

### *Corporate knowledge management infrastructure roles*

The logistics coordinator handles administrative matters for a community:

- Coordinates calendars, schedules meetings and events
- Coordinates facilities
- Obtains required equipment

The "infomediary" acts as information broker:

- Gleans data across communities for relevance
- Connects data across communities
- Acts as liaison with related projects and CoPs

The project historian is not part of a community of practice. The historian documents project decisions and events to ensure the information can be reused by the organization. The historian may be a member of an individual project team, a business process reengineering or enterprise resource planning effort, or play a role in other activities. He or she captures project history: activities, discussions, decisions, contacts, etc.

## Sample Community Orientation Workshop Agenda

- Objectives:
  - Solidify community identity
  - Prioritize knowledge needs
  - Develop plan to satisfy highest priority knowledge need
- Opening activities:
  - Welcome by functional sponsor
  - Introductions
  - Review objectives and agenda
- Guest speaker:
  - Presentation
  - Questions and answers
- Relationship-building exercise
- Community identity:
  - Clarify purpose
  - Consider success criteria
  - Consider community norms
  - Identify additional prospective members
- Clarify community intent:
  - Review types of communities
  - Determine intent and focus of community
- Knowledge needs:
  - Review prioritized knowledge needs
  - Build consensus on prioritization technique
  - Determine top knowledge needs
- Plan of action
- Collaborative environment:
  - Describe tools available for community use
  - Determine member needs for installation, training, or access
- Wrap-up:
  - Review action items and next steps
  - Review meeting objectives
- Plan next meeting

## Relationship-Building Exercise

**Title of exercise:** Connect community members
**Purpose:** Build personal relations between members; begin to answer (1) what we know, (2) what we need to know, and (3) who knows it
**Group size:** Five to forty members
**Estimated time:** Twenty to sixty minutes, depending on group size

**Props:** Set of blank index cards strung on a loose ring (or community key ring) for each member

1. Organize participants into groups of four to six based on group size.
2. Explain that the goal is to learn about community members' unique backgrounds and perspectives and get to know each other better.
3. Give each participant a set of blank ("factoid") index cards and give directions. Each subgroup should convene for ten minutes to complete a factoid card for each member.
4. After ten minutes, disperse subgroup members and regroup into new subgroups. Ensure that every member speaks with every other member of the subgroup.
5. Rotations should last just long enough for members to gather information, but want more time to whet their appetites for information.
6. Repeat subgroup formation until each member has completed a card for each member.

*Tips: Provide a complete set of blank cards to each new member and encourage him or her to complete cards by talking with each existing member. Also, provide blank cards to existing members and encourage them to complete cards for new members and add them to their rings.*

## Community of Practice Early Progress Checklist

1. Does the community have a common purpose? Is the purpose compelling to leadership, prospective members, and their functional managers?
2. Is the common purpose aligned with the enterprise strategy?
3. Is the right sponsorship in place—a respected leader who is willing to contribute to the community?
4. Does the functional sponsor agree with the community's scope, purpose, and membership?
5. Are core group members and the community leader strong content experts, enthusiastic, and able to develop the community?
6. Do members' functional managers agree that time away from the job is valuable?
7. Does the community have the right content experts to provide perspective and meaning to the membership?
8. Is there a shared space and context for dialogue, advice, and work?
9. Does the community have enough members to stay alive?
10. Are collaborative tools in place and easily accessible? Are members set to use them?
11. Are needed resources (meeting space, VTC, budget for traveling to conferences) available?

## Lessons-Learned Report

| **Lessons Learned** | |
|---|---|
| Situation | |
| Observer | |
| Date | |
| What Went Right? | |
| | |
| | |
| | |
| | |
| | |
| What Went Wrong? | |
| | |
| | |
| | |
| | |
| | |
| Suggestions | |
| | |
| | |
| | |
| | |
| | |

## Community of Practice Experience Locator Template

With today's email and Internet technologies, knowledge can be rapidly transferred. But how does someone know who to contact to learn more about a specific topic? Consider the following true anecdote:

> "I joined the organization on March 16, 1998, without previous experience. After one week of training, I joined a project team. After one day

> of training on the project, I was assigned a task to learn a particular technology that was new to everyone on the team. I was given a bunch of books and told that I had three days to learn how to create a project using this technology.
>
> "In my first week of training, I remembered learning about the company's expertise database. I sent an email to four people I found in the database asking for their help. One of them sent me a document containing exactly what I wanted. Instead of *three days, my task was completed in one-half a day.*"

How do you connect knowledge seekers with knowledge holders and facilitate knowledge exchange? One method common in industry today is using experience locators or "corporate yellow pages." Each community should post a CoP descriptor on the corporate website. The descriptor should be easily accessible by employees and provide the following information:

- Name of community
- Purpose and scope of community
- Name of functional sponsor (organization, location, phone number, email)
- Name of community leader (organization, location, phone number, email)
- Names of core group members (organization, location, phone number, email)
- Membership contact information (organization, location, phone number, email) or direct links to members
- Membership profiles (key information about experience (relevant jobs, fields of expertise, project experience, education, training, certifications, and publications)
- Listings of or links to community knowledge assets

Some interactive play may enhance the usefulness of a CoP experience locator, for example, key word search capabilities, the ability to conduct an instant messaging session with a community member identified as a subject matter expert, or contact experts via email if the expert is not online at that moment.

## 3 Creating Knowledge

### *Purpose*

This section will provide your community with suggested tools to help it create, capture, and share knowledge. A tool in this context is not an automated system for transferring information. These tools are techniques or forums for thinking—for generating ideas, building relationships, and promoting knowledge flow and transfer. The following tools are discussed in this section:

- Ad hoc sessions
- Roadmap to generating new knowledge (problem solving and brainstorming)
- Learning history
- Interviews
- Action learning
- Learning from others
- Guest speakers
- Relationship building
- Systems thinking

The inventory, storage, and migration of explicit knowledge (publications, documents, and patents) are addressed in Section 4.

### *Efforts to create and transfer knowledge cannot be neglected even if resource intensive*

Converting tacit knowledge to commonly held community knowledge may be resource intensive, but the gains can be extraordinary. To cite industry examples, companies have saved millions by transferring knowledge from organization area to another. Ford claims a $34 million saving in one year from transferring ideas between operation plants. Texas Instruments saved enough from transferring knowledge between wafer fabrication plants to pay for a new building. Chevron reduced its costs on capital projects alone by $186 million. Transferring common knowledge and creating new knowledge cannot be neglected; the transfers are critical to maintain viability, and new knowledge is required for future viability. A CoP offers a mechanism for continuously growing and transferring knowledge, as shown in Figure B.1.

## *Expected Outcomes*

After common knowledge is gained, a second cycle would leverage this knowledge across an organization, translating gained knowledge into usable forms and

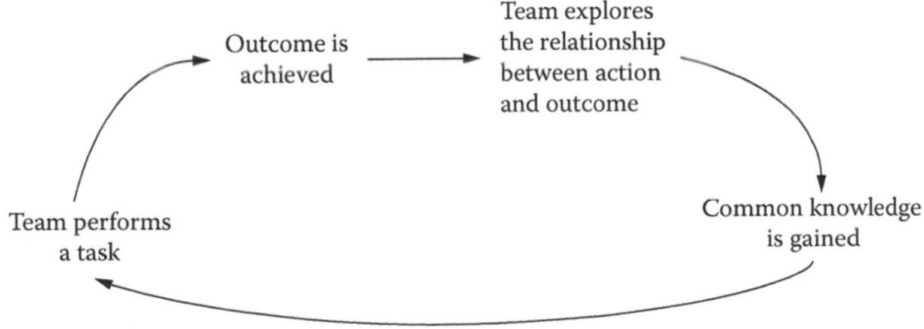


**Figure B.1 Common knowledge.**

transferring it to others who can adapt it for their own use. Expected outcomes include (1) designs for community forums for critical thinking and knowledge flow, and (2) practical techniques for knowledge creation, capture, and transfer.

## *What technique should I use?*

This section introduces the tools and provides brief descriptions. Where noted, supplemental information or templates are provided at the end of this section. A matrix of possible learning need scenarios is presented. For example, a community member may want to learn how to perform a particular task. The matrix would suggest two techniques: conducting interviews and action learning sets.

### Ad hoc sessions

One possible success criterion discussed earlier was the ability of a community to mobilize rapidly in response to a member's request for help. The ability to pull a group together quickly for a thirty-minute brainstorming or sounding board discussion is a priceless resource. Instant messaging is a great device for calling a quick session. Instant messaging, email, conference calls, VTC, or chat rooms can also be used in lieu of meetings for obtaining rapid input. In general, any or all of these technologies can be used inside a single network security domain. However, if, for example, the instant messaging or chat room protocols must traverse one or more firewalls to include all desired participants, this situation must be investigated ahead of time to ensure that the firewall is already configured to pass the required protocols. If the firewall blocks these signals, further analysis is required to ensure that opening a firewall port will not create unacceptable security vulnerabilities in the network. In this case, a *prior* consultation with the local information system security manager (ISSM) is strongly recommended.

*Tip: The community's experience locator is a useful tool when a member needs quick contact with someone who "has done this before."*

### Roadmap to generating new knowledge

An excellent approach to creating and sharing knowledge about best practices is to host facilitated, collaborative problem-solving meetings that serve many purposes: (1) solving relevant, day-to-day problems; (2) building trust among members as they help each other; and (3) solving problems in a public forum, thus creating a common understanding of tools, approaches, and solutions.

Often during problem-solving discussions, communities discover areas that need common standards or guidelines. These discoveries may be assigned to smaller, more focused work groups to develop detailed standards for incorporation into best practice recommendations. This is an example of how communities naturally trigger continuous process improvement.

A five-step roadmap for problem solving as a means to generate new knowledge is provided at the end of this section. It works well for best practices that can easily be reused (methodologies, analytical models, diagnostic approaches, case studies, and benchmark data).

## Learning history

A learning history is a very useful tool to capture tacit knowledge of individuals. A learning history is a retrospective of significant events in an organization's recent past, described in the voices of people who took part in them. Researched through a series of reflective interviews, a learning history uses feedback from employees at all levels to help an organization evaluate its progress.

## Technique to capture tacit knowledge of individuals

Organizations can learn by reviewing their successes and failures, assessing them systematically, and recording the lessons in a form that employees find open and accessible. To quote the famous philosopher, George Santayana, "Those who cannot remember the past are condemned to repeat it." Learning from mistakes can lead to subsequent success. Failure is the ultimate teacher.

Recording staff members' experiences with technical projects, operations, change programs, technical conferences, leadership conferences, workshops, site visits, etc., can ensure that useful knowledge is shared and that mistakes are not repeated. In debriefings, interviewees recall their experiences in their own words and in a way that reflects their collective learning experiences.

An interview can be transcribed into a question-and-answer format or as a standardized document or preserved as a video. Regardless of the medium, the important issue is to ensure that a record is made while events are still fresh and ideally before a project concludes. In effect, an interview record allows access to immediate hindsight, not hindsight tempered by poor memory recall and defensive reasoning.

At Ford, learning histories are used by a car parts division, an assembly plant, and in product design and development. In the assembly plant, Ford notes quality improvements of 25% per year since 1995, compared with under 10% achieved by competitors. A six-step approach to creating a learning history is provided at the end of this section.

## Storytelling

Storytelling, the construction of fictional examples to illustrate a point, can be used to transfer knowledge effectively. An organizational story is a detailed narrative of management actions, employee interactions, or other internal events that is communicated informally within the organization.

Conveying information in a story provides a rich context, remaining in the conscious memory longer and creating more memory traces than information not in context. Therefore a story is more likely than normal communications to be acted upon. Storytelling in a personal or organizational setting connects people, develops creativity, and increases confidence. The use of stories in organizations can build descriptive capabilities, increase organizational learning, convey complex meanings, and communicate common values and rule sets.

### Interviews

Conducting interviews with subject matter experts, stakeholders, process performers, customers—anyone who can shed new light on a topic—is an excellent method to gather knowledge for the community and its knowledge base. Guidelines are provided at the end of this section.

### Action Learning

Action learning is a new way to approach learning. The simple concept revolves around the fact that people learn by doing. It involves the formation of a small group of people (action learning set) who share common issues, goals, or learning needs. The set works to resolve issues and achieve goals together. Members meet regularly, about once a month, to reflect on progress, issues, and solutions and refine the way forward. They can brainstorm on alternative approaches or offer advice to an individual on proceeding to achieve specific goals. Emphasis is on trying new methods and evaluating the results. A methodology for action learning is provided at the end of this section.

Action learning is task oriented and may be useful for approaching narrowly focused issues. However, a community is neither expected nor encouraged to undertake large, task-oriented projects such as re-engineering, system requirement definitions, and policy overhauls. When the community recognizes a need for a major project, it should route the candidate project to leadership for direction. The community may wish to volunteer its subject expertise to a subsequent project team if appropriate.

### Learn from others and share relentlessly

Not all learning is derived from reflection and analysis. Power insights may arise from looking outside a realm or industry to acquire a new perspective. Organizations stop changing when people stop learning and get stuck in knowing. Consider benchmarking to identify better ways to do business; site visits or tours demonstrate how a practice is applied in a specific environment; and interactions with customers clarify their problems, preferences, and feedback about services or products.

*Tip: The American Productivity and Quality Center offers a benchmarking methodology and a wealth of information about best practices on its website (http://www.apqc.org).*

Your community should learn from external sources and leverage existing knowledge within your organization. Seek existing sources of knowledge (work products from other departments and communities, exhibitors at knowledge fairs, commissioned studies). One objective of KM is to make these resources easily available to individuals and to the community.

### Guest speakers

Inviting guest speakers to community forums is an opportunity to bring a fresh perspective into a community. Selection of speakers should be based upon relevance to community purpose or targeted areas of interest.

- Solicit ideas for speakers or topic areas from community members.
- Consider internal *and* external sources for relevant speakers. Other sources include professional associations, sister organizations, supplier and partner organizations, project historians.
- When appropriate, consider inviting representatives from other communities to speak. This will encourage links across communities.

### Relationship-building exercises

The strongest communities are built upon strong relationships. Relationships typically form naturally when people work together over time. It may helpful, on occasion, to add a relationship-building exercise into community forums. Several exercises are provided at the end of this section.

### Systems thinking

Systems thinking provides an approach for managing complexity. It helps decision makers understand cause-and-effect relationships among data, information, and people. It identifies archetypes (or patterns) involved in decision making. In short, it expands individual thinking skills and improves both individual and group decision making. Additional information on systems thinking is provided at the end of this section.

## *Tools*

- Suggested techniques for scenarios
- Roadmap to generating new knowledge
- Learning history: overview

- Storytelling; white paper
- Interview guidelines
- Action learning
- Relationship building exercises
- Systems thinking

## Suggested Techniques for Scenarios

| *Scenario* | *Ad Hoc Sessions* | *Roadmap* | *Learning History* | *Story Telling* | *Interviews* | *Action Learning* | *Learn from Others* | *Guest Speakers* | *Relationship Building* | *Systems Thinking* |
|---|---|---|---|---|---|---|---|---|---|---|
| No information available | | | | | ✓ | ✓ | ✓ | ✓ | | |
| Practice performed differently by many with varying levels of success; seeking best practice for adoption by all | | ✓ | ✓ | | ✓ | | ✓ | ✓ | | |
| Common problem with many alternatives; seeking best practice | | ✓ | ✓ | ✓ | ✓ | | | | | ✓ |
| Energizing community with new ideas | | | | ✓ | | | | ✓ | | ✓ |
| Method to test or prototype alternatives; find best practice | | ✓ | | | | ✓ | | | | |
| One or more members must learn specific task | | | | | ✓ | ✓ | | | | |
| New tasking from command leadership; finding best way to implement | | ✓ | | | | ✓ | | | | ✓ |
| Problem identified but not yet understood; finding root cause | | ✓ | ✓ | | ✓ | | | | | ✓ |
| Need for immediate answer or bouncing idea to colleagues | ✓ | | | | ✓ | | | | | |

| *Scenario* | *Ad Hoc Sessions* | *Roadmap* | *Learning History* | *Story Telling* | *Interviews* | *Action Learning* | *Learn from Others* | *Guest Speakers* | *Relationship Building* | *Systems Thinking* |
|---|---|---|---|---|---|---|---|---|---|---|
| Exercise or event occurred; was it successful? | | | ✓ | ✓ | ✓ | | | ✓ | | |
| Build consensus on topic with high levels of conflict or controversy | | ✓ | | | | | | | Brain writing | ✓ |
| Need to generate and evaluate ideas | | | | | | | | | Brain writing | |
| Prepare group to derive lessons learned; think beyond the obvious | | ✓ | | ✓ | | | | | Moral of story? | |
| Think creatively; see same issue in new light | | ✓ | | ✓ | | | ✓ | | New product offering | ✓ |

## *Roadmap to Generating New Knowledge*

This roadmap is a variation on an approach commonly used for problem solving. It may be useful to a community trying to solve a problem shared by many members or developing a best practice for adoption by members. The roadmap leads the community through a series of steps: define problem, conduct analysis, generate ideas, select best practice or solution, and capture knowledge in explicit form. Groups and individuals can use this approach by following the same steps.

### *Problem Exploration and Definition*

Explore the problem and determine whether additional information is needed. For example, members may decide to observe specific practices or research existing information on a topic. Other methods to collect more information may include interviews with impacted individuals or subject matter experts. Jumping to a conclusion without understanding a problem may save time but can also waste time if you solve the wrong problem. Before following a wrong conclusion, consider the following:

- Examine a problem from all angles; try to see it from the perspective of an employee, a customer, or a supplier.

- Separate fact from fiction. Perception is important but must be distinguished from fact.
- Identify key players: those affected by the problem, those responsible for solving it, and those who have the authority to accept a solution.
- Dissect or decompose the situation; break the problem into pieces.
- Devise plan for gathering information: surveys, interviews, observations, brainstorm sessions, benchmark reviews.

Clearly defining a problem in clear, plain English is like having your finger on its pulse. A clear definition builds a strong foundation for subsequent fact finding, communication, and analysis. A good definition

- Distills a situation into a brief, concise statement
- Uses key words to "get to the bottom" of the situation
- States what a problem is rather than what it isn't
- States a problem in terms of needs, not solutions

## *Analysis*

Typically, what you know is only the tip of the iceberg: the symptoms of a problem rather than its root cause. It is important to distinguish cause from effect to ensure that you act on the source of a problem and do not simply address its symptoms. Consider a medical analogy. You have many symptoms of a common cold, but in fact you have a sinus infection that can only be cured with an antibiotic. Although you use over-the-counter cold medicines to alleviate your symptoms, your infection worsens. The same process occurs in an organization. By addressing only the symptoms, you miss the root cause and the condition persists and may worsen.

Discovering the root cause of a problem can be tricky. Sound questioning techniques represent a good start. Using your problem definition statement, answer the following questions:

- Why does the problem persist?
- Where did it start, and where did it come from?
- Why doesn't it resolve itself or just go away?
- What caused it?
- What changed right before it started?
- Why do we keep returning to the situation?
- Why won't things improve no matter what we try?

Still not sure? Don't move to the solution phase until you are sure you know the root cause. Test your tentative conclusion using the questions in the table that follows. The proposed root cause must pass the entire test to be a true root cause. If the results of the questionnaire are not conclusive, continue analysis until you can answer yes to each question.

## *Questionnaire for Determining Root Cause*

| *Desired Response* | *Test Question* | *Yes/No* |
|---|---|---|
| Dead end | You reached a dead end when you asked what created the proposed root cause. | |
| Conversation ends | All conversation reached a positive end. | |
| Feels good | Everyone involved feels good, is motivated and uplifted emotionally. | |
| Agreement | All agree the root cause keeps the problem from resolving. | |
| Explains | The root cause fully explains why the problem exists from all points of view. | |
| Beginnings | The earliest beginnings of the situation were explored and are understood. | |
| Logical | The root cause is logical, makes sense, and dispels all confusion. | |
| Control | The root cause can be influenced, controlled, and dealt with realistically. | |
| Hope | Finding the root cause restored the hope that something constructive can be done. | |
| Workable solution | Suddenly workable solutions, not outrageous demands, begin to appear. | |
| Stable resolution | A stable, long-term, once-and-for-all resolution now appears feasible. | |

Analytic techniques such as diagramming and process modeling may be applied during the analysis stage. A few additional techniques for analyzing a problem include

- Play Napoleon. Imagine you are someone else to gain new perspectives.
- Morphological analysis. Systematically examine each attribute of the problem.
- Create a deadline.
- Sleep on the problem.

## *Idea Generation*

After the root cause is identified, possible solutions should be generated. This is a time to be creative. One useful way to generate a storm of ideas with a group is a facilitation technique called brainstorming that works in two ways: it enhances the flow of ideas and innovations and builds consensus and commitment via participation. Four rules must be followed for a truly effective brainstorm session:

- Quantity versus quality: The more ideas, the greater the likelihood of finding a useful one.
- Free-wheeling thinking: Open the gate and allow ideas to freely flow; build on the ideas even if they seem wild or outrageous.
- Defer judgment: The surest way to shut down creative thinking is to judge each idea. Brainstorming is thinking imaginatively, not choosing suitable ideas.
- Hitchhike: If the idea flow stops, try making more out of what has already been said, changing it a little, adding to it. For example, if a client meeting was suggested, add ideas for structuring it. Voila, a new idea!

## *Useful Brainstorming Steps*

- Frame a session with an idea-seeking question (what are all the ways . . .) or by posting a general question or topic where everyone can see it.
- Clearly state purpose (to generate a storm of ideas) and brainstorming rules.
- Establish a time limit, usually twenty to thirty minutes.
- Try a round-robin to encourage participation, allowing members to pass or "green light" participants to speak in any order that naturally occurs.
- Encourage participants to build on others' ideas.
- Post all ideas.
- Allow no evaluation, criticism, or discussion while ideas are generated; do not allow comments that kill ideas.
- Allow participants time to think. Do not allow a lull in the idea storm stop the session.
- After all ideas have been generated, reduce the list by questioning, categorizing, and consolidating.

Remember: the goal is to think creatively and view a problem from a new perspective. The Nobel Prize winning physician, Albert Szent-Gyorgyi, said, "Discovery consists of looking at the same thing as everyone else and thinking something different." Another creative genius, Albert Einstein, said that, "Problems cannot be solved at the same level of consciousness that created them." Before generating ideas, try some creativity exercises. When generating ideas, avoid mental locks ("I already have the answer"). The table that follows lists common mental locks and possible techniques to overcome them.

| *Mental Lock* | *Consider* |
|---|---|
| The right answer | There is often more than one right answer. |
| That's not logical | Excessive logical thinking can short-circuit your creative process—be curious, look for surprises. |
| Follow the rules | Challenge the rules. "Slaying sacred cows makes great steaks" according to philosopher Dick Nicolosi. |
| Be practical | Ask "what-if" questions. Use them as stepping stones. |
| Play is frivolous | Use play to fertilize your thinking. Make a game of it. |
| That's not my idea | Specialization limits you. Develop an explorer's attitude. Leave your own turf. |
| Don't be foolish | Foolish thinking can get you out of a rut. |
| Avoid ambiguity | Too much specificity can stifle your imagination. |
| To err is wrong | Don't be afraid to fail. Inventor Grace Hopper said, "A ship in port is safe, but that's not what ships are built for." |
| I'm not creative | Believe in the worth of your ideas. |
| I don't have time | You don't have time not to. |

### *Solution Selection*

The goal at this point is to narrow the list of ideas into feasible, creative, and win–win alternatives. Using an objective, criterion-based method to select ideas will facilitate the decision-making process because the terms for reaching consensus have been defined. The process therefore becomes fact-based and less emotionally charged.

Establishing objective criteria is similar to judging a sporting event. Olympic judges use consistent, objective criteria to evaluate performances and select winners. In addition to establishing criteria, you may want to prioritize them. For example, some criteria may be mandatory and some optional. Another technique is setting acceptable ranges. For example, if an idea meets fewer than 80% of the criteria, it is removed from the running. If no clear winner emerges, identify the best and worst outcomes and/or the pros and cons for each idea. Another method is to validate a proposed practice with stakeholders or peers. For a final check, ask the following:

- Is the best practice or alternative based on good, sound reasoning and data?
- Were the right people involved in the problem-solving process?

This roadmap will help you create new knowledge that will improve your job, the overall performance of your organization, and the jobs of peers in other organizations.

### Knowledge Capture

All new knowledge or best practices generated by a community should be presented with certain specific pieces of information. Readers with questions about written material should be encouraged to call the point of contact (originator) or community members to gain better understanding of the topic. Knowledge information should include

- Date prepared
- Point of contact (name, organization, and contact information)
- Members who participated in developing project and their contact information
- Problem statement
- Background describing research conducted during the exploration phase and a summary of significant findings, including findings from root cause analysis
- Alternatives considered; list significant ideas considered and explain reasons for rejection

For a best practice, provide sufficient information to ensure clarity. If additional materials (models, business rules, etc.) were developed, include them. Consider how graphics could enhance knowledge transfer.

## Learning History: Overview

A learning history is a retrospective covering significant events in an organization's recent past described by people who took part in them. Based on a series of reflective interviews, a learning history uses feedback from employees at all levels to help an organization evaluate its progress. This tool goes beyond simply gathering best practices and lessons learned. A learning history

- Provides the time and space for participants to openly reflect on learning from the initiative or exercise
- Enhances the reflection process so that team members make new connections and see how their actions ultimately produce final outcomes
- Gathers information from a variety of perspectives to reduce bias
- Analyzes data to elicit key themes
- Contains accurate, validated information
- Uses the words of participants, not paraphrases of consultants
- Provides a vehicle to promote discussion among participants

## *Approach*

A learning history is a structured process for gathering information related to a project, mission, or initiative. The steps to create a learning history are depicted in Figure B.2.

### Step 1: Select interview candidates

Interview candidates are selected to give a variety of perspectives. The selection of interview candidates through a thorough learning history should include those who initiated, participated in, or were affected by the project in any way.

### Step 2: Conduct interviews

Interviews may be conducted in person or by telephone if an in-person interview is not possible. An interview generally lasts about forty-five minutes. It is advisable to use the same interviewers to ensure consistency. The interviews should be reflective and allow an interview candidate to speak freely without the constraints of a structured interview. No more than six general questions should be prepared. Additional questions should develop during the interview to yield more specific information based on responses to prepared questions. General interview questions might include

- What was your role in the exercise or initiative?
- How would you judge the success of the initiative?
- What would you do differently if you could?
- What are your recommendations for other people who may pursue a similar project?
- What innovative methods were developed or could have been developed?

### Step 3: Record and transcribe interviews

Interviews are recorded to ensure the accuracy of quotes used in the learning history. Interviews are transcribed to enable analysis of the data obtained.

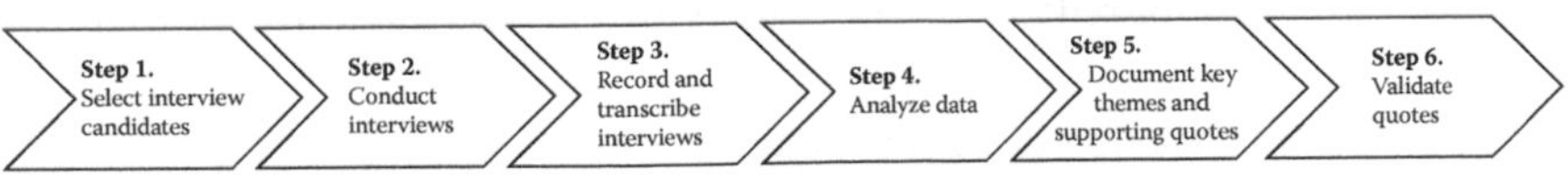


**Figure B.2 Gathering information for learning history.**

### Step 4: Analyze data

Interview data should be sorted and analyzed to identify themes and sub-themes. Quotes are identified to support the major themes from balanced perspectives.

### Step 5: Document key themes and supporting quotes

This step requires assembly and recording of the themes and supporting quotes into the right-hand column of the history document (see next section on format). The quotes do not have to follow a particular order; they should provide a picture of the theme from the various perspectives of the interview candidates.

Now develop the left-hand column of each section for additions of commentaries and potential questions related to the adjacent quotes. The left-hand column commentary does not reflect the questions asked during the interview; it includes comments, questions, and conclusions posed by the author of the document to foster further reflection by readers.

### Step 6: Validate quotes

The final interview step is validating quotes cited in the learning history with the interview candidates. Although interviews were recorded and quotes appear as anonymous in the history, validation ensures that they were not taken out of context and truly represent the intent of the speaker. Quotes are sent to each interviewee for correction and a signature indicating approval.

## *Format of Learning History Document*

Part 1 describes the theme and related practices of successful organizations.

Part 2 presents quotes describing the theme in the right-hand column. The quotes presented in the learning history are not inclusive; they represent selections of quotes illustrating the perspectives of interview candidates and information gathered through the interview process.

The left-hand column of the document does not list questions asked during the interview, but records commentary and questions posed to the reader by the author for further consideration when reading the document. The commentary on the left relates to the adjacent quote or quotes. The commentary is presented to provide the reader with ideas for reflection. The readers are encouraged to record their own thoughts and questions as they read.

Part 3: The final section of the theme is a summary of the key points from the quotes in Part 2. Questions for further consideration relating to the theme are presented at the end of this section.

The format of each section is depicted below:

| Theme title | |
|---|---|
| Part 1: Overview (theme, practices of other organizations) | |
| Part 2: Analysis of interview responses | |
| Commentary, conclusions, potential questions relating to adjacent quotes | Quotes that represent key responses to interview questions |
| Part 3: Brief summary of quotes heard during interview; additional questions to provide clarity to theme | |

## *Use of Storytelling*

Storytelling, the construction of fictional examples to illustrate a point, can effectively transfer knowledge. An organizational story is a detailed narrative of management actions, employee interactions, or other internal events that are communicated informally inside the organization.

A variety of story forms exist naturally and include scenarios and anecdotes. Scenarios articulate possible future states based on the imaginative limits of the author. While scenarios may illustrate alternatives and are valuable simply for that reason, they may also be used as planning tools for possible future situations. The plan becomes a vehicle for responding to recognized objectives in a scenario. An anecdote is a brief sequence captured in the field or arising from a brainstorming session. To reinforce positive behavior, sensitive managers can seek out and disseminate true anecdotes that embody the values of an organization. The capture and distribution of anecdotes across organizations has great value. Based on a critical number of anecdotes captured from a community, a set of values or rules underlying the behavior of the community can be determined. Understanding these values allows utilization of informal and formal aspects of the organization.

Conveying information in a story provides a rich context that remains in the conscious memory and creates more memory traces than information not in context. A story is more likely to be acted upon than normal means of communications. Storytelling in a personal or organizational setting connects people, develops creativity, and increases confidence. The use of stories by organizations can build descriptive capabilities, increase organizational learning, convey complex meanings, and communicate common values and rule sets.

Stories increase our descriptive capabilities—a strength in this age of uncertainty that requires us to describe our environments and acquire the self-awareness to describe our individual capabilities. Description capabilities are essential in strategic thinking and planning, and enhance awareness of what may be achieved. Fictional stories can be powerful because they provide a mechanism by which an organization can learn from failure without attributing blame. Some organizations actually create characters from archetypes taken from a large number of anecdotes and use and reuse the characters that eventually become natural vehicles for organizational learning and repositories for organizational memory.

A well-constructed story can convey a high level of complex meaning. The use of sub-text can convey this meaning without making it obvious. A sub-text is an unstated (not explicit) message in the dialogue of a story. Analogies are often used to help transfer complex information and give the human mind something to relate to. This form of learning has been used throughout history to transfer complex concepts and core values.

Finally, because stories communicate common values and rule systems, they provide mechanisms to build organic organizational responses to emerging requirements. As new situations and challenges arise in response to an ever-changing world, a common set of values will drive responses at every level of the organization. Snowden explains that to operate in a highly uncertain environment, we must have common values and rule systems that support networks of communities self-organizing around a common purpose. Stories act as a catalyst to that process. Snowden states that old skills such as stories and other models drawn from organic rather than mechanical thinking are survival skills, not "nice-to-haves."

The World Bank has used what it calls a springboard story in recent years to transform itself into a knowledge organization. The springboard story, a powerful method of communicating knowledge about norms and values, is a transformational tool that enables a listener to take a personal leap in understanding how an organization, community, or complex system may change. The intent of this type of story is not to transfer information, but to serve as a catalyst for creating understanding by a listener. These stories enable listeners to easily and quickly grasp ideas as a whole in a nonthreatening way. In effect, they invite listeners to see analogies from their own histories, their own contexts, and their own fields of expertise.

Springboard stories are told from the perspective of a single protagonist known to the audience and in the predicament cited in the story. Elements or strangeness or incongruity to the listeners help capture their attention and imagination. The story must have a degree of plausibility and a prediction about the future. And a happy ending. Happy endings make it easier for listeners to take imaginative leaps from the explicit story to the implicit meaning.

The Internet and intranets provide more opportunities to use stories to bring about change. Electronic media add moving images and sound as context setters. Hypertext capabilities and collaboration software invite groups, teams, and communities to co-create their stories. New multiprocessing skills are required to navigate this new world, skills such as quick and sure assimilation of and response to fast-flowing images, sounds, and sensory assaults.

## *Interview Guidelines*

These guidelines serve as a reference for conducting interviews to gather information effectively. Certain steps should be followed.

### Prepare

- Determine purpose of interview and types of information to be collected.
- Identify the categories of interview questions (knowledge requirements, knowledge sharing and interaction, knowledge exchange).
- Specify data necessary to meet objectives of interview.
  - Attempt to meet at interview candidate's workspace in case he or she must access data located there.
  - Notify candidate in advance of your data requirements.
- Ask open-ended questions: How can the process be improved?
- Ensure clarity of meaning by eliminating ambiguity How would you rate the professionalism of your staff? [*Professionalism* can have various meanings.]
- Keep questions simple: State whether you agree or disagree that "Our staff was both fast and friendly."
- Avoid biased questions that may be difficult to detect and hinder insight: Do you wish me to pass any compliments on to our CEO?

### Conduct interview

- Introduce yourself, your objective, and the agenda of the interview.
- Determine whether an interviewee has his or her own objectives for the interview or KCO implementation. The interviewee's objectives are important because you can use them to motivate or enable the implementation of the KCO in the organization.
- Ask whether the interviewee has any general questions about the project.
- Explain how the information gathered will be used.
- Put the interviewee at ease about note-taking by explaining that the notes will serve as references about subjects discussed. Try to capture exact wording, particularly if you think it may be very important. Ensure understanding throughout the interview and paraphrase statements to indicate you understood what the interviewee said.
- Utilize the funnel technique to move from general ideas to detail. Start with broad questions: Tell me about.... Describe.... Then seek more detail: Who? What? When? Where? How? Proceed to very detailed questions that require yes or no answers to verify information.

## Post-interview

Document your finding as soon as possible and follow up with the interviewee to clarify areas of uncertainty.

Send the interviewee a summary of his or her comments (if relevant) to confirm what you heard and how you interpreted an interview statement.

## Ladder of inference

The ladder of inference is a model that describes an individual's mental process of observing situations, drawing conclusions, and taking action. When we say, "The fact is . . ." we really mean, "The fact, as I understand it based upon my data selection process, cultural and personal background, judgments, beliefs, and assumptions is . . ." Why is this distinction important? Many steps occur between acquiring data and taking action based on the data. By allowing others to explore our thinking processes, we may reveal more effective and higher leverage solutions.

After an event, human mental processing immediately screens out a certain percentage of the data. In other words, our mental vision is naturally blurred and absorbs only a certain amount of the data representing a life event. When we look at the data we collected, we attach our own personal meanings and cultural biases to it. Thus, no data is pure; it is influenced by the person who analyzes it. Based on meanings we attach to data collected, we make inferences or judgments and arrive at conclusions and the process influences behavior. A single bit of data can produce as many different conclusions as there are people analyzing it. Over time, the conclusions we reach from an event or pattern of events develop our belief systems. We become fixated on certain ways of viewing how the world works, creating our own mental models that reappear every time an event takes place.

All too often, people fall into the "competency trap"—a problem-solving routine that succeeded initially and is used over and over with little regard for how accurately it fits a current problem. The ladder of inference provides an easy tool for breaking out of the trap. Simply ask, "What assumptions am I making about this particular situation that may limit my deeper understanding of the problem?" As we work to clarify a problem, we may be able to reframe it. The ladder of inference helps us understand why it is important to make our reasoning steps explicit. By consciously reviewing the data that supports our conclusions, we can improve our ability to explore complex problems and not jump to conclusions based on incomplete data.

People often behave defensively by trying to control situations and never saying, "I don't know." A tool that allows us to say, "As I understand what you're saying, x leads to y, which results in z. Am I on track with your thinking?" prevents us from trying to defuse complex issues and trying to cover up our lack of information. When people in organizations jointly practice skilled incompetence, the result is the formation of defensive routines. A mutually acceptable tool allows us to analyze someone's thinking without resorting to rudeness.

A very powerful application of the ladder of inference is to introduce it at the beginning of a project. When team members commit to individually and collectively examine their beliefs and assumptions and make them explicit, a great deal of time spent arguing and going around in circles can be eliminated.

## Left-Hand Column

The left-hand column is the basic premise that two conversations actually take place when people talk. One conversation is explicit and consists of the words spoken throughout the exchange between two or more persons. The other conversation involves what the individuals are thinking and feeling but not saying. The "left-hand column" term was derived from an exercise designed to explore what was thought about but not said in the course of a conversation. It is a tool for studying conversations so that we can redesign them to be more effective in creating the results we want. People need an introduction to this tool before they can begin using it effectively in a team situation. The following is an exercise for introducing it to a team.

**Step 1: Choosing a problem** — Select a difficult problem you encountered during the last month or two. Write a brief paragraph describing it. What were you trying to accomplish? Who or what blocked you? What might happen? Perhaps the rest of the organization resisted your idea, or you believe they will resist a change you want to implement, or your team is paying too little attention to the most crucial problem

**Step 2: Right-hand column (what was said)** — Recall a frustrating conversation you had about the problem. Take several pieces of paper and draw lines down the centers. In the right-hand column, write the statements made in the conversation that occurred or write a conversation you're pretty sure *would have* occurred occur if you raised this issue. The discussion may go on for several pages. Leave the left-hand column blank at this point.

**Step 3: Left-hand column (what you were thinking)** — Use the left-hand column to describe what you thought and felt but did not say.

**Step 4: Individual reflection (using left-hand column as resource)** — You can learn a lot simply from writing about a case, putting the writing away for a week, and then looking at it again. As you reflect, ask yourself several questions:

- What led me to think and feel this way?
- How might my comments have contributed to the difficulties?
- Why didn't I say what was in my left-hand column?
- What assumptions am I making about the other person or people?
- How can I use my left-hand column as a resource to improve our communications?

**Step 5: Pair or small group discussion** — Pairs or small groups review one or more of the left-hand columns written in Step 3. The conversation should focus on exploring the assumptions behind both speakers' words, discussing alternative ways in which the participant could have conducted the conversation so that he or she would have been more satisfied with the outcome.

## Action Learning

### Overview

Action learning is a new way of approaching learning. It is a very simple concept revolving around the ability of people to learn by doing. Put simply, action learning involves the formation of a small group of people who share common issues, goals, or learning needs. The group or action learning set works to resolve issues and achieve goals together, meeting regularly, about once a month, to reflect on progress, issues, and solutions and refine the way forward. The team brainstorms alternative approaches and offers advice as needed for achieving specific goals. Action learning emphasizes trying new things and evaluating the results. Action learning is cyclical. It consists of six steps: (1) identifying the task and learning opportunity, (2) planning together, (3) doing, (4) reflecting, (5) sharing learning, and (6) closing out.

#### Identifying task and learning opportunity

Determine the objectives of the action learning program. Form the action learning set. Discuss with the team the development needs and job challenges that may be addressed by action learning. Not all set members will have the same development needs but their needs should be similar. It is important for the group to understand the development needs of the individual members and the development needs of the group as a whole. An action learning set ideally consists of five to eight people to encourage discussion during sessions. Someone should be assigned to facilitate the group meetings, asking questions to draw out the key learning points. Define how often the group will meet and set ground rules for meetings. Identify any subject matter experts who might talk to the group.

#### Planning together

The official start of an action learning program should be a start-up workshop held ideally off site to allow participants to avoid the usual distractions of the workplace. Included in the agenda for the workshop should be time for the following activities:

- Developing personal learning plans and a common view of the purpose of the action learning set.
- Declaring individual objectives for membership of the set and identifying medium- and short-term actions to progress toward the objectives. Set

members should be asked how they will know when objectives have been reached or how will they plan to measure progress.
- Identifying opportunities to apply new ideas and learning points in the workplace.
- Introduction to the practice of reflection and keeping a learning log to capture key learning activities and progress.
- Reviewing at the end of a session what went well and what could be done to improve the format for future sessions.

## Doing

Doing is time spent working on a task. The members of the action learning set spend time experimenting with new approaches and testing new ideas developed during their meetings, all with the aim of making progress on a problem, project, or issue of importance. The following instructions apply to this phase:

- Refer back to the action plans developed during the planning workshop.
- Before taking action, reflect on what you think the outcome will be. If possible, record the expected outcome in the learning log.
- Take action. Try the approach as planned. This is where you do your normal work with the added benefit of advanced planning and documenting your expectations before you act.
- Look for evidence of how effective you have been. What did you observe?
- Note your observations in the learning log. This creates opportunities to learn by reflecting on observations made by you and others and discussing them at the next set meeting.

## Reflecting

Reflection takes place at a regular session in which members of the action learning set meet to consider their progress. It is a time for challenging assumptions, exploring new ways of thinking about problems, and planning what to do next. It is also an opportunity for set members to bring up specific issues of their work that they would like others to think through and also offer their support for exploring the issues and problems raised by others.

- Plan reflection sessions on a regular basis and as far in advance as possible to ensure maximum attendance.
- Book enough time to allow thorough exploration of issues of importance. Try thirty minutes per person plus an extra thirty minutes as an estimate when planning reflection sessions.
- Make sure that participants have prepared for reflection by updating learning logs and notifying the facilitator of any key issues they wish to discuss.

- The facilitator should ensure that all members declare what actions they intend to take after they leave the reflection session and what outcomes they expect from these actions.

## Sharing

This is where new knowledge, skills, and experiences can be shared beyond the action learning set to allow other individuals and teams to benefit. Capturing the knowledge from an action learning experience contributes to the intellectual capital of the organization. As new knowledge is added to the KCO website over time, users will find more content that is timely and applicable to their current learning needs.

- Newsgroup and/or threaded discussion features can be included on the KCO website to allow action learning set members to collaborate online. This can open up the set to allow others to see what is being achieved.
- The KCO website should keep a running list of all action learning sets. Each entry should list basic information about the members, the set's objectives, meeting schedules, and contact information for the set facilitator.
- Some action learning sets may decide to create a learning history to describe the day-to-day work of the team and attempt to capture the evolution of learning during the project.
- At the conclusion of the action learning set, the team members and their facilitator select the information from their experience that others may find valuable and post it to the KCO website. Suggested topics include objectives, conclusions, recommendations, experts consulted, and planning documents such as agendas.

### *Closing Out*

The purpose of a close-out event is to ensure that the action learning set reflects on the time spent together and reviews the progress made against the original objectives. The close-out session is facilitated in the same way as regular reflection sessions and includes the administrative tasks associated with disbanding the set. The most important task is deciding which resources and learning points are to be shared with the rest of the organization.

- Plan the event to allow time to reflect on both the tasks performed between sessions and the individual and team learning throughout the process.
- Before the close-out, all set members should be asked to share their reflections. The facilitator may choose to issue a structured questionnaire for this use. What has become clearer to you since the start of the action learning program? How has your perspective of the task or problem changed during the time you spent as a member? What were the defining moments of the set? At what points did major breakthroughs take place?

## *Relationship Building Exercises*

**Title of exercise:** Brain writing
**Purpose:** Collaborate on an idea or issue that may involve sensitivities or conflicts; gather ideas and opinions in a nonthreatening manner
**Group size:** 4 to 8 people in situations where ideas or working are important; up to 20 people if intent is to gather ideas and opinions
**Estimated time:** 4 to 8 people: 10 minutes; up to 20 people: 20 minutes to write and 10 minutes to discuss
**Props:** Blank paper and writing utensils for all participants

1. Pose or frame a question, issue, or problem facing the group. Ask each person to start writing at the top of the paper:
   - An answer (if a question is posed)
   - A resolution (if an issue is presented)
   - An idea (if a problem is confronted)
   - Proposed wording (if a mission or other statement is being crafted)
2. Ask each person to pass his or her paper to the person on the left.
3. Each person should comment on the paper in front of him or her by rewriting a suggestion below the original or stating his or her opinion of the suggestion. When complete, the paper is passed to the person on the left.
4. The comment and rewrite process should continue until the papers return to their originators.
5. Discuss the findings. Most often, consensus will have built around a small number of suggestions, thus narrowing the discussion field.

**Variations** — If ideas have already been generated, post each one on a sheet of flip-chart paper and hang the papers around the room. Give people markers and have them travel around the room to write comments about as many items as desired. When the activity dies down, review each chart to determine whether the comments led to a common conclusion.

*Tips: Suggest that people use checkmarks to indicate agreement with a idea. This technique may be used to assess group opinion and narrow the field prior to voting.*

**Title of exercise:** What's the moral of the story?
**Purpose:** Sift through information to derive lessons learned
**Group size:** 8 to 20 people
**Estimated time:** 8 to 10 minutes
**Props:** Fables

1. Ask participants to pair up.
2. Distribute fables.

3. Explain that fables and folktales are short fictional narratives that illustrate morals or lessons. A fable is an indirect way to tell truths about life and thus has a level of meaning beyond the surface story.
4. Give the pairs five minutes to read two fables and add a humorous moral to each fable.
5. After five minutes, ask members to discuss possible morals to the stories.

**Variation** — Use fables without known morals and ask the group to develop morals.

*Tip: The following fables from Aesop are suggested.*

**The cock and the jewel** — A cock scratching for food for himself and his hens found a precious stone and exclaimed: "If your owner had found thee, and not I, he would have taken thee up, and have set thee in thy first estate; but I have found thee for no purpose. I would rather have one barleycorn than all the jewels in the world." *Moral: The ignorant despise what is precious only because they cannot understand it.*

**The crow and the pitcher** — A crow perishing with thirst saw a pitcher and, hoping to find water, flew to it with delight. When he reached it, he discovered to his grief that it contained so little water that he could not possibly reach it. He tried everything he could think of to reach the water, but all his efforts were in vain. At last he collected as many stones as he could carry and dropped them with his beak into the pitcher, until he brought the water within his reach and thus saved his life. *Moral: Necessity is the mother of invention.*

**The ass and his shadow** — A traveler hired an ass to convey him to a distant place. The day was intensely hot and the sun was strong. The traveler stopped to rest, and sought shelter from the heat under the shadow of the ass. The shadow afforded protection for only one person. The traveler and the owner of the ass both claimed the space. A violent dispute concerned which of them had the right to the shadow. The owner maintained that he had rented only the ass and not the ass' shadow. The traveler asserted that the hire of the ass included the ass' shadow. The quarrel proceeded from words to blows and while the men fought, the ass galloped off. *Moral: In quarreling about the shadow, we often lose the substance.*

**Title of exercise:** New product offering
**Purpose:** Allow members to "see things differently" and better understand varying perspectives members bring to the community
**Group size:** 8 to 24 people
**Estimated time:** 30 minutes; varies with number of sub-groups
**Props:** Common object such as a feather duster, stapler, or yoyo

1. Explain to the group that the object they see before them can be anything except what it is. Their job is to name the product, describe its uses, create a marketing strategy including price, and present their new product to the community.
2. Organize participants into sub-groups of three to five members.
3. Allow the subgroups to develop their ideas and practice their presentations (about twenty minutes).
4. Each sub-group introduces its new product offering to the group.

*Tip: Lead the group in clapping after each performance.*

## Purpose of Systems Thinking

As a tool for collective inquiry and coordinated action, systems thinking

- Fosters team learning and collaboration
- Tells compelling stories that describe how the system works
- Discovers the system structures behind problems
- Describes our mental models and those of others about why a system performs as it does
- Tests possible strategies against intended results and for unintended consequences
- Identifies higher leverage interventions

Systems thinking enables us to

- Understand how organizations and other complex systems really function
- Change our own thinking to match the ways such systems operate
- Change behaviors to work with instead of against complex forces to create what we want
- Develop greater appreciation for the impact of our strategies on others in the system
- Understand impacts of time delays and the need to balance short- and long-term objectives and strategies
- Anticipate unintended consequences of well-intentioned strategies

Systems thinking is composed of several steps:

1. State the issue and tell the story. Begin your inquiry with the evidence. What facts convince you and others that there is an issue?
2. Graph performance patterns over time. What are the trends?
3. Establish creative tension and draft a focusing question. When a trend is visible, we can state how this reality differs from our vision. A good focusing

question describes the patterns in the context of what we want. For example, why, despite our efforts to improve quality, do we continue to miss deadlines?
4. Identify structural explanations. What are key causes and consequences of the trends we observe? How do the consequences, particularly our own responses, become the causes of more problems?
5. Apply the going-deeper questions. What are the deeper structures that keep this set of causes and consequences in place? Does this system successfully accomplish a purpose other than the stated one? Are beliefs and values causing the situation to persist?
6. Plan an intervention: Based on our understanding of the structure, what is our hypothesis about how to change it? What general approaches are needed? What specific actions?
7. Assess results. Because our intervention is based on a theory of the situation, the results of our attempts to improve things provide new data, allowing us to repeat the steps if necessary.

Systems thinking usually adds value when situations are problematic, long-standing, and resistant to intervention or change. Systems thinking is often helpful as a planning resource. A systems view can help planning for growth, anticipate limits to growth, predict and avoid actions that can undermine partnerships, and avoid "shooting yourself in the foot" by producing a worse situation than you already have.

Systems thinking rarely helps us find a single right answer; other problem-solving tools are more efficient for problems that truly have only one answer. Systems thinking provides the most value when it illuminates possible choices embedded in complex, divergent problems, and their likely consequences. The final choice is ours.

Use systems thinking to

- Identify or clarify a problem.
- Increase creative discussion.
- Promote inquiry and challenge preconceived ideas.
- Determine validities of multiple perspectives.
- Make assumptions explicit.
- Sift out major issues and factors.
- Find systemic causes of stubborn problems.
- Test the viabilities of previously proposed solutions.
- Explore short- and long-term impacts of alternative or newly proposed solutions.

Do not use systems thinking to

- Impress people or win an argument.
- Validate prior views.
- Hide uncertainties.
- Impose blame.

**Comparison Traditional Approach and Systems Thinking**

| *Traditional Approach* | *Systems Thinking* |
|---|---|
| Connection between problems and their causes is obvious and easy to trace. | Relationship between problems and their causes is indirect, not obvious. |
| Others (within or outside organization) are to blame for problems; they must change. | We unwittingly create our own problems and have significant control or influence in solving them by changing our behavior. |
| Policy designed to achieve short-term success will also assure long-term success. | Most quick fixes make no long-term difference or make matters worse in the long run. |
| To optimize the whole, we must optimize the parts. | Focus on policies that optimize the whole rather than individual parts. |
| Aggressively tackle many independent initiatives simultaneously. | Target and orchestrate a few key changes over time. |

# 4 Building Knowledgebase

## *Purpose*

Provide a framework for building your community's knowledge base.

## *Expected Outcomes*

- Establish knowledge inventory and folder structure.
- Develop process for capturing documents for content management systems.
- Devise framework to continually improve business processes leveraging lessons learned and reusing best practices.
- Identify target efficiencies in mission-related measures such as cycle time, customer service, and total ownership cost.

## *Roles and Responsibilities*

A CoP's knowledge base requires specific roles to ensure successful implementation. The roles were discussed in detail in Section 2 and are listed below:

- Community sponsor
- Community leader

- Community members
- Facilitator
- Logistics coordinator

## Products

- Requirements traceability matrix (RTM) of groupware functions on which the CoP will focus for its first release of the knowledge base
- List of identified community media (documents, presentations, spreadsheets, etc.) that cites specific documents
- List of folders for organizing community media
- Graphical model and supporting narrative of as-is media flow between the community and stakeholder organizations
- List of community members and folders assigned to them for life-cycle development
- Groupware electronic repository containing all functions listed in the RTM, all identified media, and completed folder structure (media will have been migrated to groupware application per assigned folder structure)
- List of asset rules to ensure that all groupware transactions are consistent across CoP
- Graphical model and supporting narrative of projected media flow between community and stakeholder organizations that includes list of business performance measures and expected efficiencies (e.g., cycle time = 8 weeks; goal = 4-week reduction)

## Key Tasks

- **Requirements**: Map identified collaborative tool functions to business requirements to simplify deployment, narrow training scope, and ensure more efficient use of groupware.
- **Inventory**: Define knowledge assets in a business process context and identify whether created by the community or borrowed from other business owners.
- **Taxonomy**: Develop business context classification structure for organizing inventory that should provide an intuitive navigation scheme for members and other interested communities
- **Flow Model**: Model as-is business processes based on flow of inventory assets to and from customers. Focus on how assets are created and disseminated.
- **Migrate**: Provide necessary technical support to migrate existing inventory assets in legacy repositories. Inventory should be organized, classified as relevant, and mapped to a classification owner. Owners are typically subject matter experts within the community.
- **Map**: Identify owners of inventory folders and designate life-cycle responsibility at folder structure level.

- **Asset Rules**: Establish business rules for the use of the groupware to maintain consistency during business transactions. Designate groupware functionalities to be used to process specific transactions.
- **Transformation**: Identify, in priority order (high value–low risk), business processes that provide the best value based on customer service, cycle time reduction, and total ownership cost. Members should focus on measures that correlate to related business performance measures.
- **Training**: Secure computer-training facilities to allow hands-on training for members. Transformed business processes will be simulated in a training environment for user testing and acceptance.
- **Help Desk**: Enable a functional help desk specifically for community members.

## *Key Task 1: Requirements*

### Narrow functional scope of groupware application

### Base assessment on past experience and lessons learned

This task should narrow the functional scope of the selected groupware application to only those functions that allow achievement of mission-related measures (e.g., reduction in cycle time). Conduct a functional analysis of each specific groupware application. At a minimum, the analysis should include (1) function name, (2) function description, and (3) release details.

List all functions that the groupware application can perform (e.g., adding new documents). This list should not include extended or custom functionalities. Focus only on the base functionality of the groupware.

After a list is prepared, convene the members to review the list. Leaders should try to achieve consensus about functions that meet the general requirements of the community's needs for inclusion in the first release of the knowledge base. Enter 1 for release if the community requires the function in the first release. Enter 2 or 3 if the community feels that a specific function may be postponed to a later release. The community is expected to base its function decisions on lessons learned and past experiences.

### Work product: Requirements traceability matrix

Excel spreadsheet containing: REQ ID, REQUIREMENT (or function name), DESCRIPTION, RELEASE (version of implementation that will contain the corresponding function), NEW or EXISTING, FULL/PARTIAL, COMMENTS, DOCUMENTS.

### *Key Task 2: Inventory*

#### Inventory all community media

#### Conduct both group and individual inventories

An inventory allows members to identify all media associated with established business processes. With the help of a facilitator or community leader, convene a session of community members and brainstorm media that serve as inputs or outputs of the community's business processes. After the list is developed, assign each member the responsibility of reviewing the baseline list and adding media not captured during the session. Compile the baseline list along with the individual inputs from members. This will serve as the community's baseline inventory.

#### Work Product: Inventory list

Excel spreadsheet containing ASSET ID#, NAME, DESCRIPTION, BEST PRACTICE, RECORDS MANAGEMENT META DATA.

### *Key Task 3: Taxonomy*

#### Build group and individual lists

#### Consolidate lists and assign inventory items to categories

*Tip: Limit consolidated list to about nine categories; limit sub-categories to three levels.*

The objective of taxonomy building is devising an intuitive structure for users who want to obtain information from or contribute to a community's practice. First, convene the community to brainstorm a list of categories based on the prepared inventory list to develop as complete a list as possible. Disregard the length of the list. The list can be finalized at a separate session. After the group has developed a list, distribute it to members and have them assess it. They may add, consolidate, or recommend deletions. Community leaders will consolidate the group and individual lists into a single list. When that is completed, begin assigning inventory items to their respective categories.

#### Work product: Taxonomy list

Excel spreadsheet containing FOLDER ID #, CATEGORY, LEVEL, OWNERS, STATUS, DESCRIPTION, and REVISION NOTES.

## *Key Task 4: Flow Model*

Easy way to identify business processes

Layout stakeholder organizations

Illustrate inventory path between community and stakeholder

Model all core processes and associated inventory

Flow modeling is intended to graphically illustrate how inventory items are transferred between organizations as business transactions are conducted. The model view will allow easy identification of as-is business processes. To begin, model the organizations involved in the inventory exchange as depicted in Figure B.3. Using the baseline inventory list, illustrate how each item travels between community and organization. Some inventory items may traverse several paths between organization and community until the business process cycle is completed.

The as-is flow model is complete when each of the inventory items has been illustrated on the model (Figure B.4). The leader then writes a narrative that describes the paths of community inventory items. A member should write a narrative incorporating details that are not readily apparent within the model.

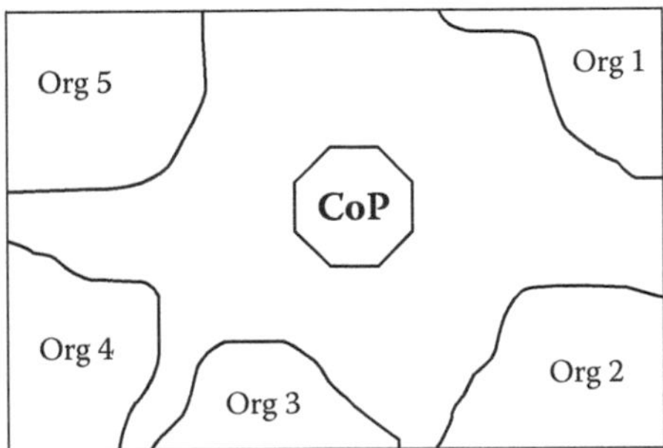


**Figure B.3 Sample flow model.**

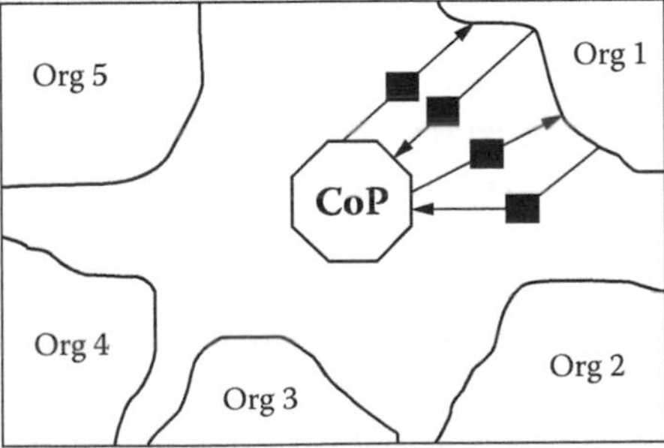


**Figure B.4 Sample flow model with path example.**

### Work products: As-is model and narrative

The narrative describes the business processes and the knowledge assets transacted by the processes. It should also describe the community, stakeholders or customers, and direction flows of assets between services and customers.

## *Key Task 5: Map*

### Community members share the responsibility of maintaining community workspace

### Assign primary and alternate members to folders

Mapping provides a means for the community to maintain its data. Members should be designated as points of contact for specific categories of data within the knowledge base. All members must participate in the maintenance and upkeep of the community locale. Likewise, the groupware community will share the responsibility of maintaining its community.

Mapping is a relatively quick and informal process. Convene a meeting of community members. Using the established taxonomy list, have members volunteer for folders that fall within their areas of responsibility. Record these assignments in the ASSIGNED OWNER column of the taxonomy list. Additionally, have members volunteer to serve as alternate points of contact for specific folders so that each folder will have two community members familiar with its structure, content, and access privileges.

### Work product

See taxonomy list (Key Task 3). Excel spreadsheet containing ASSET CLASSIFICATIONS and ASSIGNED OWNER.

## *Key Task 6: Migration*

Migration of data is important for demonstrating the capabilities of the groupware application and validating work relating to data organizations. Finally, it provides a context for discussing how inventory and taxonomy contribute to the community's business processes. Migration begins with validation of the inventory and taxonomy lists to ensure that results to date accurately reflect the needs of the community. Convene the community and conduct a quick review of both lists. Pay particular attention to inventory items that are not associated to a business process and are not products of the community. Items not associated to a business process may be considered for removal. Items that are not community products may be products of an adjacent community. If so, eliminate the redundancies. After the lists are validated, begin populating the project workspace according to the taxonomy. Data can be populated manually or in batches. Tools are available for large-scale conversions.

### Work product

Tool user accounts for all core group members and operational prototype of current release of collaborative workspace.

## *Key Task 7: Asset Rules*

Asset rules provide members with groupware guidelines for moving data in and out of the knowledge base. They also designate groupware functions for supporting specific transactions in a business processes. An example of an asset rule is using a compound document instead of a folder to collect and present periodic volume releases of a newsletter. In this case, two different groupware functions could be used to achieve similar results. Establishing asset rules provides a consistent means for interacting with the knowledge base.

Sets of asset rules exist for each business process supported. Regardless of process size, rules must be put in place to avoid differences in usage. Asset rules will most commonly be identified with a business process. However, in some cases, specific documents may have their own asset rules. Begin by listing the different processes or documents that will require asset rules and all transactions conducted within the groupware application will require asset rules that provide guidance to the community members. For example, a community maintains a community calendar within its groupware application. The document format of the calendar is a Microsoft Word file. To provide guidance to the community on the use of this document, the following asset rules have been created:

- Calendar must be maintained only by assigned owner.
- Community members who need to add a date will use the groupware's document check-in/check-out function.
- The community will maintain a three-month calendar (one month of past events and two months of future events).
- All community members will create change notifications on the community calendar so that they receive email notifications of calendar updates.

A set of asset rules should be developed for each process or document involved in a community business transaction. Asset rules should be reviewed periodically to ensure applicability and effectiveness.

### Work product: Set of asset rules

Excel spreadsheet containing RULE NUMBER, RULE, DESCRIPTION, REVISION, STATUS, and COMMENTS.

## *Key Task 8: Transformation*

Transformation is key to achieving value from the knowledge base. The use of a knowledge base process implies a transformation of how communities do business. If transformation is not achieved, the community has done no more than increase its burden via another data repository.

To transform, begin by selecting high value–low risk inventories identified in the flow model stage. The flow selection should be based on that which the community believes will yield the best value at the lowest risk to the community's mission. List and prioritize flows to be transformed into the groupware application such that all future transactions relating to the selected process will be conducted via the groupware. After the processes are listed and prioritized based on value and risk, prepare an assessment or gap analysis of the as-is processes and the future processes to include

- List of stakeholders who will be affected by the process change
- Changes (steps required) to complete the process; document the changes
- Measures and metrics for assessing the value achieved by transforming the as-is processes to the groupware application environment
- Document asset rules associated with conducting the process in future (to-be) environment

### Work product: To-be model and narrative

Model and narrative should cover business processes transacted and include a gap analysis identifying changes to as-is model and documented asset rules.

## *Key Task 9: Training*

Training ensures that all community members possess the necessary skills to function in a collaborative work environment. Community leaders should not assume that members understand and can operate within the knowledge base without training and support. Training in this context extends beyond application training. It includes context-based training rooted in business processes, i.e., members are trained to use the groupware application and understand the business processes it supports to ensure training is relevant and immediately applicable.

Training can be accomplished within the community by selecting a training lead among the members. Typically, this person will possess an above-average aptitude for information technology and a good grasp of business processes. The trainer will use the requirements traceability matrix (RTM) developed earlier in the process to design a course for community members. The RTM provides the basis for the training. It lists groupware topics the trainer will cover. The trainer selects the business contexts of the functional topics and should develop a group of use cases or scenarios to show members how the groupware will be utilized within the community's business environment. An example of a use case is updating the group calendar based on the following steps:

- Log in to groupware
- Check out calendar
- Add new calendar entry
- Check in calendar

There is no replacement for hands-on training. Where possible, utilize a training center to deliver training to members. Sessions should be brief and specifically geared to business processes. Training sessions exceeding 1.5 hours are ineffective. If training seems to long, scale back on the coverage areas. Keep training manageable, applicable, short, and enjoyable.

## *Tools*

- Sample Requirements Traceability Matrix
- Sample Taxonomy and Mapping Template
- Sample Asset Rule Template

**Sample Requirements Traceability Matrix**

| *Req ID* | *Requirement* | *Description* | *Release* | *(N)ew/ (E)xisting* | *(F)ull/ (P)artial* | *Source* | *Comments* | *Documents* |
|---|---|---|---|---|---|---|---|---|
| **1.0** | SECURITY | | | | | | | |
| 1.1 | Login | Used to verify user authorization. Also helps keep track of who adds, modifies, views, and accesses content. | 1 | | | | | |
| 1.2 | Change password | Allows users to change secure encrypted password. | 1 | | | | | |
| 1.3 | Logout | Prevents unauthorized access; users are encouraged to log out when finished. | 1 | | | | | |
| **2.0** | SITE SEGMENTS | | | | | | | |
| 2.1 | Enterprise workspace | Central repository of organization's knowledge. Stores documents and other information meant to be generally available. | 1 | | | | | |

| | | | | | | | | |
|---|---|---|---|---|---|---|---|---|
| 2.2 | Project or workgroup workspace | Team collaborative environment for projects to share and exchange specific project-related information. | 1 | | | | | |
| 2.3 | Personal workspace | Allows users to create customized views of personal data, project data, and enterprise data and share workspace with other designated users. | 2 | | | | | |
| **3.0** | NAVIGATION | | | | | | | |
| 3.1 | Standard navigational controls on workspaces | Provides consistent means of navigating site and quick links to specific site content. | 1 | | | | | |
| 3.2 | Provide consistent access to context sensitive help | Makes help link available in every view. | 1 | | | | | |

**Sample Taxonomy and Mapping Template**

| *Folder ID#* | *Category* | *Level* | *Owner(s)–Mapping* | *Status* | *Description* | *Revision Notes* |
|---|---|---|---|---|---|---|
| | | | | | | |
| | | | | | | |
| | | | | | | |
| | | | | | | |
| | | | | | | |
| | | | | | | |
| | | | | | | |

**Sample Asset Rule Template**

| *BR#* | *Business Rule* | *Description* | *Revision* | *Status* | *Comments* |
|---|---|---|---|---|---|
| 1.0 | Update | Classification owners designated as first points of contact have final approval authority over all content posted to assigned area. | 1.0 | A | |
| 2.0 | Event expiration | Dated assets such as event or training schedule items will be scheduled for expiration one day after item date. | 1.0 | A | |
| 3.0 | Periodicity | Update periodicity for an asset will be determined by first and second points of contact assigned to classification area. | 1.0 | A | |
| | | If an asset requires updating, first point of contact will perform update or reset asset periodicity. | | | |
| 4.0 | Gatekeeper | Gatekeeper will have access to all classification areas. Access includes ability to update, delete, restrict access, and renew asset update periodicities. | 1.0 | A | |

# 5 Sustaining Communities

## Purpose

Congratulations! Your community has met and begun to form. The members are working together to develop and share best practices. How do you keep the community moving in a forward direction? How do you keep members coming back for more?

This section is designed to help community leadership assess progress, recognize the natural evolution of community interactions, recognize and reward both individual and community contributions, and continuously foster innovation and growth.

## Expected Outcomes

- Process adjustments
- Continuous infusion of new knowledge

## Key Tasks

- Assess community progress
- Understand community evolution
- Recognize community contribution
- Spark new knowledge creation and sharing

### Key Task 1: Assess Community Progress

After your community is up and running, leadership should periodically review progress. The Community of Practice Early Progress Checklist was introduced in Section 2. This section will expand that tool to assess ongoing community effectiveness. The expanded Community of Practice Regular Progress Checklist is provided at the end of this section.

As the community evolves, so may the strategic objectives of its members' organizations. A community should ask itself whether it satisfied the highest priority knowledge needs. Do remaining needs still reflect strategic objectives? Have our knowledge needs changed? Community members should be polled periodically to gain insights on how they believe the community is performing. Is it serving its members, the organization, and the enterprise?

One relatively simple method to gather member feedback is to facilitate occasional lessons-learned discussions. A template to capture this information was provided in Section 2. A second approach is collecting written responses via a survey. A generic Community Member Satisfaction Survey is provided at the end of this section. The survey should be tailored to your community's purpose and success criteria.

## *Key Task 2: Understand Community Evolution*

Similar to the stages of group development (forming, norming, storming, and performing), communities also undergo evolutionary stages. As communities of practice evolve, their states of development are characterized by different levels of interaction among members and different kinds of activities.

## *Key Task 3: Recognize Community Contribution*

When you reward people for certain behaviors such as sharing knowledge, they will want to continue the behavior. Therefore, developing meaningful rewards is essential to sustaining community goals and achieving a knowledge-centric organization.

### If you use it, say so

Meaningful recognition can come from leadership and from peers. Community members should be encouraged to acknowledge individual and organizational contributions on a personal level. If knowledge culled from the knowledge base is useful to an individual's work, he or she should reach out to the contributor and personally acknowledge the contribution. A simple phone call or email expressing appreciation is sufficient.

### Peer nomination for rewards can be especially valued

People, if properly motivated and encouraged, will freely contribute if they know they are truly adding value to an enterprise. Peer nomination for rewards can be especially valued. An example might be a team of individuals contributing lessons learned on a particular assignment to the knowledge base. A second team utilizes these lessons on a similar assignment, resulting in improved decision-making capability and improved results. They nominate the first team for reward and recognition based on these results.

### Blow your own horn

The community leader and core group should continuously promote and publicize individual and community contributions to organizational goals via newsletters, websites, staff meetings, luncheons, etc. Consider hosting or participating in knowledge fairs to publicize successes.

### Personal acknowledgments from senior leadership

Another mechanism for community leadership recognition of contributors is to inform senior leadership of success stories. The information should be accompanied by a request for a personal note of appreciation to the individuals and/or communities involved to commend their work and acknowledge their contributions to the bottom line.

Incorporate knowledge management expectations into formal performance evaluations and incentive compensation systems. Ernst & Young evaluates its consultants along several dimensions, including their contributions to and utilizations of the knowledge assets of the firm. At Bain, a consulting firm, the partners are evaluated yearly on a number of performance issues, including how much direct help they provide to colleagues. The extent of partners' high-quality personal dialogues can account for as much as one fourth of their annual compensation.

### Not invented here but I did it anyway!

Create a new award that promotes desired behaviors. Texas Instruments (TI) created the NIHBIDIA (Not Invented Here But I Did It Anyway) Award. TI's annual Best Practices Celebration and Sharing Day (all the best practice teams staff booths to publicize and answer questions about their practices) culminates in an award ceremony for organizations that most successfully shared best practices and knowledge and produced great results. The organizations involved receive awards from senior executives for collaborating on exchanges of best practices. The award is highly prestigious at TI because it reinforces the process and the results. Rewards and recognition may be healthy and useful in the early stages of building enthusiasm for transfer, but in the long run to maintain sustainable effort, employees must also find the work rewarding.

## *Key Task 4: Spark New Knowledge Creation and Sharing*

Members should be continuously polled to identify new areas of interest or challenge. As needs evolve, the core group should seek interesting ways to bring knowledge to the community. Be creative by reaching outside the organization for relevant seminars, training opportunities, tours and site visits to relevant operations, and guest speakers.

### If only we knew what we know

Consider sponsoring cross-community forums to gain additional insights. Understanding the purpose and inventories of knowledge assets owned by other communities may help expand your community's knowledge base.

### Look outside for innovations

Most professional disciplines foster relevant publications, websites, associations, and other activities. Who has time to read all the available information? Perhaps your community could assign members to scan specific information sources regularly to cull interesting knowledge nuggets for the benefit of the community. If you have a corporate KM infomediary, use this resource for scanning across knowledge bases to identify valuable and relevant information.

### Don't just stockpile new knowledge in a database

To counter the "if I build it, they will come" mentality, consider other vehicles to "push" knowledge gains throughout an enterprise. As best practices are identified, have them reviewed and edited by professional writers and embed them in various places—training programs, policies and procedures—to cover as many different dimensions of the organization as possible.

### Get to work and start talking

Try to create informal settings for member interactions. Coordinate Bring Your Own Lunch (BYOL) sessions, typically held in a meeting room. This approach to discussion takes little time away from busy schedules. Members can come and go as they please, and prospective members can visit and check out the activities. The emphasis is open dialogue—informal weekly meetings without agendas or pressure to produce results. Attendees can get input on any topic. The only structure relates to the time and place.

Your community may decide to adopt this easy approach to informal networking and knowledge sharing. Have the community select a regular BYOL day and time such as every other Wednesday at noon. To foster the process, the core group or community leader should find a room that is always available for BYOL day. Until attendance becomes habit, the leader should personally invite members and prospective members to drop in.

## *Tools*

- Community of Practice Regular Progress Checklist
- Community Member Satisfaction Survey

**Community Member Satisfaction Survey**

| Community name: | *Yes* | *No* |
|---|---|---|
| Is there a common purpose that galvanizes community members to contribute to the knowledge base? | | |
| Are you likely to recommend the community to your professional colleagues? | | |
| Does your manager recognize and value your involvement in the community? | | |
| Are community activities part of your job? | | |
| Is there an acknowledged member base? | | |
| Does the community share a mutual understanding of its identity? | | |
| Does the community sustain common methodology, process, and language? | | |
| Does the community scan external sources for new ideas and innovations? | | |
| Is the community free of the "not invented here" syndrome? | | |

| | *Rating* | | | | |
|---|---|---|---|---|---|
| | *5* | *4* | *3* | *2* | *1* |
| Technology is leveraged to support collaboration. | | | | | |
| The community serves as a reliable source for workable solutions and/or best practices. | | | | | |
| Needed information is quickly accessed and easy to apply. | | | | | |
| Community members enjoy open channels of communication. | | | | | |
| Community participation contributes to your individual success. | | | | | |
| Members enjoy continuous learning. | | | | | |
| Resources and effort are invested to develop supporting infrastructure for the community. | | | | | |
| The community quickly mobilizes for ad hoc discussions. | | | | | |

Ranking: 5 = exceeds expectations, 1 = does not meet expectations.

- What do you like best about the community?
- What do you like least about the community?
- How would you improve the community?

# Appendix C

# Knowledge Discovery Techniques

Knowledge can be transmitted between or among people but this does not mean that it can only be copied. People learn rather than are taught, and the knowledge transferred is recreated by the recipient. It can change as it replicates and will not always take the same form. The key concept is to understand the extent to which useful knowledge can be codified. One of the simpler concepts is the difference between explicit and tacit knowledge.

A large number of organizations have seized on this concept as a way to capture knowledge residing in their organizations that they hope will prove valuable assets. Sometimes knowledge is limited to programs of managing a firm's intellectual property. This form of knowledge management (KM) has been characterized as defensive—concerned with protecting some aspect of organization activity.

However, other forms of knowledge are not so easily amenable to codification. Typically, these are skills or abilities, sometimes physical in nature, that resist easy replication. Sports stars are common examples cited to explain this difference but the concept can also be illustrated by examples from "creative" occupations and from design and engineering work. It is important to understand that some forms of knowledge do not exist outside their contexts and some forms are created socially. Because some forms of knowledge or experience cannot easily be codified, the experiences of one person or a group of people cannot always be written and passed on in written form for another group to replicate. Learning from the experiences of others may require additional approaches and other skills. Table C.1 lists some of the techniques discussed in this appendix.

Innovation is one of the key drivers of KM and other collaborative activities in commercial organizations. It is a critical factor in research-based industries such as pharmaceutical production, where new developments are converted

**Table C.1 Knowledge Discovery Techniques**

| *Technique* | *Basic (B) or Advanced (A)* | *Cultural Change Required?* |
|---|---|---|
| Exit interviews | B | N |
| Speed dating | B | N |
| Mind mapping | B | N |
| After-action review | B | N |
| Project review | B | N |
| Baton passing | B | Y |
| Virtual team | B | Y |
| Coaching and mentoring | B | N |
| Intellectual capital | B | Y |
| Communities of practice | B | Y |
| Social network analysis | A | N |
| Complex adaptive system | A | Y |
| Knowledge audit | A | N |
| Design of space | A | Y |
| Knowledge harvesting | A | Y |
| Domain knowledge mapping | A | Y |
| Storytelling | A | Y |

into major financial assets such as patents. However, other forms of innovation include improved internal processes and new services to offer. KM is a collection of approaches designed to answer two questions: How do we know what we know? How do we get to know what we need to know?

Understanding the sources of existing knowledge is not the only component of a successful KM strategy. Creating new knowledge is in the longer term even more important. Understanding the sources of knowledge to support service improvement is another vital issue. A diverse set of knowledge sources fall into three categories: your customers, your organization, and others.

**Learning from customers** — Customers are major sources of knowledge about service improvement. The skill, however, lies in understanding what to ask and how to interpret the answers. Many organizations use customer complaint systems but how they generate lessons that lead to service improvement is not always clear. This is where customer relationship management technology is useful. It goes beyond the recording of customer interactions. It requires mining of the data. This is the KM dimension—the need to combine insights from a number of sources to gain a better understanding of pathways to innovation.

**Learning from your organization** — In most organizations, the chief sources of expertise and the well-springs of innovation come from within the organization. Although every organization produces some of its organizational capital in the form of manuals and procedure documents, most of its actual capital is contained in the minds and behaviors of its employees. The chief issues in liberating this capital is achieving buy-in from staff members who control access to this learning. They may need to receive value such as a material reward or recognition in return for their learning. Such expertise may reside in organizational areas other than the ones that provide the specific knowledge providing services. Management may represent the biggest problem in opening learning sources, because of distrust on the part of the individuals or groups with access to this capability or because new ways of working may threaten existing power structures. Knowing where the expertise lies is another major inhibitor to effective organizational learning. Ways of addressing these inhibitors involve adopting some of the methods identified as useful for capturing tacit knowledge.

**Learning from other organizations** — Other organizations constitute the largest, most complex, and most diffuse sources of knowledge. Organizations can usually learn a great deal from comparable organizations. These other organizations do not need to be of the same type. Dissimilar organizations may be great sources of learning. However, to take advantage of learning sources, organizations must be able to learn from the experiences of others.

## Knowledge Management Techniques

An important area for sharing knowledge and expertise lies in solving specific problems. A number of basic techniques have been developed for this.

**Exit interviews** — Such interviews are normally seen as basic HR activities. They are relevant to knowledge sharing and collaboration as links to retaining specialist knowledge within the organization and further links to retaining intellectual property. From an HR perspective, exit interviews provide insights into how employees see the organization and identify potential areas for improvement. Interest in the potential of exit interviews as KM tools is growing. A number of organizations now realize that much valuable information about techniques and customer expectations (tacit rather than explicit knowledge) is locked inside the heads of employees and will be lost if they leave the organization without recording or passing on their understanding and expertise. A traditional, HR-focused exit interview may be conducted in person, by telephone, by questionnaire, or even via the Internet. However, for KM objectives, a face-to-face interview is the only realistic answer.

No single approach applies to conducting knowledge-focused exit interviews. An organization can develop an approach that fits its circumstances. The principal value of exit interviews lies in simplicity. However, their successful use depends on how well the process is integrated with other knowledge sharing activities. The results from the interviews must be incorporated into other developmental processes to ensure that the value of any knowledge gained is immediately accessible throughout the organization. Exit interviews are part of a spectrum that includes other forms of knowledge elicitation such as blogging and more elaborate forms of knowledge harvesting discussed later in this appendix.

**Speed dating** — This technique is intended to elicit the largest number of potential solutions to a problem. The person with the problem can then sift the responses to see whether any offer solutions. It is possible to organize speed dating in any way that is convenient but one basic method is as follows:

1. A range of people from different backgrounds are arranged into groups.
2. People who have problems and seek potential solutions visit each group in turn.
3. A person with a problem has a short time (five to ten minutes) to explain it.
4. A group offering solutions then has a short time (ten to fifteen minutes) to suggest as many solutions as it can devise.

The chief benefit of this technique is that, apart from the cost of bringing people together, it is economical. It allows a range of different people to contribute to potential solutions. At its simplest, it involves someone with a specific problem presenting it briefly to a group of individuals from different backgrounds. The listening group has a short time to suggest possible answers. To be effective, the process must be repeated several times with other groups.

**Mind mapping** — This is a well-established graphic technique developed in the 1960s by Tony Buzan. It allows one individual or a group to visualize the relationships among a range of related topics and to represent them in the form of a diagram. Its primary purpose is to clarify thinking and understanding. Tony Buzan (http://www.mind-map.com/EN/mindmaps/how_to.htm) has written extensively on this technique, and various printed guides available document the steps.

Successful mind maps help visualize the relationships of different components of an issue. The maps can be very personal but can also be used to reveal and discuss differences in understanding of people who must collaborate on a specific issue.

The potential application of mind mapping to organizational improvement is in the structure it offers to allow groups of people to explore or clarify thinking and thus access or share knowledge, particularly by identifying linkages across different components. The method offers some interesting links to Ishikawa ("fishbone") diagrams used in quality improvement activities and the linking of corporate objectives to detailed performance measures at the heart of the balanced scorecard used to support strategic management.

## *Organizational Learning Approaches*

Organizational learning is a key component of any KM strategy or attempt to harness the experience of an organization to improve its performance. A major overlap exists between organizational learning approaches and collaboration. A number of the techniques developed to support organizational learning are therefore of direct use for KM projects.

**After-action reviews** — This is one of the simplest ways to learn by doing. It was developed by the U.S. military to learn lessons from combat. An after-action review (AAR) is a professional discussion of an event, focused on performance standards that enables participants to discover what happened, why it happened, and how to sustain strengths and improve on weaknesses. This definition presents several important points. The first is the emphasis on a "professional" discussion. That means the discussion is structured and based on the expectation that a plan was to be followed and preexisting standards were to have been observed in carrying out the tasks. Finally, and most importantly, AAR use must feed into performance management and service improvement activities. It is not a stand-alone activity.

An AAR is both an art and a science. The art is in the attainment of mutual trust so that people speak freely. Innovative behavior should be the norm. Problem solving should be pragmatic, and employees should not be preoccupied with status, territory, or second guessing what the leader will think. There is a fine line between keeping a meeting from falling into chaos and accomplishing nothing, and enforcing a formal and polite exchange that masks issues (especially with the boss) and again nothing is accomplished. An AAR consists of several basic questions:

1. What was supposed to happen?
2. What actually happened?
3. Why was there a difference?
4. What did we learn?

To be effective, this approach must be removed from any attempt to assign blame. The major advantage of AAR is its independence of technology and adaptability for many situations from very small reviews to large meetings.

**Project reviews** — A project review is a somewhat more sophisticated version of an after-action review. In general, project reviews apply to larger areas of work than AARs and are often linked to complex methodologies for large-scale project management. Project review is a major technique for codifying knowledge because it attempts to capture learning points from the experience of delivering a project and may be linked to other performance management activities.

**Baton passing** — This involves passing on the lessons from a recently experienced process to another team about to face the same process. It was developed by Victor Newman of the European Pfizer Research University. It is a more sophisticated technique for passing lessons learned than the methods outlined earlier. It is critical that the team that just successfully completed a process records its experiences immediately, so the key feature is the just-in-time knowledge transfer. The technique was developed to allow project teams to pass on their lessons learned to a team about to embark on a similar activity. The reason for the just-in-time requirement was to capture the experiences of a group that successfully completed an unusual project. It is important to capture such knowledge before it is lost even though it is not likely to be useful to the successful team for some time. The key steps are

1. Build, identify, and capture experiences.
2. Review and exchange experiences of outgoing and incoming teams to connect learning and questions.
3. Produce an action plan for implementing the lessons.
4. Commit the plan to action.

The applicability of this technique to service improvement is using learning gained in one area to prepare the next area for the same test.

## *Organizational Design Approaches*

A number of approaches to collaboration and sharing knowledge have strong components of organizational change and redesign. These are more formal approaches than those cited above.

**Virtual teams** — The distinguishing characteristic of a virtual team is that it consists of groups or individuals who are physically apart and must collaborate across physical boundaries. Often they are assigned to a specific project but this approach is productive in other circumstances. Team collaboration is vital in research-based activities, for example, in pharmaceutical companies to maximize resources or more usually to generate new areas of knowledge from existing ones. A virtual team brings together distributed resources to work on a number of projects. It offers greater flexibility in the use of resources and the ability produce new expertise from old. Key needs for successful virtual teams are

1. Occasional personal contact at the outset of a project because some degree of contact is important for communication and building trust as confirmed by a number of research studies.
2. Addressing cultural differences among team members. Multinational firms involve a number of different cultures. Direct personal contact and socialization can break down the barriers.

The effective use of technology can also be a key determinant of the success or failure of a virtual team. Effective information systems can allow collaboration; ineffective sisters will hinder efficient communication. Email tends to be the simplest method currently employed. More elaborate technologies include collaboration software and video conferencing technologies.

The value of virtual teams to performance improvement is in the direction of resources to solving specific tasks. It is usual in organizations that specialized experience or expertise is restricted to one organizational unit, and the only way to release it to another unit is to transfer staff members.

Virtual teams allow individuals or groups to collaborate without changing organizational boundaries. The teams differ from many matrix management structures in that they do not require changes in formal reporting structures. However, creating and maintaining virtual teams present challenges. Several key areas must be addressed:

1. Job design. Team working methods and expectations must be dealt with explicitly and cover job accountability and decision-making authority.
2. Team design. Virtual teams are meant to overcome the limitations of traditional organization boundaries and thus need new criteria such as identifying the purpose of the team and selecting members who fit. More importantly, the team requires a clear identity and a defined statement of purpose.
3. Communication methods are essential to the success of virtual teams because physical contact is kept to a minimum. Communications must be comprehensive (members must keep each other fully informed), frequent, and preferably consist of short messages. Quality of communication is the most important aspect.
4. Leadership exerts a key impact on the success of a virtual team. The leader must set clear goals and provide continuous feedback on performance.
5. Trust. Trust is at the heart of most successful KM practices and is best established by social interaction, particularly at the start of a project.
6. Cultural awareness. The cultural dimension should be tackled at the outset to improve coherence and minimize misunderstanding.
7. Technology. Appropriate technology is a key enabler to ensure frequent contact. Advanced technology will be required to support collaboration.

**Coaching and mentoring** — Coaching and mentoring are well-known HR and organizational development techniques. Their relevance to knowledge-based work lies in the opportunities they provide for direct assimilation. The processes are similar to the way apprentices traditionally learned their crafts.

Not all useful information can be conveyed by capturing tacit knowledge and codifying it, for example, as a guide or handbook. Certain types of knowledge are best provided by observing someone else at work and, where possible, copying the activity and asking questions. The principal advantages of mentoring and coaching are

1. The personal contact and opportunities for socialization and internalizing knowledge.
2. The processes can strongly reinforce cultural aspects of work by allowing feedback and development.

The corresponding disadvantages are

1. Coaching and mentoring can be intensive and time consuming and may in some cases interfere with normal work activities.
2. The strength is in imparting existing knowledge but development of new knowledge or expertise may be hindered.

For these reasons, coaching and mentoring are often restricted to highly regarded areas such as senior management development.

### *Cultural Approaches*

Several effective knowledge management approaches are based on understanding the cultural aspects of organizational behavior and concentrate on improving the cultural bias toward sharing knowledge or other information.

**Identifying intellectual capital** — The concept of intellectual capital continues to gain acceptance in commercial organizations but is not yet common in the public sector except where the concentration is on organizational development. Intellectual capital may be traced back to work carried out for the Skandia Corporation by Leif Edvinsson. The model developed was intended to demonstrate the importance of nonfinancial assets to the value and performance of a company. The nonfinancial forms of capital are usually intangible assets that represent value. Customer capital is a measure of the value of customers to the organization, particularly their contributions to future income and profits. Customer capital can also be represented as feedback or ideas obtained via consultations, surveys, or reviews of complaints.

Structural capital encompasses the nonhuman and nonfinancial aspects of an organization, such as proprietary processes and procedures. In the commercial world, processes and procedures provide competitive advantages. Human capital is easier to explain and consists of all intangible assets contributed by employees (skills, experience, knowledge, and current and potential abilities). In service-based organizations, human capital is often the key source of improvement and innovation. It may be increased or renewed by staff turnover or by education, development, and acquisition of new skills. A number of difficulties surround the measurement of human capital in an organization and its financial valuation. Some progress has been made on valuation of human capital in areas such as transfer fees for athletes market valuations of companies whose intellectual assets far outweigh their tangible ones. This has long been true of consultancy operations and companies such as Microsoft.

Social capital covers a set of processes that stresses the importance of the relationships built and maintained by individuals who work together to provide goods or services. Most people will recognize this in the strength of working relationships and goodwill present in effective teams. Social capital is intangible but real. It describes the value generated by the interactions of people and is essential to exploiting intellectual capital because much of the knowledge of individuals is created in social contexts rather than by acting alone. Social capital is one of the major contributions of teams to the efficiency and effectiveness of organizations.

Intellectual capital is not applied directly. It constitutes analyzing and interpreting the basic capacity of an organization. It helps identify assets that may be used to improve an organization's effectiveness and its ability to change and to innovate. The key to determining intellectual capital is developing a measurement and reporting system that values these assets in a reasonably objective fashion.

**Building communities of practice** (CoPs) — These tools are comparatively new but very powerful for developing links among individuals and groups that lead to sharing experiences across wider groups. A CoP is essentially a social network or group of individuals who understand and express needs to share knowledge or collaborate in a specific area. The term is new but the concept is very old, and the use of CoPs continues to grow.

The strength of CoPs is that they can be formed around any topic of interest or concern. The communities can exist for long or short times, depending on the nature of their interest. Although a typical CoP is formed by people from similar backgrounds, the approach is also effective for connecting disparate people to share knowledge and experience to tackle a new problem—the questions must be formulated and the answers are not yet clear. CoPs differ from teams and workgroups in significant ways. Teams usually have specific goals with targets or demonstrable objectives. CoPs concentrate on wider areas of interest that can develop over time. Teams are usually formal parts of organizations; CoPs are more amorphous and often voluntary.

Although CoPs are not dependent on technology, the wider availability of IT has clearly boosted their importance. The key technologies of a community are email, bulletin boards, and collaboration software. Commercial experience with CoPs indicates that managerial organization is unlikely to lead to their success, and that most successful CoPs tend to be self-organizing. This presents challenges to very hierarchical or highly structured organizations. The potential contribution of CoPs to performance improvement is clear. They allow members to learn directly from more experienced individuals and provide a space where ideas can be proposed and explored without being put directly into practice.

## Advanced Techniques

**Social network analysis** — This analysis is both a specific academic technique and a useful way of analyzing the flow of communications through an organization. As an analytical activity, it illuminates the ways social relationships can improve or impede the flow of knowledge. It has no preferred model; the analysis demonstrates the situation.

KM staff who wish to design a preferred outcome must mold the organizational structure. Social network analysis is essentially an analytical technique that may be used diagnostically. However, the key skill required for its successful application is designing questionnaires required to elicit the basic data. Accurate and relevant data is critical to proper mapping of the network. The resulting map is a visual description as shown in Figure C.1.

**Knowledge audit** — This is a complex but potentially effective approach to identifying and describing the creation and storage of knowledge in an organization. The audits cannot be open ended and must be based on a thorough analysis of knowledge types and flows.

**Design of space** — The design of working space is a very powerful aspect of KM intended to make work more effective. A body of research in a range of settings demonstrates the impact of working space design on working relationships and collaboration. Working space should allow individuals a degree of freedom to meet so that spontaneous conversations can develop (the "water cooler approach"). A design should provide neutral spaces and wide corridors to enable chance meetings without concerns about interrupting work. One analysis of the approach to

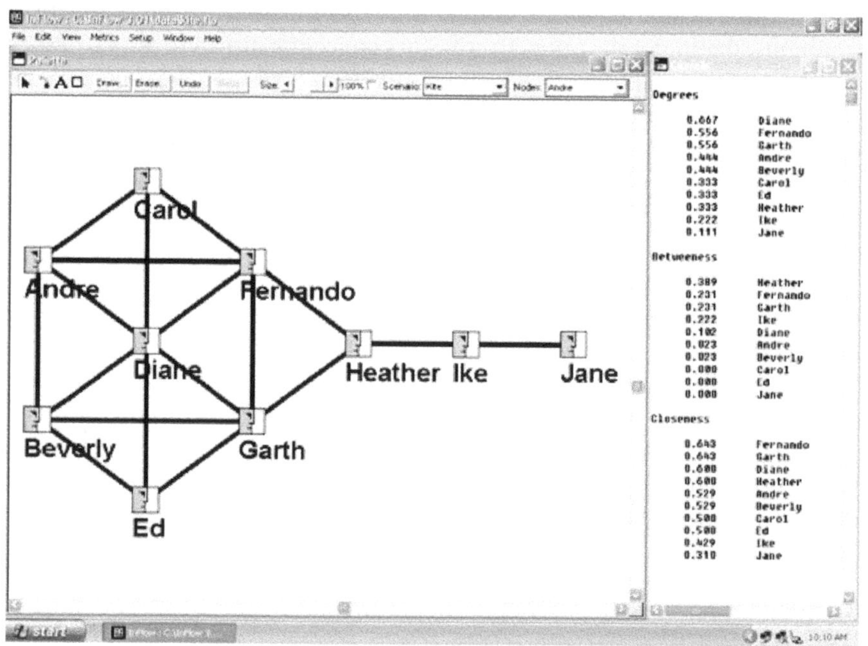


**Figure C.1 Social network analysis.**

designing office space can be found in *The New Office*, a book by Francis Duffy. The book cites four office space classifications:

- The hive, an open plan humming with activity
- The club, styled after eighteenth-century coffee houses to promote deals, ideas and bonding
- The den, for intense communicative work among a small number of people
- The cell, where an individual works contemplatively

**Knowledge harvesting** — A range of techniques is used to recover knowledge assets from many forms of tacit knowledge within an organization. Several approaches focus on capturing tacit knowledge and codifying it (turning it into explicit knowledge). The principal techniques include developing communities of interest (parallel activities to CoPs) and encouraging activities such as web logging (blogging). Another technique is using resources such as internal directories as guides to likely sources of expertise.

**Domain knowledge mapping** — This is a somewhat complicated approach to identifying knowledge considered important but poorly defined. It is often useful for beginning to record knowledge in newly developed fields. Domain knowledge mapping often concentrates on developing high-level knowledge models to obtain an overview of available and missing knowledge in core business areas. Knowledge mapping is a good example of a useful KM activity based on existing knowledge acquisition and modeling techniques. It concentrates on the visualization of relationships, particularly in new or complex areas of study.

**Storytelling** — Organizations use stories as communication tools to share knowledge. The approach is deceptively simple but is considered an advanced technique because its effective use is a complex undertaking. Most people are attracted to stories but few are good at telling them. Stories must be chosen based on appropriateness, content, and presentation. Storytelling skills often take years to acquire and develop into useful techniques.

## Tools for Organizing Knowledge Assets

A wide range of software is available for organizing knowledge assets.

**Tools based on database technologies** — These tools are very heavily influenced by computing theories and rely frequently on relational database models. They are optimized for highly structured data and have difficulty in dealing with unstructured data. However, newer RDBMs often have support for other structures.

**Electronic document management systems (EDMS)** — These systems are hailed as the answers to all KM problems, largely because they work with both highly structured and unstructured information.

**Metadata management systems** — Metadata is a key component of all comprehensive management systems but few metadata schemes relate to service improvement or performance management. One area of development is in metadata layers of business intelligence and other reporting tools. In addition to allowing mappings between object names used in service areas with usually less meaningful table names and views, these metadata layers may support the creation of new objects derived from underlying values in the base data to create standard approaches for deriving or calculating performance indicators or other values.

**Generalized retrieval systems** — A variety of technologies can handle generalized retrieval systems, but very sophisticated probabilistic searching methods, often based on Bayesian inference, are becoming increasingly popular. A popular area for deploying searching tools is in support of CRM systems, to allow multiskilled agents to access organizational information. These developments are managed in several ways. Suppliers of CRM and help desk software often include what they describe as knowledge management software to extend the capability of a basic system by allowing agents to record how new or unusual problems were dealt with and making the resulting knowledge available to colleagues who may face the same problem.

**Tools for collaboration** — These tools are less structured and in some ways less highly developed than tools for organizing knowledge. The two main categories of collaboration software are systems written for specific groups and those for specific purposes. They include, for instance, project management software, which has moved from task recording and scheduling packages for producing Gantt charts and calculating critical paths to repository-based collaborative systems.

Collaborative tools range from development systems such as Lotus Notes and Domino to systems designed to provide enterprise information portals. The recent concentration on portals illustrates the issues that must be addressed to devise generic solutions to knowledge work and collaboration issues. Portals offer a range of services. A user simply plugs into a portal and information services are made available to desktops throughout the organization. In reality, however, portals are complex software environments that require considerable programming for proper utilization. The choice of the basic platform is a critical success factor for a portal project.

Another significant IT component involving both knowledge asset organization and collaboration is the intranet. In a strict context, an intranet deploys Internet technologies within a single organization. In practice, however, intranet is a shorthand term for a collection of information management and collaboration tools delivered to a set of desktops. Many organizations encountered difficulties deploying intranets:

1. Poor information management. Duplication exists and information is allowed to become stale.
2. Intranets and the Internet are subject to Gresham's law: less useful material is easy to find and genuinely useful material is not in regular circulation.
3. A proliferation of intranets based on organizational units reinforce internal barriers instead of trying to break down problems of cultural fit between the

technology and the wider organizational culture. The latter needs to support a degree of openness in the use of the technology or effective collaboration is unlikely to result

## *Frameworks*

The KM literature is replete with proposed frameworks of varying degrees of complexity. The two major approaches are (1) maturity models and (2) strategy or implementation frameworks.

The maturity models are common outside KM and purport to describe a journey from less sophisticated to more sophisticated approaches. A good example of a maturity model is Siemens' KMMM model (http://w4.siemens.de/ct/en/technologies/ic/beispiele/kmmm.html). Based on the well-known capability maturity model (CMM) from the Software Engineering Institute, KMMM includes analysis and development models. Implementation frameworks can be simple or complex, depending on the organization. One well-regarded framework devised by British Petroleum (BP) consists of three steps:

1. Create awareness
2. Build knowledge assets
3. Leverage knowledge assets

When considering the application of KM to process improvement, managers should seek the simplest possible approach that is congruent with organizational goals. That predisposes them to frameworks such as the BP model.

## *Producing Corporate KM strategies*

KM strategies are highly problematic. They tend to imply that a well-defined path leads to achieving KM and that concept is arguable. The very useful model of George von Krogh (2000) suggests certain enablers:

1. Instill a knowledge vision
2. Manage conversations
3. Mobilize knowledge activists
4. Create the right context
5. Globalize local knowledge

Theories of knowledge (epistemologies) constitute a huge area of debate involving philosophy, psychology, and now information theory. These theories reach from the ancient world to the present and cross many cultures. Basic approaches to understanding the nature of knowledge—and knowledge creation in particular—may be of use in planning to introduce KM initiatives.

**Cognitive model** — This model treats knowledge as essentially objective and transferable. It stresses the capturing of tacit knowledge and embedding it into more explicit forms. The resulting knowledge can then be shared and reused. This model is very strongly linked to approaches that stress explicit knowledge as a form of intellectual property and lies behind most IT installations sold as knowledge management systems. Such systems treat KM as a more complex form of information processing. Cognitive abilities are seen as major inputs to be transformed by technology into the desired outputs.

**Social (also community or connectiveness) model** — Knowledge creation is essentially a social process. This model emphasizes the importance of social interaction to create and disseminate knowledge—a common view of social scientists and researchers and professionals who concentrate on organizational development and HR processes. The most important formulation of the theory appears in *The Knowledge Creating Company*, a 1995 book by Nonaka and Takeuchi. Their book relies on both Eastern philosophies and modern business practices and makes the point that the types of knowledge required to drive innovation are essentially social. The Nonaka and Takeuchi model sees KM as an iterative process whereby tacit knowledge is often shared in social contexts before becoming explicit, and explicit knowledge is often internalized before it helps create new forms of tacit knowledge.

**Autopoietic model** — This recent development has elicited a lot of interest. *Autopoiesis* means *self-creation* based on the work of two biologists, Humberto Maturano and Francisco Varela, to explain a theory about the development of organisms. Their book titled *The Tree of Knowledge* (1987) proposed a theory of knowledge creation based on the interactions of individual organisms with their environment. In their model, knowledge does not exist independently of the organism (as it does in the cognitive model). It is created by an individual organism, not by its interactions with other organisms (as in the social model). The autopoietic model imposes implications for any systematic view of KM. The model has been criticized for a number of reasons. The most significant may be the assumption that what applies to simple organisms may not hold for complex, self-aware, higher organisms.

KM should be pursued for practical reasons, for example,

1. To provide a degree of protection for intellectual property or assets. These approaches tend to concentrate on knowledge harvesting or turning tacit knowledge into explicit knowledge. They represent a survival strategy.
2. To provide continuing or future competitive advantages based on creating new knowledge or finding new ways to exploit existing knowledge. This approach emphasizes collaboration and may also be called an advancement strategy.

Innovation is critical for commercial organizations. In industries such as pharmaceutical production, innovation is the major motivation for investing in KM initiatives. The knowledge proposition states that significant additional stakeholder value and competitive advantage will result if the expertise, information, and ideas of employees, partners, and customers are continually developed and used in all business and decision-making processes.

## References

Maturano, H., and Varela, F. (1992). *The Tree of Knowledge*. Boston: Shambhala Publications.

Nonaka, H., and Takeyuchi, I. (1995). *The Knowledge Creating Company*. New York: Oxford University Press.

Van Krogh, G., Ichijo, K., and Nonaka, I. (2000). *How to Unlock the Mystery of Tacit Knowledge and Release the Power of Innovation*. Oxford: Oxford University Press.

# Appendix D

# Staff Competency Survey

Directions: Rate your perception of your abilities on a scale of 1 to 5 (1 = lowest; 5 = highest). Please use the same scale to rate the importance of this trait in your current work environment.

## Communications

1. Professionals must communicate in a variety of settings using oral, written, and multimedia techniques.

   Your self rating:

   Low High

   1 2 3 4 5

   Importance of this trait to your organization:

   Low High

   1 2 3 4 5

## Problem Solving

2. Professionals must be able to choose from a variety of problem-solving methodologies to analytically formulate a solution.

   Your self rating:

   Low High

   1 2 3 4 5

   Importance of this trait to your organization:

   Low High

   1 2 3 4 5

3. Professionals must think creatively in solving problems.

   Your self rating:

   Low High

   1 2 3 4 5

   Importance of this trait to your organization:

   Low High

   1 2 3 4 5

4. Professionals must be able to work on project teams and use group methods to define and solve problems.

   Your self rating:

   Low High

   1 2 3 4 5

   Importance of this trait to your organization:

   Low High

   1 2 3 4 5

## Organization

5. Professionals must have sufficient background to understand the functioning of organizations because the product or service must be congruent with and supportive of the strategy, principles, goals, and objectives of the organization.

   Your self rating:

   Low High

   1 2 3 4 5

   Importance of this trait to your organization:

   Low High

   1 2 3 4 5

6. Professionals must understand and be able to function in the multinational and global context of today's information-dependent organizations.

   Your self rating:

   Low High

   1 2 3 4 5

   Importance of this trait to your organization:

   Low High

   1 2 3 4 5

## Quality

7. Professionals must understand quality, planning, and steps in the continuous improvement process as they relate to the enterprise, and tools to facilitate quality development.

   Your self rating:
   Low High
   1 2 3 4 5

   Importance of this trait to your organization:
   Low High
   1 2 3 4 5

8. Error control, risk management, process measurement, and auditing are functions that professionals must understand and apply.

   Your self rating:
   Low High
   1 2 3 4 5

   Importance of this trait to your organization:
   Low High
   1 2 3 4 5

9. Professionals must possess a tolerance for chance and skills for managing change.

   Your self rating:
   Low High
   1 2 3 4 5

   Importance of this trait to your organization:
   Low High
   1 2 3 4 5

10. Education must be continuous.

    Your self rating:
    Low High
    1 2 3 4 5

    Importance of this trait to your organization:
    Low High
    1 2 3 4 5

11. Professionals must understand mission-directed, principle-centered mechanisms to facilitate aligning individual and group missions with organizational missions.

    Your self rating:
    Low High
    1 2 3 4 5

    Importance of this trait to your organization:
    Low High
    1 2 3 4 5

## Groups

12. Professionals must interact with diverse user groups in team and project activities.

    Your self rating:
    Low High
    1 2 3 4 5

    Importance of this trait to your organization:
    Low High
    1 2 3 4 5

13. Professionals must possess communication and facilitation skills for team meetings and related activities.

    Your self rating:
    Low High
    1 2 3 4 5

    Importance of this trait to your organization:
    Low High
    1 2 3 4 5

14. Professionals must understand the concept of empathetic listening and utilize it proactively to solicit synergistic solutions in which all parties to an agreement can benefit.

    Your self rating:
    Low High
    1 2 3 4 5

    Importance of this trait to your organization:
    Low High
    1 2 3 4 5

15. Professionals must be able to communicate effectively with a changing workforce.

    Your self rating:

    Low High
    1 2 3 4 5

    Importance of this trait to your organization:

    Low High
    1 2 3 4 5

# Appendix E

# Behavioral Competencies

Companies interested in stimulating learning and growth among employees may utilize this list of behavioral competencies for employees and managers.

## For Employees

### *Communicates effectively*

1. Listens to others in a patient, empathetic, nonjudgmental way; acknowledges their ideas in a respectful manner; questions appropriately.
2. Is straightforward and direct; behavior is consistent with words.
3. Discusses concerns and conflicts directly and constructively.
4. Communicates in a timely fashion.

### *Promotes teamwork*

1. Networks with other employees within and outside his or her area; makes internal referrals to connect people.
2. Readily volunteers to serve on teams.
3. Is a participating and equal partner on teams; has the same purpose as the team; encourages cohesion and trust.
4. Is receptive to and solicits advice and ideas from other team members.
5. Keeps supervisor and team informed of status of work to minimize surprises.
6. Verbally and nonverbally supports established decisions and actions; represents collective stance.

## Presents effectively

1. Understands audiences and is sensitive to their values, backgrounds, and needs.
2. Presents ideas clearly so that others can easily understand them.
3. Delivers presentations with the appropriate level of expression and confidence.
4. Incorporates humor when appropriate and in good taste.

## Makes sound decisions

1. Knows when a decision is necessary and makes decisions in a timely manner.
2. Connects decisions to strategic plans; separates essential from nonessential information; considers all logical alternatives when generating conclusions.
3. Seeks and considers input from others who are close to a situation before establishing a course of action.
4. Considers the relevance and impact of a decision on others prior to deciding.

## Uses resources wisely

1. Considers need and cost before making resource-related requests and decisions.
2. Makes maximum use of available resources by efficient and creative use of people, time, materials, and equipment.
3. Reduces waste, and reuses materials and recycles appropriately.
4. Functions within budget.

## Takes initiative and accepts accountability

1. Is proactive; plans ahead; sees what needs to be done and handles on own initiative and on time.
2. Accepts responsibility and consequences for his or her decisions and actions.
3. Follows through on commitments; does what he or she promises the first time.
4. Acknowledges, accepts, and learns from mistakes.

## Lives company values

1. Demonstrates the organizational and professional code of ethics related to honesty, respect, dignity, caring, and confidentiality.
2. Demonstrates and consistently applies organizational principles, policies, and values to all employees and situations.
3. Respects and operates within the boundaries established for his or her job and personal boundaries set by others.
4. Promotes a positive work environment.

## *Demonstrates customer-first approach to internal partners and external customers*

1. Anticipates customer needs; facilitates customers to express their needs; listens to customer and hears what they say.
2. Promptly attends to customer needs (answers phone, returns calls within a reasonable time).
3. Treats customers with respect, politeness, and dignity while maintaining appropriate boundaries.
4. When appropriate, provides customers with options for action in response to their needs.

## *Generates new ideas*

1. Generates imaginative and original ideas that will bring about positive change.
2. Seizes opportunities to expand on other people's ideas to create something new and add value.
3. Encourages others to create new ideas, products, or solutions that will add value to the organization.

## *Demonstrates flexibility*

1. Adapts to and accepts changing work schedules, priorities, challenges, and unpredictable events in a positive manner.
2. Is visible and accessible; is approachable even when interruptions are inconvenient.
3. Is receptive to new ideas that are different from his or her own.
4. Offers to help others when circumstances necessitate sharing workloads.

## *Demonstrates professional demeanor*

1. Demonstrates acceptable hygiene and grooming; dresses appropriately for job.
2. Uses proper verbal and nonverbal communications and tones with internal partners and external customers.
3. Places work responsibilities and priorities before personal needs while at work.
4. Maximizes positive and professional communication with internal partners and external customers; minimizes complaining and nonfactual communication.

## *Stimulates and adapts to change*

1. Stimulates positive attitudes about change; pushes change processes along.
2. Takes personal responsibility for adapting to and coping with change.
3. Commits quickly when change reshapes his or her area of work.
4. Accepts ambiguity and uncertainty; can improvise and still add value.

### *Continually improves processes*

1. Seeks and anticipates opportunities to improve steps in the development and delivery of products or services; takes logical risks that may lead to improvement and change.
2. Examines his or her work for conformance to predetermined plans, specifications, and standards.
3. Freely shares and promotes new ideas that may lead to improvement and positive change, even when the ideas may be unpopular.
4. Seeks input from those closest to a situation when making improvements.

## For Managers

### *Organizational acumen*

1. Demonstrates thorough knowledge of company model, organizational history, and values.
2. Applies knowledge of services, products, and processes to understand key issues in own division and work unit.
3. Demonstrates understanding of and ability to influence organizational culture, norms, and expectations.
4. Contributes to, fosters, and supports changes resulting from organizational decisions and initiatives.

### *Strategic direction*

1. Integrates own work and work of his or her unit with the organization's mission, values, and objectives.
2. Analyzes and utilizes customer, industry, and stakeholder inputs in strategic and operating plan processes.
3. Establishes workgroup priorities to support strategic objectives.
4. Gathers input from internal and external resources to analyze business unit needs.
5. Promotes and embraces innovation and creativity to achieve organizational and work unit goals.
6. Develops work unit plans and measures aligned with division and organization strategic objectives.
7. Defines operational goals for work unit.
8. Integrates strategies and plans with other areas.
9. Promotes and supports the use of corporate and cross-functional teams.
10. Ensures customer and employee confidentiality by monitoring access to information to individuals who have need, reason, and permission for such access.

## *Systems improvement*

1. Demonstrates understanding of the "big picture" encompassing interrelationships of divisions, departments, and work units.
2. Incorporates a broad range of internal and external factors in problem solving and decision making.
3. Solicits and incorporates customer and stakeholder needs and expectations into work unit planning.
4. Applies and encourages the use of process improvement methods and tools.
5. Encourages and supports innovative and creative problem solving by others.
6. Integrates process thinking into management of daily operations to enhance quality, efficiency, and ethical standards.
7. Utilizes data in decision making and managing work units.

## *Communication*

1. Communicates company mission, values, structure, and systems to individuals, groups, and larger audiences.
2. Provides leadership in communicating up, down, and across the organization.
3. Reinforces organization's key messages.
4. Creates a work environment for and models open expression of ideas and diverse opinions.
5. Routinely includes a communications plan in work and project planning.
6. Applies, communicates, and educates others about organization policies and procedures.
7. Keeps employees informed of industry trends and implications.
8. Understands, communicates, and administers compensation and benefits to employees.

## *Employee and team direction*

1. Anticipates and assesses staffing needs.
2. Maintains and updates staff job descriptions, linking job descriptions and projects to unit, division, and corporate strategies.
3. Recruits, selects, and retains high-performing individuals.
4. Provides information, resources, and coaching to support individual and team professional and career development.
5. Applies knowledge of team dynamics to enhance group communication, synergy, creativity, conflict resolution, and decision making.
6. Assures staff has training to fully utilize technological tools necessary for job performance.
7. Delegates responsibilities to, coaches, and mentors employees to develop their capabilities.

8. Involves staff in planning and reporting to ensure integration with operational activities and priorities.
9. Coaches employees by providing positive and constructive feedback and realistic pictures of their performance.
10. Ensures that core functions in areas of responsibility will continue during short- or long-term absences of staff members.
11. Recognizes and acknowledges successes and achievements of others.

## *Financial literacy*

1. Partners with financial specialists in planning and problem solving.
2. Develops and meets financial goals using standard budgeting and reporting processes.
3. Continually finds ways to improve revenue, reduce costs, and leverage assets in keeping with the organization's strategic direction and objectives.
4. Uses financial and quantitative information in work unit management.
5. Communicates unit budget expectations and status to employees.
6. Coaches employees on financial implications of work processes.

## *Professional development*

1. Keeps up to date with external environment through professional associations, conferences, journals, etc.
2. Nurtures and maintains working relationships with colleagues across the organization.
3. Demonstrates commitment to professional development; aligns development with current and future needs of the organization when possible.
4. Models self-development and healthy work–life balance for employees.

# Appendix F

# Balanced Scorecard Metrics

All metrics are accompanied by targets. For the most part, targets are percentages ascertained via calculations based on entry of raw data. Some targets have "baselines" encoded to indicate that the metrics are informational: only raw values aggregated by specified weekly, monthly, or other period will be displayed. The targets should be set to default (0 for baselined targets). The entirety of metrics provided is greater than the norm for a typical balanced scorecard that usually shows only a few key metrics per perspective. Many metrics can be modified to measure systems developed using social software engineering methods. In particular, note the social software engineering metrics listed at the end of the learning and growth perspective.

## Financial

| *Objective* | *Measure* | *Target* | *KPI* |
|---|---|---|---|
| Optimize purchasing cost efficiency | Cost-to-spend ratio [1] | <1% | F1 |
| | Negotiated cost savings [2] | ≥20% | F2 |
| | Costs avoided/total costs [3] | ≥10% | F3 |
| | Percentage of goods and services obtained via competitive procurement practices [4] | ≥19% | F4 |

| *Objective* | *Measure* | *Target* | *KPI* |
|---|---|---|---|
| Control costs | Dollar amount under budget | Baseline | F5 |
| | Dollar amount over budget | Baseline | F6 |
| | Budget as percentage of revenue | ≤30% | F7 |
| | Expenses per employee | ≤$35,000 | F8 |
| | Cost of technology acquired or developed in house | ≤50% | F9 |
| | % new products or services with break-even points within one year | 80% | F10 |
| | Total cost of ownership [5] | ≤$6,000/ device/year | F11 |
| | Overtime ratio [6] | ≤25% | F12 |
| | Cost performance index [7] | ≤1 | F13 |
| | Average break-even point [8] | ≤1.5 years | F14 |
| | Schedule performance index [9] | ≤1 | F15 |
| | Total cost reductions from use of technology | ≥33% | F16 |
| | Workforce reduction from use of new products | ≥10% | F17 |
| | Contractor utilization [10] | ≥35% | F18 |
| Increase business value | Revenue from new products or services [11] | Baseline | F19 |
| | Average ROI [12] | ≥1 | F20 |
| | % resources devoted to strategic projects | ≥55% | F21 |
| | % favorable rating of project management by top management | ≥93% | F22 |
| | Average cost–benefit ratio | ≥22% | F23 |
| | Net present value [13] | ≥1 | F24 |
| | Assets per employee | Baseline | F25 |
| | Revenues per employee | Baseline | F26 |
| | Profits per employee | Baseline | F27 |

| *Objective* | *Measure* | *Target* | *KPI* |
|---|---|---|---|
| Improve technology acquisition | Total expenditures | Baseline | F28 |
| | Total expenditures/industry average expenditures | ≥1 | F29 |
| | Amount of new technology from mergers and acquisitions | Baseline | F30 |

[1] Operational costs/purchasing obligations (goods and services purchased).

[2] Cost savings compared to total costs.

[3] Costs avoided compared to total costs. Avoid costs by reusing hardware and software, utilizing partners, etc.

[4] Difference between average qualified bid and cost of successful bid. The sum of each calculation is aggregated into a new savings ratio for all transactions.

[5] Additional capital costs = software, IT support software, network infrastructure. Technical support costs = hardware and software deployment, help desk staffing, system maintenance. Administration costs = financing, procurement, vendor management, user training, asset management. End-user operations costs = downtime costs, end users supporting other end users instead of support from help desk technicians.

[6] Overtime hours/regular hours worked.

[7] Ratio of earned value (EV) to actual cost. EV, also known as budgeted cost of work performed, is an estimate of the value of work completed based on original planned project cost.

[8] Break-even analysis. All projects have associated costs and associated benefits. At the outset, costs will far exceed benefits, but at some point the benefits will start outweighing the costs. This is the break-even point. Break-even analysis determines when the break-even point will occur.

[9] SPI = ratio of earned value to planned value. It is used to determine whether a project is on target. (See Note [7] for definition of EV.)

[10] Cost of external contractors/cost of internal resources.

[11] Use real dollars if systems are external customer facing. Use internal budget dollars for internal customer-facing systems.

[12] Return on investment (ROI). Most organizations select projects that yield positive ROIs. The ROI represents earnings above costs. The formula is ROI = (Benefit – Cost)/Cost.

[13] NPV is a method of calculating expected monetary gain or loss by discounting all expected future cash inflows and outflows to the present time. If financial value is a key criterion, an organization should consider only projects with positive NPVs because a positive NPV indicates that return from a project exceeds the cost of capital (the return available by investing elsewhere). Higher NPVs are more desirable than lower NPVs. The formula is NPV = II + [OCF/(1 + R(r))t] + [TCF/(1 + R(r))n], where II = initial investment, OFC = operating cash flows in year t, t = year, n = life span (in years) of project, and R(r) = project required rate of return. (*Source:* http://www.mtholyoke.edu/~aahirsch/howvalueproject.html)

[14] Use research from a company such as http://www.infotech.com/

## Customer

| *Objective* | *Measure* | *Target* | *KPI* |
|---|---|---|---|
| Increase customer satisfaction | % of customers satisfied with system timeliness (speed) | ≥92% | C1 |
| | % of customers satisfied with responsiveness to questions | ≥92% | C2 |
| | % of customers satisfied with quality | ≥92% | C3 |
| | % of customers satisfied with sales and/or customer service representatives | ≥92% | C4 |
| | Time required to resolve disputes | ≤4 hours | C5 |
| Conform to customer requests | % of baselined projects with plan | ≥90% | C6 |
| | % customer requests satisfied | ≥90% | C7 |
| Increase customer base | Customer lifetime value ($) | Baseline | C8 |
| | Share of wallet (%) [1] | ≥25% | C9 |
| | Retention % | ≥80% | C10 |
| | Win-back percent | ≥85% | C11 |
| | New/current customers | ≥10% | C12 |
| | Rate of defection | ≤43% | C13 |
| Enhance customer-facing systems | Average number of searches per order or query | Baseline | C14 |
| | Average number of support calls per order or query | Baseline | C15 |
| | Average elapsed time to select product and order | Baseline | C16 |
| | Average elapsed time to search website | Baseline | C17 |
| | Number of steps required to select and purchase | Baseline | C18 |
| | Average time to answer incoming call | Baseline | C19 |
| | % availability of customer-facing applications | ≥98% | C20 |
| | Average cost to service customer transaction | Baseline | C21 |

| *Objective* | *Measure* | *Target* | *KPI* |
|---|---|---|---|
| Support internal customers | % better decisions | ≥90% | C22 |
| | % time reduction in making decisions | ≥90% | C23 |
| | Average time to answer support phone call | Baseline | C24 |

[1] Compare to competition using service such as http://www.lexisnexis.com/marketintelligence/

## Internal Business Processes

| *Objective* | *Measure* | *Target* | *KPI* |
|---|---|---|---|
| Improve data quality | Forms input | Baseline | I1 |
| | Data entry error rate | ≤3% | I2 |
| | Age of current data | Baseline | I3 |
| | % of employees who have up-to-date data | ≥98% | I4 |
| Improve balance between technical and strategic activities | % of time devoted to maintenance | ≤20 | I5 |
| | Strategic project counts | Baseline | I6 |
| | % of time devoted to ad hoc activities | ≤15% | I7 |
| Increase product quality and reliability | % reduction in demand for customer support | ≥25% | I8 |
| | Number of end-user queries handled | Baseline | I9 |
| | Average time to address end-user problem | ≤4 hours | I10 |
| | Equipment downtime | ≤1% | I11 |
| | Mean time to failure | ≤1000 hours | I12 |
| | % remaining known product faults | ≤5% | I13 |
| | % of projects with lessons learned in database | ≥95% | I14 |
| | Fault density [1] | ≤3% | I15 |
| | Defect density [2] | ≤3% | I16 |

| *Objective* | *Measure* | *Target* | *KPI* |
|---|---|---|---|
| Increase product quality and reliability (continued) | Cumulative failure [3] | Baseline | I17 |
| | Number of fault days [4] | ≤1 | I18 |
| | Functional test coverage [5] | ≥95% | I19 |
| | Requirements traceability [6] | ≥98% | I20 |
| | Maturity index [7] | ≥1 | I21 |
| | % conflicting requirements | ≤5% | I22 |
| | Test coverage [8] | ≥92% | I23 |
| | Cyclomatic complexity [9] | ≤20 | I24 |
| | % project time for quality testing | ≥15% | I25 |
| Reduce risk | % definitional uncertainty risk [10] | ≤10% | I26 |
| | % technological risk [11] | ≤45% | I27 |
| | % developmental risk [12] | <10% | I28 |
| | % non-alignment risk [13] | ≤4% | I29 |
| | % service delivery risk [14] | ≤5% | I30 |
| | Number of fraudulent transactions | ≤1% | I31 |
| | % systems with risk contingency plans | ≥95% | I32 |
| | % systems assessed for security breaches | ≥95% | I33 |
| Improve processes | % resources devoted to planning and review of product development activities | ≥25% | I34 |
| | % resources for R&D | Baseline | I35 |
| | Average time required to develop new product or service | Baseline | I36 |
| | Person-months of effort or project | Baseline | I37 |
| | % requirements fulfilled | ≥90% | I38 |
| | Pages of documentation | Baseline | I39 |
| | % on-time implementations | ≥97% | I40 |
| | % expected features delivered | >98% | I41 |
| | Average time to provide feedback to project team | ≤1 day | I42 |

| *Objective* | *Measure* | *Target* | *KPI* |
|---|---|---|---|
| Improve processes (continued) | Project development time | ≥50% | I43 |
| | % project backlog | ≤10% | I44 |
| | % project cancellation rate | ≤20% | I45 |
| | Ratio of support personnel to development personnel | ≥35% | I56 |
| Enhance resource planning | Number of supplier relationships | Baseline | I47 |
| | Decision speed | <5 days | I48 |
| | Paperwork reduction | ≥10% | I49 |
| Monitor change management | Number of change requests per month | Baseline | I50 |
| | % change to customer environment | Baseline | I51 |
| | Changes released per month | Baseline | I52 |
| Enhance applications portfolio | Age distribution of projects | Baseline | I53 |
| | Technical performance of project portfolio [15] | Baseline | I54 |
| | Rate of product acceptance | ≥95% | I55 |

[1] Faults of a specific severity per thousand.
[2] Total number of unique defects detected.
[3] Failures per period.
[4] Number of days that faults spend in the system (from creation to removal).
[5] Number of requirements for which test cases have been completed over total number of functional requirements.
[6] Number of requirements met over number of original requirements.
[7] Number of functions in current delivery (additions + changes + deletions) over number of functions in current delivery.
[8] [Implemented capabilities/Required capabilities] × [Capabilities tested/Total capabilities] × 100%.
[9] Cyclomatic complexity, also known as V(G) or graph theoretic number, equals the number of decisions plus one. It is calculated by simply counting the number of decision statements. A high cyclomatic complexity denotes a complex procedure that is difficult to understand, test, and maintain. Every procedure involves a relationship between cyclomatic complexity and risk.
[10] Low degree of project specification. Rate risk probability from 0 to 100%.
[11] Use of bleeding-edge technology. Rate risk probability from 0 to 100%.
[12] Lack of development skillsets.
[13] Resistance of employees or end users to change. Rate risk probability from 0 to 100%.
[14] System delivery problems such as interface difficulties. Rate risk probability from 0 to 100%.
[15] Rate on a scale of 1 to 2: 1 = unsatisfactory; 2 = satisfactory.

## Learning and Growth

| *Objective* | *Measure* | *Target* | *KPI* |
|---|---|---|---|
| Create quality workforce | % of employees meeting mandatory qualification standards | ≥95% | L1 |
| | % voluntary separations | ≥98% | L2 |
| | % leaders' time devoted to mentoring | ≥45% | L3 |
| | % employees with certifications | ≥54% | L4 |
| | % employees with degrees | ≥75% | L5 |
| | % employees with 3 or more years of experience | ≥75% | L6 |
| | Average appraisal rating | Baseline | L7 |
| | Number of employee suggestions | Baseline | L8 |
| | % expert in currently used technologies | ≥95% | L9 |
| | Rookie ratio [1] | ≤10% | L10 |
| | % expert in emerging technologies | ≥75% | L11 |
| | Proportion of support staff | ≥35% | L12 |
| | Availability of strategic information | ≥100% | L13 |
| | Intranet searches | Baseline | L14 |
| | Average years of experience with team | Baseline | L15 |
| | Average years of experience with language | Baseline | L16 |
| | Average years of experience with software | Baseline | L17 |
| | % employees whose performance evaluation plans are aligned with organization goals and objectives | ≥98% | L18 |
| | % conformity with HR roadmap as basis for resource allocation | ≥95% | L19 |
| | % critical positions with current competency profiles and succession plans in place | ≥98% | L20 |
| | % Number of net meetings compared to offline meetings | ≥20% | L21 |
| | Number of new templates, procedures, tools to increase productivity | Baseline | L22 |

| *Objective* | *Measure* | *Target* | *KPI* |
|---|---|---|---|
| Increase employee satisfaction | % employees satisfied with work environment | ≥98% | L23 |
| | % employees satisfied with professionalism, culture, values, and empowerment | ≥98% | L24 |
| | Employee overtime | Baseline | L25 |
| | Employee absenteeism | Baseline | L26 |
| | Discrimination charges | Baseline | L27 |
| | Employee grievances | Baseline | L28 |
| | Tardiness | Baseline | L29 |
| | Number of employee suggestions implemented | Baseline | L30 |
| | % in-house promotions | ≥90% | L31 |
| Enhance employee training | % technical training goals met | ≥90% | L32 |
| | Number of training sessions attended per employee | Baseline | L33 |
| | Training budget as percentage of overall budget | ≥20% | L34 |
| | Frequency of use of new skills | ≥85% | L35 |
| Enhance R&D | Research budget as percent of total budget | ≥35% | L36 |
| | Number of quality improvements | Baseline | L37 |
| | Number of innovative processes | Baseline | L38 |
| | % R&D directly in line with business strategy | ≥98% | L39 |
| | Number of technologies owned | Baseline | L40 |
| | Number of new patents generated by R&D | Baseline | L41 |
| | Number of patentable innovations not yet patented | Baseline | L42 |
| | Number of patents protecting core of specific technology or business area | Baseline | L43 |
| | Number of entrepreneurs in company [2] | Baseline | L44 |

| *Objective* | *Measure* | *Target* | *KPI* |
|---|---|---|---|
| Enhance R&D (continued) | % workforce currently dedicated to innovation projects | ≥5% | L45 |
| | Number of new products, services, and businesses launched | Baseline | L46 |
| | % employees trained in innovation | ≥5% | L47 |
| Social software engineering | Number of wikis | Baseline | L48 |
| | Number of blogs | Baseline | L49 |
| | Number of group workspaces | Baseline | L50 |
| | Number of collaborative project plans | Baseline | L51 |
| | Number of collaborative spreadsheets | Baseline | L52 |
| | Number of teams using social software engineering | Baseline | L53 |
| | Number of team members using social software engineering | Baseline | L54 |
| | Maturity of collaboration | Baseline | L55 |
| | Degree of communication efficiency | Baseline | L56 |
| | Collaborative lessons learned | Baseline | L57 |

[1] Rookie = new, inexperienced, or untrained personnel.
[2] Number of individuals who previously started a business.

# Appendix G

# Glossary

**Advocacy:** Creating a movement of "net-fluencers" to influence conversation, actions, or motives in support of an objective.

**Aggregation:** Gathering and remixing content from blogs and other websites that provide RSS feeds; typically displayed in an aggregator like Bloglines or Google Reader or directly on a desktop using software (often called a newsreader). Beneficial for breaking news. CNN uses such tools. Digg and Reddit are examples of aggregator sites.

**Ajax (asynchronous JavaScript and XML):** Development technique for creating interactive web applications.

**Alert:** Search result sent to a user via email by Google or other search engine. The user specifies words, phrases, or tags to be searched periodically.

**API (application programming interface):** Source code interface (set of routines, protocols, and tools for building software applications) provided by a computer system or program library to support requests for services from a computer program.

**Archive:** Collection of items usually organized by week or month; users may be able to comment on archived items.

**Audio–video interleave (AVI):** Microsoft multimedia video format using waveform audio and digital video frames (bitmaps) to compress animation.

**Authenticity:** A sense that something or someone is real. Blogs enable people to publish content and engage in conversations showing their interests and values, thus helping them develop authentic voices online. Agencies should always be transparent and authentic online.

**Avatar:** Graphic image of person in the new media. A virtual character has a body, clothing, behavior, gender, and name and may or may not be an authentic representation.

**Back channel communication:** Private email or other message sent by a facilitator or participant during public conferencing. Such communications significantly affect public conversations.

**Badges and buttons:** Graphics embedded into a web page (similar to widgets, sometimes called widgets) that link to online content elsewhere. They act as content syndication tools, to lead to content on other sites.

**Bandwidth:** Capacity of an electronic line such as a communications network or computer channel to transmit bits per second (bps).

**Blog:** Websites self-published by bloggers showing dated content in reverse chronological order. Items (posts) may have associated keyword tags; they are usually available as feeds and often allow commenting. Blogs may be moderated by a host or allow any material to be posted.

**Blogosphere:** All blogs on the Internet and conversations in the sphere.

**Blogroll:** List of sites displayed in the sidebar of a blog that show what a blogger reads regularly.

**Bookmarking:** Web-based service that lets users create and store links by saving a website address or item of content in a browser or on a social bookmarking site like Delicious. Adding tags allows others to find the research; the social bookmarking site becomes an enormous public library.

**Bulletin board:** Early vehicle for online collaboration. Users connected to a central computer could post and read email-like messages.

**Categories:** Prespecified ways to organize content, for example, a set of keywords that may be used but not altered when posting on a site.

**Champion:** Enthusiast or group of enthusiasts who start conversations by posting messages, responding to messages, or helping others.

**Chat:** Website interaction of a number of people who add text items into the same space at (almost) the same time. A chat room (place for chat) differs from a forum because conversations happen in real-time as they do in face-to-face encounters.

**Cloud computing:** Using applications hosted across the Internet by an independent service provider. An example is Google Doc in which a word processing program is accessible through a web browser and the document content resides in Google servers.

**Community, online:** Group of people who communicate mainly via the Internet.

**Community building:** Recruiting potential community or network participants to help them find shared interests and goals, use technology, and develop useful conversations.

**Computing over Internet:** Cloud computing supports business processes via Internet-based services. In the future, personal computer software and data will "float around" on a server and be accessed via the Internet. *Cloud* is a metaphor for the Internet, based on Internet depictions in computer network diagrams. Cloud computing provides resources as Internet services, usually common business applications online accessed from a web browser. Software and data are stored on servers. Cloud computing may be a free, subscription-based, or pay-per-use service. Two examples are Google Docs and Zoho. Google Docs is a free web-based word processor, spreadsheet, presentation, and form application. Documents are created within the application, imported via a web interface, or sent via email. They can also be saved to Google servers or to a user's computer in several formats. Collaboration is a feature. Documents can be shared, opened, and edited simultaneously by multiple users. Spreadsheet users can be notified of changes via email. Zoho is a Google Docs competitor offering free office programs for personal use and professional versions for a fee.

**Conference, online:** Conversation of members of a web forum, often organized around topics, threads, and themes.

**Constructive:** Application of new media viral mapping to a specific public affairs issue to determine a projected outcome; educating readers on projected paths.

**Content management system:** Software suite offering the ability to create static web pages, document stores, blogs, wikis, and other tools.

**Conversation:** Social networking currency; exchanging information by blogging, commenting or contributing to forums.

**Cookie:** Web (URL) address information created by a web server and stored on a user's computer that allows websites view a user's browsing pattern and preference history. Browsers can be set up to accept or not accept cookies.

**Copyright:** Intellectual property that gives the author of an original work exclusive rights of publication, distribution, and adaptation for a certain period.

**Creative common:** Not-for-profit organization and licensing system offering creators the ability to fine-tune their copyrights to specify how others may use their works.

**Crowdsourcing:** Collective skills and enthusiasm of those outside an organization who can volunteer their time to contribute content and solve problems.

**Cyberculture:** Collection of cultures and cultural products on or made possible by the Internet along with stories told about these cultures and cultural products.

**Digital story:** Short personal nonfiction narrative told from a narrator's view and composed on a computer, often for publishing online or to a DVD.

**Domain name:** Identification of a computer address. An email address has a domain indication suffix: *.edu* denotes an account affiliated with an educational institution, *.com* denotes a personal or business account, and *.gov* denotes a government account.

**Email list:** Important networking tool offering the ability to "starburst" a message from a central postbox to any number of subscribers and allowing them to respond.

**Embedding:** Inserting a video or photo to a website or email.

**Enterprise 2.0:** New suite of emergent technologies—wikis, blogs, tagging, etc. in the business environment.

**Facilitator:** Individual who helps online group or forum members manage their conversations.

**Feed:** Method by which you can read, view, or listen to items from blogs and other RSS-enabled sites without visiting a site via subscription and use of an aggregator or newsreader.

**Flash:** Animation software used to develop interactive graphics for websites, desktop presentations, and games.

**FOAF:** Friend of a friend; machine-readable ontology describing persons, their activities, and their relations to other people and objects. Anyone can use FOAF to describe himself or herself. FOAF allows groups of people to describe social networks without a centralized database.

**Folksonomy:** System of classification derived from the practice and method of collaboratively creating and managing tags to annotate and categorize content; also known as collaborative tagging, social classification, social indexing, and social tagging. See *Tag*.

**Forum:** Website discussion area where people can post messages or comment on existing messages asynchronously (independently of time or place).

**Friends:** Contacts whose profiles are linked to a user profile, thus creating a network. Some sites require a user to accept a link.

**Group:** Collection of individuals with some sense of unity via activities, interests, or values. A group is bounded; people are in or not. Groups differ from networks, which are dispersed and defined by nodes and connections.

**Hyperlink:** Text, images, or graphics that when activated by a mouse or keystrokes will connect a user to a new website. The link is usually obvious, such as underlined text or a "button" of some type.

**Instant messaging (IM):** Chatting with one other person using an IM tool like AOL Instant Messenger, Microsoft Live Messenger, or Yahoo Messenger. The tools let a user show availability for a chat. IM is a good alternative to emails for a rapid exchange. Problems arise when people in a group use IM tools that do not connect.

**iPod:** Apple's portable media (music, books, pictures, videos) player.

**iPod Touch:** Apple's portable media player, personal digital assistant, and Wi-Fi mobile platform.

**Kindle:** Amazon.com's software and hardware platform for reading electronic books (ebooks). Three hardware devices (Kindle, Kindle 2, and Kindle DX) and an iPhone application (Kindle for iPhone) support this platform.

**Listening:** Setting up searches that monitor blogs to determine when an organization receives a mention or reference; skimming feeds to the blogosphere to find out what topics "bubble up."

**Listserv:** List of email addresses of people with common interests. Software enables people on a list to send messages to the group without typing a series of addresses into the message header.

**Lurker:** Forum member who reads but does not contribute or add comments. The 1% rule states that 1% of people contribute new content, another 9% comment, and the rest lurk.

**Malware:** Malicious software designed to infiltrate a computer without the owner's informed consent. The expression covers a variety of forms of hostile, intrusive, or annoying software or program code. *Computer virus* is a catchall phrase covering all types of malware, including true viruses.

**Mashup:** Mix of technology, audio, video, and maps that combine several tools to create a new web service. For example, a mashup would be a Google map showing average housing prices drawn from a city assessor's online database.

**Microblog:** Extremely short blog posts in the vein of text messaging. Messages are available to any person or group the user chooses. Twitter, a popular microblog client, allows posts of up to 140 characters, uploaded and read online or through instant messaging or mobile devices via text messaging.

**MP3:** Digital audio player (DAP) consumer electronic device for storing, organizing, and playing audio files (music, books, etc.). Some DAPs are called portable media players as they allow image viewing and/or video play. MP3 is a patented digital audio encoding format, the most common format for consumer audio storage, and the standard of digital audio compression for the transfer and playback of music on DAPs.

**Network:** Structure defined by nodes and connections between nodes. Nodes of social networks are people and the connections are their relationships. Networking is the process of developing and strengthening such relationships.

**Newsgroup:** Internet "site" centered on a specific topic or course. Some newsreader software can "thread" discussion to center various topics on a central theme.

**Newsreader:** Website or desktop tool that acts as an aggregator, gathering content from blogs and similar sites using RSS feeds so content may be read in one place instead of on different sites.

**Ontology:** Formal representation of knowledge as a set of concepts within a domain and the relationships between concepts. It is used to reason about the entities within a domain, and may be used to describe the domain.

**Open-source software:** Software available under a license that permits users to study, change, improve, and redistribute it in modified or unmodified form. Open source describes a broad general type of software license that makes source code available to the general public with relaxed copyright restrictions or without restrictions. An open source may not impose restrictions on the use or distribution by any organization or user. Open-source software (OSS) projects are built and maintained by a network of volunteer programmers. Examples are Productivity, Open Office, and Neo Office. ILS examples are Evergreen, Koha, OPALS, Open Biblio. Linus is an OS; Firebox is a browser.

**Peer-to-peer:** Direct interaction between two people in a network. Each peer connects to other peers to allow further sharing and learning.

**Permalink:** Address (URL) of an item of content, for example, a blog post instead of a web page address containing lots of items, usually found at the end of a blog post.

**Phishing:** Fraudulent criminal activity; attempting to acquire sensitive information such as usernames, passwords, and credit card details by masquerading as a trustworthy entity in an electronic communication. Communications purporting to be from popular social websites are used to lure unsuspecting users. Phishing typically occurs by email or instant messaging and may direct users to enter details on a fake website whose look and feel are almost identical to the legitimate one. Even with server authentication, great skill is required to detect a fake website.

**Photo sharing:** Uploading images to a website like Flickr, Picasa, SmugMug, BubbleShare, and Photobucket, adding tags and offering people the opportunity to comment or even reuse photos if an appropriate copyright license is added.

**Podcast:** Series of digital media (audio or video) files released episodically and downloaded through web syndication. The mode of delivery differentiates podcasts from other ways of accessing media files (simple downloads or streamed webcasts) over the Internet. Special client software applications known as podcatchers (iTunes, Zune, Juice, and Winamp) automatically identify and download new files in a series when released by accessing a centrally maintained web feed that lists all files associated with the series. New files are downloaded automatically and stored locally on a user's computer or other device for offline use, allowing simpler access to episodic content.

**Post:** Item on a blog or forum.

**Presence online:** Availability for contact by instant messaging, voice over IP, or other synchronous method of communication; degree to which an individual's name appears in online search.

**Profile:** Personal information provided by users when they engage a social networking site. Along with a picture, a profile may include personal and business interests, a "blurb and" and tags to find like-minded people.

**Remixing:** Combining separate items of content, identified by tags and published through feeds, in different ways.

**RSS (really simple syndication):** System that allows subscribers to receive content from blogs and other social media sites delivered via a feed.

**Shockwave:** Three-dimensional (3D) animation technology format.

**Sharing:** Offering the use of text, images, videos, bookmarks, and other content by adding tags and applying copyright licenses that encourage use of content.

**Smartmob:** Gathering of users for an activity or event arising from an online connection or network.

**Smartphone:** Mobile phone offering advanced capabilities, often with PC-like functionality. No standard industry definition exists. Many smartphones are phones with advanced features like email, Internet, and ebook readers. Some are miniature computers with phone capabilities. Examples are the iPhone, Blackberry, and Google Android.

**Social network analysis (SNA):** Social relationships viewed in terms of network theory consisting of nodes and ties (also called edges, links, or connections). Nodes are the individual actors in networks. Ties are the relationships between actors. The resulting graph-based structures may be very complex because many types of ties connect nodes. Research in a number of academic fields has shown that social networks operate on levels from families to nations and play a critical role in determining how problems are solved, organizations are run, and the degrees of success in achieving goals.

**Social networking site (SNS):** Online community whose users can create profiles and socialize using a range of social media tools including blogs, videos, images, tags, lists of friends, forums, and messages. A social network service focuses on building online communities of people who share interests or activities or want to explore the interests and activities of others. Most social network services are web based and provide several ways for users to interact such as email and instant messaging services. Users of Facebook (http://www.facebook.com) can join networks organized by city, workplace, school, and region. People can also add friends and send them messages, and update their personal profiles. The site name refers to the paper facebooks depicting members of a campus community given by some U.S. colleges and preparatory schools to incoming students, faculty, and staff as a way to get to know people. Facebook is targeted to college-age levels and started at Harvard University. The website is free to users and generates revenue from advertising. Myspace (http://www.myspace.com) is an interactive, international, user-submitted network of friends, personal profiles, blogs, groups, photos, music, and videos for teenagers and adults. MySpace was overtaken internationally by Facebook in April 2008, based on monthly unique visitors. MySpace operates solely on revenues generated by advertising. Its user model possesses no paid-for features for end users. Twitter (http://www.twitter.com) is a free social networking and microblogging service that enables its users to send and read updates known as tweets. Tweets are text-based posts up to 140 characters in length displayed on a user's profile page and delivered to subscribers (followers). Users can send and receive tweets via the Twitter website, short message service (SMS), or external applications. The service is free over the Internet, but

SMS use may incur phone service provider fees. LinkedIn (http://www.linkedin.com) is an interconnected network of experienced professionals representing 170 industries and 200 countries. It is a business-oriented social networking site intended to allow registered users to maintain a list of contact details about people they know and trust in business. Second Life (http://secondlife.com/), also known as SL, is a three-dimensional virtual world accessible via the Internet. A free client program called the Second Life Viewer enables its users (residents) to interact through avatars. Residents can explore, meet other residents, socialize, participate in individual and group activities, and create and trade virtual property and services, or travel the world (grid).

**Streaming medium:** Video or audio intended to be listened to online but not stored permanently.

**Tag:** Keyword added to a blog post, photo, or video to help users find related topics or media. The activity of labeling resources of interest is known as tagging. See *Folksonomy*.

**Thread:** Strand of conversation.

**Tiny URL:** Web service that provides short aliases for redirection of long URLs.

**Trackback:** Facility for bloggers to leave calling cards automatically instead of commenting. Blogger A may write on Blog A about an item on Blogger B's site, and through the trackback facility leave a link on B's site back to A. The collection of comments and trackbacks on a site facilitates conversations.

**Transparency:** Ability to enhance searching, sharing, self-publishing, and commenting across networks to search recent events wherever online activity occurs.

**Troll:** Hurtful, but possibly valuable person who is both obsessed by and offended by everything written on a blog.

**URL (unique resource locator):** Technical term for a web address.

**Video sharing:** Sharing videos for others to view and comment on. Video sharing sites let viewers embed or display others' video on their own sites. Sharing sites include YouTube, Blip.tv, and Vimeo.

**Virtual world:** Online site like Second Life on which you can create a representation (avatar) of yourself and socialize with other residents. Basic activity is free, but you can buy virtual currency to purchase "land" and trade with other residents. Some organizations use Second Life to run discussions, virtual events, and fundraising.

**Web 2.0:** O'Reilly Media invented the Web 2.0 term in 2004 to describe blogs, wikis, social networking sites, and other Internet-based services that emphasize collaboration and sharing instead of the less interactive Web 1.0 system. The concept of Web 2.0 is use of the Internet as a platform.

**Widget:** Window gadget, a stand-alone application that can be embedded in other applications like a website or desktop or viewed on a PDA. A widget may help subscribe to a feed, perform a specialized search, and even make a donation. A widget may link to a display of news and weather, a map program, or photos.

**Whiteboard:** Online equivalent of a write-on-and-/wipe-off glossy surface; a tool that lets one write or sketch on a web page.

**Wiki:** Web page with editing capability that lets users contribute to a body of information. The best known example is Wikipedia, an encyclopedia created by thousands of contributors worldwide. After people obtain appropriate permissions from owners, they can create pages and add to and alter existing pages.

**WMA (Windows media audio):** Proprietary audio data compression technology developed by Microsoft. It forms part of the Windows Media framework. It was conceived to compete with the popular MP3 and RealAudio codecs.

**Worm:** Self-replicating computer program that uses a network to send copies of itself to other nodes (computers on the network) without intervention by a user. Unlike a virus, it does not have to attach itself to an existing program. Worms nearly always harm a network, if only by consuming bandwidth, whereas viruses corrupt or devour files on a targeted computer.

**XML:** Extensible Markup Language system for organizing and tagging elements of a document so that it may be transmitted and interpreted between applications and organizations. Human-readable XML tags define what it is and HTML defines how it looks. XML allows designers to create their own tags.

**Zune:** Microsoft version of the popular MP3 player. SanDisk's Sansa View, Clip, and Fuze are others.

# *Appendix H*

# Brief EMML Reference

## Declarations and Statements: Links to Syntax Topics

This appendix lists EMML declarations and statements with links to their syntax topics. See http://www.openmashup.org/omadocs/v1.0/emml/emmlReference.html for more detail.

| | |
|---|---|
| <annotate> | Adds attributes or children elements to selected node of a variable and assigns values using XPath expression; typically used to add metadata to mashup result or to intermediate variable. |
| <appendresult> | Appends well-formed structure of nodes to the result of mashup or to intermediate variable; typically used in repeating loops to handle results with repeated sections. |
| <assert> | Defines logical assertion comparing variables, literals, counts, or element depths. Assertions must be true to continue mashup processing. |
| <assign> | Copies and optionally transforms one variable or variable fragment to another variable; uses XPath 2.0 expressions to identify source nodes to copy and optionally applies XPath functions to transform result; statement can also assign literal values. |

| | |
|---|---|
| <break> | Explicitly break out of looping statements. |
| <constructor> | Creates a well-formed structure for the result of mashup or intermediate variable; user defines nodes of result and uses mashup expressions to define data from variable to fill the nodes. |
| <datasource> | Defines connection information to one database for use with direct SQL commands. |
| <directinvoke> | Invokes publically accessible service or website. Only REST, SOAP, and syndication (RSS or Atom) services are currently supported. |
| <display> | Sends message to log and console, optionally including value of a variable or portion of variable defined in XPath 2.0 expression. |
| <emml-meta> | Defines metadata for mashup specific to EMML. |
| <filter> | Filters set of nodes in a variable based on filter expression in XPath 2.0. |
| <for> | Processes loop of mashup statements based on count. |
| <foreach> | Processes loop of mashup statements based on set of nodes from a variable; set of nodes is an XPath 2.0 sequence defined by an expression; loops may be processed sequentially (default) or concurrently. |
| <group> | Sorts and optionally filters a set of nodes in a variable and constructs a result document based on the groups; the command supports multiple levels of grouping and calculations or other transformations on groups. |
| <if> | Handles if–elseif–else processing for mashup script based on a condition defined in XPath 2.0; user can include any mashup statement in any section of <if>. |
| <include> | Make common macros from macro library file accessible in specific mashup script or in another macro library. |

| | |
|---|---|
| <input> | Defines parameter to use as input to mashup or macro. |
| <invoke> | Reserved for future use to invoke services hosted or governed by another system that may not be publicly accessible. |
| <join> | Joins results of two or more services; statement works much like a database join in which results may be disparate but must have key nodes that determine how data is joined. Structure and nodes may be defined for inclusion in result of join. |
| <macro> | Allows definition of custom statements for use in one or many mashups; virtually any mashup statement may be used in a macro but macros cannot be nested. |
| <macros> | Root node for macro libraries containing macro definitions for use in any mashup. |
| <macro:custom-macro-name> | Instruction to use custom mashup statement. |
| <mashup> | Root element for mashup script. |
| <merge> | Merges results of two or more services that have homogeneous result models; works much like a database union; results of all services must have identical structures. |
| <operation> | Optional name for mashup service operation. |
| <output> | Defines name and type for result of mashup. |
| <parallel> | Processes each <sequence> child concurrently as separate parallel flows; statements within <sequence> are processed sequentially; <sequence> can contain variable declarations and other mashup statements. |
| <script> | Calls user-defined script to execute at runtime at specified location in mashup processing; user can include scripting code directly or point to external file on local server. |

| | |
|---|---|
| <select> | Creates structure for mashup result or intermediate variable with only selected nodes from repeating set of items. |
| <sort> | Sorts set of nodes in a variable based on sort keys and sorting expression in XPath 2.0. |
| <sql> | Executes SQL queries directly against data source; can also invoke stored procedures that return result sets. |
| <sqlBeginTransaction> | Begins transaction for SQL commands to single data source. |
| <sqlCommit> | Commits transaction for SQL commands to single data source. |
| <sqlRollback> | Rolls back transaction for SQL commands to single data source. |
| <sqlUpdate> | Executes any other SQL statement against data source; can also invoke stored procedures that do not return result sets. |
| <template> | Defines XPath expressions dynamically for passing into generic mashup scripts. |
| <user-meta> | Allows definition of metadata for mashup or macro. |
| <variables> | Contains one or more definitions of variables to hold input, output, or intermediate data for mashup statement. |
| <while> | Processes loop of mashup statements as long as specified condition is true; condition defined in XPath 2.0 expression. |
| xmlns on <mashup> or <macro> | Declares namespace used in mashup script or macro. |
| <xslt> | Transforms document-type input variable using XSLT 2.0 style sheet. |

## Common Content Model Groups

The following common content model groups are used in many EMML statements.

### *Declarations Group*

Declarations define the parameters and metadata used in a mashup. They include inputs and results of a mashup. Metadata may be user or system defined. See *Variables Group* for additional declarations. Valid content for this group is any choice of the following:

- emml-meta
- input
- output
- user-meta

### *Macroincludes Group*

Macros define custom statements for use in a specific mashup or a mashup hosted by a specific EMML engine. They are mini-mashups. *Include* statements allow inclusion of macro definitions from a macro library in a mashup or in another macro library. Valid content for this group is any choice of the following:

- include
- macro

### *Statements Group*

Statements are actions to be performed by a mashup. Valid content for this group is any choice of the following:

- annotate
- appendresult
- assign
- assert
- constructor
- directinvoke
- display
- filter
- for
- foreach
- group
- if

- invoke
- join
- merge
- parallel
- script
- select
- sort
- sql
- sqlBeginTransaction
- sqlCommit
- sqlRollback
- sqlUpdate
- template
- while
- xslt

## Variables Group

This group contains additional declarations that define variables and data sources used in a mashup. See *Declarations Group* for other types of declarations. Valid content for this group is any choice of the following:

- datasource
- variable
- variables

# Appendix I

# Computer Use Policy

In consideration of being authorized by ________________ (hereinafter referred to as "Company") to use and access Company computers, communications facilities, internal and external social networks and resources (hereinafter referred to as "Company facilities and resources'), I agree to comply with the conditions set forth in paragraphs (a) through (j) below:

(a) Use of and access to Company facilities and resources are provided only for Company business. I will use or access Company facilities and resources only in ways that are cost-effective and in the Company's best interest. I will not attempt to use or access resources or data that I have not been authorized to use or access.

(b) When a user ID is assigned to me I will change the password so that it is not easily guessed. I will not share, write down, electronically store (without strong encryption), or otherwise disclose the password, authentication code, or any other device associated with any user ID assigned to me. I will take precautions to ensure that no other person makes use of any Company facilities and resources with any of my user IDs.

(c) All data stored on or originating from, and all communications transmitted or received using, Company facilities and resources are considered the property of the Company. Such data and communications are subject to monitoring or review by authorized personnel designated by Company Management. The term "private" as referred to in operating systems, application software, or electronic mail does not refer to personal privacy of an individual's data or mail. I also acknowledge that my use of or access to Company facilities and resources may be monitored at any time to assure that such use or access is in compliance with these conditions.

(d) Company information in any form shall be safeguarded. I will not copy, or distribute to others, any Company-sensitive information except as authorized. I will not upload, publish, transmit, or otherwise disclose any such information concerning the Company, its operations and activities, on or through non-Company networks without prior approval of authorized Company Management.
(e) I will respect and observe the customs, traditions, and laws of the __________ and other countries where ______________ has computer assets. I will not use Company facilities and resources to access or attempted access any computer data or computer site, or send or knowingly receive any electronic transmission that contains political, religious, pornographic, indecent, abusive, defamatory, threatening, illegal, or culturally offensive materials. I will report any such material with the source of the site name of such material to the concerned organization.
(f) I will not use Company facilities and resources for unauthorized access to, interference with, or disruption of any software, data, hardware or system available through Company facilities and resources. I will use standard Company procedures to check all downloaded files for viruses or destructive code prior to using the files on Company facilities and resources.
(g) I will not copy or download any material or any portion thereof protected by copyright without proper authorization from the copyright owner.
(h) I will not connect or use any channel of communication not authorized in compliance with Company policy and guidelines. For any situation in which I am uncertain of what behavior is expected of me in regard to using or accessing company facilities and resources, I will contact the concerned organization.
(i) I will not utilize unauthorized Internet access connections.
(j) I acknowledge that any violations of the above paragraphs (a) through (i) may result in disciplinary action including loss of access to Company facilities and resources, termination of my employment, my contract or my employer's contract, legal action or other measures, as appropriate.

## Acknowledgment

I acknowledge that I have read and understood the ________________ Computer Use Policy as set of forth above and I shall abide by it while using or accessing company Computer and Communication facilities and resources.

______________________________

Employee Name

______________________________

Employee Signature

______________________________

Date

*Appendix J*

# Best Practices Security Checklist

**General**

| | *Vulnerability* | | *Description Criteria* | *Documentation Criteria* | *Demonstration Criteria* |
|---|---|---|---|---|---|
| 1 | **Does vendor have documented and provable IT security policy?**<br>List of Items to be included:<br>1. Statement of purpose<br>2. Organization structure<br>3. Physical security<br>4. Hiring and termination procedures<br>5. Data classification<br>6. Access control<br>7. Operating systems<br>8. Hardware and software<br>9. Internet use<br>10. Email<br>11. Technical support<br>12. Virus protection, firewall, VPN, remote access | | No IT security policy or cannot describe policy = 0<br>Can describe policy = 1 | No policy, policy is not documented, or is documented but does not include any listed items = 0<br>Documented, includes 9 or fewer of 18 items = 1<br>Documented, includes more than 10 of 18 items = 2 | No policy or site cannot demonstrate policy = 0<br>Site can demonstrate policy but does not include any listed items = 1<br>Site can demonstrate policy including fewer than 9 of 18 items = 2<br>Site can demonstrate policy including more than 10 of 18 items = 3 |

| | | | | | |
|---|---|---|---|---|---|
| | 13. Backups, disaster recovery<br>14. Intrusion detection. incident response<br>15. Personnel security<br>16. Software development<br>17. Outsourcing (off shore)<br>18. Help desk development | | | | |
| | | Score | | | |
| 2 | **Is policy reviewed and updated regularly?**<br>Question to ask:<br>1. How often is policy updated? | | Does not have policy or cannot describe review and update process = 0<br>Can describe review and update process = 1 | Does not have policy or review and update process not documented = 0<br>Can document review and update required less frequently than yearly = 1<br>Can document review and update yearly or more frequently = 2 | NA |
| | | Score | | | |

**General (continued)**

| | *Vulnerability* | | *Description Criteria* | *Documentation Criteria* | *Demonstration Criteria* |
|---|---|---|---|---|---|
| 3 | **Does vendor have management buy-in to security?** | | Does not have corporate security policy with management approval or cannot describe corporate security policy = 0<br>Can describe corporate security policy = 1 | Does not have corporate security policy with management approval or cannot provide documentation of corporate security policy = 0<br>Can provide documentation of corporate security policy = 2 | NA |
| | | Score | | | |
| **Access Control** | | | | | |
| 4 | **Is application PKI enabled for client?** | | Application not PKI enabled for client = 0<br>Can describe how application uses PKI for client = 1 | Cannot provide documentation describing PKI-enabled application for client = 0<br>Can document use of PKI = 2 | Cannot demonstrate PKI enabled = 0<br>Can demonstrate the application uses PKI = 2 |
| | | Score | | | |

| | *Vulnerability* | | *Description Criteria* | *Documentation Criteria* | *Demonstration Criteria* |
|---|---|---|---|---|---|
| 5 | **Is application PKI enabled for server and configured to require PKI for authentication?** | | Application not PKI enabled for server or configured to require PKI for authentication = 0<br>Can describe how application is PKI enabled for server and configured to require PKI for authentication = 1 | Application not PKI enabled for server or configured to require PKI for authentication or cannot provide documentation = 0<br>Can provide documentation to show application is PKI enabled for server and configured to require PKI for authentication = 2 | Application not PKI enabled for server and configured to require PKI for authentication or cannot demonstrate = 0<br>Can demonstrate PKI enabled for server and configured to require PKI for authentication = 2 |
| | | Score | | | |
| 6 | **Does vendor have robust revocation checking?** | | No robust revocation checking = 0<br>Has robust revocation checking = 1 | No robust revocation checking or cannot provide documentation = 0<br>Can provide documentation = 2 | No robust revocation checking or cannot demonstrate = 0<br>Can demonstrate process = 3 |
| | | Score | | | |

**Access Control (continued)**

| | *Vulnerability* | | *Description Criteria* | *Documentation Criteria* | *Demonstration Criteria* |
|---|---|---|---|---|---|
| 7 | **Is registration process for new users in place?**<br>Question to ask:<br>1. Is registration required for new users? | | No registration process for new users = 0<br>Has registration process for new users = 1 | No registration process for new users or process not documented = 0<br>Has documentation; not provided to new users = 1<br>Has documentation and provides it to new users = 2 | No registration process for new users or cannot demonstrate registration = 0<br>Can demonstrate new user registration = 3 |
| | | Score | | | |
| 8 | **Does vendor have access request form?**<br>List of Items to be included:<br>1. * Type of request (initial, modification, deactivation)<br>2. * System name<br>3. System location<br>4. * Date | | No form = 0<br>Can describe form = 1 | No form or cannot provide form = 0<br>Can provide blank form that contains all starred items = 1<br>Can provide blank form that contains all starred and non-starred items = 2 | No form or cannot provide form = 0<br>Can provide form including all starred items = 1<br>Can provide completed form containing all starred items and one to four |

| | | | | | |
|---|---|---|---|---|---|
| | 5. * Name<br>6. Social security number and/or employee number<br>7. Organization<br>8. Phone number<br>9. * Email address<br>10. Job title<br>11. Physical address<br>12. * Citizenship<br>13. User agreement<br>14. * Justification for access/need to know<br>15. * Type of access<br>16. * Supervisor approval<br>17. * Security manager verification<br>18. * Verification of need to know | | | | of seven non-starred items = 2<br>Can provide completed form containing all starred items and five to seven of seven non-starred items = 3 |
| | | Score | | | |

**Access Control (continued)**

| | *Vulnerability* | | *Description Criteria* | *Documentation Criteria* | *Demonstration Criteria* |
|---|---|---|---|---|---|
| 9 | **Does vendor have role-based policy for user access?**<br>Questions to ask:<br>1. Do administrators have an account for administrator work only and have an additional account for other purposes?<br>2. Are administrator privileges only granted to administrators and not to all users?<br>3. Are limits put on each user who has access to the application?<br>4. Are user privileges based on need to know?<br>5. Are permissions periodically reviewed to include superusers? | | No role-based policy for user access or cannot describe role-based policy = 0<br>Can describe role-based policy for user access = 1 | No role-based policy for user access, cannot provide documentation, or can provide documentation that answers only one or two questions = 0<br>Can provide documentation that includes answers to three or four questions = 1<br>Can provide documentation that includes answers to all five questions = 2 | No role-based policy for user access or cannot demonstrate policy = 0<br>Can demonstrate answers to one or two of five questions = 1<br>Can demonstrate answers to three or four of five questions = 2<br>Can demonstrate answers to all five questions = 3 |
| | | Score | | | |

| | *Vulnerability* | | *Description Criteria* | *Documentation Criteria* | *Demonstration Criteria* |
|---|---|---|---|---|---|
| 10 | **Is there a process for checking for inactive and terminated users?** | | No process for checking for inactive and terminated users or cannot describe process = 0<br>Can describe process for checking for inactive and terminated users = 1 | No process for checking for inactive and terminated users or process is not documented = 0<br>Can provide documentation for manual process = 1<br>Can provide documentation for automated process = 2 | No process for checking for inactive and terminated users or process cannot be demonstrated = 0<br>Can demonstrate manual process = 2<br>Can demonstrate automated process = 3 |
| | | Score | | | |

**Access Control (continued)**

| | *Vulnerability* | | *Description Criteria* | *Documentation Criteria* | *Demonstration Criteria* |
|---|---|---|---|---|---|
| 11 | **What is period for user revocation (length of contract, 1 year, whichever comes first)?**<br>Question to ask:<br>1. How long is revocation period? | | No revocation period or cannot describe period of revocation = 0<br>Can describe period of revocation = 1 | No user revocation period or cannot provide documentation = 0<br>Can provide user revocation documentation; period is less than length of contract or one year = 1<br>Can provide user revocation documentation; period is length of contract, one year, or more frequently = 2 | No user revocation period or cannot demonstrate that users are revoked = 0<br>Can demonstrate revocation of users; period is less frequent than length of contract or one year = 2<br>Can demonstrate revocation of users; period is length of contract, one year, or more frequent = 3 |
| | | Score | | | |

| | | | | | |
|---|---|---|---|---|---|
| 12 | **Does vendor have strong password policy?**<br>List of items to be included:<br>1. Minimum of nine characters<br>2. Includes at least one uppercase alphabetic character<br>3. Includes at least one lowercase alphabetic character<br>4. Includes at least one non-alphanumeric (special) character<br>5. Includes at least one numeric character<br>6. Expires after 60 days<br>7. Is different from previous ten passwords used<br>8. Is changeable by administrator at any time<br>9. Is changeable by associated user only once in 24-hour period (for human user accounts)<br>10. Is changeable only by administrator or user with which password is associated | | No password policy or cannot describe policy = 0<br>Can describe password policy = 1 | No password policy or policy is not documented = 0<br>Has documented policy that includes one to five of listed items = 1<br>Has documented policy that includes six to ten of listed items = 2 | No password policy or cannot demonstrate policy = 0<br>Can demonstrate policy including one to four listed items = 1<br>Can demonstrate policy including five to seven listed items = 2<br>Can demonstrate policy including eight to ten listed items = 3 |
| 12 | | Score | | | |

**Access Control (continued)**

| | *Vulnerability* | | *Description Criteria* | *Documentation Criteria* | *Demonstration Criteria* |
|---|---|---|---|---|---|
| 13 | **Does vendor permit use of default accounts, default passwords, community strings, or other default access control mechanisms?** | | Uses default access control mechanisms or cannot describe prohibition of listed mechanisms = 0<br>Can describe how they do not use default access control mechanisms = 1 | Uses default access control mechanisms or cannot provide documentation for prohibiting these mechanisms = 0<br>Can provide documentation that no default access control mechanisms are used = 2 | Uses default access control mechanisms or cannot demonstrate that mechanisms are not in use = 0<br>Can demonstrate that no default access control mechanisms are used = 3 |
| | | Score | | | |
| 14 | **Does vendor permit use of shared accounts?** | | Permits shared accounts or cannot describe how shared accounts are not permitted = 0<br>Can describe how shared accounts are not permitted = 1 | Permits shared accounts or cannot provide documentation prohibiting shared accounts = 0<br>Can provide documentation prohibiting shared accounts = 2 | Permits shared accounts or cannot demonstrate that no shared accounts are used = 0<br>Can demonstrate that no shared accounts are used = 3 |
| | | Score | | | |

**Confidentiality**

| | *Vulnerability* | | *Description Criteria* | *Documentation Criteria* | *Demonstration Criteria* |
|---|---|---|---|---|---|
| 15 | **Does vendor utilize appropriate file permissions on sensitive data?**<br>Question to ask:<br>1. Are file permissions based on roles and need to know? | | No appropriate file permissions for sensitive data or cannot describe file permissions on sensitive data = 0<br>Can describe file permissions and they are appropriate for sensitive data = 1 | No appropriate file permissions for sensitive data or cannot provide documentation on permissions = 0<br>Can document requirement for system file permissions for sensitive data = 1<br>Can document requirement for system file and application file permissions for sensitive data = 2 | No appropriate file permissions on sensitive data or cannot demonstrate file permissions = 0<br>Can demonstrate that system file permissions are appropriate for sensitive data = 2<br>Can demonstrate that system and application file permissions are appropriate for sensitive data = 3 |
| | | Score | | | |

**Confidentiality (continued)**

| | *Vulnerability* | | *Description Criteria* | *Documentation Criteria* | *Demonstration Criteria* |
|---|---|---|---|---|---|
| 16 | **Are authentication credentials stored in encrypted format?** | | Authentication credentials not stored in encrypted format or cannot describe use of encryption to store authentication credentials = 0<br>Can describe how authentication credentials are stored in encrypted format = 1 | Authentication credentials not stored in encrypted format or cannot provide documentation of requirement = 0<br>Can provide documentation that authentication credentials are stored in encrypted format = 2 | Authentication credentials not stored in encrypted format or cannot demonstrate that authentication credentials are stored in encrypted format = 0<br>Can demonstrate that authentication credentials are stored in encrypted format = 3 |
| | | Score | | | |

| | | | | | |
|---|---|---|---|---|---|
| 17 | **Is SSL used with sensitive web traffic?** | | Cannot describe how SSL is used = 0<br>Can describe how SSL is used with sensitive web traffic = 1 | SSL not used for sensitive web traffic = 0<br>Can provide documentation of SSL use with unclassified sensitive web traffic = 2 | SSL not used for sensitive web traffic or cannot demonstrate how it is used = 0<br>Can demonstrate that SSL is used with sensitive web traffic = 3 |
| | | Score | | | |
| 18 | **Is SSL used to protect sensitive data and data in transit?** | | SSL not used to protect sensitive data and data in transit or cannot describe how it is used = 0<br>Can describe how SSL is used to protect sensitive data and data in transit = 1 | SSL not used to protect sensitive data and data in transit or cannot provide documentation stating requirement = 0<br>Can provide documentation showing SSL is used to protect sensitive data and data in transit = 2 | SSL not used to protect sensitive data and data in transit or cannot demonstrate requirement = 0<br>Can demonstrate that SSL is used to protect sensitive data and data in transit = 3 |
| | | Score | | | |

**Confidentiality (continued)**

| | *Vulnerability* | | *Description Criteria* | *Documentation Criteria* | *Demonstration Criteria* |
|---|---|---|---|---|---|
| 19 | **Are authentication credentials encrypted during transmission?** | | Authentication credentials not encrypted during transmission or cannot describe how they are encrypted = 0<br>Can describe how authentication credentials are encrypted during transmission = 1 | Authentication credentials not encrypted during transmission or cannot provide documentation of requirement = 0<br>Can provide documentation that authentication credentials are encrypted during transmission = 2 | Authentication credentials not encrypted during transmission or cannot demonstrate requirement = 0<br>Can demonstrate encryption of authentication credentials during transmission = 3 |
| | | Score | | | |

| | | | | | |
|---|---|---|---|---|---|
| 20 | **Does vendor maintain separation of data to prevent disclosure of information?** | | Does not maintain separation of data or cannot describe how data will be separated = 0<br>Can describe how to maintain separation of data = 1 | Does not maintain separation of data or cannot provide documentation requiring separation of data = 0<br>Can provide documentation showing separation of data = 2 | Does not maintain separation of data or cannot demonstrate separation of data = 0<br>Can demonstrate separation of data = 3 |
| | | Score | | | |
| **Integrity** | | | | | |
| 21 | **Does vendor have a trust mark or site seal to validate users who reach vendor site?** | | No trust mark or site seal or cannot describe trust mark or site seal = 0<br>Has trust mark or site seal = 1 | No trust mark or site seal or requirement not documented = 0<br>Can provide documentation of trust mark or site seal = 2 | No trust mark or site seal or cannot show trust mark or site seal = 0<br>Can show trust mark or site seal = 3 |
| | | Score | | | |

**Integrity (continued)**

| | *Vulnerability* | | *Description Criteria* | *Documentation Criteria* | *Demonstration Criteria* |
|---|---|---|---|---|---|
| 22 | **Are documents loaded to vendor site scanned for viruses prior to posting?** | | Does not scan for viruses before posting or cannot describe scanning process = 0<br>Can describe process for virus scanning documents prior to posting = 1 | Does not scan for viruses before posting documents or process is not documented = 0<br>Can provide documentation of virus scanning of documents prior to posting = 2 | Does not scan for viruses before posting or cannot demonstrate scanning = 0<br>Can demonstrate virus scans prior to posting = 3 |
| | | Score | | | |
| 23 | **Are virus signatures updated at least every 14 days?**<br>Question to ask:<br>1. Is process manual or automated? | | Virus signatures not updated every 14 days or less or cannot describe update process = 0<br>Can describe process used to update virus signatures at least every 14 days = 1 | Virus signatures not updated at least every 14 days or update process not documented = 0<br>Can provide documentation that virus signatures are updated at least every 14 days via manual process = 1 | Virus signatures are not updated at least every 14 days or update process cannot be demonstrated = 0<br>Can demonstrate that virus signatures are updated at least every 14 days via manual process = 2 |

| | | | | | |
|---|---|---|---|---|---|
| | | | | Can provide documentation that virus signatures are updated at least every 14 days via automated process = 2 | Can demonstrate that virus signatures are updated at least every 14 days via automated process = 3 |
| | | Score | | | |
| 24 | **Does vendor regularly scan servers for viruses?**<br>Question to ask:<br>1. How often does vendor scan for viruses? | | Does not scan for viruses regularly or cannot describe scanning process = 0<br>Can describe virus scanning process and frequency = 1 | Does not scan for viruses regularly or cannot provide documentation of scanning process = 0<br>Can provide documentation of virus scans less frequently than weekly = 1<br>Can provide documentation of virus scans weekly or more frequently = 2 | Does not scan for viruses regularly or cannot demonstrate scanning = 0<br>Can demonstrate virus scans less frequently than weekly = 2<br>Can demonstrate virus scans weekly or more frequently = 3 |
| | | Score | | | |

**Integrity (continued)**

| | *Vulnerability* | | *Description Criteria* | *Documentation Criteria* | *Demonstration Criteria* |
|---|---|---|---|---|---|
| 25 | **Does vendor regularly scan server for spyware?**<br>Question to ask:<br>1. How often does vendor scan for spyware? | | Does not scan for spyware regularly or cannot describe scanning process = 0<br>Can describe process of scanning for spyware and frequency = 1 | Does not scan for spyware regularly or cannot provide documentation of process = 0<br>Can provide documentation of spyware scans less frequently than weekly = 1<br>Can provide documentation of spyware scans weekly or more frequently = 2 | Does not scan for spyware regularly or cannot demonstrate scanning process = 0<br>Can demonstrate spyware scans less frequently than weekly = 2<br>Can demonstrate spyware scans weekly or more frequently = 3 |
| | | Score | | | |

| | | | | | |
|---|---|---|---|---|---|
| 26 | **Does vendor regularly scan servers for adware?**<br>Question to ask:<br>1. How often does vendor scan for adware? | | Does not scan for adware regularly or cannot describe scanning process = 0<br>Can describe process to scan for adware and frequency = 1 | Does not scan for adware regularly or cannot provide documentation of scanning = 0<br>Can provide documentation of adware scans less frequently than weekly = 1<br>Can provide documentation of adware scans weekly or more frequently = 2 | Does not scan for adware regularly or cannot demonstrate scanning = 0<br>Can demonstrate adware scanning less frequently than weekly = 2<br>Can demonstrate adware scans weekly or more frequently = 3 |
| | | Score | | | |

**Availability**

| | *Vulnerability* | | *Description Criteria* | *Documentation Criteria* | *Demonstration Criteria* |
|---|---|---|---|---|---|
| 27 | **Does vendor have policy for backups?**<br>List of items to be included:<br>1. Schedule for regular backups<br>2. Backups to be stored off-site<br>3. Recovery plan<br>4. Clearly defined activities and responsibilities of individuals<br>5. Policy should be tested annually<br>6. Personnel trained annually<br>7. Backups should maintain separation of data | | No policy for backups or cannot describe backup policy = 0<br>Can describe policy for backups = 1 | No policy for backups, cannot provide documented policy, or policy does not include any items listed = 0<br>Can provide documentation of policy that includes one to three listed items = 1<br>Can provide documentation of policy that includes four to seven of listed items = 2 | No policy for backups or cannot demonstrate backups = 0<br>Can demonstrate policy including one or two listed items = 1<br>Can demonstrate policy including three or four listed items = 2<br>Can demonstrate policy including five to seven listed items = 3 |
| | | Score | | | |

| | | | | | |
|---|---|---|---|---|---|
| 28 | **Does vendor have documented, executable process for backups?**<br>Question to ask:<br>1. Is process manual or automated? | | No backup process or cannot describe process = 0<br>Can describe backup process = 1 | No backup process or cannot provide documentation of backup process = 0<br>Can provide documentation of manual backup = 1<br>Can provide documentation of automated backup = 2 | No backup process or cannot demonstrate process = 0<br>Can demonstrate manual backup process = 2<br>Can demonstrate automated backup process = 3 |
| | | Score | | | |

**Availability (continued)**

| | *Vulnerability* | | *Description Criteria* | *Documentation Criteria* | *Demonstration Criteria* |
|---|---|---|---|---|---|
| 29 | **Does backup process include operating system files?**<br>Question to ask:<br>1. Is process manual or automated? | | Backup process does not include operating system files or cannot describe process = 0<br>Can describe backup process and it includes operating system files = 1 | Backup process does not include operating system files or cannot provide documentation of process = 0<br>Can provide documentation of manual backup process that includes operating system files = 1<br>Can provide documentation of automated backup process that includes operating system files = 2 | Backup process does not include operating system files or cannot demonstrate process = 0<br>Can demonstrate manual backup process including operating system files = 2<br>Can demonstrate automated backup process including operating system files = 3 |
| | | Score | | | |

| | | | | | |
|---|---|---|---|---|---|
| 30 | **Does backup process include user data?**<br>Question to ask:<br>1. Is process manual or automated? | | Backup process does not include user data or cannot describe process = 0<br>Can describe backup process and it includes user data = 1 | Backup process does not include user data or cannot provide documentation of process = 0<br>Can provide documentation of manual backup process = 1<br>Can provide documentation of automated backup process = 2 | Backup process does not include user data or cannot demonstrate process = 0<br>Can demonstrate manual backup process = 2<br>Can demonstrate automated backup process = 3 |
| | | Score | | | |
| 31 | **Is backup process tested regularly?** | | Backup process not tested regularly or cannot describe test of process = 0<br>Can describe backup process tested regularly = 1 | Backup process not tested regularly or cannot provide documentation of testing backup process = 0<br>Can provide documentation of regular testing = 2 | Backup process not tested regularly or cannot demonstrate regular testing = 0<br>Can demonstrate that backup process is tested regularly = 3 |
| | | Score | | | |

**Availability (continued)**

| | *Vulnerability* | | *Description Criteria* | *Documentation Criteria* | *Demonstration Criteria* |
|---|---|---|---|---|---|
| 32 | **Are results of backup process verified?** | | Backup process results not verified or cannot describe verification = 0<br>Can describe backup verification = 1 | Backup process results not verified or cannot provide documented verification of backups = 0<br>Can provide documentation showing verification of backup process results = 2 | Backup process results not verified or cannot demonstrate verification of backup = 0<br>Can demonstrate verification of backup process results = 3 |
| | | Score | | | |
| 33 | **Are backups stored off-site?** | | Backups not stored off-site or cannot describe where they are stored = 0<br>Can describe off-site storage of backups = 1 | Backups not stored off-site or cannot provide documentation requiring off-site storage = 0<br>Can provide documentation of off-site storage = 2 | Backups not stored off-site or cannot demonstrate storage off-site = 0<br>Can demonstrate storage off-site = 3 |
| | | Score | | | |

| | | | | | |
|---|---|---|---|---|---|
| 34 | **Does vendor have restore and recovery processes?**<br>Issues to consider:<br>1. Restore and recovery node<br>2. High availability failover<br>Question to ask:<br>1. Is process manual or automated? | | No restore and recovery processes or cannot describe them = 0<br>Can describe restore and recovery processes = 1 | No restore and recovery process or cannot provide documentation of process = 0<br>Can provide documentation of manual restore and recovery process = 1<br>Can provide documentation of automated restore and recovery process = 2 | No restore and recovery process or cannot demonstrate process = 0<br>Can demonstrate manual restore and recovery process = 2<br>Can demonstrate automated restore and recovery process = 3 |
| | | Score | | | |
| 35 | **Are restore and recovery processes tested regularly?** | | Does not test restore and recovery processes or cannot describe testing process = 0<br>Can describe testing of restore and recovery processes = 1 | Does not test restore and recovery process or cannot provide documentation of process = 0<br>Can provide documentation of testing restore and recovery process = 2 | Does not test restore and recovery process or cannot demonstrate = 0<br>Can demonstrate testing of restore and recovery process = 3 |
| | | Score | | | |

**Availability (continued)**

| | *Vulnerability* | | *Description Criteria* | *Documentation Criteria* | *Demonstration Criteria* |
|---|---|---|---|---|---|
| 36 | **Have results of restore and recovery processes been verified?** | | Results not verified or cannot describe verification process = 0<br>Can describe verification of results = 1 | Results not verified or cannot provide documentation of verification = 0<br>Can provide documentation of verification of results = 2 | Results not verified or cannot demonstrate verification of results = 0<br>Can demonstrate verification of results = 3 |
| | | Score | | | |
| 37 | **Does application support maximum number of concurrent users based on contract requirements without impacting availability of application?**<br>Issue to consider:<br>1. Scalability | | No maximum number of concurrent users or cannot describe maximum number of concurrent users = 0<br>States that application has maximum number of concurrent users = 1 | No maximum number of concurrent users or cannot provide documentation of number = 0<br>Can provide documentation of maximum number of concurrent users but maximum is not scalable = 1 | No maximum number of concurrent users or cannot demonstrate maximum number of concurrent users = 0<br>Can demonstrate maximum number of concurrent users but maximum is not scalable = 2 |

| | | | | | |
|---|---|---|---|---|---|
| | | | | Can provide documentation of maximum number of concurrent users and maximum is scalable = 2 | Can demonstrate maximum number of concurrent users but maximum is scalable = 3 |
| | | Score | | | |
| 38 | **Does application limit maximum number of concurrent sessions per user?** | | No maximum number of concurrent sessions per user or cannot describe maximum number = 0<br>States that application has maximum number of concurrent sessions per user = 1 | No maximum number of concurrent sessions per user or cannot provide documentation = 0<br>Can provide documentation that application has maximum number of concurrent sessions per user = 2 | No maximum number of concurrent sessions per user or cannot demonstrate maximum number sessions = 0<br>Can demonstrate maximum number of concurrent sessions per user = 3 |
| | | Score | | | |

**Availability (continued)**

| | *Vulnerability* | | *Description Criteria* | *Documentation Criteria* | *Demonstration Criteria* |
|---|---|---|---|---|---|
| 39 | **Does vendor have alternative or uninterruptible power supply to support application and data transmissions?** | | No alternative or uninterruptible power supply or cannot describe alternative power supply = 0<br>Can describe alternative or uninterruptible power supply = 1 | No alternative or uninterruptible power supply or cannot provide documentation of power supply = 0<br>Can provide documentation of alternative or uninterruptible power supply = 2 | No alternative or uninterruptible power supply or cannot demonstrate power supply = 0<br>Can demonstrate alternative or uninterruptible power supply = 3 |
| | | Score | | | |
| 40 | **Does vendor provide appropriate levels of redundancy of all application components based on contract requirements?** | | No appropriate redundancy or cannot describe redundancy = 0<br>Can describe how appropriate redundancy is provided = 1 | No appropriate redundancy or cannot provide documentation of redundancy = 0<br>Can provide documentation of appropriate redundancy = 2 | No appropriate redundancy or cannot demonstrate redundancy = 0<br>Can demonstrate appropriate redundancy = 3 |
| | | Score | | | |

| | | | | | |
|---|---|---|---|---|---|
| 41 | **Does vendor utilize system performance monitoring tool to analyze performance in real-time?** | | Does not utilize system performance tool or cannot describe use of tool = 0<br>Can describe how tool is utilized to monitor system performance = 1 | Does not utilize system performance tool or cannot provide documentation of utilizing tool = 0<br>Can provide documentation of system performance tool = 2 | Does not utilize system performance tool or cannot demonstrate tool = 0<br>Can demonstrate system performance tool = 3 |
| | | Score | | | |
| **Non-Repudiation** | | | | | |
| 42 | **Does vendor use cryptography to implement encryption, key exchange, digital signature, and hash?** | | Does not use cryptography or cannot describe how it used = 0<br>Can describe how cryptography is used in application = 1 | Does not use cryptography or cannot provide documentation of cryptography use = 0<br>Can provide documentation of cryptography = 2 | Does not use cryptography or cannot demonstrate use = 0<br>Can demonstrate use of cryptography = 3 |
| | | Score | | | |

**Non-Repudiation (continued)**

| | *Vulnerability* | | *Description Criteria* | *Documentation Criteria* | *Demonstration Criteria* |
|---|---|---|---|---|---|
| 43 | **Does vendor perform auditing?**<br>List of items to be included:<br>1. Operating system<br>2. Application<br>3. Web server<br>4. Web services<br>5. Network devices<br>6. Database<br>7. Wireless | | Does not perform auditing or cannot describe how it is performed = 0<br>Can describe auditing process = 1 | Does not perform auditing or cannot provide documentation requiring auditing = 0<br>Can provide documentation of auditing; auditing includes one to three listed items = 1<br>Can provide documentation auditing and auditing includes four to seven listed items = 2 | Does not perform auditing or cannot demonstrate auditing = 0<br>Can demonstrate auditing that includes one or two listed items = 1<br>Can demonstrate auditing that includes three of four listed items = 2<br>Can demonstrate auditing that includes five to seven listed items = 3 |
| | | Score | | | |

| | | | | | |
|---|---|---|---|---|---|
| 44 | **Does vendor audit successes and failures of log-on attempts to the application?** | | Does not audit successful and failed log-on attempts or cannot describe how attempts are audited = 0<br>Can describe audits of successful and failed log-on attempts to application = 1 | Does not audit successful and failed log-on attempts to application or cannot provide documentation of auditing = 0<br>Can provide documentation of auditing successful and failed log-on attempts = 2 | Does not audit successful and failed log-on attempts or cannot demonstrate auditing of these events = 0<br>Can demonstrate auditing of successful and failed log-on attempts = 3 |
| | | Score | | | |

**Non-Repudiation (continued)**

| | *Vulnerability* | | *Description Criteria* | *Documentation Criteria* | *Demonstration Criteria* |
|---|---|---|---|---|---|
| 45 | **Does vendor have policy for reviewing audit logs?**<br>Issue to consider:<br>1. Frequency of review (daily, weekly) | | No policy for reviewing audit logs or cannot describe policy = 0<br>Can describe policy for reviewing audit logs = 1 | No policy for reviewing audit logs or cannot provide documentation of policy = 0<br>Can provide policy for reviewing audit logs; reviews less frequently than daily = 1<br>Can provide policy for reviewing audit logs; reviews daily or more frequently = 2 | No policy for reviewing audit logs or cannot demonstrate policy = 0<br>Can demonstrate reviewing logs less frequently than weekly = 1<br>Can demonstrate reviewing logs weekly or more frequently but less frequently than daily = 2<br>Can demonstrate reviewing logs daily or more frequently = 3 |
| | | Score | | | |

| 46 | **What events does vendor log?**<br>List of items to be included:<br>1. Audit all failures<br>2. Successful log-on attempt<br>3. Failure of log-on attempt<br>4. Permission changes<br>5. Unsuccessful file access<br>6. Creating users and objects<br>7. Deletion and modification of system files<br>8. Registry key/kernel changes | | Does not audit, audit does not include listed items, or cannot describe audited events = 0<br>Can describe events audited = 1 | Does not audit, audit does not include listed items, or cannot provide documentation of events in log = 0<br>Can provide documentation of auditing that includes one to four items = 1<br>Can provide policy for auditing that covers five to eight items = 2 | Does not audit, audit does not include listed items, or cannot demonstrate events in log = 0<br>Can show audit log covering one or two listed items = 1<br>Can show audit log covering three or four listed items = 2<br>Can show audit log covering five to eight listed items = 3 |
|---|---|---|---|---|---|
| | | Score | | | |

**Non-Repudiation (continued)**

| | *Vulnerability* | | *Description Criteria* | *Documentation Criteria* | *Demonstration Criteria* |
|---|---|---|---|---|---|
| 47 | **What events are logged by application?**<br>List of items to be included:<br>1. Startup and shutdown<br>2. Authentication<br>3. Authorization/permission granting<br>4. Actions by trusted users<br>5. Process invocation<br>6. Controlled access to data by individually authenticated user<br>7. Unsuccessful data access attempt<br>8. Data deletion<br>9. Data transfer<br>10. Application configuration change<br>11. Application of confidentiality or integrity labels to data<br>12. Override or modification of data labels or markings<br>13. Output to removable media<br>14. Output to printer | | Application does not audit or cannot describe what application logs = 0<br>Can describe what application audits = 1 | Application does not audit or cannot provide documentation for application audit = 0<br>Can provide documentation for application audit that includes one to seven listed items = 1<br>Can provide documentation for application audit that includes eight to fourteen listed items = 2 | Application does not audit or cannot demonstrate what application logs = 0<br>Can show application audit log covering one to five listed items = 1<br>Can show application audit log covering six to ten listed items = 2<br>Can show application audit log covering eleven to fourteen listed items = 3 |
| | | Score | | | |

| Protection | | | | | |
|---|---|---|---|---|---|
| 48 | **Does vendor follow guidance to secure its computing and network infrastructure?** | | Follows no guidance for securing network and computing infrastructure or cannot describe guidance followed = 0<br>Follows guidance for securing network and computing infrastructure and can describe guidance = 1 | Follows no guidance for securing computing and network infrastructure or cannot provide documentation of guidance = 0<br>Can provide guidance; it lacks defense in depth = 1<br>Can provide copy of guidance covering defense in depth = 2 | Follows no guidance for securing computing and network infrastructure or cannot demonstrate guidance = 0<br>Can demonstrate security guidance that lacks defense in depth = 2<br>Can demonstrate security guidance that includes defense in depth = 3 |
| | | Score | | | |

**Protection (continued)**

| | *Vulnerability* | | *Description Criteria* | *Documentation Criteria* | *Demonstration Criteria* |
|---|---|---|---|---|---|
| 49 | **Does vendor employ a firewall?** | | Does not employ firewall or cannot describe firewall = 0<br>Employs firewall and can describe it = 1 | Does not employ firewall or cannot provide firewall documentation = 0<br>Can provide firewall documentation = 2 | Does not employ firewall or cannot demonstrate use of firewall = 0<br>Can demonstrate use of firewall = 3 |
| | | Score | | | |
| 50 | **Are firewall ACLs set to deny by default, allow by exception?** | | Firewall ACLs not set to deny by default, allow by exception, or cannot describe firewall ACLs = 0<br>Firewall ACLs set to deny by default, allow by exception, and can describe ACLs = 1 | Firewall ACLs not set to deny by default, allow by exception, or cannot provide documentation of firewall ACLs = 0<br>Can provide documentation of firewall ACLs; not set to deny by default, allow by exception = 1<br>Can provide documentation of firewall ACLs set to deny by default, allow by exception = 2 | Firewall ACLs not set to deny by default, allow by exception or cannot demonstrate firewall ACLs = 0<br>Can demonstrate firewall ACLs not set to deny by default, allow by exception = 2<br>Can demonstrate firewall ACLs set to deny by default, allow by exception = 3 |
| | | Score | | | |

| | | | | | |
|---|---|---|---|---|---|
| 51 | **Does vendor deploy and monitor network intrusion detection tools?** | | Does not deploy and monitor network intrusion detection tools = 0<br>Deploys and monitors network intrusion detection tools = 1 | Does not deploy and monitor network intrusion detection tools = 0<br>Can provide documentation for deploying and monitoring network intrusion detection tools = 2 | Does not deploy and monitor network intrusion detection tools = 0<br>Can demonstrate deployment and monitoring of network intrusion detection tools = 3 |
| | | Score | | | |
| 52 | **Does vendor deploy and monitor host-based intrusion detection tools?** | | Does not deploy and monitor host-based intrusion detection tools or cannot describe use of HIDs = 0<br>Can describe use of host-based intrusion detection tools = 1 | Does not deploy and monitor host-based intrusion detection tools or cannot provide documentation of deployment and monitoring = 0<br>Can provide documentation for deploying and monitoring host-based intrusion detection tools = 2 | Does not deploy and monitor host-based intrusion detection tools or cannot demonstrate HIDs = 0<br>Can demonstrate deployment and monitoring of host-based intrusion detection tools = 3 |
| | | Score | | | |

**Protection (continued)**

| | *Vulnerability* | | *Description Criteria* | *Documentation Criteria* | *Demonstration Criteria* |
|---|---|---|---|---|---|
| 53 | **Does vendor have strong two-factor authentication for management and administrative traffic?**<br>Issues to consider:<br>1. Something you have<br>2. Something you are<br>3. Something you know | | No strong two-factor authentication for management and administrative traffic or cannot describe two-factor authentication = 0<br>Can describe strong two-factor authentication for such traffic = 1 | No strong two-factor authentication for management and administrative traffic or cannot provide documentation of strong two-factor authentication = 0<br>Can provide documentation of strong two-factor authentication for management and administrative traffic = 2 | No strong two-factor authentication for management and administrative traffic or cannot demonstrate authentication = 0<br>Can demonstrate strong two-factor authentication for management and administrative traffic = 3 |
| | | Score | | | |

| | | | | | |
|---|---|---|---|---|---|
| 54 | **Does vendor have patch management process?** | | No patch management or cannot describe process = 0<br>Can describe patch management process = 1 | No patch management process or cannot provide documentation for process = 0<br>Can provide documentation for patch management process = 2 | No patch management process or cannot demonstrate process = 0<br>Can demonstrate patch management = 3 |
| | | Score | | | |
| 55 | **What is vendor's patch management process?**<br>Questions to ask:<br>1. Does vendor subscribe to application vendor hardware/ software notification sites for latest patch notifications?<br>2. Are patches applied on a schedule?<br>3. Are patches tested before applying to productions?<br>4. Is the degree of vulnerability considered when determining timeliness of applying patches? | | No patch management process or cannot describe process = 0<br>Can describe patch management process = 1 | No patch management process or cannot provide documentation of process = 0<br>Can provide documentation of patch management addressing one or two questions = 1<br>Can provide documentation of patch management addressing three or four questions = 2 | No patch management process or cannot demonstrate process = 0<br>Can demonstrate patch management process addressing one or two questions = 2<br>Can demonstrate process addressing three or four questions = 3 |
| | | Score | | | |

**Protection (continued)**

| | *Vulnerability* | | *Description Criteria* | *Documentation Criteria* | *Demonstration Criteria* |
|---|---|---|---|---|---|
| 56 | **Does vendor have verification process to ensure patches have been applied?** | | No verification process or cannot describe process = 0<br>Can describe verification process = 1 | No verification process or cannot provide documentation of verification = 0<br>Can provide documentation requiring application of patches = 2 | No verification process or cannot demonstrate application of patches = 0<br>Can demonstrate application of patches = 3 |
| | | Score | | | |
| 57 | **Does vendor perform security self-assessments regularly?**<br>Question to ask:<br>1. How often does vendor perform self-assessments? | | Does not perform self-assessments or cannot describe process = 0<br>Performs self-assessments = 1 | Does not perform self-assessments or cannot provide documentation of self-assessment requirement = 0<br>Can provide documentation requiring self- | Does not perform self-assessments or cannot demonstrate process = 0<br>Can demonstrate self-assessments performed less frequently than monthly = 2 |

| | | | | | |
|---|---|---|---|---|---|
| | | | | assessments less frequently than monthly = 1<br>Can provide documentation requiring self-assessments monthly or more frequently = 2 | Can demonstrate self-assessments performed monthly or more frequently = 3 |
| | | Score | | | |
| 58 | **Are self-assessment results reviewed regularly?** | | Does not review self-assessment results or cannot describe review or results = 0<br>Can describe review of self-assessment results = 1 | Does not review self-assessment results or cannot provide documentation of reviews = 0<br>Can provide documentation requiring review of results = 2 | Does not review self-assessment results or cannot demonstrate review of results = 0<br>Can demonstrate review of self-assessment results = 3 |
| | | Score | | | |

**Protection (continued)**

| | *Vulnerability* | | *Description Criteria* | *Documentation Criteria* | *Demonstration Criteria* |
|---|---|---|---|---|---|
| 59 | **Does vendor require sanitation of equipment and media prior to disposal?** | | Does not require sanitation of equipment and media prior to disposal or cannot describe sanitation process = 0<br>Can describe sanitation of equipment and media prior to disposal = 1 | Does not require sanitation of equipment and media prior to disposal or cannot provide documentation of sanitation = 0<br>Can provide documentation of sanitation of equipment and media prior to disposal = 2 | Does not require sanitation of equipment and media prior to disposal or cannot demonstrate sanitation = 0<br>Can demonstrate sanitation of equipment and media prior to disposal = 3 |
| | | Score | | | |
| 60 | **Do vendor's security policies and processes include guidance for maintaining and monitoring baseline configuration?** | | No guidance for baseline configuration or cannot describe baseline configuration = 0<br>Can describe guidance for baseline configuration = 1 | No guidance for baseline configuration or cannot provide documentation of guidance = 0<br>Can provide documentation of baseline configuration = 2 | No guidance for baseline configuration or cannot demonstrate baseline configurations = 0<br>Can demonstrate baseline configuration = 3 |
| | | Score | | | |

| | | | | | |
|---|---|---|---|---|---|
| 61 | **Does vendor have process in place to routinely verify baseline configuration?** | | No process for routinely verifying baseline configuration or cannot describe process = 0<br>Can describe process for routinely verifying baseline configuration = 1 | No process for routinely verifying baseline configuration or cannot provide process documentation = 0<br>Can provide process documentation requiring routine verification of baseline configuration = 2 | No process for routinely verifying baseline configuration or cannot demonstrate process = 0<br>Can demonstrate process for verifying baseline configuration = 3 |
| | | Score | | | |
| 62 | **Does vendor employ a baseline configuration tool?** | | No baseline configuration tool or cannot describe tool = 0<br>Can describe employment of baseline configuration tool = 1 | No baseline configuration tool or cannot provide documentation of use of baseline configuration tool = 0<br>Can provide documentation requiring use of baseline configuration tool = 2 | No baseline configuration tool or cannot demonstrate use of tool = 0<br>Can demonstrate use of baseline configuration tool = 3 |
| | | Score | | | |

| Detection | | | | | |
|---|---|---|---|---|---|
| 63 | **Does vendor's security policy contain guidance for scheduled routine security audits by external party?**<br>List of items to be included:<br>1. Operating systems<br>2. Web servers<br>3. Browsers<br>4. Web services<br>5. Database<br>6. Network sensors<br>7. Firewalls<br>8. Applications<br>9. Wireless | | Policy does not contain guidance for regularly scheduled routine security audits by external party or cannot describe policy = 0<br>Can describe policy and it contains guidance for regular routine security audits performed by external party = 1 | Does not contain guidance for regularly scheduled routine security audits by external party or cannot provide documentation of policy = 0<br>Can demonstrate security policy requiring routine security audits by external party but policy does not include all listed items = 1<br>Can demonstrate security policy requiring routine security audits by external party; policy includes all listed items = 2 | Does not contain guidance for regularly scheduled routine security audits by external party or cannot demonstrate policy = 0<br>Can demonstrate security policy requiring routine security audits by external party but covers only operating systems = 1<br>Can demonstrate security policy requiring routine security audits by external party; policy covers operating systems but not all listed items = 2<br>Can demonstrate security policy requiring routine security audits by |

| | | | | | |
|---|---|---|---|---|---|
| | | | | | external party and covering all listed items = 3 |
| | | Score | | | |
| 64 | **Does vendor perform verification of perimeter router policies?**<br>Question to ask:<br>1. How often does vendor verify perimeter router policies? | | Does not verify perimeter router policies or cannot describe verification process = 0<br>Can describe verification = 1 | Does not verify perimeter router policies or cannot provide documentation of verification = 0<br>Can provide documentation requiring verification of perimeter router policies less frequently than monthly = 1<br>Can provide documentation requiring verification of perimeter router policies monthly or more frequently = 2 | Does not perform verification of perimeter router policies or cannot demonstrate verification = 0<br>Can demonstrate verification of perimeter router policies less frequently than quarterly = 1<br>Can demonstrate verification of perimeter router policies quarterly or less frequently than monthly = 2<br>Can demonstrate verification of perimeter router policies monthly or more frequently = 3 |
| | | Score | | | |

**Detection (continued)**

| | *Vulnerability* | | *Description Criteria* | *Documentation Criteria* | *Demonstration Criteria* |
|---|---|---|---|---|---|
| 65 | **Is vendor firewall or network sensor configured to alert for unauthorized access attempts and privilege escalation?** | | Firewall or network sensor not configured to alert or cannot describe how firewall or network sensor is configured to alert = 0<br>Can describe how firewall or network sensor is configured to alert for unauthorized access attempts and privilege escalation = 1 | Firewall or network sensor not configured to alert or cannot provide documentation alert configuration of firewall or network sensor = 0<br>Can provide documentation on how firewall or network sensor is configured to alert = 2 | Firewall or network sensor not configured to alert or cannot demonstrate how firewall or network sensor is configured to alert = 0<br>Can demonstrate how firewall or network sensor is configured to alert = 3 |
| | | Score | | | |

| | | | | | |
|---|---|---|---|---|---|
| 66 | **Does vendor routinely check that no new ports, protocols, or services are activated without approval by configuration management board?** | | Does not routinely check whether PPS are activated without approval or cannot describe check process = 0<br>Can describe process to routinely check that no new PPS are activated without approval = 1 | Does not routinely check whether PPS are activated without approval or cannot provide documentation of check process = 0<br>Can provide documentation for routine checks whether new PPS are activated without approval = 2 | Does not routinely check whether PPS are activated without approval or cannot demonstrate checking process = 0<br>Can demonstrate checking whether new PPS are activated without approval = 3 |
| | | Score | | | |
| 67 | **Does vendor comply with ports, protocols, and services guidance?** | | Does not comply with guidance or cannot describe compliance method = 0<br>Can describe compliance with guidance = 1 | Does not comply with guidance or cannot provide documentation on method = 0<br>Can provide documentation on compliance method = 2 | Does not comply with guidance or cannot demonstrate how compliance is achieved = 0<br>Can demonstrate compliance methods = 3 |
| | | Score | | | |

**Detection (continued)**

| | *Vulnerability* | | *Description Criteria* | *Documentation Criteria* | *Demonstration Criteria* |
|---|---|---|---|---|---|
| 68 | **Does the vendor's security policy require routine review of HIDs, NIDs, and firewall rules for accuracy, efficiency, and their ability to withstand new attacks?**<br>Question to ask:<br>1. How often are reviews completed? | | Does not require routine review of HIDs, NIDs, and firewall rules or cannot describe policy requiring them = 0<br>Can describe routine reviews of HIDs, NIDs, and firewall rules = 1 | Does not require routine review of HIDs, NIDs, and firewall rules or cannot provide policy showing requirement = 0<br>Can provide documentation showing routine review of HIDs, NIDs, and firewall rules; review less frequently than monthly = 1<br>Can provide documentation on routine review of HIDs, NIDs, and firewall rules; review monthly or more frequently = 2 | Does not require routine review of HIDs, NIDs, and firewall rules or cannot demonstrate policy with requirement = 0<br>Can demonstrate routine review of HIDs, NIDs, and firewall rules; review occurs less frequently than quarterly = 1<br>Can demonstrate routine review of HIDs, NIDs, and firewall rules; review occurs quarterly or more frequently but less frequently than monthly = 2 |

| | | | | | |
|---|---|---|---|---|---|
| | | | | | Can demonstrate routine review of HIDs, NIDs, and firewall rules; review occurs monthly or more frequently = 3 |
| | | Score | | | |
| **Reaction** | | | | | |
| 69 | **Does vendor have documented incident response program?** | | No documented incident response program or cannot describe program = 0<br>Can describe incident response program = 1 | No documented incident response program or cannot provide documentation of program = 0<br>Can provide documentation of incident response program = 2 | No documented incident response program or cannot demonstrate program = 0<br>Can demonstrate incident response program = 3 |
| | | Score | | | |

**Reaction (continued)**

| | *Vulnerability* | | *Description Criteria* | *Documentation Criteria* | *Demonstration Criteria* |
|---|---|---|---|---|---|
| 70 | **Does vendor have documented incident response policy?**<br>List of items to be included:<br>1. Statement of management commitment<br>2. Purpose and objectives of policy<br>3. Scope of policy<br>4. Definition of computer incident and their consequences<br>5. Organizational structure<br>6. Roles, responsibilities, and level of authority<br>7. Prioritization or severity rating of incident<br>8. Performance measures<br>9. Methods of secure communication<br>10. Reporting and contract forms | | No documented incident response policy or cannot describe policy = 0<br>Can describe incident response policy = 1 | No documented incident response policy, policy does not include any of listed items, or cannot provide policy = 0<br>Can provide incident response policy that includes one to five listed items = 1<br>Can provide incident response policy that includes six to ten listed items = 2 | No documented incident response policy, policy does not include listed items, or cannot demonstrate policy = 0<br>Can demonstrate incident response policy that includes one to three listed items = 1<br>Can demonstrate incident response policy that includes four to seven listed items = 2<br>Can demonstrate incident response policy that includes eight to ten listed items = 3 |
| | | Score | | | |

| | | | | | |
|---|---|---|---|---|---|
| 71 | **Does vendor have documented incident response procedures?**<br>List of items to be included:<br>1. Standard operating procedures (SOPs)<br>2. Identification of incident<br>3. Reporting of incident<br>4. Actions to be taken<br>5. Containment of incident<br>6. Eradication of incident<br>7. Recovery of incident<br>8. Contact Information (internal and external parties)<br>9. List of threats to guard against and respond to<br>10. Incident reporting forms (internal)<br>11. Incident reporting forms (External)<br>12. Equipment list<br>13. Checklists | | No documented incident response procedures or cannot describe procedures = 0<br>Can describe incident response procedures = 1 | No documented incident response procedures or cannot provide documentation of procedures = 0<br>Can provide incident response procedures including one to seven listed items = 1<br>Can provide incident response procedures including eight to thirteen listed items = 2 | No documented incident response procedures or cannot demonstrate procedures = 0<br>Can demonstrate procedure that includes one to five listed items = 1<br>Can demonstrate procedure that includes six to ten listed items = 2<br>Can demonstrate procedure that includes eleven to thirteen listed items = 3 |
| | | Score | | | |

**Reaction (continued)**

| | *Vulnerability* | | *Description Criteria* | *Documentation Criteria* | *Demonstration Criteria* |
|---|---|---|---|---|---|
| 72 | **Are incident response procedures published in hard copy?** | | Not published in hard copy or cannot describe requirement for hard copy publishing = 0<br>Can describe requirement to publish incident response procedures in hard copy = 1 | Not published in hard copy or cannot document requirement for publishing in hard copy = 0<br>Can provide hard copy of incident response procedures = 2 | Not published in hard copy or cannot demonstrate publishing in hard copy = 0<br>Can demonstrate published incident response procedures = 3 |
| | | Score | | | |
| 73 | **Are incident response procedures published on intranet or other shared medium?** | | Not published on intranet or shared medium or cannot describe requirement for intranet or shared media publishing = 0<br>Published on intranet or shared medium = 1 | Not published on intranet or shared medium or cannot provide documentation of requirement intranet or shared media publishing = 0<br>Can document requirement for intranet or shared media publishing = 2 | Not published on intranet or shared medium or cannot demonstrate publication on intranet or shared medium = 0<br>Can demonstrate publication on intranet or shared medium = 3 |
| | | Score | | | |

| | | | | | |
|---|---|---|---|---|---|
| 74 | **Is incident response policy reviewed and updated regularly?**<br>Question to ask:<br>1. How often is policy reviewed and updated? | | Not reviewed or updated or cannot describe process for reviewing and updating = 0<br>Can describe how policy is reviewed and updated = 1 | Not reviewed and updated or cannot describe process for review and update = 0<br>Can describe process for review and update performed less frequently than yearly = 1<br>Can describe process for review and update performed yearly or more frequently = 2 | Not reviewed and updated or cannot demonstrate process to review and update = 0<br>Can demonstrate process to review and update policy less frequently than yearly = 2<br>Can demonstrate process to review and update policy yearly or more frequently than yearly = 3 |
| | | Score | | | |
| 75 | **Is initial incident response training provided to user community?** | | Not provided to users or cannot describe initial incident response training requirement = 0<br>Can describe requirement for providing initial incident response training = 1 | Not provided to users or cannot provide documentation of initial incident training = 0<br>Can provide documentation of initial incident response training = 2 | Not provided to users or cannot demonstrate initial incident response training of users = 0<br>Can demonstrate initial incident response training of user = 3 |
| | | Score | | | |

**Reaction (continued)**

| | *Vulnerability* | | *Description Criteria* | *Documentation Criteria* | *Demonstration Criteria* |
|---|---|---|---|---|---|
| 76 | **Is refresher incident response training provided periodically to user community?**<br>Question to ask:<br>1. How often is training provided? | | Not provided to users or cannot describe refresher training requirement = 0<br>Can describe requirement for providing refresher incident response training = 1 | Not provided to users or cannot provide documentation of refresher training = 0<br>Can provide documentation of refresher training provided less frequently than yearly = 1<br>Can provide documentation of refresher training provided yearly or more frequently = 2 | Not provided to users or cannot demonstrate refresher training of users = 0<br>Can demonstrate refresher training of users less frequently than yearly = 2<br>Can demonstrate refresher training of users yearly or more frequently = 3 |
| | | Score | | | |

| | | | | | |
|---|---|---|---|---|---|
| 77 | **Is incident response reporting mechanism in place?**<br>List of items to be included:<br>1. Who discovered incident<br>2. How incident was recognized<br>3. Nature of incident<br>4. When incident occurred<br>5. When incident was detected<br>6. Impact on clients<br>7. Parties involved<br>8. Evidence recovered<br>9. Where incident occurred<br>10. Affected computer description<br>11. Why incident happened<br>12. How incident occurred<br>13. Team activities<br>14. Internal and external parties notified<br>15. Resolution | | No incident response reporting mechanism or cannot describe mechanism = 0<br>Can describe incident response reporting mechanism = 1 | No incident response reporting mechanism or cannot provide documentation of mechanism = 0<br>Can provide documentation of incident response reporting mechanism covering one to eight listed items = 1<br>Can provide documentation of incident response reporting mechanism covering eight to fifteen listed items = 2 | No incident response reporting mechanism or cannot demonstrate mechanism = 0<br>Can demonstrate reporting mechanism that includes one to six listed items = 1<br>Can demonstrate reporting mechanism that includes seven to eleven listed items = 2<br>Can demonstrate reporting mechanism that includes twelve to fifteen listed items = 3 |
| | | Score | | | |

**Reaction (continued)**

| | *Vulnerability* | | *Description Criteria* | *Documentation Criteria* | *Demonstration Criteria* |
|---|---|---|---|---|---|
| 78 | **Is incident response reporting mechanism on computer database, paper, or both?** | | Reporting mechanism not published on paper, in database, or both or cannot describe publishing requirement for reporting mechanism = 0<br>Can describe requirement to publish reporting mechanism in database, on paper, or both = 1 | Reporting mechanism not published on paper, in database, or both or cannot provide documentation of requirement for such publishing of mechanism = 0<br>Can provide documentation of reporting mechanism on paper only = 1<br>Can provide documentation of requirement for reporting mechanism on paper and database = 2 | Reporting mechanism not provided on computer database of paper = 0<br>Can demonstrate reporting mechanism on paper only = 1<br>Can demonstrate reporting mechanism on database only = 2<br>Can demonstrate reporting mechanism on paper and database = 3 |
| | | Score | | | |

| | | | | | |
|---|---|---|---|---|---|
| 79 | **Are incident response reports sent to management regularly?**<br>Question to ask:<br>1. How often are reports sent to management? | | Not sent to management regularly or cannot describe how reports are sent to management = 0<br>Can describe how reports are sent to management regularly = 1 | Not sent to management regularly or cannot provide documentation requiring reports to be sent to management regularly = 0<br>Can provide documentation of requirement for sending reports to management regularly; reports sent less frequently than monthly = 1<br>Can provide documentation of requirement for sending reports to management regularly; reports sent monthly or more frequently = 2 | Not sent to management regularly or cannot demonstrate requirement for sending reports to management regularly = 0<br>Can demonstrate requirement to send reports to management regularly; reports sent yearly or less frequently = 1<br>Can demonstrate requirement to send reports to management regularly; reports sent quarterly or less frequently but more frequently than yearly = 2<br>Can demonstrate requirement to send reports to management regularly; reports sent monthly or less frequently but more frequently than quarterly = 3 |
| | | Score | | | |

**Reaction (continued)**

| | *Vulnerability* | | *Description Criteria* | *Documentation Criteria* | *Demonstration Criteria* |
|---|---|---|---|---|---|
| 80 | **Are incident response procedures tested periodically by exercise or simulation?**<br>Question to ask:<br>1. How often are procedures tested? | | Not tested periodically or cannot describe how procedures are tested periodically = 0<br>Can describe how procedures are tested periodically = 1 | Not tested periodically or cannot provide documentation on periodic testing = 0<br>Can provide documentation on periodic testing; procedures tested less frequently than monthly = 1<br>Can provide documentation on periodic testing; procedures tested monthly or more frequently = 2 | Not tested periodically or cannot demonstrate periodic testing = 0<br>Can demonstrate how procedures are tested yearly or less frequently = 1<br>Can demonstrate how procedures are tested quarterly or less frequently but more frequently than yearly = 2<br>Can demonstrate how procedures are tested monthly or less frequently but more frequently than quarterly = 3 |
| | | Score | | | |

| 81 | **Does incident response team include members from all key functional areas?**<br>List of items to be included:<br>1. Senior management<br>2. Human resources<br>3. Information technology and information security<br>4. Technical staff<br>5. Budget or finance | | Does not have members from all key functional areas or cannot describe make-up of incident response team = 0<br>Can describe make-up of incident response team = 1 | Does not have members from all key functional areas or cannot provide documentation for team make-up = 0<br>Can provide documentation of make-up of team that includes one to three listed items = 1<br>Can provide documentation of make-up of team that includes four or five of listed items = 2 | Does not have members from all key functional areas or cannot demonstrate make-up of team = 0<br>Can demonstrate make-up of team that includes one or two of listed items = 1<br>Can demonstrate make-up of team that includes three or four of listed items = 2<br>Can demonstrate make-up of team that includes five listed items = 3 |
|---|---|---|---|---|---|
| | | Score | | | |

| Configuration Management | | | | | |
|---|---|---|---|---|---|
| | *Vulnerability* | | *Description Criteria* | *Documentation Criteria* | *Demonstration Criteria* |
| 82 | **Does configuration management plan include hardware, operating system, utility software, communication, network device changes, application and facilities?** | | No plan, plan does not include all items, or cannot describe configuration management plan = 0<br>Can describe configuration management plan and it includes all items = 1 | No plan, plan does not include all items, or cannot provide documentation of plan = 0<br>Can provide documentation of plan = 2 | No plan, plan does not include all items, or cannot demonstrate configuration management plan = 0<br>Can demonstrate configuration management plan = 3 |
| | | Score | | | |
| 83 | **Does configuration management plan contain necessary items?**<br>List of items to be included:<br>1. Describe configuration change<br>2. Follow approval process<br>3. Review configuration change<br>4. Schedule configuration change<br>5. Track implementation<br>6. Track system impact of configuration change | | No configuration management plan or cannot describe plan = 0<br>Can describe configuration management plan = 1 | No configuration management plan or cannot provide documentation of plan = 0<br>Can provide documentation of configuration management plan that includes one to five listed items = 1<br>Can provide | No configuration management plan or cannot demonstrate plan = 0<br>Can demonstrate configuration management plan that includes one to four listed items = 1<br>Can demonstrate configuration management plan |

| | | | | | |
|---|---|---|---|---|---|
| | 7. Record and report change to appropriate party<br>8. Back-out plan if change does not work as planned<br>9. Provide for meeting minutes<br>10. Emergency change procedures<br>11. List of team members from key functional areas | | | documentation of configuration management plan that includes six to eleven listed items = 2 | that includes five to eight listed items = 2<br>Can demonstrate configuration management plan that includes nine to eleven listed items = 3 |
| | | Score | | | |
| 84 | **Is configuration management process automated or manual?** | | No configuration management process or cannot describe process = 0<br>Can describe configuration management process = 1 | No configuration management process or cannot provide documentation of process = 0<br>Can provide documentation of configuration of manual process = 1<br>Can provide documentation of configuration of automated process = 2 | No configuration management process or cannot demonstrate process = 0<br>Can demonstrate manual configuration management process = 2<br>Can demonstrate automated configuration management process = 3 |
| | | Score | | | |

| Vulnerability Management | | | | | |
|---|---|---|---|---|---|
| | *Vulnerability* | | *Description Criteria* | *Documentation Criteria* | *Demonstration Criteria* |
| 85 | **Does vendor's security policy contain guidance for regularly scheduled internal vulnerability audits?**<br>Question to ask:<br>1. How often are vulnerability audits performed? | | Does not require regularly scheduled internal vulnerability audits or cannot describe requirement = 0<br>Can describe requirement for regularly scheduled vulnerability audits = 1 | Does not require regularly scheduled internal vulnerability audits or cannot describe requirement = 0<br>Can provide documentation requiring regularly scheduled internal vulnerability audits performed less frequently than monthly = 1<br>Can provide documentation requiring regularly scheduled internal vulnerability audits performed monthly or more frequently = 2 | Does not require regularly scheduled internal vulnerability audits or cannot describe requirement = 0<br>Can demonstrate requirement for regularly scheduled vulnerability audits performed yearly or less frequently = 1<br>Can demonstrate requirement for regularly scheduled vulnerability audits performed quarterly or less frequently but more frequently than yearly = 2<br>Can demonstrate requirement for regularly scheduled vulnerability audits |

| | | | | | |
|---|---|---|---|---|---|
| | | | | | performed monthly or less frequently but more frequently than quarterly = 3 |
| | | Score | | | |
| 86 | **Does vendor utilize network vulnerability scanner?**<br>Question to ask:<br>1. How often is network scanned? | | Does not utilize network vulnerability scanner or cannot describe how scanner is used = 0<br>Can describe how scanner is used = 1 | Does not utilize network vulnerability scanner or cannot provide documentation of scanner use = 0<br>Can provide documentation of how scanner is used; scans performed less frequently than monthly = 1<br>Can provide documentation of how scanner is used; scans performed monthly or more frequently = 2 | Does not utilize network vulnerability scanner or cannot demonstrate how scanner is used = 0<br>Can demonstrate how scanner is used; scans performed yearly or less frequently = 1<br>Can demonstrate how scanner is used; scans performed quarterly or less frequently but more frequently than yearly = 2<br>Can demonstrate how scanner is used; scans performed monthly or less frequently but more frequently than quarterly = 3 |
| | | Score | | | |

**Vulnerability Managment (continued)**

| | *Vulnerability* | | *Description Criteria* | *Documentation Criteria* | *Demonstration Criteria* |
|---|---|---|---|---|---|
| 87 | **Are results of network vulnerability scans regularly sent to management?** | | Results not sent to management or cannot describe requirement for sending network vulnerability scan results to management = 0<br>Can describe requirement for sending network vulnerability scan results to management = 1 | Results not sent to management or cannot provide documentation of requirement to send network vulnerability scan results to management = 0<br>Can provide documentation of requirement to send network vulnerability scan results to management = 2 | Results not sent to management or cannot demonstrate requirement for sending network vulnerability scan results to management = 0<br>Can demonstrate sending of network vulnerability scan results to management = 3 |
| | | Score | | | |

| | | | | | |
|---|---|---|---|---|---|
| 88 | **Is process in place to regularly correct discovered vulnerabilities and configuration discrepancies?** | | No process to correct discovered vulnerabilities and configuration discrepancies or cannot describe process to correct discovered vulnerabilities and configuration discrepancies = 0<br>Can describe process to correct discovered vulnerabilities and configuration discrepancies = 1 | No process to correct discovered vulnerabilities and configuration discrepancies or cannot provide documentation of process to correct discrepancies = 0<br>Can provide documentation of process to correct discrepancies = 2 | No process to correct discovered vulnerabilities and configuration discrepancies or cannot demonstrate process to correct discrepancies = 0<br>Can demonstrate process to correct discovered vulnerabilities and configuration discrepancies = 3 |
| | | Score | | | |

**Vulnerability Managment (continued)**

| | *Vulnerability* | | *Description Criteria* | *Documentation Criteria* | *Demonstration Criteria* |
|---|---|---|---|---|---|
| 89 | **Does vendor have verification process for ensuring vulnerabilities and configuration discrepancies have been corrected?** | | No process to ensure vulnerabilities and configuration discrepancies have been corrected or cannot describe correction process = 0<br>Can describe process to correct vulnerability and configuration discrepancies = 1 | No process to ensure correction of vulnerabilities and configuration discrepancies or cannot provide documentation of correction process = 0<br>Can provide documentation of correction process = 2 | No process to ensure vulnerabilities and configuration discrepancies are corrected or cannot demonstrate correction process = 0<br>Can verify corrections = 3 |
| | | Score | | | |
| 90 | **Does vendor routinely run port scanning tool to ensure no new or unexpected ports, protocols, or services are discovered?**<br>Question to ask:<br>1. How often are ports scanned? | | Does not utilize port scanner to ensure no new or unexpected PPS are discovered or cannot describe how scanner is used = 0<br>Can describe how scanner is used = 1 | Does not utilize port scanner to ensure no new or unexpected PPS are discovered or cannot provide documentation of requirement to use a port scanner = 0<br>Can provide | Does not utilize port scanner to ensure no new or unexpected PPS are discovered or cannot demonstrate how scanner is used = 0<br>Can demonstrate how scanner is used; scans |

| | | | | | |
|---|---|---|---|---|---|
| | | | | documentation of requirement to use port scanner; scans performed less frequently than monthly = 1<br>Can provide documentation of requirement to use port scanner; scans performed monthly or more frequently = 2 | performed yearly or less frequently = 1<br>Can demonstrate how scanner is used; scans performed quarterly or less frequently but more frequently than yearly = 2<br>Can demonstrate how scanner is used; scans performed monthly or less frequently but more frequently than quarterly = 3 |
| | | Score | | | |
| 91 | **Is vendor's application compliant with ports, protocols, and services (PPS) CAL?** | | Is not compliant with CAL or cannot describe compliance measures = 0<br>Can describe compliance with PPS CAL = 1 | Is not compliant with PPS CAL or cannot describe how operation is compliant = 0<br>Can provide documentation of compliance with PPS CAL = 2 | Is not compliant with PPS CAL or cannot describe method of compliance = 0<br>Can demonstrate compliance with PPS CAL = 3 |
| | | Score | | | |

**Vulnerability Managment (continued)**

| | *Vulnerability* | | *Description Criteria* | *Documentation Criteria* | *Demonstration Criteria* |
|---|---|---|---|---|---|
| 92 | **Are results of port scans sent to management regularly?** | | Results not sent to management or cannot describe requirement for sending port scan results to management = 0<br>Can describe requirement for sending port scan results to management = 1 | Results not sent to management or cannot provide documentation of requirement to send port scan results to management = 0<br>Can provide documentation of requirement to send port scan results to management = 2 | Results not sent to management or cannot demonstrate requirement to send port scan results to management = 0<br>Can demonstrate sending of port scan results to management = 3 |
| | | Score | | | |
| 93 | **What ports, protocols, and services are necessary for access to application from outside local enclave?** | | Note PPS and Compliance statement here: | | |
| | | Score | | | |

| | | | | | |
|---|---|---|---|---|---|
| 94 | **Does vendor routinely run web-scanning tool to check for new web vulnerabilities?** | | Does not utilize web scanner to find new web vulnerabilities or cannot describe how web scanner is used = 0<br>Can describe how web scanner is used = 1 | Does not utilize web scanner to find new web vulnerabilities or cannot provide documentation of requirement to scan web = 0<br>Can provide documentation of requirement to scan web; scans performed less frequently than monthly = 1<br>Can provide documentation of requirement to scan web; scans performed monthly or more frequently = 2 | Does not utilize web scanner to check for new web vulnerabilities or cannot demonstrate how web scanner is used = 0<br>Can demonstrate how web scanner is used; scans performed yearly or less frequently = 1<br>Can demonstrate how web scanner is used; scans performed quarterly or less frequently but more frequently than yearly = 2<br>Can demonstrate how web scanner is used; scans performed monthly or less frequently but more frequently than quarterly = 3 |
| | | Score | | | |

**Vulnerability Managment (continued)**

| | *Vulnerability* | | *Description Criteria* | *Documentation Criteria* | *Demonstration Criteria* |
|---|---|---|---|---|---|
| 95 | **Are results of web scans sent to management regularly?** | | Results not sent to management or cannot describe requirement for sending web scan results to management = 0<br>Can describe requirement for sending web scan results to management = 1 | Results not sent to management or cannot provide documentation of requirement to send web scan results to management = 0<br>Can provide documentation of requirement to send web scan results to management = 2 | Results not sent to management or cannot demonstrate requirement to send web scan results to management = 0<br>Can demonstrate sending of web scan results to management = 3 |
| | | Score | | | |
| 96 | **Does vendor routinely run password checking tool?** | | Does not utilize password checking tool or cannot describe how tool works = 0<br>Can describe how | Does not utilize password checking tool or cannot provide documentation of requirement for tool = 0 | Does not utilize password checking tool or cannot demonstrate how tool works = 0<br>Can demonstrate how |

| | | | | | |
|---|---|---|---|---|---|
| | | | password checking tool works = 3 | Can provide documentation of requirement for password checking tool run monthly or more frequently or uses PKI = 3 | password checking tool works; check is run monthly or more frequently or PKI is used = 3 |
| | | Score | | | |
| 97 | **Are results of password checks sent to management regularly?** | | Results not sent to management or cannot describe requirement for sending password check results to management = 0<br>Can describe requirement for sending password checking results to management = 1 | Results not sent to management or cannot provide documentation of requirement to send password check results to management = 0<br>Can provide documentation of requirement to send password check results to management = 2 | Results not sent to management or cannot demonstrate requirement to send password checking results to management = 0<br>Can demonstrate sending of password checking results to management = 3 |
| | | Score | | | |

**Vulnerability Managment (continued)**

| | *Vulnerability* | | *Description Criteria* | *Documentation Criteria* | *Demonstration Criteria* |
|---|---|---|---|---|---|
| 98 | **Does vendor subscribe to applicable vendor security notification sites for latest security vulnerability notifications?** | | Does not subscribe to security notification sites or cannot describe requirement for subscribing to sites = 0<br>Can describe requirement for subscribing to security notification sites = 1 | Does not subscribe to security notification sites or cannot provide documentation of requirement for subscribing to sites = 0<br>Can provide documentation of requirement to subscribe to security notification sites = 2 | Does not subscribe to security notification sites or cannot demonstrate subscriptions to sites = 0<br>Can demonstrate subscriptions to security notification sites = 3 |
| | | Score | | | |
| **Personal Security** | | | | | |
| 99 | **Does vendor have documented requirement for background security investigations?**<br>Question to ask:<br>1. What type of background security investigation is required? | | No requirement for background security investigation or cannot describe investigation = 0<br>Can describe background security investigation = 1 | No requirement for background security investigation or cannot provide documentation of requirement for background security investigation = 0 | No background security investigation requirement or cannot demonstrate performance of background security investigations = 0<br>Can demonstrate |

| | | | | | |
|---|---|---|---|---|---|
| | | | | Can provide documentation of requirement for background security investigation = 1 | performance of background security investigation = 1 |
| | | Score | | | |
| 100 | **Does vendor regularly perform background security investigations?**<br>Question to ask:<br>1. How frequently are background investigations performed? | | No regular background security investigation or cannot describe investigation = 0<br>Can describe regular background security investigation = 1 | No background security investigation or cannot document background security investigation = 0<br>Can provide documentation of background security investigation performed less frequently than every 5 years = 1<br>Can provide documentation of background security investigation performed every 5 years or more frequently = 2 | No background security investigation or cannot demonstrate performance of background investigation = 0<br>Can demonstrate performance of security investigation less frequently than every 5 years = 2<br>Can demonstrate performance of security investigation every 5 years or more frequently = 3 |
| | | Score | | | |

**Personal Security (continued)**

| | *Vulnerability* | | *Description Criteria* | *Documentation Criteria* | *Demonstration Criteria* |
|---|---|---|---|---|---|
| 101 | **Can vendor prove it performs background security investigations?**<br>Issue to consider:<br>1. Is having a clearance a requirement in statement of work? | | Cannot prove it perfoms background investigations = 0<br>Can prove it performs background investigations = 2 | NA | NA |
| | | Score | | | |
| 102 | **Does vendor's background security investigation include pertinent areas?**<br>List of items to be included:<br>1. Does employment process restrict hiring convicted felons?<br>2. Does investigation cover participation or membership in subversive activities or groups?<br>3. Does investigation research credit backgrounds of potential employees?<br>4. Does employment process require drug screenings? | | No requirement for background security investigation or cannot describe investigation = 0<br>Can describe background investigation = 1 | No requirement for background security investigation or cannot provide documentation of background investigation = 0<br>Can provide documentation of background investigation covering one or two listed items = 1<br>Can provide documentation of background | No requirement for background security investigation or cannot demonstrate background investigation = 0<br>Can demonstrate background investigation covering one or two listed items = 1<br>Can demonstrate background covering three listed items = 2<br>Can demonstrate |

| | | | | | |
|---|---|---|---|---|---|
| | | | | investigation covering three or four listed items = 2 | background covering four listed items = 3 |
| | | Score | | | |
| 103 | **Are vendor personnel subject to background checks?**<br>List of items to be included:<br>1. System administrators<br>2. Help desk<br>3. Administrative personnel<br>4. Management<br>5. Janitorial staff | | Not subject to background check or cannot describe background check = 0<br>Can describe background check = 1 | Not subject to background check or cannot provide documentation of background check = 0<br>Can provide documentation of background check; system administrators and help desk subject to background check = 1<br>Can provide documentation of background check covering all five listed items = 2 | Not subject to background check or cannot demonstrate check = 0<br>Can demonstrate background check; system administrators and help desk are subject to background check = 1<br>Can demonstrate background check; system administrators, help desk, and management subject to check = 2<br>Can demonstrate background check; all listed items subject to check = 3 |
| | | Score | | | |

**Personal Security (continued)**

| | *Vulnerability* | | *Description Criteria* | *Documentation Criteria* | *Demonstration Criteria* |
|---|---|---|---|---|---|
| 104 | **Do personnel assigned to conduct background checks have security clearances?** | | No security clearance or cannot describe requirement for such personnel to have clearance = 0<br>Can describe requirement for personnel who require clearance = 1 | No security clearance or cannot provide documentation of requirement for these personnel to have clearance = 0<br>Can provide documentation of requirement for these personnel to have clearance = 2 | No security clearance or cannot demonstrate requirement for these personnel to have clearance = 0<br>Can demonstrate these personnel have clearance = 3 |
| | | Score | | | |
| **Physical Security** | | | | | |
| 105 | **Is access control present at every physical access point to vendor facility?** | | No access control at every access point or cannot describe access control = 0<br>Can describe access control at every access point = 1 | No access control at every access point or cannot provide documentation requiring access control at every access point = 0<br>Can provide | No access control at every access point or cannot demonstrate how every physical access point has access control = 0<br>Can demonstrate access control at |

| | | | | | |
|---|---|---|---|---|---|
| | | | | documentation requiring access control at every access point = 2 | every physical access point = 3 |
| | | Score | | | |
| 106 | **Does equipment facility housing have a separate access control zone to restrict unauthorized personnel?** | | No separate access control zone to restrict unauthorized personnel or cannot describe how separate access control zone restricts unauthorized personnel = 0<br>Can describe how separate access control zone restricts unauthorized personnel = 1 | No separate access control zone to restrict unauthorized personnel or cannot provide documentation of requirement to have separate access control zone to restrict unauthorized personnel = 0<br>Can provide documentation of requirement to use separate access control zone to restrict unauthorized personnel = 2 | No separate access control zone to restrict unauthorized personnel or cannot demonstrate how separate access control zone restricts unauthorized personnel = 0<br>Can demonstrate how separate access control zone restricts unauthorized personnel = 3 |
| | | Score | | | |

**Physical Security (continued)**

| | *Vulnerability* | | *Description Criteria* | *Documentation Criteria* | *Demonstration Criteria* |
|---|---|---|---|---|---|
| 107 | **Does equipment facility housing have additional security measures (key control)?**<br>Items to Consider<br>1. Locking area with key when not manned.<br>2. All interior and exterior doors have closed-circuit television (CCTV) or motion detectors<br>3. Area staffed 24/7, alarmed when not staffed , or locked with GSA approved system when not staffed | | No additional security measures or cannot describe additional security measures = 0<br>Can describe additional security measures in facility housing equipment = 1 | No additional security measures or cannot provide documentation requiring additional security measures = 0<br>Can provide documentation requiring additional security measures = 2 | No additional security measures or cannot demonstrate additional security measures = 0<br>Can demonstrate additional security measures at facility housing equipment; area is locked with key lock when not staffed = 1<br>Can demonstrate additional security measures at facility housing equipment; all doors have CCTV or motion detectors = 2 |

| | | | | | |
|---|---|---|---|---|---|
| | | | | | Can demonstrate additional security measures at facility housing equipment; area is staffed 24/7, is alarmed when not staffed, or is locked when not staffed = 3 |
| | | Score | | | |
| 108 | **Does facility have disaster recovery plan?**<br>Question to ask:<br>1. Is plan documented and tested annually? | | No disaster recovery plan or cannot describe plan = 0<br>Can describe disaster recovery plan = 1 | No disaster recovery plan or cannot provide plan = 0<br>Can provide disaster recovery plan that is documented and not tested = 1<br>Can provide disaster recovery plan that is documented and tested annually = 2 | No disaster recovery plan or cannot demonstrate plan = 0<br>Can demonstrate disaster recovery plan; plan is only documented = 2<br>Can demonstrate disaster recovery plan that is documented and tested annually = 3 |
| | | Score | | | |

**Physical Security (continued)**

| | *Vulnerability* | | *Description Criteria* | *Documentation Criteria* | *Demonstration Criteria* |
|---|---|---|---|---|---|
| 109 | Does facility have environmental controls?<br>Items to include:<br>1. Fire suppression<br>2. Climate-controlled computer facility | | No environmental controls or cannot describe controls = 0<br>Can describe environmental controls = 1 | No environmental controls or cannot provide documentation of environmental controls = 0<br>Can provide documentation of environmental controls covering one listed item = 1<br>Can provide documentation of environmental controls covering two listed items = 2 | No environmental controls or cannot demonstrate controls = 0<br>Can demonstrate environmental controls covering one listed item = 2<br>Can demonstrate environmental controls covering two listed items = 3 |
| | | Score | | | |

| Security Awareness and Training | | | | | |
|---|---|---|---|---|---|
| 110 | Do employees receive general security training?<br>Questions to ask:<br>1. Are training materials available?<br>2. Are initial and annual training sessions conducted and documented? | | No general security training or cannot describe training = 0<br>Can describe general security training = 1 | No general security training or cannot provide documentation of training = 0<br>Can provide documentation of general security training via available training materials = 1<br>Can provide documentation of initial and annual general security training; training is documented = 2 | No general security training or cannot demonstrate general security training = 0<br>Can demonstrate general security training achieved by making training materials available = 2<br>Can demonstrate initial and annual general security training; training is documented = 3 |
| | | Score | | | |

**Security Awareness and Training (continued)**

| | *Vulnerability* | | *Description Criteria* | *Documentation Criteria* | *Demonstration Criteria* |
|---|---|---|---|---|---|
| 111 | **Do privileged users receive additional security training specific to their duties?**<br>Questions to ask:<br>1. Are privileged users given additional training?<br>2. Are system administrators, security personnel, and other privileged users required to be certified? | | No additional security training for privileged users or cannot describe additional training = 0<br>Can describe privileged users' additional training = 1 | No additional security training or cannot provide documentation of privileged users' additional training = 0<br>Can provide documentation of privileged users' additional training = 1<br>Can provide documentation of additional training of system administrators, security personnel, and privileged users = 2 | No additional general security training or cannot demonstrate training = 0<br>Can demonstrate privileged users' additional training = 2<br>Can demonstrate additional training of system administrators, security personnel, and privileged users = 3 |
| | | Score | | | |

*Appendix K*

# User Interface Design Guide*

## 1.0 Introduction: How to Use Guidelines

The guidelines on user interface design found in this document are necessarily generic. They are meant to apply across a wide range of applications. To do so, they must be worded at a relatively high level. The first step is to select guidelines that are meaningful in the context of the user interface to be developed. Next, each guideline must be developed to the point of defining a clear, specific design rule. The full set of design rules then constitutes the project's style guide.

## 1.1 Developing Style Guide

The process for developing a style guide includes the following steps:

- Identify relevant guidelines. From the overall set of guidelines, select those that pertain to the application under development.
- Narrow the subset of pertinent guidelines. The subset of guidelines selected in the first step may include some that conflict. The choice of guidelines to retain may be based on relative importance or impact in relation to time and budget constraints.

* Adapted from User-Interface Guidelines. January 30, 1996. Goddard Space Flight Center. Data Systems Technology Division.

- Develop design rules from guidelines. Translation is required to move from high-level guidelines to specific design rules. One guideline may require a whole set of design rules. If a guideline requires displays to be formatted consistently, for example, a set of design rules should specify the locations of such display features as menu titles, icon labels, dialog boxes, and error messages. Design rules take the guidelines down to a concrete, highly specific level.

Because a particular guideline can be translated in numerous ways, translation requires designers to define interface components, application components, and constraints that must be met.

- Document and distribute design rules. Each member of the design and development team needs unambiguous guidance on the rules to be followed. The goal of collecting design rules in a style guide is to encourage consistency in the look and feel of the application.
- Allow reasonable exceptions. As the design rules are applied during design, some rules may conflict with others or may simply be inapplicable due to design constraints. In such cases, the group can agree to make exceptions, record and distribute the rationales for exceptions, and perhaps revise the rules in question.

Occasionally, a conflict may arise between guidelines. Sometimes the development team can decide which guideline to accept simply by considering whether one or the other is more appropriate for the application. When the answer is not clear, the team can use a more formal decision-making process, according to the following steps:

- Identify attributes of user performance that may be affected by conflicting guidelines (e.g., color discrimination, target detection, speed of response).
- Weight the importance of those attributes for overall system performance. Weightings are likely to vary from project to project.
- Rate the conflicting guidelines for expected effect on each performance outcome. The rating scale should have at least three alternatives (high = 1, moderate = 2, low = 3) but should always have an odd number of alternatives so that a mid-point is defined.
- Multiply ratings by weights and add the products. Select the guideline with the higher total.

## 1.2 From Guidelines to Design Rules

Several examples follow to illustrate the transition from guideline to design rule:

- Guideline example for buttons. When the same buttons are used for different windows, consistently place them in the same location and keep related buttons together.
- Transition questions. Which buttons are involved? Are there related buttons? Where should these buttons be placed in this application?
- Sample design rule: Place window-level buttons at bottom of window.
- Guideline example for labels: Label each data field to inform users of entries to be made. Keep labels close to associated data fields; separate them by at least one space. For more clarity, employ additional cues in a field label or in the field.
- Transition questions: How can we aid users to know where a label ends and an entry field begins? How many spaces should be inserted between label and data?
- Sample design rule: Use three-dimensional (3D) shading to delineate data field.
- Guideline example for graphical aids: Provide graphical or textual aids to assist users in maintaining their orientation within underlying menu structure.
- Transition questions: Will a graphical or textual aid benefit users? If the aid is to be graphical, what should it include? Should the aid be displayed continuously or not?
- Sample design rule: At user request, display a small schematic of entire menu structure. Use the schematic provided by the menu project manager. As the user proceeds through the menu structure, highlight the path taken in yellow.

Design rules should be specific enough that different developers will produce exactly the same features when applying them. For this reason, rules should be pretested to ensure that developers will agree on interpretation. Leave little room for variety of interpretations.

## 2.0 User-Centered Design Principles and Guidelines

User productivity can be enhanced by providing consistent and comprehensible displays, flexibility to change or structure a system, informative feedback, error tolerance, and reduced demands on short-term memory—all of which give a user a sense of competence, mastery, and control over the system. The following principles are offered as general guidance in designing a user interface. They represent a condensation of the many general principles articulated in the literature on user-interface design.

## 2.1 Maintain Consistency in Look and Feel

Consistent visual appearance and consistent response to user input are required throughout the user interface. Interface characteristics should be uniform and familiar, with consistent sequences of actions in similar situations. Terminology must be consistent to avoid confusing users. A user interface becomes intuitive by consistently meeting users' expectations.

### 2.1.1 Consistent Interface Characteristics

Allow the user to build up expectations and predict system actions based on the system's performance of other actions.

2.1.1.1 Permit the user to take the general knowledge and skills learned in one system and transfer them to another like it, without requiring extensive learning and training exercises. Positive transfer may be based on any or all of the following:

- Analogy with manual methods (e.g., file cabinet for a collection of files)
- Experience with similar systems
- Previous experience in life or culture (e.g., red = danger)
- Experience with this system's consistent look and feel

2.1.1.2 Maintain consistency in following design areas:

| |
|---|
| Display:<br>Icon design and meaning<br>Title field location<br>Menu bar location<br>Message location<br>Cursor shape and function<br>Cursor home position<br>Field delimiters<br>Color meanings<br>Data entry prompt |
| System control:<br>Command terminology<br>Command meanings<br>Editing procedures<br>Function keys<br>Command keys |
| Labeling terminology |
| Abbreviations |

| Mnemonics |
|---|
| Acronyms |
| Alarms and warnings |
| Visual coding |

2.1.1.3 Occasional departures from consistency may be necessary to support user task performance or convenience. If such departures are necessary, try to minimize the extent of inconsistency with the rest of the interface.

## 2.2 Provide Shortcuts and Flexibility

The experienced user needs the ability to go directly to specific locations in the user interface (UI) structure. The UI should be flexible enough to accommodate different user styles of performing tasks.

### *2.2.1 Number of Interactions*

Limit the number of interactions a frequent user must perform. Based on their knowledge, skill, and experience, users should have the flexibility to change or structure a system to suit their particular requirements.

### *2.2.2 Self-Pacing*

Ensure that the pacing of inputs is controlled by the user.

### *2.2.3 Keyboard Commands*

Provide keyboard commands for use by more experienced users as alternatives to cursor pointing and selection.

### *2.2.4 Loading on User Memory*

To support job performance, mnemonics, codes, special or long sequences, and detailed instructions should be kept to a minimum.

### *2.2.5 Log-On and Log-Off*

Support ease of logging on and logging off by

- Providing means to log on and log off by single action.
- Prior to accepting log-off, informing user of pending actions.

- For automatic log-off, providing audible signal prior to log-off.
- Permitting user to save contents of task document before log-off.

## 2.3 Present Informative Feedback

Learning and user confidence result from feedback. Feedback informs the user when processing is in progress or when the system has completed a request. Feedback also indicates user selection of a displayed element such as a menu option.

### *2.3.1 Automatic Validation*

For data processing, provide automatic validation to check for entries of correct content and/or format. If incorrect data are entered, a message should request a revised entry.

### *2.3.2 Temporary Deferral*

For the user who wants to defer a required data item, provide a special symbol to be entered by the user to indicate that the item has been temporarily omitted and not ignored. Upon a request to process entries that include deferred data items, inform the user of the omission(s) and permit immediate entry of missing items or allow for further deferral.

### *2.3.3 Clarity and Brevity*

Present information in a manner that is understandable and concise.

2.3.3.1 When displaying text for user guidance, use simple and clear wording.
2.3.3.2 Begin sentences with main topic. Keep sentences short and simple.
2.3.3.3 Use distinct words. Avoid contractions or combined forms.

### *2.3.4 Rules of Message Composition*

2.3.4.1 Use affirmative rather than negative command statements.
2.3.4.2 Use active rather than passive voice.
2.3.4.3 Phrase a sequence of events in corresponding word order.
2.3.4.4 Display a series of related items in a list, not as continuous text (Table K.1).
2.3.4.5 Base level of detail on user's knowledge and experience. Examples of messages for inexperienced users are illustrated in the "Better" column of Table K.2.

**Table K.1 List of Related Items**

| *Not Good* | *Better* |
|---|---|
| Create new log-on by entering user ID, entering your full name, entering organization code, and pressing save button. | To Create A New Log-on:<br>• Enter user ID<br>• Enter your full name<br>• Enter organization code<br>• Press save button |

**Table K.2 Messages for Novice Users**

| *Not Good* | *Better* |
|---|---|
| Position cursor on save and click. | Click on save button. |
| Date: | Date mm/dd/yy: _ _/_ _/_ _ |
| Press up or down arrows to move up or down. | To move up: Press up arrow.<br>To move down: Press down arrow. |
| Pressing ESC will cause you to exit. | To exit, press esc button. |

### *2.3.5 Message Location*

Provide consistent location for messages, such as a designated line at the bottom of the screen or a window.

2.3.5.1 Make messages distinct from other displayed information using techniques such as highlighting, reverse video, or different fonts.

2.3.5.2 Display messages in mixed case.

## 2.4 Design for Recovery from Error

When an error occurs, tell the user what the error is and how to correct it.

### *2.4.1 Undo Function*

When possible, permit easy reversal of actions. It benefits a user to know that an error can be undone.

2.4.1.1 Provide an undo command that immediately enables the user to reverse the previous control, entry, change, or delete action.

2.4.1.2 Make an undo action reversible. A second undo action should reinstate whatever was just undone.

### 2.4.2 Meaningful Error Messages

2.4.2.1 An error message should state the nature of the error and provide possible solutions. Error messages should be brief and worded in terms of the task.

2.4.2.2 Enable a user to inquire about the error in more detail and/or request additional information on the operation in progress.

### 2.4.3 Backup Function

Make it possible to back up in a transaction sequence to correct errors and/or make changes.

### 2.4.4 Minor Deviations

Accept minor deviations. Under some circumstances, there are acceptable deviations such as equating *exit* with off, log-off, quit, or bye.

## 2.5 Reduce Memory Demands

Human capacity for information processing has limitations. Short-term memory provides a limited mental "scratchpad" for information processing and problem solving. Too many facts and decisions may overload short-term memory.

### 2.5.1 Length and Complexity

Do not require users to remember lengthy lists of codes and complex command strings.

### 2.5.2 Amount of Input Activity

Require fewer input activities to increase user productivity.

### 2.5.3 Selection through Recognition

Provide selections from a list of choices. This eliminates memorization, structure decision making, and typographical errors. Selecting from a pull-down menu is an example of recognition that places little demand on short-term memory when compared to unaided recall of command strings.

## 2.6 Design for Task Relevance

Present information that pertains to the user's task. Any arrangement of items on the screen (in menus, lists, tables, etc.) should reflect task requirements.

### *2.6.1 Task-Related Capabilities*

Use system capabilities to support task performance. For example, use color, highlighting techniques, and graphics only to enhance user task accomplishment.

2.6.1.1 Make the design focus on the task, not on what the user must do with the hardware and software to accomplish the task.
2.6.1.2 Use dialog techniques that reflect the user's view and conception of what needs to be done.

### *2.6.2 Familiar Terms*

Use terminology that is familiar to the user. Abbreviations, icons, mnemonics, codes, and acronyms should stem from specific job-related terminology or a known logic. Avoid the technical language of designers and programmers.

## 2.7 Aid Orientation and Navigation

Provide orientation aids and instructions to help users maintain a sense of where they are in the system, what they can do, and how they can get out.

### *2.7.1 Descriptive Title*

Include a descriptive title placed in a consistent location on each screen, window, and menu.

2.7.1.1 Provide a clear, distinctive, and short title that reflects the content and purpose of a screen. Avoid words such as *form* and *screen* and connecting words like *of* in the title.
2.7.1.2 Center the title on the screen.
2.7.1.3 Display the screen title in capital letters or mixed case.

Use a numbering scheme to identify the currently displayed page and the total number of pages in a multipage display (e.g., 2 of 20).

### *2.7.2 Screen Identifiers*

2.7.2.1 Locate screen identifiers consistently, preferably to the right of the screen title.

### 2.7.3 Site or System Map

When appropriate, provide a site map or system map to show users where they are in the system.

### 2.7.4 Anticipation of User Actions

Anticipate possible user actions. In preparation for possible actions, provide the user with

- A uniform starting point for control entries
- Available transaction options
- Task-relevant menus and consistently located control options
- Editable fields that are distinct from noneditable fields
- Default values, displayed automatically in appropriate data fields
- User-interrupt, continue, and abort functions.
- A simple means of navigating between windows

### 2.7.5 Exiting

Provide the user with a means to log off by a single action (e.g., menu option, command input).

2.7.5.1 Inform users of pending actions that will be lost upon log-off.

2.7.5.2 Permit a user to exit a file without saving changes; require a confirmation to exit without saving changes.

2.7.5.3 Give a user a means to stop interacting with any type of file by a single exiting action (e.g., menu option, command input).

## 2.8 Provide Online Help

Provide users with online help that can be entered whenever needed. Tailor help to task context and requirements. Presenting an entire user manual in response to a help query will only frustrate the user. Effective help can serve as a data-protection resource.

### 2.8.1 Multilevel Help

Provide multilevel help, beginning with summary information and providing more detailed explanations on request.

### *2.8.2 Access to Help*

Permit the user to enter help at any point.

### *2.8.3 Request for Help*

Use a simple, standard action for requesting help.

### *2.8.4 Help Browser*

Permit the user to browse help topics.

### *2.8.5 Context-Sensitive Help*

Tailor available help to task context and requirements.

### *2.8.6 Automatic Help*

Activate the help function automatically (or offer help) when a user makes repeated errors.

### *2.8.7 Return to Task*

Provide an easy means of returning to the task after accessing help.

## 2.9 Maintain User-Centered Perspective

Focusing on user requirements is the key to maintaining a user-centered perspective. Every element of a design should be traceable to user requirements. From this perspective it is counterproductive to introduce "bells and whistles" simply because it is technically possible to implement them. Capabilities not needed by the user will remain unused or may cause confusion.

### *2.9.1 User in Control*

Keep the user in charge. A system that gives users a sense of control and responds to their actions builds trust and acceptance.

### *2.9.2 Decision Assistants*

Design any required decision aids as assistants to (not replacements for) the user's flexible decision-making capabilities.

# 3.0 Guidelines for Basic User Interface Components

Basic components of alphanumeric user interfaces include such elements as text fields, tables, and lists. Graphical user interfaces add lines, shapes, pushbuttons, icons, and dialog boxes. Both types of user interfaces (UIs) incorporate one or more cursors, and labeling is important for both. The key design challenge is to select and integrate all UI components into a seamless whole.

## 3.1 Cursors

Cursors enable a user to move the focus of input or attention on a screen. Cursor control should provide fast movement and accurate placement. A placeholding cursor should be easy to see and should not interfere with detection of any adjacent symbol or character. A second pointing cursor should be visually distinct from the placeholding cursor.

### *3.1.1 Placeholding Cursor*

On the screen, a cursor is typically positioned for quick and easy start of the keying process. The placeholding cursor is a mark on the display indicating the current position for attention.

3.1.1.1 Place the cursor at the first data entry field to which the user must provide input and advance it to the next data field when the user has completed entry in the current field.

3.1.1.2 Use only one placeholding cursor in each window in which the user enters alphanumeric characters.

3.1.1.3 Make a placeholding cursor the same height or width as the adjacent alphanumeric character.

### *3.1.2 Pointing Cursor*

The pointing cursor has the advantage of permitting a user to point at display information and select an item. This direct manipulation approaches commands that do not have to be learned, reduces the chances of typographic errors on a keyboard, and keeps attention on the display.

3.1.2.1 Do not make the pointing cursor blink.

3.1.2.2 Make the pointing cursor completely graphic. Do not use a label.

3.1.2.3 Do not allow pointing cursor to move without input from the user.

3.1.2.3.1 Ensure that the step size of cursor movement is both horizontally and vertically consistent.

3.1.2.4 Use a cursor to enable a user to move the focal point of input or attention within a display.
3.1.2.5 Make the pointing cursor available at all times. It should not obscure other, critical information.
3.1.2.6 Use crosshairs when fine positioning accuracy is required.
3.1.2.7 Use multiple cursors only if required by the task.
3.1.2.8 Make multiple cursors visually distinctive.
3.1.2.9 Provide a visual indication of the cursor being controlled.

## 3.2 Text

The user interface presents text, for example, in menus, labels, help windows, and message areas. The user may need to enter brief text, as in naming a file or making control entries, or enter continuous text, as in writing a comment or maintaining an online event log. The user needs simple editing capabilities (e.g., for correcting typographical errors and making word substitutions) that do not require going into a separate edit mode.

### *3.2.1 Text Fields*

Present text fields in a consistent format, from one display to another.

3.2.1.1 Enable the use of text fields to execute commands such as spell check, grammar check, search, find, and replace.
3.2.1.2 Ensure that control entries (e.g., keyed menu selections or commands) are distinguishable from displayed text to prevent the user from entering controls as text.
3.2.1.3 Permit users to specify units of text as (e.g., words, paragraphs) modifiers for control entries.
3.2.1.4 Highlight specified units of text to indicate boundaries of the text affected by control entries.

### *3.2.2 Continuous Text*

Give users reasonable control over justification, line spacing, page structure (e.g., headers, margins, tab stops, and footers), and print options.

3.2.2.1 Left justify all lines of continuous text. Do not permit right justification with nonproportional spacing.
3.2.2.2 Maintain constant spacing between words. Do not use proportional spacing.
3.2.2.3 Use 150% of character height as default line spacing.
3.2.2.4 Display continuous text in upper- and lowercase letters (i.e., mixed case.)

3.2.2.5 Provide automatic line breaks for entry and editing of unformatted text. Permit user to override automatic line breaks by inserting page or section breaks when formatting and editing text.

3.2.2.6 For predefined page structures, provide standard format automatically.

3.2.2.7 Allow users to label and store frequently used text formats and segments for future use.

3.2.2.8 Provide automatic pagination, but permit the user to override pagination to specify page numbers anywhere within a document. Enable users to control for the number of lines in a paragraph that will be permitted to stand alone as orphans or widows at the tops or bottoms of pages.

3.2.2.9 Provide capability for the display of annotations to displayed text. Make annotations easy to distinguish from text.

3.2.2.10 Permit user to specify portions of text for printing (e.g., single page or range of pages). Allow user to display text as it will be printed, including underlining, boldface, subscript, superscript, special characters, special symbols, and different styles and sizes of type. Inform user of the status of requests for printouts. For example, notify user when printout has been completed.

## 3.3 Fonts and Typography

The legibility of displayed text is a major UI issue. Reading from a screen can be considerably slower than reading from paper. The following guidelines assume adequate display contrast, depending on lighting conditions.

### *3.3.1 Font Sizes and Styles*

Improve legibility by the use of well-formed letter shapes and type sizes that are appropriate for viewing distances.

3.3.1.1 For a nominal viewing distance of 18 inches, the minimum recommended size for a font is 0.08 inch (just slightly less than 1/16th of an inch).

3.3.1.2 Where alphanumeric characters; are displayed, select font styles to allow discrimination of similar characters, such as letter l and number 1, letter Z and number 2.

3.3.1.3 Do not use varying sizes or styles of fonts for any reason other than coding (for example, text as labels, text as data, text as command input).

3.3.1.4 Use selected fonts consistently throughout the interface, and provide upper- and lowercase with full descenders.

3.3.1.5 Avoid type faces that have extended serifs, internal patterns, stripes, italics, stenciling, shadowing, three dimensions; fonts that appear handwritten or like Old English script; and fonts that are distorted to look tall and thin or wide and fat.

## 3.4 Tables

In general, users should not be required to search through lengthy tabular data to find required values. That is a job for the software. The following guidelines apply when there is no alternative to tabular presentation or when a brief table will support task performance.

### 3.4.1 *Information Presented*

Present information that compares detailed sets of data in recognizable order. A consistent design is required to facilitate scanning and assimilation.

### 3.4.2 *Headings*

Use row and column headings that reflect information the user had before consulting the table.

3.4.2.1 For large tables exceeding one screen, provide column and row labels in all displayed sections of the table.

### 3.4.3 *Arrangement*

Arrange rows and columns according to some logic (e.g., chronological, alphabetic).

### 3.4.4 *Scanning Cues*

Provide adequate separation between columns (at least three spaces) and between groups of rows (blank line inserted after every fifth row).

## 3.5 Lists

Display a series of related items in a list to support quick, accurate scanning.

### 3.5.1 *Number of Columns*

A single column is usually recommended; that is, each item in the list starts on a new line.

3.5.1.1 For a more compact display of a long list, use multiple columns and order items vertically within each column.

### 3.5.2 Order of Items

Maintain the same order of items for each instance of a particular list. Base the order on natural logic such as frequency of use, related functionality, or normal sequence of user actions. If no logical basis for ordering is apparent, list them alphabetically.

3.5.2.1 If a single item in a list continues onto another line, mark the item to indicate the continuation; for example, use an ellipsis (. . .).

3.5.2.2 If a list is very long, use a hierarchical structure to partition it into a set of more compact lists.

### 3.5.3 Orderly Format

Attention to alignment and labeling can improve UI consistency.

3.5.3.1 Align decimal points when listing numbers with decimal values.

3.5.3.2 When decimal values are not used, numbers should be flush right.

3.5.3.3 Alphabetic listings should be flush left.

3.5.3.4 Labels describe the contents of the lists and should be flush left or centered.

## 3.6 Pushbuttons

Maintain consistency in the design of pushbuttons. Although pushbuttons can vary in size and shape, the design of a particular type should remain consistent throughout an application. Standard names and uses for common pushbutton functions are listed in Table K.3.

### 3.6.1 Pushbutton Captions

Provide captions on pushbuttons, specifically stating the actions they are intended to perform.

**Table K.3 Names and Uses for Pushbutton Functions**

| *Names* | *Uses* |
|---|---|
| OK | Confirms any information changed in a window; window is closed. |
| Apply | Any changes in a window will occur and be displayed in the window. |
| Reset | Cancels changes that have not been submitted. |
| Cancel | Closes window after no changes are submitted. |
| Help | Displays contextual help for an item or for an entire window. |

### *3.6.2 Information Prior to Action*

If additional information must be supplied by the user before the system can carry out a pushbutton action, provide an ellipsis (. . .) after the pushbutton caption to indicate that a query will be presented.

### *3.6.3 Arrangement of Pushbuttons*

To the extent possible, arrange pushbuttons by frequency of use. For example, position frequently used action buttons to the left of or above other displayed buttons. When the same buttons are used for different windows, consistently place them in the same location and keep related buttons together.

## 3.7 Icons

Icons are pictorial representations of objects or actions that reflect the controlling metaphor of an application (desktop, office environment, wiki, etc.). Although it seems obvious that icons should look like what they represent, this is not always easy to achieve in practice. An icon that means one thing to a developer may mean something entirely different to a user. It is important to pre-test icons with users to verify that they convey the intended meanings.

### *3.7.1 Representation*

Use icons whose shapes have clear meanings and pictorially reflect the objects or actions represented. To the extent possible, use icons that are already familiar to users.

3.7.1.1 Make each icon represent a single object or action.

3.7.1.2 Make each icon a simple, closed figure. Use as few graphical components as necessary. Avoid ornamentation.

3.7.1.3 Do not use purely abstract designs for icons.

3.7.1.4 Use the same icons for the same objects and actions across applications.

3.7.1.5 If it is necessary to create a new icon, consult standard symbol sets available from the American National Standards Institute (ANSI) and other sources to find established icons that may meet the need.

3.7.1.6 If no existing icons are satisfactory, create shapes that are meaningful to users, easily recognizable, and visually distinct from each other.

3.7.1.7 Use humor in icon design only if all users will get the joke and none will be confused or offended.

### 3.7.2 Size

Make icons big enough to be seen, recognized, and selected easily.

3.7.2.1 Make all icons within a related set the same size.

3.7.2.2 Determine size requirements imposed by UI style guides, software used (e.g., web browser), and standards for legibility.

### 3.7.3 Number

For most applications, display fewer than twenty icons simultaneously on the same screen.

### 3.7.4 Labeling

Give each icon a text label corresponding to the object or action. Do not let labels obscure the icons.

3.7.4.1 Place the caption or label directly beneath the icon.

### 3.7.5 Grouping

Group related icons using similar shapes and colors to depict a common relationship.

3.7.5.1 Provide a default arrangement, but permit users to rearrange icons within the context of their tasks.

### 3.7.6 Highlighting

Highlight icons selected by the user.

### 3.7.7 Documentation

Provide a glossary in online help containing a list of standard icons and their associated objects and actions.

### 3.7.8 Testing

Prior to implementation, measure the effectiveness of icons by testing them with a representative group of users to ensure quick recognition and ease of learning. Re-design and re-test until usability objectives are met.

## 3.8 Labels

The quality of labeling employed throughout a user interface can impact user performance. Labels should be as meaningful and detailed as possible.

### 3.8.1 *Wording*

Give each data field, data group, message, pushbutton, icon, and window a descriptive label or caption, generally not a number.

3.8.1.1 Spell words in full, using the simplest possible words as labels. Do not use contractions, abbreviations, or punctuation in labels (unless absolutely necessary for meaning or to accommodate space restrictions or the label chosen is an accepted standard in the user environment).

3.8.1.2 Display labels and titles in mixed case.

### 3.8.2 *Location*

Locate a label as close as possible to the item it describes (e.g., adjacent to, immediately above, or below the item).

3.8.2.1 Integrate labels with graphics, using the same type style for labels and text.

### 3.8.3 *Orientation*

Display labels in a left-to-right (horizontal) orientation. Do not display labels vertically or in any other off-horizontal orientation.

### 3.8.4 *Differentiation*

Differentiate labels from other screen elements in a unique and consistent manner (e.g., bold, underlined).

### 3.8.5 *Spacing*

Separate labels from one another by at least two standard character spaces.

### 3.8.6 *Consistency*

Make labels consistent in wording, location, orientation, differentiation, and spacing throughout an application or set of applications.

## 3.9 Checkboxes and Radio Buttons

Use checkboxes or radio buttons to present multiple options. Multiple options are often presented in panels of checkboxes or radio buttons, but their use is not interchangeable. Checkboxes allow users to select several options. Radio buttons permit only one selection from a group of options.

### *3.9.1 Labeling*

Descriptions of alternative choices for checkboxes and radio buttons should be fully and clearly spelled out and positioned to the right of each box or button.

3.9.1.1 Display descriptors (labels) in mixed case.
3.9.1.2 Capitalize the first letter of each major word in multiword labels.

### *3.9.2 Choice Indication*

Indicate a choice of a box or button by means of a checkmark, fill-in, or highlighting.

### *3.9.3 Checkboxes*

Use checkboxes for nonexclusive options. When options are not mutually exclusive, checkboxes allow more than one selection. Checkboxes are usually displayed as square or rectangular boxes with option labels inscribed alongside each box.

3.9.3.1 Provide labels for each set of checkboxes.
3.9.3.2 Arrange checkboxes in logical order so that the most frequently used boxes are at the top or at the left, depending on how the boxes are oriented.
3.9.3.3 A columnar orientation is generally preferred for checkboxes, with the boxes aligned to the left. If space is limited, a horizontal orientation may be used with adequate separation (three spaces) between each box.
3.9.3.4 Within a group of checkboxes, make the boxes equal in height and width.
3.9.3.5 Label style and orientation should remain consistent to the extent possible.
3.9.3.6 Use the method of indicating selected options consistently across all panels of checkboxes in an application or set of applications.

### *3.9.4 Radio Buttons*

Use circular or diamond-shaped radio buttons for mutually exclusive options. Avoid rectangular radio buttons because they may be confused with checkboxes. When options are mutually exclusive, radio buttons permit the selection of only one item at a time.

3.9.4.1 Provide labels for each set of radio buttons. If a screen or window contains only one panel of radio buttons, the screen or window title may serve as the panel label (if there is no question of user confusion).

3.9.4.2 Limit to eight the number of options presented in a panel of radio buttons. When nine or more options must be presented, consider using a scrollable list or a drop-down list.

3.9.4.3 Arrange options in a logical or expected order, beginning at the top of the panel.

3.9.4.4 Left-align the radio buttons and their labels in the preferred columnar format. If the buttons must be arranged horizontally, provide at least three spaces between an option label and the next button.

3.9.4.5 When a particular option is not available, display it as subdued or grayed-out in relation to the brightness of the available options.

3.9.4.6 Make the selection target area include the radio button and its label. When the cursor has been moved to an option, making it available for selection, highlight only the label (not the button) using a technique such as reverse video, reverse color, or a dashed box around the label.

3.9.4.7 Use the method chosen to indicate selection consistently across all panels of radio buttons in the application or set of applications.

## 3.10 Dialog Boxes

Dialog boxes ask users to specify preferences and acknowledge messages from the system.

### *3.10.1 Dialog Box Basics*

The two basic categories of dialog boxes are modal and modeless. Modal dialog boxes require a response before any further action can be taken by the user. Modeless dialog boxes allow the user to perform parallel dialogs. Switching between the modeless dialog box and its associated window is permitted. Palettes and toolbars are modeless dialog boxes.

3.10.1.1 Give each dialog box a title.

3.10.1.2 Match pushbuttons to the function of the dialog box.

3.10.1.3 Size dialog boxes to be smaller than application windows.

3.10.1.4 Locate each dialog box uniquely, depending on the scope of its relationship to system or application elements.

### 3.10.2 Message Boxes

When a warning of an unexpected event or information regarding an irreversible state is presented to the user, a message box provides space for user acknowledgment.

## 4.0 Guidelines for Screen Layout and Design

This section is concerned with orderly design to support the exchange of information between user and computer. Of interest are screen format and content—where information is placed, how information is structured, and what information is included. Achieving consistency in screen design throughout an application's UI is a key challenge for a development team.

## 4.1 General Layout

The objective is to achieve a screen layout that meets user information requirements while appearing well organized and uncluttered.

### 4.1.1 Presentation of Information

Present information in a directly usable form; the user should not have to cross-reference other resources or perform mental transformations of data.

4.1.1.1 To the extent possible, put all the data related to one task on a single screen. Users should be able to see the whole page on which they are working. If all the required data will not fit on a single screen, divide it into logical units so that the data needed first are presented first, followed by a screen or screens containing the data needed later in the task. Indicate display continuation when display output is presented on more than one screen. Label each screen of a multiscreen display to show its relationship to the others. Display functionally related data items on the same screen. Do not require the user to jump back and forth in a set of screens or windows to find required data.

4.1.1.2 Reserve special areas of the screen for commands, status messages, and input fields. Locate these areas consistently on all screens.

4.1.1.3 To the extent possible, do not require users to perform mental comparisons or other analyses of data. Present the information integrated into the form needed for task performance (e.g., trends over time). When there is no alternative to requiring users to detect similarities, differences, trends, and relationships across sets of data, format the screen so that the data are grouped to facilitate analysis and comparison.

## *4.1.2 Emphasis between Elements*

Use contrasting display features to emphasize differences among elements (1) different screen components such as dialog boxes, windows, menus; (2) items being acted upon; and (3) urgent items.

## *4.1.3 Visual Guidance through Grouping*

Guide users through the screen with bordering lines formed by display elements, and provide symmetry and balance through the use of white space.

4.1.3.1 Group data in ways that support a user's logical train of thought in performing tasks. Group particularly important data items, and display them at the top of the screen. Group frequently used data items and display them near the top of the screen (below the important items).
When data are used in some spatial or temporal order, group by sequence of use. When sets of data are associated with particular questions or are related to particular functions, group each set to illustrate the functional relationships. Use general-to-specific grouping for hierarchical relationships among data elements, with general elements preceding specific elements. If there is no other known logic for grouping data, based on cognitive task analysis, use a standard grouping technique (e.g., chronological, alphabetical).

4.1.3.2 Use grouping to make the screen appear as an organized collection of smaller identifiable elements. Demarcate groups of information by spacing, drawing lines, color coding, or other means. Do not clutter a display with too many lines or colors. For critical tasks, use at least one character space above and below, and two character spaces before and after critical information.

## *4.1.4 Visual Appearance*

Be consistent with visual appearance and procedural usage.

4.1.4.1 Place recurring data fields in consistent relative positions within displays.

4.1.4.2 When appropriate for users, use the same format for input and output. (Determine appropriateness through the task analysis and discussions with users.)

4.1.4.3 When appropriate, match data entry formats and source document formats. (Determine appropriateness through the task analysis and discussions with users.)

4.1.4.4 In general, keep screen density below 50% and preferably below 25%. In displays used for critical tasks, minimize screen density (ratio of filled to unfilled pixels).

### 4.1.5 Output Displays

Based on results of task analysis, provide the user with all the data needed for any transaction, making such data available for display. Use task analysis to determine the user's detailed information requirements. Users should not have to recall data from one output display to the next.

4.1.5.1 Continue to provide prior data when necessary so that users do not have to remember previous values when interpreting new data.

4.1.5.2 Use familiar, task-oriented terms on displayed data and labels. Ensure that carefully chosen words and the same grammatical structure are used consistently within and across displays.

4.1.5.3 Use complete words instead of abbreviations whenever possible. If you must use abbreviations, they should be common and familiar to the user. Do not use the same abbreviation with more than one meaning; make sure abbreviations are distinctive. Minimize punctuation of abbreviations and acronyms; for example, display USA instead of U.S.A. Use a standard method to form abbreviations. Special abbreviations are used only when required for clarity. If an abbreviation must deviate from the standard method, make the deviation minimal. Keep abbreviations as short as possible. Provide a dictionary of abbreviations and acronyms in online help and in the user's guide.

4.1.5.4 Define the frequency of displaying a data field as required or optional. A required field is always displayed when a screen is used. An optional field is displayed when information is requested but not necessarily required. Alternatively, display both required and optional fields, but code them differently (e.g., place parentheses around the label of an optional field).

### 4.1.6 Entry Screens

If forms of any type are used for data entry, they should be compatible with those used for data output. Use the same item labeling and ordering for both. Data should be entered in units that are familiar to the user.

4.1.6.1 Ensure that screen titles reflect the names of the data elements. Clarification of titles on system worksheets may be required.

4.1.6.2 Minimize the amount of data to be entered. A user should not have to enter the same data more than once. Correct items are saved and should not have to be re-entered when incorrect items are changed. Preserve the context of each data entry transaction.

4.1.6.3 Design data entry transactions and associated displays so that users follow a single method of entry. If data entry is assigned to specific areas, provide clear visual definition of the entry fields. Provide a sufficient number of lines and line length to support entry and editing tasks. Permit users to change previous entries by delete-and-insert (cut-and-paste) methods. If direct character substitution (typeover) is included, make the data changes consistently available wherever substitution is required. For cancellation of data entry, have the computer confirm completion of a transaction with a message stating that the cancellation was successful or an error occurred. When the user requests changes or deletion of data, offer the option of maintaining the old value before making the change.

4.1.6.4 Provide the user with the means for selection and entry (e.g., point to and click on; move to and select) of a position on a display, or of a displayed item.

4.1.6.5 To aid entry of data in a hierarchical structure with various sections and levels of detail, provide computer aids such as (1) question-and-answer dialogues or form filling to maintain data relationships, (2) arrows on flowcharts that automatically connect lines, and (3) indicators of current positions when panning a map. For orientation, consider displaying a defined data structure with branches and levels labeled for reference. For complex data structures, provide computer prompts so that the user can make appropriate data entries at different levels.

## 4.2 Alphanumerics

The display of continuous text, numbers, and combined alphanumeric codes raises numerous design and layout issues. Designers and developers should have a detailed understanding of user needs for alphanumeric displays before proceeding with a particular approach.

### *4.2.1 Continuous Text*

Reading from a computer screen can be noticeably slower than reading from paper. The challenge in designing and displaying continuous text is to support the user's reading speed and comprehension.

4.2.1.1 If a user must read continuous text from a screen, present at least four lines of text at a time, displayed in mixed upper and lower case.

4.2.1.2 Present text in wide lines containing forty to sixty characters per line. Avoid narrow columns of short lines. Make the display space wide enough to present full lines of text. Do not require horizontal scrolling to uncover hidden text.

4.2.1.3 Number paragraphs, and separate them by at least one blank line.

### 4.2.2 Letter Combinations and Special Characters

4.2.2.1 Do not use restricted alphabetic sets for alphabetical data entry.

4.2.2.2 When special characters are chosen for keying (@, /, =, #), select characters that do not require frequent keyboard shifting.

### 4.2.3 Numbers

Present data in digital form only if the user needs specific numerical values.

4.2.3.1 Use six or fewer characters in numeric codes.

4.2.3.2 Use Arabic (not Roman) numerals when numbering items in a list.

4.2.3.3 Right-justify integers for ease of viewing and scanning.

4.2.3.4 Give users the option to enter or omit the decimal point at the end of an integer. The system should recognize entries of *45* and *45.* as equivalent. If a decimal point is required for data processing, program the computer to append one as needed. When displayed in columns, decimal numbers should be decimal aligned.

4.2.3.5 Permit users the option of entering or omitting leading zeros for general numeric data. In a field that is four characters long, *45* should be recognized by the system without requiring the user to enter *0045*.

4.2.3.6 Separate long numbers into groups of three or four digits. Use standard separators or spaces. For example, social security numbers and telephone numbers use hyphens; bank account numbers are often divided by spaces.

### 4.2.4 Scales

Use a linear scale for numerical data, not the more difficult to interpret logarithmic scale or nonlinear scales.

4.2.4.1 Begin scaling numeric data at zero.

4.2.4.2 Use a familiar, meaningful approach for determining scale intervals. For example, use standard intervals of 1, 2, 5, or 10 to label scale divisions.

### 4.2.5 Alphanumeric Codes

To aid user comprehension of textual and numeric codes such as acronyms and abbreviations, use meaningful codes in preference to arbitrary codes.

4.2.5.1 Do not choose frequently confused characters and character pairs. For example, the letters *O* and *I* should not be used in codes because they can be confused with the numbers zero *0* and *1*. Similarly, the number *8* can be confused with the letters *B* and *S*.

4.2.5.2 When a user must recall alphanumeric codes, limit the code to five characters.

4.2.5.3 Group letters and numbers together rather than interspersing letters and numbers. Group characters in blocks of three to five characters, separated by at least one blank space or other separating character.

4.2.5.4 Use all uppercase or all lowercase for alphanumeric codes.

4.2.5.5 Use punctuation in alphanumeric codes only when a code may be confused with a word.

4.2.5.6 When designing alphanumeric commands, consider the effects of possible typographical errors. Ask whether mistyping a command will produce another valid but undesired command. Prevent the entry of inappropriate characters into a field (e.g., an alphabetic character into a field reserved for numeric characters).

## 4.3 Graphics

Displaying data in graphical formats can often, but not always, aid a user's visual detection and comprehension of relationships of data. If the displayed data reflect spatial or temporal relationships, consider displaying them graphically instead of using numerical tables or text descriptions. Because the benefits of graphics are task dependent, any planned graphical display should be tested for usability.

### *4.3.1 Visual Balance*

To make displays readily scannable, balance their elements in as organized a pattern as possible and maintain that organization across the application. Base the organizing principle on users' expectations and understanding of the logic underlying the displayed information.

4.3.1.1 Balance the left side of the display against the right side, and the top against the bottom, as shown in Figure K.1. Consider using a layout grid to achieve both

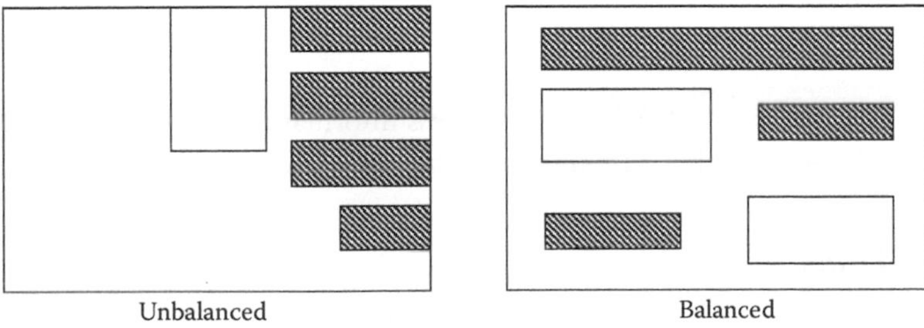


**Figure K.1 Visual balance.**

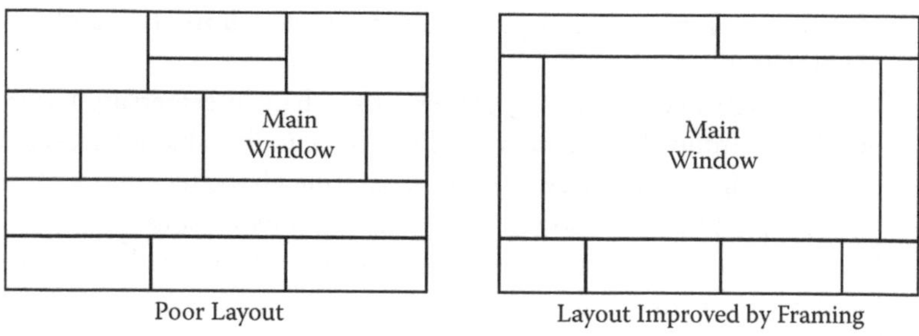


**Figure K.2 Use of framing.**

visual and conceptual balance of displayed elements. Use symmetry (even distribution of elements to the left and right of center) to convey stability. If you use an asymmetric layout to emphasize contrast or convey movement, balance the distribution of displayed elements via color, size, and shape.

4.3.1.2 Display short messages in wide, shallow spaces.

4.3.1.3 Display graphics in square or slightly rectangular areas. Use recommended proportions of length to width (e.g., 1:1, 1:1.414, 1:1.618). Avoid irregular shapes.

4.3.1.4 Frame the central display area with smaller functional elements. See Figure K.2.

4.3.1.5 Leave at least one character space between the contents of a window and the window borders.

## 4.4 Hypertext and Hypermedia

Hypertext documents are based on a design metaphor that likens the screen to a deck of cards or a series of planes through which the user can scroll or pan. The primary features of a hypertext system are nodes (text, graphics, sound, video) and links between nodes. In hypermedia systems, the user controls traversal among nodes.

### *4.4.1 Access to Information*

Provide alternative means for the user to access information in a hypermedia document (e.g., following links, searching, or using contextual cues).

### *4.4.2 Links*

Links between nodes enable a user to move nonlinearly through available information. A common problem to avoid is the inclusion of so many links that the user becomes overwhelmed.

4.4.2.1 Base the creation of links between related information on the user's need for information in a particular context.

4.4.2.2 Indicate the presence of links using a link marker (such as an icon) or highlighting.

4.4.2.3 Present linked graphical materials with appended text defining the graphical material and its text links.

4.4.2.4 To the extent possible, provide links across media (i.e., in addition to text linking, use graphics linking, sound linking, and video linking).

### *4.4.3 User Orientation*

To avoid user disorientation in navigating hypermedia documents, employ (1) maps or browsers that indicate the user's position within the network, or (2) tags, markers, or milestones that represent locations within the network.

### *4.4.4 Collaborative Authoring*

In collaborative authoring of hypermedia documents, use an authoring system that provides ways to read, link, and edit the document while allowing authors to protect their work from unauthorized access or changes.

## 5.0 Guidelines for Interaction Styles and Data Protection

Depending on the user's task environment, one or more styles of interaction may be appropriate. The varieties of interaction styles include alphanumeric dialogs (fill-in forms) and graphical dialogs (menu selection and direct manipulation). Many user interfaces combine textual and graphical styles. The key design challenges are matching interaction style to the user's task domain and protecting data integrity.

## 5.1 Fill-In Forms

Fill-in forms are used to enter predefined items into labeled fields. The screens resemble paper forms that allow a user to fill in the blanks. The screens provide necessary cues so that novice users can correctly determine what must be keyed, enter appropriate information, and review it. Major issues include design of entry fields and transactions.

### 5.1.1 Compatible Forms

Design forms so that data items are ordered in a way that is familiar to the user.

5.1.1.1 If transcriptions from source documents are used in data entry, ensure that form-filling displays are compatible with such documents related to ordering, data grouping, and labeling.

### 5.1.2 Entry-Field Basics

Design data entry fields consistently within and across applications. Use consistent approaches to labeling, prompting, highlighting, justification, and spacing.

5.1.2.1 Label each data field to inform users of entries to be made. Keep labels close to associated data fields; separate them by at least one space. Ensure consistency in field labels by using the same label for the same kind of data entry. Protect field labels from keyed entry by having the cursor skip over them when the user is spacing or tabbing. Use descriptive wording, standard terms, codes, and/or abbreviations when labeling data fields. For more clarity, employ additional cues in a data field label. Include a unit of measurement as part of the field label when the unit (e.g., $, °, mph) is part of a particular data field. The units of measurement employed should be familiar to users. When alternative units of measurement are used, provide space to distinguish the units entered.

5.1.2.2 In form-filling operations, require one explicit entry action at the end of the transaction sequence for the entry of logically related items, to avoid the separate entry of each item. Allow the user to enter multiple data items without keying special separator or delimiter characters. Permit the user to review, cancel, or back up multiple data items entered as a single transaction.

5.1.2.3 If a delimiter is to be used, be consistent in the employment of a standard character. Choose a character that does not require shifting keys or one that does not occur as part of any data entry. Do not require users to remove delimiters or otherwise enter keystrokes for all positions within a variable length field.

5.1.2.4 Select a standard means of prompting users for keyed entry, such as highlighting the entry field with beveled edges or shadows. Ensure that the method used for highlighting is visually different from screen error messages. Highlight entry fields consistently across screens.

5.1.2.5 Clearly distinguish between required and optional entry fields. For example, dashes might indicate required fields, and dots, optional fields. Provide a means for indicating when a fixed or maximum length is specified for data entry (Figure K.3). Use field delineation cues, such as coding the labels of required and optional entry fields. If the data entry does not completely fill the markers because length is variable, ignore the remaining

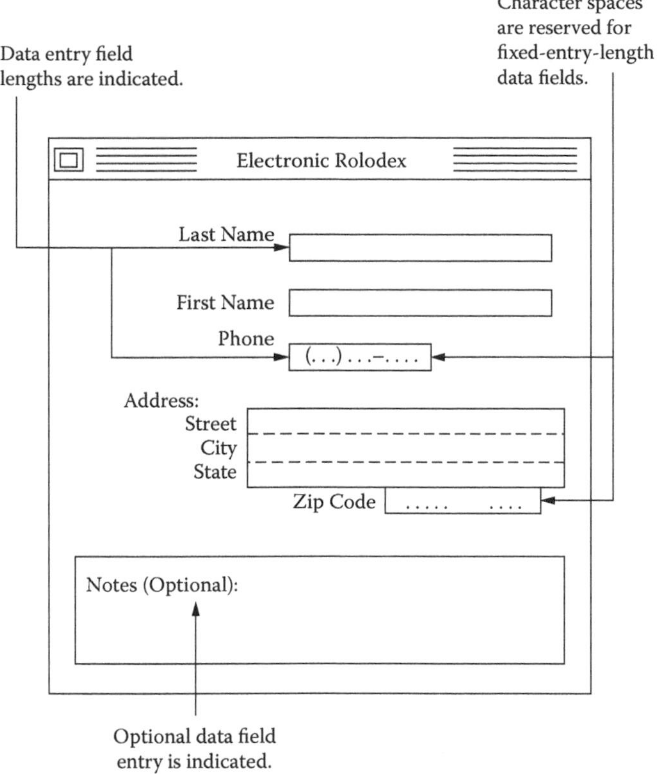


**Figure K.3 Data entry design.**

field markers in computer processing. Do not accomplish data entry by overwriting a set of characters within a field.

5.1.2.6 To speed data entry, offer default values that can be defined for data entry in a specific task. In the event of a series of defined default values, permit the user to accept defaults for all entries or to default until reaching the next required, non-default entry. When it is not possible to predict what default values will be useful, permit the user to define, change, or remove default values for any data entry field, without changing default definitions for subsequent transactions. At the beginning of a data entry transaction, display default values in the appropriate fields.

5.1.2.7 Provide automatic updating to free the user from entering the same data twice.

5.1.2.8 Limit data items to five to seven characters when the user must code data or enter numbers. If the data items must be longer, partition them into shorter clusters for entry and display. For example, ten-digit telephone numbers are partitioned into three groups: XXX-XXX-XXXX.

| Organization: _ _ _ _<br>Account Code: _ _ _ _<br>Password: _ _ _ _ | Logon Account Code: _ _ _ _<br>Report Number: _ _ _ _<br>Date: _ _/_ _/_ _ |
|---|---|

Alternative Justification of Caption and Entry Fields

**Figure K.4 Justification.**

| | |
|---|---|
| 1. Project #: _ _ _ _ _ | 4. Project #: _ _ _ |
| 2. Project #: _ _ _ _ _ | 5. Project #: _ _ _ |
| 3. Project #: _ _ _ _ _ | 6. Project #: _ _ _ |

Horizontal Spacing of Entry Fields

| | |
|---|---|
| Employee Number: | _ _ _ _ _ |
| Social Security Number: | _ _ _ _ _ _ _ _ _ |
| Grade: | _ _ |
| Department: | _ _ _ _ _ _ _ _ _ _ |
| Division: | _ _ _ |
| | |
| Title: | _ _ _ _ _ _ _ _ _ _ |
| Years in Service: | _ _ |
| Salary: | _ _ _ _ _ _ |

Vertical Spacing of Entry Fields

**Figure K.5 Horizontal and vertical spacing.**

5.1.2.9 Use a consistent approach to the justification of data entry fields. Left justify the caption and the entry fields, with one space between the longest caption and the entry field. Alternatively, right justify the captions and left justify the entry fields. See Figure K.4.

5.1.2.10 For horizontal viewing, provide a minimum of five spaces between the longest entry field in one column and the left-most caption in the adjacent column. For vertical viewing, provide one blank line between groups of related information. See Figure K.5.

## 5.1.3 Command Keystrokes

Across interaction styles, when speed of command input is important, use command keystrokes (i.e., a limited number of keystrokes combined with pressing a command key to access a command language term).

## 5.1.4 Function Keys

Use function keys for tasks with unique control entries or as adjuncts to other interaction styles for functions that occur frequently, must be quick, and allow minimal syntax errors.

## 5.2 Question-and-Answer Interface

A question-and-answer interface is a combination of menu and fill-in form interfaces in a dialog style. The dialog proceeds in a step-by-step continual interaction. Typically, prompting is included with questions. Sometimes questions and answers are scrolled on the screen, enabling a user to view much of the dialog. In other cases, new questions individually refresh the screen, omitting from view previous questions and answers. Question-and-answer dialogs are used for

- Tasks requiring routine data entry
- Known data items where ordering can be constrained
- Novice system users
- Relatively fast computer response time

### *5.2.1 Wording of Questions*

Ensure questions are in clear, simple language. Grammatical form should be consistent throughout.

5.2.1.1 Avoid negatives statements (e.g., *If the claim is not related to an accident, check here.*). Phrase questions in a positive manner: *Check here if the claim is related to an accident.*

### *5.2.2 Mnemonic Codes and Abbreviations for Answers*

Use simple mnemonic codes for answers to questions. A user should not have to perform translations to correctly answer a question. For example, when the user is asked for marital status, the user indicates married or single via a simple mnemonic code.

5.2.2.1 When a question requires only two possible answers (*Are you an employee or visitor?*), provide mnemonic codes such as *e* for employee and *v* for visitor.

5.2.2.2 Minimize typing requirements by requesting abbreviated answers, such as *m* for married and *y* for yes. Avoid capital letters if possible; for example, do not require *M* for married and *Y* for yes).

### *5.2.3 Recapitulation of Prior Answers*

Display interrelated, computer-posed questions so that answers to previous questions are visible to a user. This often helps a user answer questions that follow.

### 5.2.4 *Visible Titles*

Display the dialog title continuously even if questions scroll off the screen as the dialog progresses.

### 5.2.5 *Visual Coding of Dialog Parts*

Use visual cues and white spaces to allow users to distinguish between questions, prompts, instructions, and input. Upper- versus lowercase letters, indentations, and spatial location are other methods that can identify dialog parts.

### 5.2.6 *Navigation Instructions*

Include instructions for using navigation capabilities; otherwise a user may never find or use them.

### 5.2.7 *Scanning Capabilities*

Provide the capability to return to and edit previous answers, scan through future questions, quit the session before completion of dialog, and re-enter the dialog where a user left off.

## 5.3 Menus and Visual Cues

The key objectives of menu design are minimizing user search-and-selection time and optimizing user ability to navigate the menu structure.

### 5.3.1 *General*

Consider using menus when

- User tasks involve selecting from a constrained set of alternative actions.
- User tasks require only occasional data entry.
- Users have little experience or training.
- Computer response is reasonably fast.
- Commands from a large command set are used infrequently.

5.3.1.1 Locate menus and menu options consistently when they appear in different displays.

5.3.1.2 Provide a means for an experienced user to bypass the menu structure by using direct keyboard commands. Display alternative keyboard commands (accelerators) to the right of the menu option label. Do not use arbitrary numbers for accelerator codes.

5.3.1.3 If logical grouping of options is not possible, display up to eight options appropriate to any particular transaction. If selection must be made from a list of more than eight options or sequential selection is required, consider using a hierarchical menu structure. If logical categories can be established for a set of more than eight options, as many as sixty-four categorized options may be presented in one menu.

5.3.1.4 Dim (or gray out) unavailable or invalid options.

### *5.3.2 Phrasing Menu Options*

Use direct, unambiguous wording that reflects the actions to be executed. Use verbs or verb phrases (not nouns or noun phrases) to denote actions (e.g., edit, view, insert).

5.3.2.1 Where possible, use wording that is familiar to users; do not use familiar terms to mean something different from their common usage in the user community.

### *5.3.3 Formatting Menu Options*

Menu options can be formatted linearly in a vertical or horizontal list or spatially in a circle, rectangle, or other geometric shape (e.g., pie menus). The following guidelines apply to the layout, organization, and grouping of vertically formatted menu options.

5.3.3.1 Format a menu list as a single column, wide enough to accommodate the widest option plus its keyboard accelerator.

5.3.3.2 Arrange menu and submenu options in separate, cascading columns; list options left justified beneath each other.

5.3.3.3 Use logical sequence, criticality, or frequency of use to establish option order in a brief menu. Make the most likely selection in a menu list the default option. Within hierarchical menus, permit immediate access to critical or frequently selected options.

5.3.3.4 If basing menu organization on frequency of use, place the following options at the bottom: (1) less frequently used options; (2) destructive commands such as delete or exit.

5.3.3.5 Within a longer menu, group logically related options, and draw a solid line between groups. Make the solid line the same color as the option labels.

5.3.3.6 If a set of menu options has no inherent logical order, alphabetize the options, but do not place options for opposing actions adjacent to each other. For example, a delete option should not be next to a save option.

### 5.3.4 Pull-Down Menus

Pull-down menus appear in response to a user's selection of an option from a menu bar. They are also called drop-down menus. Pull-down menus should be used when space is limited, when users must view menu options only when selecting them, and when required information on the screen will not be obscured by the menu. Pull-down menus include various options such as command actions, settings or toggles, submenus, and cascades.

5.3.4.1 Use pull-down menus to open top-level menus listed in the menu bar.
5.3.4.2 Place the pull-down directly below the option selected from the menu bar. The higher-level option serves as the title for the pull-down.
5.3.4.3 Present the pull-down in the same foreground and background colors used for the menu bar. The colors should contrast sufficiently with the background of the application area or screen body.
5.3.4.4 Outline the pull-down with a border or drop shadow.
5.3.4.5 To the extent possible, present all options to minimize scrolling.
5.3.4.6 Present the pull-down menu options in initial capital letters followed by lowercase letters (mixed case) or via self-explanatory graphics (fill-in patterns, colors) appropriate to the task.
5.3.4.7 Display a pull-down menu until the user makes a selection.
5.3.4.8 Do not place instructions in pull-down menus.
5.3.4.9 If a pull-down option leads to a second-level, cascading pull-down, follow the option label with a right-pointing arrow. Position the cascading pull-down to the right of the highlighted option in the previous pull-down.

The recommended number of levels of cascading pull-downs varies between one (Apple) and three (DEC windows). To support a user's sense of orientation within the menu structure, minimize the number of levels.

### 5.3.5 Pop-Up Menus

Each window or displayed object may have an associated pop-up menu that appears on demand in response to a user action (e.g., point and click on a designated screen area or menu icon). A pop-up menu resembles a pull-down menu, but is not associated with the top-level menus listed in the menu bar. A pop-up menu typically contains five to ten options listed vertically. In some environments, pop-up menus may cascade and include keyboard accelerators.

5.3.5.1 Provide some indication of a pop-up menu (for example, highlight the portion of the display that can be selected to access the hidden menu; provide a textual message indicating that a hidden menu is available; or change the shape of the cursor when it is moved to a clickable or selectable area).

5.3.5.2 Place a pop-up menu directly below the pointer used to select it and near the object or higher-level menu manipulated.

5.3.5.3 Display a title for each pop-up menu.

5.3.5.4 When an option in a pop-up menu leads to a cascading menu, place a right-pointing triangle after the option label.

5.3.5.5 Make the pop-up distinct from the screen background by giving it a contrasting but complementary, background or a solid-line border.

5.3.5.6 Highlight an option selected from a pop-up menu. Continue to highlight an option that leads to a cascading menu. The highlighted option serves as the title for the cascading menu.

5.3.5.7 Because of variations in use and implementation of pop-up menus across environments, check your UI software style guide before incorporating pop-ups in the UI of your application.

## *5.3.6 Option Button Menus*

When screen space is limited, use an option button menu to present a brief set of specialized menu options (Figure K.6).

5.3.6.1 Implement an option button menu to open like a pull-down menu, allowing a user to see all possible options.

5.3.6.2 Distinguish an option button menu from a pushbutton.

## *5.3.7 Graphic Menus*

Graphic menus are sometimes called palettes. A palette is a set of unlabeled symbols, typically presented in small rectangles. Symbols may be icons, patterns, characters, or drawings that represent an operation. When activated, a symbol provides access

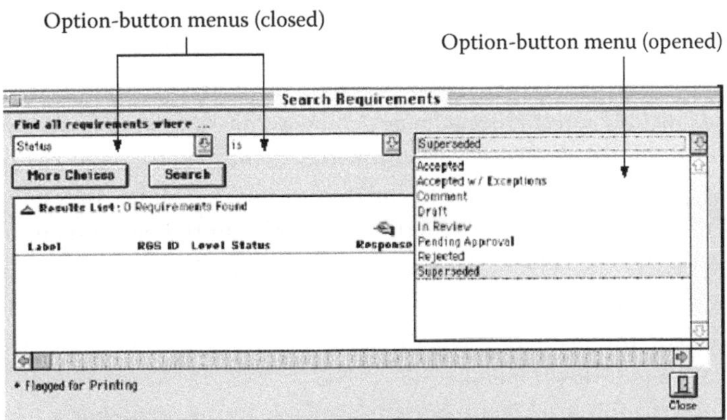


**Figure K.6 Option menu buttons.**

to a software tool (set of specialized software functions). Palettes are used widely in drawing and painting packages but have proliferated into word processing applications. A major problem for a user is not knowing what the symbols mean.

5.3.7.1 Ensure that symbols are self-explanatory, as they are not labeled.
5.3.7.2 Because selection of a symbol (tool) sends the user into a mode, display a reminder of the mode in effect (e.g., by changing the shape of the pointing cursor).
5.3.7.3 Allow a user to move and re-size the palette.
5.3.7.4 Reflect settings for the active window in the palette.

### *5.3.8 Tear-off Menus*

A tear-off menu can be "torn" from the menu bar and moved to another location on a screen where it can remain on display. Tear-off menus are also called tacked or pushpin menus.

5.3.8.1 Keep a tear-off menu posted so that the user can make multiple selections before dismissing it.
5.3.8.2 Use a graphic tear-off menu instead of a fixed palette to save display space and provide greater flexibility.

### *5.3.9 Aiding Menu Navigation*

A big problem for menu systems is getting lost in the menu structure. A key objective of menu design is to support user ability to navigate forward and backward through the structure. A number of menu navigation aids can be used singly or in combination, depending on the user's goals, tasks, and information requirements.

5.3.9.1 Provide graphical or textual aids to assist users in maintaining orientation within the underlying menu structure. Graphic aids include designated font styles, line types, or colors for different menu levels. Textual aids include numbering schemes and descriptive titles. Provide visual cues indicating current position within the menu structure and the path traveled by a user through a hierarchy of menus. Consider displaying a small schematic of the menu structure, highlighting the path taken as the user proceeds. The schematic serves as a roadmap. Consider providing a text list of the options selected as an alternative to a highlighted menu map.
5.3.9.2 Display the primary navigational aid continuously or make it available from a pull-down menu.
5.3.9.3 Keep the top-level menu options available in the menu bar.
5.3.9.4 In a hierarchical menu, allow the user to return to the next higher menu level or top-level menu with a single control action.

5.3.9.5 Provide visual indicators such as ellipses (. . .) to make menu options that branch to other submenus distinguishable from menu options that immediately perform operations.

5.3.9.6 Provide support for various user search strategies. Allow movement both forward and backward through the menu structure.

5.3.9.7 Allow experienced users to use optional shortcuts such as direct access, type ahead, jump ahead, or macros to speed traverse of the menu structure.

5.3.9.8 Consider various strategies for repositioning the search automatically when the user reaches a terminal node in a hierarchical menu without finding the target menu option. Reposition search to the next higher level that affords the widest breadth of selection. Provide a capability for users to mark points in the menu structure for possible return and a capability to return to such points via command. Reposition to intermediate landmarks instead of forcing a user to return to the root node to restart a local search.

5.3.9.9 Sequence menus according to the logical flow of control required by the task.

5.3.9.10 Consider allowing users to create their own pathways through the menu structure (e.g., by adding horizontal and diagonal links within the original structure).

## 5.4 Direct Manipulation

Users find graphical representations much easier to retain and manipulate than textual or numeric representations. By direct manipulation, a user senses that the displayed environment is acted upon rapidly and the results are continuously visible.

### *5.4.1 Manipulation Techniques*

Techniques of direct manipulation include open and close, minimize and maximize, drag and drop, resize, and scroll. Many direct manipulation tasks are initiated when a user points and clicks at an on-screen-control graphic or icon.

5.4.1.1 Continuously display graphical reminders of actions that can be performed.

5.4.1.2 Provide feedback about the action to be performed and the action as it is performed. If a selection action is to be performed, highlight the selected object. If the action is to be a movement, alter the pointing cursor shape and highlight the object to be moved. Continue to highlight the object as it is moved. In a drag-and-drop action, move the entire object as the user drags it; do not allow the object to lag behind the pointing cursor.

5.4.1.3 Permit a user to cancel a selection before executing the associated action.

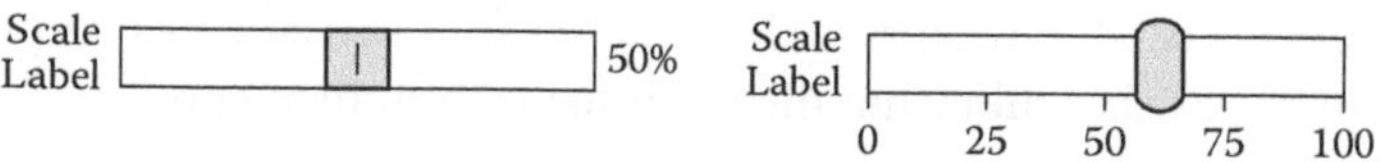


**Figure K.7 Examples of slider bars.**

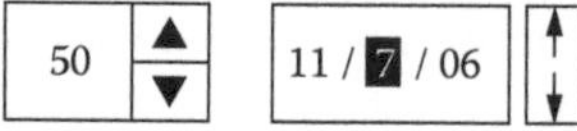


**Figure K.8 Examples of spin buttons.**

5.4.1.4 Provide smooth, even tracking between the screen pointer and input device (e.g., mouse, trackball).

5.4.1.5 Immediately display the results of direct manipulations.

5.4.1.6 Consider using a slider bar and button to allow a user to set values represented along a scale. See Figure K.7 and Figure K.8.

5.4.1.7 Consider using a spin button to allow a user to select from a long list of options that increase or decrease uniformly at constant intervals.

## *5.4.2 Browsing*

The coordination of multiple windows that can appear, change contents, and close as a result of user activity is a useful design for browsing. Techniques for browsing are based on the task for which the design is developed. Types of multiple window coordinations and procedures for browsing are described below.

5.4.2.1 Synchronized scrolling. The scroll bar of one window is linked to the scroll bar of an adjoining window. Movement of one scroll bar causes the other to scroll its window contents, allowing the browser to compare the contents of both windows simultaneously.

5.4.2.2 Hierarchical browsing. Selecting an item in the first window with a pointing device can lead to the display of an adjoining window that contains more detail. The development of coordinated windows that display different levels of information is a finer-grained approach.

5.4.2.3 Direct selection. Pointing at an icon, a word in the text, or a variable name in a program pops up an adjoining window with information about the icon, word, or variable name.

5.4.2.4 Two-dimensional browsing. A map, graphic, photograph, or other image is presented in a high-level view. The details of the view are then simultaneously presented in magnified form in another, larger window.

5.4.2.5 Dependent-window opening. The opening of dependent windows located conveniently on a display is another option. When browsing a program, opening a main procedure also opens a dependent set of procedures.

5.4.2.6 Dependent window closing. With a single action, closing a window closes its dependent windows. The advantage is the one-step process of removing from the screen the windows such as dialogs, messages, and help that are no longer applicable.

5.4.2.6 Save or open window state. Saving the state of a display as it appears on the screen with all windows intact is useful for browsing. The implementation of a save-by menu item to the file menu permits a user to access that state for future reference.

# 5.5 Data Protection

Whenever a proposed user action will interrupt a transaction sequence, it is necessary to automatically protect the data. If potential data loss cannot be prevented, warn the user and require confirmation prior to implementation. Data integrity can also be advanced by limiting access, building protection around dangerous operations, and maintaining security procedures. Providing an undo function and effective online help are major ways to protect data and transaction sequences from the unintended consequences of possible user actions.

## *5.5.1 Sequence Control*

Several interaction styles support the sequencing and completion of transactions. A transaction is one complete exchange of information between user and computer. Transactions include keystrokes and their immediate display and command entries (save, print) and their execution. A sequence is a series of user actions combined with computer logic that initiates, interrupts, or terminates a transaction. Key design objectives are to maintain consistency among control actions, limit needs for control actions, reduce loading on user memory, and provide the ability to adapt to a range of user needs. Sequence control should be in the hands of the user, with system control subordinated to user control.

5.5.1.1 Use the structure of the user's task to design a sequence of related transactions. A sequence of transactions should form a logical unit from the user's view and provide the control options needed at any point. Transaction options should match expected user goals and tasks.

5.5.1.2 Provide multiple, flexible means of sequence control so that users can accomplish necessary transactions involving data entry, display, and processing and obtain guidance as needed. Give users more than one method of controlling scrolling, and paging.

5.5.1.3 Permit users to control transaction sequencing by explicit action. Defer computer processing until the explicit action is taken. Provide a means to override control lockout due to processing.

5.5.1.4 Provide immediate system acknowledgment of every control entry.

5.5.1.5 Permit users to key a sequence of commands or option codes as a single massed or stacked command entry.

5.5.1.6 Provide interrupt or abort functions to terminate transactions. Consider the need for the following types of interrupts in addition to backup and undo:

| *Function* | *Transaction* |
|---|---|
| Cancel | Abort command or operation |
| Review | Return to first display in a sequence and permit user to step through sequence |
| Restart | Cancel all entries made in transaction sequence and return to beginning of sequence |
| End | Conclude repetitive transaction sequence |
| Pause | Interrupt transaction sequence |
| Continue | Resume paused transaction sequence without changing data entries or control logic |
| Suspend | Preserve current transaction status when user leaves system; permit resumption of work at that point on re-entry |

5.5.1.7 If different types of transaction interrupts are provided, designate each interrupt function as a separate control action with a distinct name.

5.5.1.8 Display paused or suspended status and provide prompts for resumption of a transaction sequence.

5.5.1.9 Permit users to search for specific line numbers and literal strings of alphanumeric characters.

5.5.1.10 Minimize the number of screens required to complete a transaction.

### *5.5.2 Access Security*

Include a simple, prompted log-on process to protect data from unauthorized access.

5.5.2.1 Provide for user selection of passwords and use software to enforce periodic changing of passwords. Do not display entered passwords on the screen.

5.5.2.2 Establish user authorization for data display, entry, and change at initial log-on. Do not require additional authorization when a user attempts to display data, enter data, or change data.

5.5.2.3 Limit the number and rate of unsuccessful attempts to log on.

5.5.2.4 To protect highly sensitive information, require another authentication of identity after ten minutes of inactivity.

5.5.2.5 When a record of data access is required, have the system maintain the records automatically. Do not expect the user to maintain such records manually or through the system.

### 5.5.3 Dangerous Operations

Maintain the integrity of the data. Build protection around dangerous operations such as accidental file deletion.

5.5.3.1 Prior to command execution, require users to confirm their intent to perform a critical, potentially hazardous, or potentially destructive command (including commands to destroy stored data). If a complete file is to be deleted, provide sufficient information for a user to confirm the deletion (file name, description, size, creation and modification dates).

5.5.3.2 Label a confirm action clearly and distinctively and make explicit the effects that will follow a confirmation. Require a user to wait for a prompt before entering a confirmation (i.e., do not buffer the confirm affirmation).

5.5.3.3 Require a user to select a dangerous operation instead of making it a default. This may be a deviation from design consistency but it is necessary in the interest of data integrity.

5.5.3.4 Deactivate potentially destructive function keys or other devices when not needed.

5.5.3.5 Protect display formatting features, such as field labels and delimiters, from accidental change by users.

5.5.3.6 Provide clear and consistent procedures for potentially dangerous transactions (e.g., global operations or those involving data change or deletion).

### 5.5.4 Information Security

When displayed data are classified or controlled, display a prominent indication of status.

5.5.4.1 When displayed data must be protected, maintain computer control over the display (e.g., do not allow users to change a read-only field), and display the status of the screen (e.g., read-only).

5.5.4.2 When classified or controlled data are to be displayed at an uncontrolled workstation, provide a rapid means of temporarily suppressing the screen display if privacy is threatened.

# 6.0 Guidelines for Display Control and Window Design

Resolving issues of data selection and presentation is a key concern for a development team. Display control issues become even more complex in a windowed environment. Key human factors issues center on the design of window appearance and behavior (look and feel). A design objective is to minimize time spent in window management (housekeeping).

## 6.1 Display Control

Designers are expected to determine as many user requirements for specific tasks as possible. Because a designer cannot anticipate all user requirements, users must have the flexibility to tailor their displays online by controlling data selection, data coverage within a display frame, data updating, and data suppression.

### *6.1.1 User Control*

Support user control by permitting users to control the amount, format, movement, and complexity of displayed data. Within data protection constraints, users should be able to change displayed data or enter new data.

6.1.1.1 Indicate display control options clearly and appropriately for selection. (Determine appropriateness from the task analysis and from discussions with the user group.)

6.1.1.2 To the extent possible (without crowding), include data relevant to the current transaction in one display frame or page.

6.1.1.3 Provide an easy and consistent way to move through data such as windowing, panning, paging, or scrolling. Use scrolling to support the expert user's search through continuous text. Do not use paging or windowing for this purpose. Use paging to search for logically grouped information such as data forms. Do not use panning or scrolling for this purpose. Use up and down arrows to indicate vertical scrolling direction and previous and next or left and right arrows to indicate paging direction.

6.1.1.4 Provide zoom-in and zoom-out capabilities to support a user's detailed examination of graphical displays (maps, pictures, diagrams).

### *6.1.2 Selection of Data for Display*

Enable a user to select data for display. In determining the means for specification of data output automatically or by a user, consider the following recommendations.

6.1.2.1 For general data processing systems, enable users to specify the data for displayed output.

6.1.2.2 For specific information handling applications, always allow users to select data to meet task requirements.

6.1.2.3 If a designer cannot exactly determine specific categories required by users at different stages, permit users to select the categories they need for information handling tasks.

6.1.2.4 If a response must be delayed, notify the user when display output is complete.

### *6.1.3 Updates*

When displayed data change dynamically with external events, permit a user to request an update of the change and control the update rate.

6.1.3.1 Consider highlighting data changes resulting from automatic updating. Maintain the highlighting briefly but long enough to call user attention to any changes.

6.1.3.2 Ensure that changing data values are readable.

6.1.3.3 If a user must determine trends over time or make predictions based on changing data, provide integrated trend displays and predictive displays.

### *6.1.4 Suppression*

Permit users to suppress displayed data not required for the task at hand.

6.1.4.1 After data have been suppressed from a display, remind the user of the suppressed data.

6.1.4.2 Enable a user to restore suppressed data quickly to the originally displayed form.

## 6.2 General Window Appearance

The appearance of windows in an application is generally controlled by instructions built into the UI development software. It may be possible to exercise options on window appearance or customize some aspects of window appearance.

### *6.2.1 Window Components*

A typical window is a square or rectangular area that contains a window frame, a menu bar, an application area, and window controls. Optional features are command areas and message areas. The components of the window frame may be called decorations and include a title bar, maximize and minimize buttons, a resize border, and a window menu button. A specific set of window controls may be required and built into the UI development software. Other window controls are optional.

6.2.1.1 Display a brief, unique, and descriptive title at the top center of each window unless directed otherwise by a UI toolkit style guide. Continue to display the window title while the user scrolls data in the application area.

6.2.1.2 Tailor the size of the application area to the user's needs.

6.2.1.3 Provide window controls to support

- Opening and closing a window
- Moving a window
- Resizing a window
- Shrinking a window to an icon
- Scrolling through window contents
- Zooming in and out

6.2.1.4 Provide standard buttons by which a user may control window size (minimum to variable to maximum).

6.2.1.5 Comply with the default appearance and placement of scroll bars for the environment. (Some windowing systems allow users to control placement of scroll bars.)

6.2.1.6 Display scroll bars in full contrast only for the active window (the one that displays current input).

6.2.1.7 Make the appearance of optional window controls consistent with required controls.

## 6.2.2 Primary and Secondary Windows

An application's primary or main window displays the essential data a user needs to interact with the application. Secondary windows convey context-specific information and may be called transient or child windows. A dialog box may be used to create a secondary window.

6.2.2.1 Limit the number of secondary windows to avoid user navigation problems.

6.2.2.2 Locate related window components in the same place from parent to child.

6.2.2.3 Use a secondary window to temporarily add data (such as help screens, menus, or other features) to a display, for controlling or displaying divergent information, or segregating and controlling separate operations.

### 6.2.3 Tiled and Overlapping Windows

When windows are strictly tiled, they abut each other's borders but do not overlap. The look is two-dimensional. When windows overlap, the window nearest the apparent foreground is the active window. It may obscure data "beneath" it or be made transparent so that underlying data are visible. The look of overlapping windows is close to three-dimensional, like papers stacked on a desk.

6.2.3.1 Use tiled windows to support user performance when (1) user activities focus on a single task, (2) tasks require minimal manipulation of windows, or (3) users are novices or rarely use the application.

6.2.3.2 Use overlapping windows when (1) user activities cut across independent tasks, (2) tasks require frequent window manipulation, or (3) users are experts or use the application frequently.

6.2.3.3 Use a variant of tiled or overlapping windows to limit clutter and promote efficiency while supporting access to several sources of information (Figure K.9). Variants include non-space-filling tiling, piles of tiles, automatic panning, window zooming, and cascades.

6.2.3.4 If using overlapping windows, ensure that window overlays are nondestructive; overlaid data are not permanently erased.

6.2.3.5 For tiled windows, indicate the active window by highlighting the window border, altering the background color slightly, or changing the labeling.

6.2.3.6 For overlapping windows, indicate the active window by moving it to the forefront upon activation by the user.

6.2.3.7 For overlapping windows, use a neutral background pattern instead of complex patterns that create unintended visual effects.

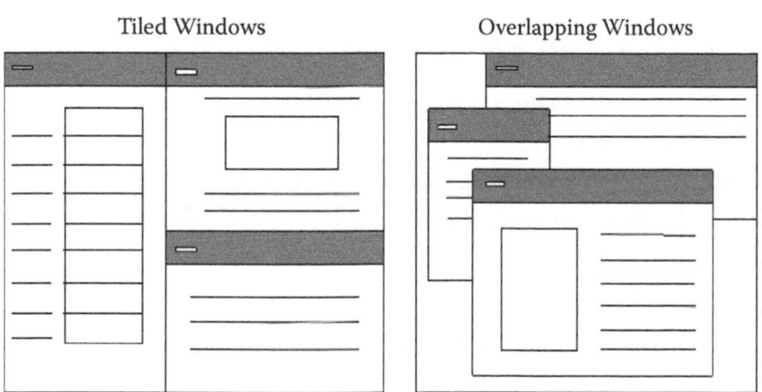


**Figure K.9 Tiled and overlapping windows.**

### 6.2.4 Decision-Supportive Window Design

User tasks will often require the integration of various kinds of information from multiple sources. Data may appear on different scales or in different units. From a user perspective of information processing capacities, an objective of window design is to increase his or her ability to integrate such multiple sets of information. If the different sets of data must be kept separate and not integrated automatically, various windowing strategies can promote productivity.

6.2.4.1 Consider using the suggested windowing strategies under these conditions:

- When a user must consider different data sets in making a decision, place the required data sets in separate windows that can be displayed simultaneously.
- When a user will benefit by seeing the same data at different levels of analysis, display each level in a separate window.
- When a user will benefit from different perspectives of the same object, show each perspective in a different window. Perspectives may be more or less concrete or abstract, for example, viewing a spacecraft design from various angles, considering its different attributes, or choosing an historical or predictive view of spacecraft operations.
- When changes made in one window affect data in other windows, link the affected windows so that the rest of the window set is updated by the changes.

6.2.4.2 Decide which decision-supportive strategies to use on the basis of a good understanding of user functions and tasks.

6.2.4.3 Use combinations of decision-supportive strategies that will best support user decision making in particular situations.

6.2.4.4 If a user must interact with a sequence of displays in close temporal proximity, use separate windows that can be displayed simultaneously.

### 6.2.5 Related versus Independent Windows

To promote the user's conceptual grouping, design related windows or sets of windows to share family characteristics. To promote differentiation of unrelated windows, windows or window sets that are independent should reflect their differences partially through appearance. (Note that independent windows may also behave differently.)

6.2.5.1 Use identical attributes for related windows (size, shape, color of foreground, background, and border). Give independent windows contrasting attributes (different sizes or shapes, different colors in foreground, background, or borders). Place related windows close to each other. Use spacing to segregate independent windows from each other.

# 6.3 General Window Behavior (Feel)

The behavior of tiled or overlapping windows may be entirely controlled by the windowing system; some behaviors may be controlled by a user. For example, a user may control the basic windowing actions (open, resize, move) and placement of scroll bars. Panning strategies may be automatic or under user control. Although user-controlled placement of windows and window elements requires additional decision-making and housekeeping, an amount of optional user control may improve subjective satisfaction with the interface. General design objectives are to limit the extent of window manipulation and preserve predictability in windowing behavior by (1) minimizing manual activity for window-manipulation tasks and (2) aiming for consistency across windowing operations.

## *6.3.1 Window Manipulation*

Systems vary in the steps required to perform window-manipulation but the steps are relatively standardized. The behavior of controls in a window frame is usually controlled by the windowing system used.

6.3.1.1 Provide common window manipulation actions as listed in Table K.4. These actions are typically performed with a mouse, but keyboard alternatives may be provided.

6.3.1.2 Following the user's open action, open the new window as close as possible to the current focus without obscuring the current focus. For example, when the user selects a control panel icon, display the open control panel just below its icon. If the user requests help on a fill-in-form field, display the help window to the side of the field without obscuring the field.

6.3.1.3 Open and close windows as smoothly and rapidly as possible.

6.3.1.4 Upon resizing, reformat text, graphics, or icon layouts to remain visible up to a standard limit set by project consensus.

6.3.1.5 Protect against obscuring of critical information during window resizing.

6.3.1.6 Provide visual feedback during movement of a window.

6.3.1.7 Follow a standard panning sequence.

6.3.1.8 If a user must frequently perform long mouse movements, provide keyboard alternatives for windowing actions.

6.3.1.9 Consider controlling window manipulation by user task actions without requiring direct window manipulation actions.

6.3.1.10 Allow keyboard and mouse input to affect only the active window.

**Table K.4 Window Manipulation**

| *Opening and Closing Windows* | |
|---|---|
| Create | Displays entirely new window |
| Delete | Removes window from screen |
| Open | Replaces iconic window with full-size window it represents |
| Close | Replaces window with iconic window |
| Bring to front | Moves window to most forward plane of screen with overlapping windows |
| Push to back | Moves window to most rearward plane of screen with overlapping windows |
| *Changing Windows* | |
| Move | Repositions window in its two-dimensional plane |
| Resize | Shows more or less data in window by contracting window or expanding it to maximum size |
| Zoom | Expands to maximum size with one action |
| Rescale | Shows more or less data in window by changing scale of image in window |
| Scroll | Selects different portion of data for viewing without resizing |
| Name/rename | Defines or changes name of window |
| Make active (change focus) | Designates window as available for interaction |

### 6.3.2 Aiding Window Arrangement and Navigation

To reduce housekeeping and support the user's sense of orientation, provide built-in aids to window manipulation and navigation between windows.

6.3.2.1 Design for maximum ease and efficiency of navigating between windows.

6.3.2.2 Consider providing a way for a user to move around among open windows with minimal manual activity.

6.3.2.3 Consider providing the ability to users to call by name a window or particular configuration of windows (window macro).

6.3.2.4 When windows are allowed to overlap, provide powerful commands to support a user's tailored arrangement of windows on the screen (create, name, and recall specific sets of windows).

6.3.2.5 Within a set of windows (parent and children), offer an indication of how far the user has progressed through the set and how many windows remain.

6.3.2.6 For a set of overlapping, open windows, allow the user to request an iconic or graphical map depicting all the open windows.

6.3.2.7 When a map of open windows is available, allow the user to designate the active window by selecting a map element. Bring the selected window forward without requiring the user to resize or move other windows.

6.3.2.8 Consider opening and closing child windows when a parent window is opened or closed.

## 7.0 Guidelines for Visual Coding Techniques

Color is a major technique to support quick detection and discrimination of displayed data elements or groupings of data. Other visual coding techniques include variations in brightness, flashing, line style, symbols, sizes, and shapes. All these techniques can be misused or overused. Visual coding should be used only for functional purposes, not for decoration. A key challenge to designers is to use these techniques to enhance task performance (Table K.5).

## 7.1 Color

Color serves several functional purposes in screen design. It (1) establishes relationships between displayed objects, (2) helps users distinguish between displayed objects, (3) communicates the organization of information, and (4) calls users' attention to system states. If color is overused, these purposes are defeated. Likewise, if color is used for decorative purposes, these functional purposes are compromised.

### *7.1.1 Number of Colors*

Limit the number of colors to be used, preferably to four or fewer.

7.1.1.1 Use task performance requirements to determine the number of colors to be presented simultaneously. Minimize the number of colors presented on the same screen. Use color to support visual search and symbol identification tasks.

7.1.1.2 Use no more than six distinct colors or three shades of gray if users must recall the meanings of colors or shades.

7.1.1.3 Use no more than six distinct colors if users must perform rapid visual searching based on color discrimination.

**Table K.5 Attention-Getting Techniques**

| *Technique* | *When To Use* | *When Not To Use* |
|---|---|---|
| Color | A powerful attention getter is needed. | Several colors are already used on the display. |
| Blinking/flashing | User must respond immediately. | Message does not require immediate attention or text is lengthy. |
| Bold | Captions or titles should stand out. | There are more than three levels of bold. |
| Reverse video | Purpose is to indicate a selected item or error. | Text is lengthy. |
| Size | A code is needed for relative quantity or importance. | There are five or more levels of size codes. |
| Font | Text items should stand out. | There are more than two to four different character types. |
| Underlining | Purpose is to draw attention to key words for instruction or to distinguish fill-in fields from text. | Too frequent use reduces legibility. |
| Shape | Purpose is to communicate urgency. | Use of shapes is not based on established standards. |
| Special characters and icons | Purpose is to draw attention to items on a screen. | Space is limited (graphic symbols take up additional screen space). |
| Proximity | White space can be used to associate items with each other (grouping). | There is no need to associate items. |
| Borders | Purpose is to identify meaningful groups, create sense of closure, and/or focus attention. | Identified groups, closure, and focus of attention are not required. |

7.1.1.4 If functional requirements dictate the use of more than the recommended number of colors or shades of gray, display a legend of color and shade meanings.

## *7.1.2 Pairing Colors*

Avoid the color combinations listed in Table K.6.

**Table K.6 Color Combinations to Avoid**

| | |
|---|---|
| Saturated red and blue | Saturated red and green |
| Saturated blue and green | Saturated yellow and green |
| Yellow on purple | Green on white |
| Yellow on green | Blue on black |
| Magenta on green | Red on black |
| Magenta on black | Yellow on white |

## 7.1.3 Foreground and Background Colors

Consult Table K.7 for recommended foreground and background colors. Use a medium achromatic background (dark or medium gray) to maximize the visibility of foreground colors.

7.1.3.1 Consider the effects of varying levels of saturation (color intensity) and varying levels of lightness (amount of white mixed with color) on color

**Table K.7 Foreground and Background Colors**

| | Background | | | | | | | | | |
|---|---|---|---|---|---|---|---|---|---|---|
| *Foreground* | *Black* | *Blue* | *Green* | *Cyan* | *Red* | *Magenta* | *Brown* | *White* | *Gray* | *Beige* |
| Black | – | | | R | | R | | R | R | R |
| Blue | – | – | – | – | – | – | – | r | r | R |
| Green | – | R | – | R | – | | | | – | – |
| Cyan | R | | | – | | | | | R | R |
| White | R | | | | | | | | – | – |
| Bold green | R | | | | | | | | R | R |
| Bold cyan | R | R | | – | R | R | | | R | R |
| Bold magenta | R | | R | | | – | | | R | R |
| Yellow | R | R | – | R | | R | | – | – | – |
| Bold white | R | | R | R | | | | – | – | – |

*R = recommended; r = some saturations acceptable; – = avoid this combination.*

discriminability and interactions. Avoid combinations that are similar in tone (navy blue on black, yellow on white).

7.1.3.2 Maintain adequate contrast between foreground and background colors to enhance color perception and perceived image resolution. Increase contrast if the screen will be viewed under dim lighting. Consider using complementary colors (yellow on dark blue; magenta on green) to maximize contrast, if appropriate for the task environment.

7.1.3.3 Consult authoritative sources for guidance on measuring color uniformity, contrast, and differences.

7.1.3.4 Test selected colors with users to verify easy discrimination. Color contrast should be at least 7:1 for foreground versus background.

### 7.1.4 Colors For Thin Lines

Consult Table K.8 for colors to make thin lines easily perceivable.

### 7.1.5 Redundant Use of Color

Be sure that the information to be coded by color is coded in another manner for color-deficient users.

7.1.5.1 Before adding color to a display, design for its use in monochrome; then use color as a redundant code to enhance an otherwise logical, well-organized design.

### 7.1.6 Consistent Use of Color

Use color consistently with common meanings for the user's culture (e.g., in Western cultures, use green for good or normal, yellow for caution, and red for danger or warning).

7.1.6.1 If the user community established meanings for various colors, retain the meanings. Do not use a color to signify a condition different from one it signified in the previous system.

**Table K.8 Colors for Thin Lines**

| *Number of Colors* | *White Background* | *Black Background* |
|---|---|---|
| 1 | Red or green | Yellow, cyan, or green |
| 2 | Red and green<br>Magenta and cyan<br>Red and blue | Green and magenta<br>Yellow and magenta<br>Cyan and magenta |
| 3 | Red, blue, and green | Cyan, magenta, and yellow |

## 7.2 Brightness

On monochrome or color displays, variations in brightness can be used to attract user attention and to differentiate categories or levels in a category. On a color display, variations on the continuum from dull to bright (brightness) are indistinguishable from variations in lightness (range from white to gray to black).

### 7.2.1 *Suggested Uses*

Use brightness coding for task-related purposes.

7.2.1.1 Consider using high brightness to call attention to errors in data entry fields and highlight answer fields on question-and-answer screens.

7.2.1.2 Consider using brightness coding to differentiate adjacent items of information or code state conditions (on and off; standby and run).

7.2.1.3 Consider using "reverse video" (brightness inversion) to highlight critical items requiring user attention. Return to normal brightness when the user has responded.

### 7.2.2 *Levels of Brightness*

Use only two levels of brightness coding (bright and dim) separated by at least a 2:1 ratio.

## 7.3 Flashing and Blinking

Flashing and blinking are powerful attention getters and should be used only rarely. Overuse will only distract users. Data or text that must be read should never blink or flash because a blinking object is not displayed continuously and can be read only when it is displayed.

### 7.3.1 *Suggested Uses*

Use flash or blink coding only to indicate an urgent need for user attention and response or to indicate an active location for data entry (placing a blinking cursor where user input will be accepted).

7.3.1.1 Allow only a very small area of the screen to flash at one time.

7.3.1.2 Instead of blinking data or text, place a small square or rectangle next to the critical information and blink only the square or rectangle.

### 7.3.2 Levels of Flashing

Use no more than two levels of flash or blink coding.

### 7.3.3 Lengths of Intervals

In general, use equal on and off duty cycles. Consider winking rather than blinking by setting the on cycle to be substantially longer than the off cycle.

## 7.4 Line Coding

Lines or rules help focus reader attention on related information and separate unrelated groupings of information. Line borders delineate the boundaries of menu bars, display control options, and entire windows. Line coding should be used sparingly.

### 7.4.1 Line Attributes

Use line thickness, width, and height or length to convey functional meaning.

7.4.1.1 Use line coding by type (solid, dashed, dotted), width, or other attribute to indicate associations of elements. Limit to four the number of variations of any one line attribute (four thicknesses, four lengths). Minimize possible interactions caused by varying line attributes. For example, use horizontal lines of equal width and vertical lines of equal height where possible.

7.4.1.2 Use line length coding for applications involving spatial categorizations in a single dimension (e.g., velocity).

7.4.1.3 Use line direction coding for applications involving spatial categorizations in two dimensions (e.g., altitude, bearing).

## 7.5 Special Symbols

Use special, standard symbols (asterisk, arrow) to draw user attention to specific items in alphanumeric displays.

### 7.5.1 Mappings

Make special symbols analogous to the event or system elements they represent based on established standards or conventional meanings.

### *7.5.2 Consistent Meanings*

Assign consistent meanings to special symbols within and across applications.

## 7.6 Symbol Sizes

Use size coding only on uncrowded displays. Use no more than three symbol sizes for coding. A larger object should be 1.5 times the height of the next smaller object (character, symbol, shape).

## 7.7 Shapes

Use shape categories (circle, triangle, square) to code related objects and support user ability to discriminate between various categories of displayed data.

### *7.7.1 Redundant Coding*

Map shapes to colors (red circles, green triangles) to achieve redundant coding (meaning conveyed both by shape and color).

### *7.7.2 Distinctiveness*

Use a distinctive shape to call attention to a single type of displayed object.

## 7.8 Type Styles

Variations in type styles include the use of bold, underlining, and different fonts.

### *7.8.1 Bolding*

Use the heavy intensity of bolding for strong emphasis. If more than one level of bold is available, avoid using more than three levels whose meanings the user must remember.

### *7.8.2 Underlining*

Use underlining for mild emphasis, not for urgent or critical information. Use it to emphasize key words, titles, or headings or to distinguish fill-in fields from surrounding text or labels.

### *7.8.3 Fonts*

Use multiple fonts to convey moderate emphasis and help users discriminate among categories of displayed information.

7.8.3.1 Limit to two or three the number of different fonts displayed on a single screen. Do not exceed four fonts.

7.8.3.2 Use variations of one font (size, style) to convey levels in a category of information. For example, large, bold letters for high-level titles; smaller, bold letters for second-level titles; still smaller, underlined letters for third-level titles.

## 7.9 Three-Dimensional Effects

Screen development tools typically provide widgets with three-dimensional features, such as drop shadows and beveled edges. Three-dimensional features cause objects to appear closer to users. Closer objects (i.e., in the foreground) take on greater importance than background elements. The user's attention goes naturally to screen elements that seem closer because they are important in the context of the task. Such features should be used sparingly on any one display screen to avoid canceling out their effects.

### *7.9.1 Drop Shadows*

Consider using drop shadows to make important elements appear closer to the user.

7.9.1.1 Place shadows at the lower right of icons and buttons as if light were coming from the upper left.

7.9.1.2 Place shadows along the bottom and right side of a pull-down menu, dialog box, or window to attract user attention.

### *7.9.2 Beveled Edges*

Consider using beveled edges to bring important screen elements to the foreground. Beveled edges may be used on icons, buttons, menus, dialog boxes, and windows. Shade the bottom and right beveled edges to enhance the three-dimensional effect.

## 8.0 Guidelines for User Guidance and Feedback

Providing effective guidance and feedback to users helps meet several general objectives of UI design:

Consistency of operational procedures

- Efficient use of system capabilities
- Limited memory load on the user
- Reduced learning time
- Flexibility in supporting different classes of users
- Error prevention

User guidance includes prompts, warnings, error messages, status information, and online help. A key design goal is to reflect the user's (not the designer's) understanding of the system. Meeting this goal requires review and usability testing by potential end users who have not been involved with system development.

## 8.1 Prompts and General Guidance Messages

Prompts are advisory messages that help navigate the user interface. General guidance messages inform users about available actions and suggest actions to be taken.

### *8.1.1 Distinctive, Consistent Prompts and Messages*

Ensure that prompts and general guidance messages are distinct from displayed data and used consistently throughout the application.

8.1.1.1 Use consistent, concise phrasing, and minimal, consistent punctuation in prompts and general guidance messages.

8.1.1.2 Use positive, clear wording and the active voice in prompts and general guidance messages.

8.1.1.3 Make prompts and user guidance explicit to eliminate the need for the user to memorize lengthy sequences or consult references. Do not include codes or references to external sources in prompts.

8.1.1.4 Do not present prompts and general guidance in a person-like or personal manner. Do not use the first person (I) or second person (you).

8.1.1.5 Where possible, provide prompts for required formats and acceptable values for data entry.

### *8.1.2 Explanations*

Use brief prompts and messages to explain required input, commands, error messages, system capabilities, display formats, procedures, and steps in a sequence.

### 8.1.3 Prompting for Coded Data Entry

Prompt users for required formats and provide values for valid data entries. For example, prompt a user to enter a color selection:

| *Prompt* | *= Color* |
|---|---|
| r | Red |
| b | Blue |
| g | Green |

### 8.1.4 Optional Guidance

Permit users to request prompts and general guidance as needed, depending on level of experience.

8.1.4.1 Design prompts and general guidance with the novice user in mind.
8.1.4.2 Allow expert users to turn off prompting and guidance.

### 8.1.5 Locations of Prompts

Locate prompts where users will input data whenever possible; otherwise, place prompts in a standard message area.

## 8.2 Cautions and Warnings

Displays of cautions and warnings should be consistent throughout the system.

### 8.2.1 Cautions

Use cautions for operations and actions that might produce undesirable results: (1) permanent data loss, (2) no data loss but unchangeable consequences, (3) conflicts with other operations, and (4) need for excessive processing time.

### 8.2.2 Warnings

Use warnings for operations and actions that may result in (1) permanent data loss, (2) data loss and unchangeable consequences with few exceptions (saving an edited file using the same name as the edited file does not require a warning), (3) threat and/or compromise of proprietary information, (4) noninterruptable processing, and (5) invocation of ancillary system actions (automatic deletion or overwriting of an original file when executing a renaming command).

### *8.2.3 Visual and Auditory Display*

Present distinctive cautions and warnings through both visual and auditory display.

## 8.3 Error Messages

Use error messages to inform the user of incorrect command or data entry.

### *8.3.1 Location*

Present the error message at the point of the error or in a consistently located message area.

### *8.3.2 Style*

Make error messages specific, informative, and brief.

8.3.2.1 Use neutral wording in error messages; keep phrasing positive and professional.

8.3.2.2 Phrase error messages in terms of the current task.

### *8.3.3 Information Content*

Include the following information in error messages:

- Reason for rejection of input
- Corrective actions for subsequent operations
- Format requirements if formatting conventions were violated

### *8.3.4 Detailed Explanation of Error*

Permit the user to request a more detailed explanation of the error and additional information about the ongoing operation.

### *8.3.5 Error Correction*

Allow a user to correct an error immediately after detection.

8.3.5.1 If an error cannot be corrected, design the system so that other transactions can still be initiated. Permit the user to store and later retrieve the transaction with the error.

## 8.4 System and Status Information

System and status messages should not be humorous or sarcastic. They should not be presented in first person (I) or second person (you).

### 8.4.1 Message Scope and Content

Display messages to indicate the following conditions:

| Keyboard lock |
|---|
| Log-on denial failure |
| File writing operations |
| Making remote connections |
| Printing progress and spooling |
| Complex, time-consuming operations |
| Processing delay |
| Save operations |
| Mail and data transmission |
| High time shared system loads |
| Complex processing completion |

8.4.1.1 Include the following information: (1) description of system state, (2) directives for user action, and (3) consequences (if any) of failure to follow directives.

### 8.4.2 Message Location

Present system and status messages in a consistent location.

### 8.4.3 Operational Mode

Inform users of current operational mode when the mode may affect their actions.

## 8.5 Task-Related Job Aids

Job aids support user productivity and performance by providing task-related guidance.

### *8.5.1 Content*

Job aids should include an online dictionary of abbreviations, acronyms, and codes along with allowable options and value ranges. Online help is a major job aid.

### *8.5.2 Dialog Aids*

Provide context-specific information on semantics and syntax of any available user dialog. Include a structured listing of (1) each command available, (2) associated menu options and keystroke alternatives (accelerators), and (3) uses and consequences of command.

### *8.5.3 Online Help*

Provide context-sensitive, self-explanatory help that permits rapid access to information about specific interactions, tasks, messages, or commands. Include information about likely user questions about all parts of the application.

8.5.3.1 While the user is viewing help in a separate, reserved window, display as much as possible of the current task display.

8.5.3.2 If the user is executing a particular command and requests help, provide information on that command (effects and alternatives).

8.5.3.3 When an error occurs and a user requests help, provide a useful description of the error and suggest at least one recovery technique.

8.5.3.4 If an online reference manual is available, open the manual at the topic corresponding to the current context when the user requests help.

8.5.3.5 Use a help icon on the screen and designate a function key as the help key. Use the help icon and the help key consistently throughout the application.

# Index

## S



## T

Milton Keynes UK
Ingram Content Group UK Ltd.
UKHW031138141024
449569UK00024B/1247